Holding Forth the Word of Life

Australian College of Theology Monograph Series

SERIES EDITOR GRAEME R. CHATFIELD

The ACT Monograph Series, generously supported by the Board of Directors of the Australian College of Theology, provides a forum for publishing quality research theses and studies by its graduates and affiliated college staff in the broad fields of Biblical Studies, Christian Thought and History, and Practical Theology with Wipf and Stock Publishers of Eugene, Oregon. The ACT selects the best of its doctoral and research masters theses as well as monographs that offer the academic community, scholars, church leaders and the wider community uniquely Australian and New Zealand perspectives on significant research topics and topics of current debate. The ACT also provides opportunity for contributors beyond its graduates and affiliated college staff to publish monographs which support the mission and values of the ACT.

Rev Dr Graeme Chatfield
Series Editor and Associate Dean

Holding Forth the Word of Life

Essays in Honor of Tim Meadowcroft

Edited by
JOHN DE JONG and
CSILLA SAYSELL

Foreword by
DAVID CRAWLEY

WIPF & STOCK · Eugene, Oregon

HOLDING FORTH THE WORD OF LIFE
Essays in Honor of Tim Meadowcroft

Copyright © 2020 Wipf and Stock Publishers. All rights reserved. Except for brief quotations in critical publications or reviews, no part of this book may be reproduced in any manner without prior written permission from the publisher. Write: Permissions, Wipf and Stock Publishers, 199 W. 8th Ave., Suite 3, Eugene, OR 97401.

Wipf & Stock
An Imprint of Wipf and Stock Publishers
199 W. 8th Ave., Suite 3
Eugene, OR 97401

www.wipfandstock.com

PAPERBACK ISBN: 978-1-7252-5876-1
HARDCOVER ISBN: 978-1-7252-5877-8
EBOOK ISBN: 978-1-7252-5878-5

Unless otherwise marked, Scripture quotations are from the New Revised Standard Version Bible, copyright © 1989 the Division of Christian Education of the National Council of the Churches of Christ in the United States of America. Used by permission. All rights reserved.

Scripture quotations marked KJV are from the King James Version (Authorized Version/King James Bible), which is in the public domain.

Manufactured in the U.S.A.   03/09/20

Contents

Contributors | ix

Foreword | xi
—David Crawley

Abbreviations | xix

Introduction | xxi
—John de Jong and Csilla Saysell

Part 1: Old and New Testament

1. Daniel Compares Notes with Jeremiah | 3
   —John Goldingay

2. Job the (Im)Pious: Theological Exegesis and Ambiguity | 17
   —James Harding

3. Was Ruth a *Festschrift*? | 31
   —Tim Bulkeley

4. The Blood Manipulation of the Sin Offering and the Logic of Defilement | 44
   —Csilla Saysell

5. Nothing Was Made without Him (John 1:3) | 58
   —Richard Neville

6. Love's Four Objects and the Pursuit of Peace | 68
   —Christopher D. Marshall

7. "Saints by Calling" in Romans 1:7 and 1 Corinthians 1:2 | 84
   —Paul Trebilco

8. ΛΟΓΟΝ ΖΩΗΣ ΕΡΕΧΟΝΤΕΣ (Holding Forth the Word of Life) | 98
   —Mark Keown

9. "You Have Come To Mount Zion . . ." (Heb 12:22): Pilgrimage to Zion and the Book of Hebrews | 118
   —Philip Church

Part 2: Women, Gender, Sexuality, and the Wider New Zealand Context

10. The Disembodied Womb and the Disappearing Mother in Hosea 13:13 | 137
    —Miriam Bier Hinksman

11. What About the Women of Ḥesed? A Reaction to the Honors Gallery in Sir 44:1—50:24 | 152
    —Karen Nelson

12. Tiptoe through the Minefields: Navigating Gender, Sexuality, and the Bible in Aotearoa New Zealand | 168
    —Caroline Blyth and Emily Colgan

13. Holy Love: Seeking a Unified Theology in a Divided Church | 184
    —Peter Carrell

14. The Gospel of John as a Defense of Jesus' Honor? Some Reflections out of Intercontextual Analysis with the Māori Concept of Mana | 199
    —Derek Tovey

15. Whakawhiti Kōrero: Theology and Social Vocation | 214
    —Mark G. Brett

Part 3: Language, Linguistics, and Hermeneutics

16. The Early Greek-Language Tradition behind the Gospels | 229
    —Allan Bell

17. Textual Criticism, the Textus Receptus, and Adoniram Judson's Burmese New Testaments | 243
    —John de Jong

18. Reception History: Signaling Change in Biblical Studies | 256
    —Donald P. Moffat

19. Is There a Fish in this Cognitive Environment? Relevance Theory, Interpretive Communities, and the Bible | 268
   —STEPHEN PATTEMORE

20. Linguistics and Hermeneutics | 284
   —STANLEY E. PORTER

21. A Mimetic Model of Hermeneutics | 300
   —MARTIN SUTHERLAND

22. The Bible as Sacred Re-Membering | 318
   —YAEL KLANGWISAN AND LISA SPRIGGENS

   Subject Index | 329

   Author Index | 335

Contributors

Allan Bell, Emeritus Professor of Language and Communication, Auckland University of Technology.

Miriam Bier Hinksman, Research Fellow and Visiting Lecturer in Old Testament, London School of Theology, London, UK.

Caroline Blyth, Senior Lecturer in Religion, University of Auckland, Auckland, New Zealand.

Mark G. Brett, Professor of Hebrew Bible at Whitley College within the University of Divinity, Melbourne, Australia.

Tim Bulkeley ✝, Senior Lecturer, Sydney College of Divinity.

Peter Carrell, Anglican Bishop of Christchurch, New Zealand.

Philip Church, Senior Research Fellow at Laidlaw College, New Zealand.

Emily Colgan, Lecturer in Biblical Studies, Trinity Theological College, Auckland, New Zealand.

David R. Crawley, Senior Lecturer in Spiritual Formation, Laidlaw College, New Zealand.

John de Jong, Lecturer in Biblical and Intercultural Studies, Laidlaw College, New Zealand.

John Goldingay, Professor of Old Testament, Fuller Theological Seminary, Pasadena, California.

James E. Harding, Senior Lecturer in Hebrew Bible/Old Testament Studies, University of Otago, Dunedin, New Zealand.

Mark J. Keown, Bible Lead Academic and Senior Lecturer New Testament, Laidlaw College, New Zealand.

Yael Klangwisan, Senior Lecturer (Education, Hebrew Bible), Head of Education, Laidlaw College, New Zealand.

Christopher Marshall, The Diana Unwin Professor of Restorative Justice, Victoria University of Wellington, New Zealand.

Donald P. Moffat, Sir Paul Reeves Lecturer in Biblical Studies, College of St. John the Evangelist, Auckland, New Zealand.

Karen Nelson, Auckland, New Zealand.

Richard Neville, Senior Lecturer in Biblical Studies, Laidlaw College, New Zealand.

Stephen Pattemore, Translations Director, Bible Society New Zealand.

Stanley E. Porter, President and Dean, Professor of New Testament, Roy A. Hope Chair in Christian Worldview, McMaster Divinity College, Hamilton, Ontario, Canada.

Csilla Saysell, Lecturer in Old Testament, Carey Baptist College, Auckland, New Zealand.

Lisa Spriggens, Head of Counselling, Laidlaw College, New Zealand.

Martin Sutherland, Dean/CEO Australian College of Theology, Sydney, Australia.

Derek Tovey, Formerly Lecturer in New Testament, College of St. John the Evangelist, Auckland, New Zealand.

Paul Trebilco, Professor of New Testament Studies, University of Otago, Dunedin, New Zealand.

Foreword

David Crawley

As one of Tim's long-term colleagues at Laidlaw College, formerly the Bible College of New Zealand, it is a privilege to offer a few reflections on his life and work, mindful that neither is yet complete! For a quarter of a century we served together under six successive national principals and experienced the privileges and challenges of working in an institution that cherishes its roots in the Bible College movement while aspiring to university-level academic performance.

Timothy John Meadowcroft was born in 1953 in Blenheim Hospital to John and Monica Meadowcroft. John was the vicar in nearby Seddon at that time. In 1956, the family set off for England, in order to prepare for ministry in Pakistan. After serving a term in Karachi, Tim's father taught for fourteen years at Gujranwala Theological Seminary in Punjab. Tim went to Murree Christian School in the foothills of the Himalayan mountains. Fellow students from the United States introduced him to basketball, igniting a love affair which has continued ever since.

Tim returned to New Zealand in 1970 in order to complete his high school years at Middleton Grange. He played representative basketball for the Canterbury Colts and Canterbury B Grade teams between 1970 and 1972. In his first year at the University of Canterbury, 1972, he met Sue, and they married in 1975 while Tim was completing his MA in English.

Having earlier vowed, "I would never be a teacher or a pastor because that's what my father was," Tim undertook secondary school teacher training in 1976. His first teaching position was at Ngaruawhahia High School in 1977, where he stayed for five years. There he taught English, coached basketball, and helped to start the Hamilton Secondary School's Basketball Association.

Tim and Sue had two daughters while in Ngaruawahia, Anna and Sarah. They then went to St. John's Theological College in Auckland in 1982, where Tim commenced ordination training, and two more daughters, Katie and Elizabeth, were born. During this time, he completed a Bachelor of Divinity degree through the University of Otago. The family then moved to Matamata, where Tim was curate at All Saints for eighteen months, before being installed as vicar at St. Peter's, Katikati, where the family stayed for four years. Alongside his ministry in these churches and active participation in the wider Anglican Church, he was active in the community, contributing columns to the local newspapers and serving on school boards.

Feeling the need for more theological study, Tim obtained a year's leave in 1990 to undertake a Master of Theology at New College, University of Edinburgh. The place of study was decided by the offer of free accommodation by Sue's uncle. During that year, he was offered a scholarship by the Faculty of Divinity, with a view to completing a PhD. This meant resigning from St. Peter's and staying in Edinburgh until the end of 1993. His doctoral thesis, "A Literary Critical Comparison of the Masoretic Text and Septuagint of Daniel 2–7," formed the basis of Tim's first book, *Aramaic Daniel and Greek Daniel: A Literary Comparison*, published two years later.[1]

Towards the end of his doctoral study, Tim wrote a letter to the national principal of the Bible College of New Zealand, Dr. John Hitchen, asking if any teaching work might be available. This coincided with John's intention to write to Tim, to sound out his availability. The conversation continued and, following the completion of his PhD in 1993, a formal invitation was extended by the college board. The family returned to New Zealand, and Tim was appointed to the faculty as a lecturer in biblical studies, to begin in 1994. He continued in this role until his retirement at the end of 2018, teaching mainly in Old Testament and Biblical Interpretation, at undergraduate and postgraduate level, along with New Testament and biblical languages (Hebrew, Greek, and Aramaic). Throughout that period, he held several senior leadership roles in the college, including Dean of Students, Head of Department, Graduate School Dean and National Dean of Studies.

---

1. Meadowcroft, *Aramaic Daniel and Greek Daniel*.

At his farewell from Laidlaw College, past and present students spoke and wrote appreciatively of Tim as an inspiring and influential teacher. He is, said one, "a great lecturer with a pastoral heart." His knowledge of his subject areas is extensive, and he has a deserved reputation for insisting on grammatical and lexical accuracy. Just as memorable for his students is his commitment to fostering a hospitable classroom environment in which students' spiritual and relational needs are important, alongside their learning.

Those who have taught in a Bible college environment will be aware of the difficulty of maintaining academic research and writing while handling a substantial teaching load. In his first year, Tim taught six papers, all in areas he had never taught before. Time for research is often squeezed by the demands of classroom work and administrative responsibilities. Yet, despite his significant teaching load and administrative responsibilities, Tim has been a productive scholar, making significant contributions through his publications and conference presentations. In 2004, he co-authored a commentary on Daniel in the Asia Bible Commentary Series.[2] Two years later he produced a commentary on Haggai in the Sheffield "Readings" series.[3] A list of publications, which follows, shows other books and edited volumes he has published in the areas of biblical interpretation and contextualization, along with a steady flow of peer-reviewed articles and book chapters. This list also reflects a progressively deepening desire on Tim's part to engage his reading of Scripture with the realities of life in a complex and unpredictable world.

In 1998, Tim was instrumental in establishing the Aotearoa New Zealand Association for Biblical Studies (ANZABS). Professor Paul Trebilco (University of Otago) recalls that Tim gave the initial paper at the inaugural meeting of the Association: "Aotearoa New Zealand Association for Biblical Studies: A Rationale," which laid out the principles for the Association. In 2017 he reviewed all that the Association had achieved in the twenty years since its beginning. Paul notes that one of Tim's slogans was "The Church needs ABS [the Association for Biblical Studies]." Professor Chris Marshall (Victoria University) observes that there is now "a whole generation of younger biblical scholars in this country" who are indebted to Tim's "leadership and loving nurture."[4]

In addition to his work with ANZABS, editorial roles for various theological journals, and involvement in other scholarly networks, Tim has made a significant contribution to the development of biblical scholarship in New

2. Meadowcroft and Irwin, *The Book of Daniel*.

3. Meadowcroft, *Haggai*.

4. Excerpts from personal tributes at the time of Tim's retirement from Laidlaw College.

Zealand through his supervision of generations of postgraduate students at master and doctoral levels. His strengths as a mentor extend beyond formal supervision of students to include the encouragement and guidance he has offered to colleagues seeking to grow their scholarship. I include myself as one of those, as a relative latecomer to doctoral and postdoctoral research. Tim has also been a source of wisdom for those exploring the intersection points of life and faith. He has been a valuable dialogue partner for the Laidlaw College School of Social Practice, for example, in conversations about ethical issues that arise in counseling. In more recent years he has contributed to the development of postgraduate theological education in Papua New Guinea at the Christian Leaders' Training College.

At times, this wisdom has been hammered out in challenging circumstances close to home. In 2014 Tim was a key player in a symposium, co-hosted by the University of Auckland and Laidlaw College, entitled "Theology, Spirituality and Cancer." Subsequently, he co-edited a volume that published papers offered at the symposium: *Spirituality and Cancer: Christian Encounters*.[5] Tim's introduction to his own chapter in that volume, "Eternity and Dust," explains that his quest for meaning with respect to cancer was occasioned by the prolonged treatment of one of his grandchildren for a severe form of neuroblastoma. Tim's input to the wider Anglican Communion on a range of issues has been earthed in his commitment to his own local church, St. Michael and All Angels, Henderson, where he serves as Assistant Priest.

Finally, some thoughts on the personal qualities that Tim has brought to his work over the last twenty-five years. His Laidlaw and Anglican contemporaries speak warmly of their experience of his friendship, collegiality, and leadership. They point to the graciousness that accompanies his academic excellence, as well as his care, wisdom, sound judgment, tenacity, humility, and faithful commitment to Christ and his church as both scholar and priest. In ways that he would not want placed in the spotlight, Tim has also offered practical support and encouragement to individuals in both spheres of his work, helping them to discover their callings and develop their gifts.

Lest this paints a picture of a rather serious fellow, it should be said that most of what Tim does is leavened with his own unique blend of humor: dry, witty, and often self-deprecating. In the various leadership positions he has occupied in my time at his colleague, I have appreciated the light touch he had brought to sometimes difficult conversations. His love of sport, basketball in particular, has never wavered, as evidenced by his loyal support for the

---

5. Meadowcroft and Blyth, *Spirituality and Cancer*.

New Zealand Breakers basketball team. I cherish a memory of joining Tim to watch my first NBA game (Atlanta Hawks vs. Boston Celtics) during the SBL and AAR conferences in Atlanta. I had little clue as to what was happening most of the time, but it was hugely entertaining! In the lunchroom, he always contributed knowledgeably to postmortem conversations about rugby, most of which were again lost on me. In his penultimate year on the staff—have I used that term correctly, Tim?—he triumphed in the Laidlaw table tennis competition, beating student contenders as well as staff. Retirement will hopefully allow more time for honing his golfing techniques, riding his electric bike, and entertaining the grandchildren.

Tim, on behalf of all your students, friends, and colleagues at Laidlaw College and beyond, thank you for all the ways you have enriched our lives and our shared service of Christ.

List of Publications

This list, categorized by type of publication and ordered from most recent to oldest, does not include book reviews or non-peer reviewed articles.

Books

Co-editor (with William Longgar). *Living in the Family of Jesus: Critical Contextualization in Melanesia and Beyond.* Auckland: Archer, 2016.

Co-editor (with Caroline Blyth). *Spirituality and Cancer: Christian Encounters.* Auckland: Accent, 2015.

Co-editor (with Joel B. Green). *Ears that Hear: Explorations in Theological Interpretation of the Bible.* Sheffield: Sheffield Phoenix, 2013.

Co-editor (with Andrew T. Abernethy, Mark G. Brett, and Tim Bulkeley). *Isaiah and Imperial Context: The Book of Isaiah in the Times of Empire.* Eugene, OR: Pickwick, 2013.

The Message of the Word of God. Bible Speaks Today Biblical Themes. Leicester: InterVarsity, 2011.

Co-editor (with P. Church, P. Walker and T. Bulkeley). *The Gospel and the Land of Promise: Christian Approaches to the Land of the Bible.* Eugene, OR: Pickwick, 2011.

Co-editor (with M. Habets). *Gospel, Truth, and Interpretation: Evangelical Identity in Aotearoa New Zealand.* Auckland: Archer, 2011.

Haggai. Readings: Sheffield: Sheffield Phoenix, 2006.

With N. D. Irwin. *The Book of Daniel.* ABCS. Singapore: Asia Theological Association, 2004.

Aramaic Daniel and Greek Daniel: A Literary Comparison. JSOTSup 198; Sheffield: JSOT, 1995.

Research Articles and Book Chapters

"Commentary 1: Connecting the Reading with Scripture," Proper 24, Jeremiah 31:27–34 and Genesis 32:22–31; Proper 25, Joel 2:23–32 and Jeremiah 14:7–10, 19–22; All Saints, Daniel 7:1–3, 15–18." In *Connections: A Lectionary Commentary for Preaching and Worship, Year C, Volume 3, Season after Pentecost*, edited by Joel B. Green et al., 391–93, 407–10, 426–28. Louisville: Westminster John Knox, 2019.

"Wise Participation in the Divine Life: Lessons from the Life of Daniel." In *The Old Testament in Theology and Teaching: Essays in Honor of Kay Fountain*, edited by Teresa Chai and Dave Johnson, 155–73. Baguio City, Philippines: Asia Pacific Theological Seminary Press, 2018.

"Is the Word 'Evangelical' Still Meaningful?: An Opinion." *Stimulus* 25/2 (2018) 10–13.

"Daniel's Visionary Participation in the Divine Life: Dynamics of Participation in Daniel 8–12." *JTI* 11 (2017) 217–38.

"'Belteshazzar, Chief of the Magicians' (NRSV Daniel 4:9): Explorations in Identity and Context from the Career of Daniel." *Mission Studies* 33 (2016) 26–48. http://booksandjournals.brillonline.com/content/journals/10.1163/15733831-12341432;jsessionid=181yds7aouoa7.x-brill-live-03

"Introduction." In *Living in the Family of Jesus: Critical Contextualization in Melanesia and Beyond*, edited by William Kenny Longgar and Tim Meadowcroft, 17–25. Auckland: Archer, 2016.

"'Belteshazzar, Chief of the Magicians': Lessons from the Career of Daniel." In *Living in the Family of Jesus: Critical Contextualization in Melanesia and Beyond*, edited by William Kenny Longgar and Tim Meadowcroft, 381–405. Auckland: Archer, 2016.

"'One Like a Son of Man' in the Court of the Foreign King: Daniel 7 as Pointer to Wise Participation in the Divine Life." *JTI* 10 (2016) 245–63.

"Speculations towards Change." *Thought Matters* 4 (2015) 151–69.

"Eternity and Dust? Considering Humanity, Cancer, and God." In *Spirituality and Cancer: Christian Encounters*, edited by Tim Meadowcroft and Caroline Blyth, 127–48. Auckland: Accent, 2015.

"Finding Hope and Yearning for Love." In *Spirituality and Cancer: Christian Encounters*, edited by Tim Meadowcroft and Caroline Blyth, 219–23. Auckland: Accent, 2015.

"Eternity and Dust? Cancer and the Creative God." *Pacifica* 27 (2014) 294–314.

"Building an Old Testament Library: Psalms-Daniel." *Catalyst* 40/3 (March 2014) 6–8.

"Foreword." In Yael Klangwisan, *Earthing the Cosmic Queen: Relevance Theory and the Song of Songs*, xi–xiv. Eugene, OR: Pickwick, 2014.

"Theological Commentary: A Diversifying Enterprise." *JTI* 7 (2013) 133–51.

"Introduction: An Interpretive Conversation." In *Ears that Hear: Explorations in Theological Interpretation of the Bible*, edited by Joel B. Green and T. J. Meadowcroft, 1–10. Sheffield: Sheffield Phoenix, 2013.

"'Exegesis as Love': Encountering Truth in John 14:15–26." In *Ears that Hear: Explorations in Theological Interpretation of the Bible*, edited by Joel B. Green and T. J. Meadowcroft, 191–203. Sheffield: Sheffield Phoenix, 2013.

"Spirit, Interpretation and Scripture: A Study on 2 Peter 1:19–21." In *Light for Our Path: The Authority, Inspiration, Meaning and Mission of Scripture*, edited by Bruce Nicholls et al., 24–33. Manila: Asia Theological Association, 2013.

"Is the God of the Old Testament a Tyrant?" In *Taking Rational Trouble Over the Mysteries: Reactions to Atheism*, edited by Nicola Hoggard Creegan and Andrew Shepherd, 192–204. Eugene, OR: Pickwick, 2013.

"Transforming Word and Empire: Isaiah 55:10–11 Considered." In *Isaiah and Imperial Context: The Book of Isaiah in the Times of Empire*, edited by Andrew T. Abernethy et al., 137–50. Eugene, OR: Pickwick, 2013.

(Co-authored with William Messenger). "The Twelve Prophets and Work." *Theology of Work Project*. https://www.theologyofwork.org/old-testament/the-twelve-prophets#introduction-to-the-twelve-prophets

"Pascal's Bus: A Conversation between Blaise Pascal and the British Humanist Association Buses." *Omega: Indian Journal of Science and Religion* 10/2 (2011) 101–12.

"The Gospel and the Land of Promise: A Response." In *The Gospel and the Land of Promise: Christian Approaches to the Land of the Bible*, edited by P. Church et al., 158–65. Eugene, OR: Pickwick, 2011.

"Hermeneutics and Evangelical Identity: A Literary Critical Appreciation." In *Gospel, Truth, and Interpretation: Evangelical Identity in Aotearoa New Zealand*, edited by Tim Meadowcroft and Myk Habets, 266–88. Auckland: Archer, 2011.

"Spirit, Interpretation and Scripture: Exegetical Thoughts on 2 Peter 1:19–21." In *The Spirit of Truth: Reading Scripture and Constructing Theology with the Holy Spirit*, edited by M. Habets, 57–72. Eugene, OR: Pickwick, 2010.

"In Whose Interests Do We Read? A Response to Miriam Bier." In *Reconsidering Gender: Evangelical Perspectives*, edited by Myk Habets and Beulah Wood, 161–70. Eugene, OR: Pickwick, 2010.

"Prince." In *NIDB* 4:614.

"A Desolate Land, People and Temple: Haggai and the Environment." *Colloquium* 40 (2008) 54–74.

"The Subtle Temptations of State Sponsored Theological Education: A New Zealand Perspective." *Teaching Theology and Religion* 10 (2007) 25–33.

"Method and Old Testament Theology: Barr, Brueggemann and Goldingay Considered." *TynBul* 57/1 (2006) 35–56.

"Between Authorial Intent and Indeterminacy: The Incarnation as an Invitation to Human-Divine Discourse." *SJT* 58 (2005) 199–218.

"Who are the Princes of Persia and Greece (Daniel 10)? Pointers towards the Danielic Vision of Earth and Heaven." *JSOT* 29 (2004) 99–113.

"History and Eschatology in Tension: A Literary Response to Daniel 11:40-45 as Test Case." *Pacifica* 17 (2004) 243–50.

"Vive la différence: Reflections on Human Sexuality from the Old Testament Creation Tradition." *Stimulus* 11/4 (2003) 25–30.

"Editorial: Let's Talk about Sexuality." *Stimulus* 11/4 (2003) 1.

"Relevance as a Mediating Category in the Reading of Biblical Texts: Venturing Beyond the Hermeneutical Circle." *JETS* 45 (2002) 611–27.

"Exploring the Dismal Swamp: The Identity of the Anointed One in Daniel 9:24–27." *JBL* 120 (2001) 429–49.

"Metaphor, Narrative, Interpretation, and Reader in Daniel 2–5." *Narrative* 8 (2000) 257–78.

"Christ and Creation in the Johannine Prologue." *Stimulus* 7/3 (1999) 34–38.

"Remembrance of Things Past." *Stimulus* 7/2 (1999) 1–2.

"Point of View in Storytelling, An Experiment in Narrative Criticism in Daniel 4." *Didaskalia* 8/2 (1997) 30–42.

"Sovereign God or Paranoid Universe? The Lord of Hosts is His Name." *ERT* 27 (2003) 113–27 (reprinted from *Stimulus* 4/1 (1996) 20–29).

"*katastrophei*, A Puzzling LXX Translation Choice in Hosea VIII 7A." *VT* 46 (1996) 539–43.

"A Literary Critical Comparison of the Masoretic Text and Septuagint of Daniel 2–7." *TynBul* 45/1 (1994) 195–99.

Abbreviations

ABD   *The Anchor Bible Dictionary.* 6 vols. Edited by David Noel Freedman. New York: Doubleday, 1992.

BDAG   Walter Bauer, Frederick W. Danker, W. F. Arndt, and F. W. Gingrich. *Greek-English Lexicon of the New Testament and Other Early Christian Literature.* 3rd ed. Chicago: University of Chicago Press, 2000.

BHS   *Biblia Hebraica Stuttgartensia.* Edited by Karl Elliger and Wilhelm Rudolph. Stuttgart: Deutsche Bibelgesellschaft, 1968–76.

DCH   *The Dictionary of Classical Hebrew.* 9 vols. Edited by D. J. A. Clines. Sheffield: Sheffield Phoenix, 1993–2014.

EDNT   *Exegetical Dictionary of the New Testament.* ET. 3 vols. Edited by Horst Balz and Gerhard Schneider. Grand Rapids: Eerdmans, 1990–93.

HALOT   Ludwig Koehler, Walter Baumgartner, and Johann J. Stamm. *The Hebrew and Aramaic Lexicon of the Old Testament.* Translated and edited under the supervision of Mervyn E. J. Richardson, 4 vols. (Leiden: Brill, 1994–1999; electronic ed. 1994–2000).

LSJ   Henry George Liddell, Robert Scott, Henry Stuart Jones. *A Greek-English Lexicon.* 9th ed. With revised supplement. Oxford: Clarendon, 1996.

NIB   *The New Interpreter's Bible.* 12 vols. Edited by Leander Keck. Nashville: Abingdon, 1994–2004.

NIDB	*The New Interpreter's Dictionary of the Bible*. 5 vols. Edited by Katharine Doob Sakenfeld. Nashville: Abingdon, 2006-9.
NIDNTT	*New International Dictionary of New Testament Theology*. 4 vols. Edited by Colin Brown. Grand Rapids: Zondervan, 1975-78.
NIDOTTE	*New International Dictionary of Old Testament Theology and Exegesis*. 5 vols. Edited by Willem A. VanGemeren. Grand Rapids: Zondervan, 1997.
TDNT	*Theological Dictionary of the New Testament*. 10 vols. Edited by Gerhard Kittel and Gerhard Friedrich. Translated by Geoffrey W. Bromiley. Grand Rapids: Eerdmans, 1964-76.
TLNT	Ceslas Spicq. *Theological Lexicon of the New Testament*. 3 vols. Translated and edited by James Ernest. Peabody, MA: Hendrickson, 1994.
TDOT	*Theological Dictionary of the Old Testament*. 14 vols. Edited by G. Johannes Botterweck and Helmer Ringgren. Translated by Geoffrey W. Bromiley et al. Grand Rapids: Eerdmans, 1974-2004.
TWOT	*Theological Wordbook of the Old Testament*. 2 vols. Edited by R. Laird Harris, Gleason L. Archer Jr., and Bruce K. Waltke. Chicago: Moody, 1980.

Introduction

John de Jong and Csilla Saysell

This volume honors Tim Meadowcroft, a man who has had many roles and worn many hats, on his retirement. Fittingly, contributors to this book include his PhD examiner, colleagues with whom he worked through his career, younger colleagues, and his PhD students who in turn have become his colleagues, albeit ones who still look to him for guidance and advice from time to time.

About mid-2018, six months before Tim was due to retire, Myk Habets, editor of the *Pacific Journal of Baptist Research*,[1] came up with the idea of dedicating an issue of the journal to Tim on his retirement. Csilla Saysell, Myk's OT colleague, contacted a small number of New Zealand biblical scholars, who each responded with suggestions of others who should contribute. There were far too many for a single journal issue, which ended up with six contributors, so plans for this volume were hatched. Five of the six articles from the journal have been reprinted in this volume, with James Harding writing a new one.

The volume grew somewhat eclectically from various people's suggestions of contributors, and as such it represents Tim's professional and scholarly environment. There are, however, some gaps. Regrettably, none

---

1. Now Pacific Journal of Theological Research. The issue, edited by Csilla Saysell and John de Jong, is titled *Essays in Recognition of the Retirement of Rev. Dr. Timothy Meadowcroft* (*Pacific Journal of Baptist Research* 13/2, 2018).

of the contributors is Māori or Pasifika. Neither does the volume include contributors from Papua New Guinea, where Tim has been involved more latterly, nor from Pakistan, where Tim grew up and to where he returned in 2018, for the first time in many decades, to help a theological college work towards developing a master's degree.

With the exception of a sole theologian who slipped in, all the chapters in this book have been written by biblical scholars, each of whom has history with Tim.

Some contributors were invited to write on specific topics that have interested Tim over his career: Daniel, Wisdom, Theological Interpretation of Scripture, Linguistics, and Language. Other contributors consist of Tim's New Zealand-based biblical studies colleagues, who were invited to write on any topic they wished. These are people with whom Tim has worked in a variety of settings: Laidlaw College; the Anglican Church of Aotearoa NZ; collegial contexts with Carey Baptist College, Auckland and Otago Universities, St. John's College; the Aotearoa New Zealand Association *for* Biblical Studies (ANZABS—woe betide anyone who substitutes the "for" with an "of" in Tim's presence). A number of these colleagues are from among Tim's former PhD students, of whom Stephen Pattemore takes pride of place as the first. All the contributors share a deep respect for Tim borne from long association, all have appreciated the opportunity to contribute to his *Festschrift*, and the contributions reflect Tim's wide-ranging interests and involvement in so many contexts.

David Crawley, Tim's long-serving Laidlaw College colleague, provides the Foreword, giving a personal tribute to Tim along with some biographical and bibliographical details.

The first major section of the book, Part 1, consists of essays on the Old and/or New Testaments, arranged in that order (OT to NT).

John Goldingay was Tim's doctoral examiner. In "Daniel Compares Notes with Jeremiah," along with an anecdote from the doctoral examination, John imagines Daniel and Jeremiah comparing notes together, coming as they do from the same literary setting. From these texts come plenty of things for us to think about as present day believers, along with some "interesting" contemporary readings of Daniel.

James Harding, in "Job the (Im)pious: Theological Exegesis and Ambiguity," reflects on the nature of true Christian exegesis and notes two associated risks: the temptation to interpret everything in the light of Christ's cross and resurrection in a way that closes down the meaning of the text on in its own terms, and the stress falling on the victorious aspect of the resurrection without acknowledging the darkness and confusion following Christ's death. He explores the genuine ambiguity in Job 3:15, which gives voice to both hope and defiance in the face of suffering. This ambiguity, James argues, is a necessity in theological interpretation because it gives voice to the wounded soul before God.

In "Was Ruth a *Festschrift*?" Tim Bulkeley argues that Ruth is a folktale with an oral prehistory to the written book, whose concern is not political (i.e., to exalt the Davidic dynasty or to oppose ethnocentric marriages). Rather, the story's focus is on the honorable and faithful actions of a couple who become betrothed. Following Alter's *typos* of an ancestor's betrothal in biblical narratives, Tim argues that the tale of Ruth is a short-story-length example of this, which may have been told and retold at contemporary betrothals. In this sense, as a work composed for the celebration of a festal occasion, it is indeed a *Festschrift*.[2]

Csilla Saysell, in "The Blood Manipulation of the Sin Offering and the Logic of Defilement," explores how the two aspects of blood manipulation unique to the sin offering function in achieving atonement for both ritual impurity and sin. She observes some intrinsic connections between ritual impurity and sin, which explains why they are grouped together under the same remedy. Further, she argues that the daubing of blood on the horns of the altar is a symbolic appeal for God's mercy originating in the act of altar asylum, while sprinkling the blood involves cleansing sancta (sacred objects including the sanctuary itself).

Richard Neville, in "Nothing Was Made without Him (John 1:3)," argues that Genesis 1 is not only consistent with John 1:3, which claims that God created everything, but is positively affirmed there. This is often missed by commentators because of the way many English translations render the prepositional phrase לְמִי- + pronominal suffix as "according to its/their kind" (e.g., Gen 1:24), rather than as "of every kind" (*Tanakh*, NRSV). Thus, the former makes the focus the differentiation rather than the comprehensiveness of creation, and this reading is supported by a whole host of evidence. Based on this shared link between Genesis 1 and John 1, Richard further explores the reasons why the writer of John chooses to start his Gospel with a retelling of Genesis 1.

Phil Church, one of Tim's former PhD students, in "You Have Come to Mount Zion," explores the meaning of Hebrews 12:22–24 against the backdrop of some Jewish and Messianic Jewish views that Isaiah 2:2–4 (and Micah 4:1–4) point to the Jews' return to the land of Israel, rather than primarily to the pilgrimage of the nations to Zion. He concludes that Hebrews' temple imagery is used of the fellowship of Christ and his followers, and the

---

2. It is with sorrow that we acknowledge Tim Bulkeley's passing before the publication of this volume.

letter identifies Mount Zion not with the earthly Jerusalem, which is under God's judgment, but with the heavenly city symbolic of Christ's presence, wherever his followers (Jews and gentiles) are gathered.

In a global village fractured by religious violence, Chris Marshall, "Love's Four Objects and the Pursuit of Peace," looks at the concept of a "common word" between adherents of different religious traditions. Looking at both the setting and content of the parable of the Good Samaritan, the common word between Jesus and the scribe was "love." But what does love mean, and to whom should it be given? In his interpretation of the parable, Chris challenges the notion that the love Jesus commands can only be "a volitional and activist commitment, not an emotional experience." Such a notion of love precludes the necessity of interpersonal contact and relationship and is not what the parable recounts—the Samaritan was "moved with compassion." Concrete relationships are the bedrock of peace-making and reconciliation, but for Chris this is not a merely theoretical concept, as Jesus challenges us: "Go *you* and do likewise."

Paul Trebilco, in "'Saints by Calling' in Romans 1:7 and 1 Corinthians 1:2," argues that in most modern English versions, the translation of the Greek phrase κλητοῖς ἁγίοις (Rom 1:7 and 1 Cor 1:2), "called to be saints," is misleading. "Called to be saints" sounds like the readers are being exhorted to be saints, rather than a description of what they have already become through what God has done for them; yet κλητοῖς ἁγίοις is rather a description of what Paul's addressees now are through Jesus Christ, "called saints." The concept of believers as already being saints does not preclude the call to grow in holiness, nor indeed trenchant rebuke of "un-consecrated" behavior. It is part and parcel of the "indicative-imperative dynamic of Paul's theology."

Examining the title of this book, Mark Keown, "Holding Forth the Word of Life," takes Tim's motto for the ministry of teaching biblical studies—literally: Mark took a copy of this text off Tim's office wall after Tim retired. While λόγον ζωῆς ἐπέχοντες, "holding forth the word of life" (Phil 2:16 KJV) has been translated along the lines of "holding fast to the word of life" in most modern English versions, Mark argues that the older reading is better. But this is much more than a philological argument for Mark, who challenges us to rediscover Paul's evangelistic zeal and to really hold forth this word of life.

Part 2 of the book consists of essays written on women, gender, sexuality, and the wider NZ context. In "The Disembodied Womb and the Disappearing Mother in Hosea 13:13," Miriam Bier Hinksman, one of Tim's former PhD students, reflects on Hosea 13:13 from a woman's perspective and asks the question: If Ephraim/Israel is the son refusing to be born, whose womb is he refusing to leave and who is his mother? She argues that the mother is God and that Hosea 13:13 may be added to a number of motherly images of God in both Hosea and the Hebrew Bible/Old Testament.

Karen Nelson, former PhD student of Tim, in "What about the Women of Ḥesed?" observes with others that Ben Sira's honors list ("the men of ḥesed") does not include any women. She adopts Sakenfeld's definitions for what constitutes "secular" and "divine" ḥesed and identifies a number of women in the Hebrew Bible/Old Testament who may be called "women of ḥesed" (as possessors, agents, or patients of ḥesed). Some qualify as wives and mothers, others also for extraordinary acts of courage and determination. Either way, Karen argues, they deserve to be honored just as much as the men in Sirach's list.

Caroline Blyth and Emily Colgan, in "Tiptoe through the Minefields: Navigating Gender, Sexuality, and the Bible in Aotearoa New Zealand," reflect on disturbing statistics of sexual violence in New Zealand and call on the church and wider Christian community, but especially academics, pastors, and students in these contexts, to respond to this situation. The cultural ideologies that perpetuate such violence, the church's responsibility to help survivors seek justice and healing, and the role of Christian teaching and traditions that have marginalized the survivors of sexual violence all need to be confronted. Emily and Caroline sensitively offer practical steps to undertake this process.

The genesis of Peter Carrell's essay, "Holy Love: Seeking a Unified Theology in a Divided Church," is in the General Synod meeting of the Anglican Church of Aotearoa, New Zealand, and Polynesia in May 2018, which legislated for permission to be given for blessing same-sex civil marriages or civil unions. He reflects that the two sides of the homosexual debate appeal to "love" on the one hand and "holiness" on the other and have not found a unifying theology of the two: "holy love." Peter takes test cases to show how a consideration of justice helps contemporary readers reinterpret holy commandments in the light of new contexts. He then offers some perspectives on a number of key passages relating to homosexuality from the point of view of justice.

Derek Tovey's "The Gospel of John as a Defense of Jesus' Honor?" compares the meaning of glory/honor in the ancient Mediterranean world with the Māori concept of *mana*, and notes the overlap of ideas, especially the way in which both see glory/*mana* as ascribed (from birth) and also achieved or acquired. He then sketches how John's Gospel defends Jesus' honor through the development of the narrative plot. Derek particularly highlights ways in which John's Gospel subverts and challenges ancient and contemporary conceptions of honor.

In dialogue with Chief Wiremu Tāmihana's 1861 speech to the British crown, Mark Brett, in "Whakawhiti Kōrero: Theology and Social Vocation," looks at the OT priestly and wisdom creation theologies for insights into forming a common life among different groups in society. These OT creation theologies present an "inclusive monotheism," which resonate with indigenous spiritualities. From these theologies, Mark sketches a social vision of loving our neighbor, however different that neighbor may be, as a fellow human made in God's image, without trying to make them the same as us.

The final section of the book, Part 3, consists of articles that address other issues in which Tim has long had scholarly interest: language, linguistics, and hermeneutics. Allan Bell, in "The Early Greek-Language Traditions behind the Gospels," argues against the dominant view in NT scholarship that Jesus' teaching given in Aramaic was translated into Greek only a generation or so later. He contends from a sociolinguistic perspective that the bilingual context in which Jesus operated would have led to the formulation of Greek traditions very soon after his death. Thus, there is a much more direct line from the canonical Gospels to the originating early Greek traditions than it is often thought.

In "Textual Criticism, the Textus Receptus, and Adoniram Judson's Burmese New Testaments," John de Jong, a former PhD student of Tim's who lived for twelve years in Yangon, Myanmar, compares two editions of Adoniram Judson's Burmese translation of the NT. The 1832 edition was an earlier iteration of the final 1840 edition, which remains the most widely used NT version in modern day Myanmar. The comparison shows Judson's changing approach to textual criticism of the NT, a discipline that was itself in a critical stage of development. While Judson incorporated most of the latest text-critical decisions in his earlier edition, he backtracked in the later one, his decisions reflecting the doctrinal struggles that were taking place in Judson's home base of New England.

In "Reception History: Signaling Change in Biblical Studies," Don Moffat, one of Tim's former PhD students, introduces reception history as an emerging hermeneutical model that is both highlighting and magnifying fault lines within historical-critical biblical studies. Don explains how, as a postmodern method and approach to biblical texts, reception history challenges the historical-critical search for an original text and the meaning of the text. "The" text is itself caught up in the process of reception, and the different contexts of reception affect how the text is interpreted. Yet reception history builds upon the results of historical criticism, and the two approaches are not mutually exclusive.

In "Is There a Fish in this Cognitive Environment? Relevance Theory, Interpretive Communities, and the Bible," Stephen Pattemore, Tim's first PhD student, looks at Stanley Fish's idea that while the meaning of a written text is not unlimited, neither is it fixed as different communities with varying conventions and interests encounter it. Stephen brings insights from Relevance Theory to agree with and critique some of Fish's ideas. Authorial intention and the intended meaning of the biblical text are important for communities of faith, and Stephen offers nuanced and helpful insights into this issue.

In "Linguistics and Hermeneutics," Stan Porter examines the relationship between linguistics and hermeneutics. He observes that, while definitions of hermeneutics touch on language and linguistics, none of them accommodates modern linguistics as usually understood. Conversely, volumes on linguistics mention topics relating to hermeneutics, yet do not acknowledge the connections overtly. He argues that both disciplines could benefit from learning from the other, as hermeneutics often operates with outmoded theories of language, while linguistics could gain from considering the larger questions around understanding and communication.

Martin Sutherland, "A Mimetic Model of Hermeneutics," takes an appreciative look at the 40-page "Prolegomena: Reading Haggai as Scripture," in Tim's 2006 commentary on Haggai. Martin pushes back, however, against Tim's use of Schleiermacher's hermeneutics, explaining how Schleiermacher "provides no support to one key element Tim's approach (the role of the reader) and fundamentally denies the possibility of a second (performance)." Instead of Schleiermacher, Martin argues that Blaise Pascal's concepts of the "geometrical" and "intuitive" minds would provide better support to Tim's interest in the role of the reader in interpretation. Martin brings Pascal's concepts into dialogue with modern hermeneutical theory and from this proposes "a 'mimetic' model of hermeneutics . . . a Christian hermeneutic which issues in action . . . which reflects the character of God."

In "The Bible as Sacred Re-Membering," Yael Klangwisan, one of Tim's former PhD students, and her Laidlaw College colleague, counseling lecturer Lisa Spriggens, look at Narrative Therapy, a critical concept related to identity development, which can be engaged to promote identity restoration and development. Narrative Therapy resists Western individualism by recognizing that the voices, stories, and memories of others are constitutive of a person's identity. Yael and Lisa ask what these insights from Narrative Therapy offer to reading the Bible, which is itself made up of just these kinds of voices, stories, and memories.

Part I

Old and New Testament

I

Daniel Compares Notes with Jeremiah

John Goldingay

WRITE SOMETHING ON DANIEL, the editors said, because Daniel is an interest that you and Tim have shared. Indeed, we have. Twenty-five years ago, I took part in Tim's PhD viva (defense, in US-speak) in Edinburgh. I remember raising with Tim a question about his interpretation of a particular tricky passage in Daniel and asking whether one might think about the passage in light of the framework suggested by the question of readerly perspectives on texts. He gave his doleful look and murmured ruefully, "Oh dear, that kind of question gives me a headache." It was funny at the time, and over the years it became funnier, because Tim was already ahead of the curve in thinking innovatively and literarily about Daniel, and during subsequent decades he has thought as much as anyone about postmodern approaches to Daniel. Which maybe gives me the excuse for the present essay, which has hints of intertextuality, canonical interpretation, postcolonial interpretation, reception history, and theological interpretation.

I myself am thinking about Jeremiah at the moment, so I wondered about relating Daniel and Jeremiah. Ironic implications attach to the idea of linking them. Daniel 9 explicitly refers to Jeremiah, and Daniel 1:1 sets Daniel in the same chronological framework as Jeremiah. On the other hand, critical commentators do not attach any historical credence to the opening verses of Daniel, with their reference to Daniel and his friends being in Jerusalem in the time running up to the moment when Jeremiah 36 has Jeremiah dictating his messages to Baruch, and they may attach little credence to Jeremiah 36 itself. Yet the book of Daniel in effect invites its readers to imagine Daniel and his friends in that setting.

Symbolic but Real Action

Daniel and Jeremiah suggest the value of symbolic action. Daniel becomes a vegan and a teetotaler (Daniel 1); Jeremiah urges people not to shop on Sunday (Jer 17:19–27). Neither commitment is a timeless or universal one. The Torah did not require either commitment. But Daniel and Jeremiah were inspired to see that these actions were the concrete expression of commitments that the Torah did advocate.

Nebuchadnezzar put Daniel and his friends under pressure in a number of ways. He forced them to migrate to a foreign country. He enrolled them in Babylonian degree programs. He allocated Babylonian food and wine to them. And he gave them Babylonian names that would speak of the names of Babylonian gods, as Israelite names such as Hananiah and Azariah spoke of the name of the God of Israel. Whether Nebuchadnezzar intended it or not, all these moves could have had the effect of making them forget where they came from. The story safeguards against this possibility in a number of ways. God gave them supernatural academic results. The story bowdlerizes their names: most obviously, Abed-nego is a distortion of Abed-nebo (servant of Nebo). And it reminds us that they outlived not only Nebuchadnezzar but the entire Babylonian empire and lived to see the ascendancy of Cyrus, who freed Judahites to go back home. But the one thing that they themselves did was take on a vegetarian and alcohol-free diet in order to avoid being defiled.

Whether or not they were specifically trying to avoid infringing the rules in Leviticus, they were working with a similar assumption to those rules: that there is something to be said for symbolic actions that express our relationship with such important realities as food—and sex and death, the other main preoccupations of those rules in Leviticus. Because we are bodily people, what we do with our bodies makes a difference, and it makes a difference to our attitudes. Food, sex, and death: what could be more important? And symbolism is important, as we recognize when we eat special food and put on special clothes for special occasions.

When Jeremiah urges people not to engage in trade on the Sabbath, he too is relating to an area of life that the Torah covers, yet not working directly with the Torah's own rules, in that the Torah forbade work on the Sabbath but made no mention of trade. Perhaps the development of urban life in Israel made it necessary to think further about the implications of Sabbath observance. Before urbanization, people mostly grew and made things for their own consumption as a family, though they would ideally have something left over for sharing with needy people and for bartering. There are now, in Jeremiah's time, people living and working in Jerusalem who need to buy provisions from people who grow them and who are in a position to sell jewelry and pottery and metal implements to the people who come into the city with the provisions. So, the Sabbath rule requires stretching to cover that situation.

Jeremiah implies two reasons for its observance, neither of which is anything to do with rest or refreshment. There is an economic reason and a theological one. A willingness to set aside productive work and trade for one day each week suggests a repudiation of the assumption that economics is everything. It suggests a turning aside from coveting, the last of the commands in the Decalogue. In harder times, it suggests a willingness to trust God for what one eats, drinks, and wears (Matt 6:24–34). The economic significance of the Sabbath is thus its spiritual significance.

Which leads into a consideration of its theological significance—or another aspect of its theological significance. Observing the Sabbath does not imply legalism. Paradoxically, it signifies a recognition that every day belongs to God, as tithing one's possessions and thus holding back from using all of them signifies a recognition that all one's possessions come from God. Tithing thus (again paradoxically) sanctifies them all. In a parallel way, keeping one day off signifies a recognition that all one's time comes from God, so that it sanctifies all one's days. It is a meaningful piece of symbolism that expresses something theological as well as something economic. It invites its readers to recognize the sacred.

A feature I have noticed in sermons is that the texts from which preachers start are often concrete in the stories they tell or the exhortations they issue, yet the exhortations the preachers issue are quite general—for example, that we must advocate for justice or for action to take better care of the world. Daniel and Jeremiah suggest we need to discern action that is concrete, symbolic, and significant; generalizations are not enough. If eating meat (particularly beef) is a major contributor to global warming, maybe we should imitate Daniel. If air travel stands alongside eating meat in this connection as one of the biggest polluters of the atmosphere and biggest generators of CO_2, supposing we were to give up air travel? Supposing we were to give up meetings of the Society of Biblical Literature? Supposing someone who left California but missed the beach and the sun gave up the idea of an occasional flying visit? Supposing someone who lived in the Antipodes stayed there?

Involvement with the Empire

Daniel and Jeremiah know how to read empires. They know that the king of Babylon is God's servant (e.g., Jer 25:9; 27:6; Dan 2:37–38), they recognize the emperor, and they win his recognition (e.g., Jer 39:11; Dan 2:46). They also know that Babylon is wicked and is doomed, and Daniel tells Nebuchadnezzar so (Jeremiah 50–51; Daniel 2; 4). Nebuchadnezzar was the second and longest-living king of the short-lived neo-Babylonian empire; he was responsible for reasserting control of the western part of the former Assyrian empire and for substantial building projects in Babylon itself. The book of Jeremiah portrays him with straight-faced seriousness; the book of Daniel lampoons him. Jeremiah discovers an ambiguity about recognizing him as God's servant: the Jerusalem administration understandably perceives his recognition as an act of treachery. The stories in Daniel do not suggest any ambiguity about Daniel's recognition of Nebuchadnezzar, though a postcolonial perspective might ask questions about the compromise inevitably involved in supporting the oppressive imperial regime. It has been argued that "it's impossible to understand Daniel unless one understands the perspective of a colonized person."[1] Decades before the word *postcolonial* existed, people in Korea during Japanese occupation particularly valued the book of Daniel, and their overlords banned it.[2] And Daniel has particularly attracted interpreters who appreciated its implied exhortation to resistance but not to violence.[3]

The stories have long been read by Christians as a handbook in civil disobedience. (Martin Luther King Jr. invoked the book of Daniel in "Letter from Birmingham Jail" to defend the virtue of protesting without a permit). But the story of Daniel also suggests that godly people can negotiate power by influencing leaders whose values differ vastly from their own. Ralph Drollinger, a former NBA player and the founder of Capitol Ministries, aimed to demonstrate the "exemplary behavior" of Old Testament figures like Daniel, "who stood their ground for God, and yet maintained respect for those in authority with whom they did not agree." What distinguished Daniel, he wrote, was his "loyal service" to and "manifest respect" for the king. Even though he served a foreigner who did not recognize his religion, Daniel made himself useful and encouraged the ruler to follow scriptural commands. Drollinger then explicitly likened Pence [Mike Pence, Donald Trump's Vice President] to Daniel. "For years, Governor Pence has

---

1. Reid, "Book of Daniel," 38.
2. Suh, *Korean Minjung in Christ*, 18.
3. See e.g., Lederach, *Daniel*; Smith-Christopher, "Book of Daniel"; Berrigan, *Daniel*.

embodied these aforesaid biblical characteristics, and God has elevated him to the number-two position in our government."[4]

The stories in Daniel might embody for the twenty-first century reader the compromise that is inevitable in political involvement, especially with a head of state who can easily be portrayed as power-crazy, volatile, and stupid. They might then suggest that one should not sit in judgment on people who are willing to make that compromise, though they do face them with the challenge to speak truth to power in the way they especially have the scope to.

Taking a Realistic View of History

Interpreters have always been able to do amazing things with the book of Daniel. Recently, Barak Obama was identified as the leopard in Daniel 7. After all, his father came from Kenya, which is where many leopards come from. A leopard is both white and black, as is Obama's ancestry. The leopard comes out of the sea, and Obama came from Indonesia and Hawaii. Further, the leopard has the feet of a bear in Revelation 13:2, and Obama comes from Chicago where the football team is the Chicago Bears.[5] Donald Trump has been found prefigured in succeeding chapters in Daniel.

In Daniel chapter 8, the prophet has another troubling vision of the end times. The vision takes place in Susa, which was then part of Persia but today lies in Iran. (Of course, Trump has been threatening war with Iran, which could easily become World War III or even a nuclear war.) Daniel sees a time when "rebels have become completely wicked" (ISIS) and in which a fierce-looking "master of intrigue" will arise. (Has there ever been a master of intrigue like Trump?) This master of intrigue will become very strong, "but not by his own power." (Trump is not a strong man, but he gains power through lies and deceit.) The master of intrigue will cause "astounding devastation" and will "destroy those who are mighty, the holy people." (Before Trump, the United States was the mightiest nation on earth and the only global superpower. The "holy people" could refer to Israel, a tiny nation which could easily be destroyed in a major war, or it could refer to American Christians who remain true to their beliefs, or perhaps to both.) Daniel says the master of intrigue will cause "deceit to prosper" and that he will consider himself superior. (This sounds exactly like Trump to me.) There is a battle between a ram with two horns (the Middle Eastern nations

---

4. Meghan O'Gieblyn, https://harpers.org/archive/2018/05/exiled/

5. See further, https://santitafarella.wordpress.com/2009/04/08/barack-obama-the-leopard-in-the-book-of-daniel/

of the ancient Medes and Persians, or modern-day Iran) and a goat with four horns (four nations descended from ancient Greece, which I take to be the four greatest Western empires: Greece, Rome, Great Britain, and the United States). The ram is powerless before the goat, and we have seen the Western nations dominating the Middle East since the end of World War I. Daniel 8:8 says "Then the male goat magnified himself exceedingly." (Again, this sounds exactly like Trump to me . . .) The fourth or final horn is the "little horn." Daniel 8:11 says the "little horn" will "set itself up to be as great as the commander of the army of the Lord." (So Trump will claim to be as great as Jesus Christ, but he has already done that by claiming that he alone can save Americans.) Daniel 8:12 says the "little horn" will "throw truth to the ground." (Once again, exactly like Trump.) The "little horn" will seem to be unstoppable (the incomparable US military) and the goat launches an air attack because its feet don't touch the ground (a remarkable metaphor for modern air warfare). But Daniel's vision of the end times concludes: "When they feel secure, he will destroy many and take his stand against the Prince of Princes. Yet he will be destroyed, but not by human power." Daniel was then informed by Gabriel that this was a prophecy of the distant future (our time, not his). But the time is nearing, according to the Bible.[6]

How appropriate, then, that the name Donald is an Anglicized form of the Gaelic Domhnall, "world ruler" (Donald I, Donald II, and Donald III were kings of the Picts and the Scots and thus of something approaching Scotland in the ninth to eleventh centuries).

The context of Brexit (the proposal that Britain should exit from the European Union) suggests different readings of Daniel. They are less innovative, in that there is a tradition of reading the European Union as a revival of the Roman Empire, assumed to be the original referent of the fourth empire in Daniel. And Daniel 2:41–42 pictures this revived empire as a loose and unstable confederation, symbolized by a mixture of clay and iron, from which one could infer that the UK does well to dissociate itself.[7]

You may think such interpretations of Daniel are simply nonsense, but there are probably more people take them seriously than there are people who take seriously the kind of scholarly work on Daniel that Tim and I do. And these interpretations are onto something in the sense that they align with Daniel's assumption concerning patterns that run through the history of empires (Assyria, Babylon, Medo-Persia, Greece, Rome, Turkey, Britain, the USA, China . . .). And if you asked Jeremiah, he might affirm that he

---

6 http://www.thehypertexts.com/Donald%20Trump%20Bible%20Prophecy%20Little%20Horn%20Beast%20666.htm.

7. See further, http://christinprophecyblog.org/2016/08/brexit-and-bible-prophecy/

saw similarities between Assyria and Babylon and that he wished that the people of God (and leaders he knew, like Josiah) who played with the empires thought more about God's relationship with them.

Being Prepared to Die

Daniel and Jeremiah know that they have to be prepared to die if that is the price of faithfulness to YHWH and to their vocation. Over the past week I have been engaged in a correspondence with a man who wonders about seeking ordination and was asking for advice on how to go about that process in the Episcopal Church in the United States, of which I was part until we moved back to Britain a few months ago. A key consideration was that (as he put it) he had been working on taking his faith and ministry deeper. People who hope to be involved in the church's ministry may well be people who want to grow as Christians and as human beings and to express the gifts that God has given them.

As far as we know, Daniel and Jeremiah had no such desires or expectations, and no such desires or expectations led to their becoming servants of God. Daniel found himself in the position he gained because he made the mistake of being born into the Judahite royal family and being among the people subjected to forced migration to Babylon. Jeremiah found himself in that position because YHWH fingered him and he found that he couldn't escape the commission that he had no desire to fulfill, and he too found himself subjected to forced migration in due course, in the opposite direction to Daniel.

In reading the stories of Jeremiah and other prophets, we may be tempted to assume that they are set before us as examples of vocation and ministry. The Scriptures give no indication of this implication. YHWH's servant in Isaiah 49, and Jesus, and Paul, indeed seem to have looked back to Jeremiah's commission and life and to have gained some of their self-understanding from him. But for ordinary mortals, the significance of Jeremiah's account of his commission is not that we should therefore understand our commissions in light of his but rather that we should take his message really seriously because his commission was so special. In the Gospels we are not Jesus, but the disciples and the Pharisees, and in Jeremiah we are not Jeremiah, and maybe not even Baruch, but the ordinary Judahites, the priests, and the other prophets.

Like the word mission (given its use by businesses or educational institutions to talk about their aims) and the word evangelical (given the way the media use it in a political context), the word vocation deserves to be dropped from Christian vocabulary. Like the words mission and evangelical, the word vocation has come to mean the opposite to what its etymology implies and what it once meant.

Jeremiah and Daniel know that vocation is not a way of fulfilling themselves. It's a way of denying themselves, of walking towards a lynching or a judicial execution. When Jeremiah said that the leadership in the community of faith had dug a pit for his life (18:20), he was speaking figuratively, but he was not exaggerating. When Daniel was conveniently missing when his three friends were thrown into a fiery grave because they wouldn't bow down to anything or anyone but YHWH, it didn't mean he escaped an equivalent fate (Daniel 3; 6). Most days, I walk past a memorial to Thomas Cranmer, Hugh Latimer, and Nicholas Ridley, who were burnt at the stake in the sixteenth century for their commitment to the gospel. Most weeks, it can seem, we read in the news about the shooting of (say) some Copts on the way to church in Egypt or about a grenade attack on people during worship somewhere in Africa (I should add that people of other faiths or convictions can also be subject to violence in such ways). The church in Europe, America, or the Antipodes doesn't have to feel guilty for not arousing such violence, but we might ask whether we are letting ourselves be shaped by God so that we would be prepared to walk towards lynching or judicial execution if necessary.

Recognizing That History Is Meaningless

What kind of hope do Daniel and Jeremiah encourage? They know that the arc of history bends towards justice, but not in the sense that people usually mean. They know that history is meaningless, that there is no progress. There used to be a set of beliefs called premillennialism and a set called postmillennialism (and a set called amillennialism). I'm not sure whether they still exist; I think we may have sent them off from Britain to the USA because we knew they were silly, like Halloween (but then they come back to bite you). Premillennialism implied the conviction that things were going to get worse and worse until Jesus came. Postmillennialism implied the conviction that things were going to get better and better until Jesus came. Thus Christians, like non-Christians, are divided about whether there is such a thing as progress. There is progress in the sense that I can sit in a warm room when it isn't quite light and drink coffee from our coffee machine and input this essay straight onto my laptop and check the exact origin of that phrase about the arc of history from abolitionist Theodore Parker.[8] In what

---

8. From Parker, *Ten Sermons on Religion*, 84–85. The actual quote is: "I do not

sense was Parker right? The abolition of slavery was certainly progress, but it was needed only because the slavery that needed to be abolished had first had to be invented a century or three earlier; there had been regress before the progress reversed it.

Daniel 11 offers a systematic exposition of the meaninglessness of history, of the way history is just one damned thing after another. It makes the point by the way it tells the story of events from the time of Alexander to the time of Antiochus Epiphanes, in which the unnamed kings of the south (Egypt) and of the north (Syria) engage in a sequence of invasions and battles that get no one anywhere. But Daniel is not depressed because he knows that a time will come when Michael will stand up, when the people of God will be rescued, when many who sleep the sleep of death will wake up, when all will be accomplished. Yes, the arc of history bends towards justice, not because humanity is progressing towards justice, but because God will see that its arc reaches its goal. It's an especially important promise for the kind of people who inhabit the story told in both Testaments, who are not people with the power to affect the policies of the empire. They cannot contribute to any progress, but they can be sure that God is in charge of the arc. And I like the fact that the last chapter ever written in the First Testament makes Daniel close with the First Testament's only promise of resurrection. I like that fact, because the progress that has certainly characterized history, since Jesus came to make resurrection possible, consists in the fact that billions of people now know that through Jesus they are going to enjoy resurrection life in the New Jerusalem, and indeed start enjoying it now insofar as Jesus has relocated them in spirit to the heavenly places.

Jeremiah is both less gloomy than Daniel and less forward-looking; he does not live in a time of persecution, unlike the visionary who is channeling Daniel in Daniel 10–12. Jeremiah expounds that astounding fact that the imperial oppressor is YHWH's servant (25:9; 27:6; 43:10). There is indeed sometimes a moral arc to the way history unfolds: Judah (among others) is up for devastation, and Nebuchadnezzar is YHWH's agent in bringing that devastation. The unfolding of the story told in Daniel 11 has no moral meaning. Judah did not deserve devastation. It was living as properly in its relationship with YHWH as it ever had. Its troubles came despite that fact, and all it could do was wait for YHWH to do something meaningful in history. The unfolding of the story of events in and around 597 and 587 has moral meaning. Judah is getting the comeuppance it deserves. That fact is kind-of encouraging, but it won't do as a final word. So it is just as well that

pretend to understand the moral universe, the arc is a long one . . . But from what I see I am sure it bends towards justice."

catastrophe is not YHWH's last word. Restoration will come. You will be my people and I will be your God. The covenant will be renewed. The people will live lives that acknowledge YHWH. Yes, YHWH is committed to making the arc of history bend towards justice.

Refusing to Give Up Praying

Daniel and Jeremiah pray even when God and the empire tell them not to. It's been suggested that prayer is the key to understanding the books in the Bible.[9] It's an exaggeration: I suggest that God is the key to understanding the books of the Bible, though you would probably not get that impression from most scholarly books about the Bible. But prayer is a prominent theme, and not least in Daniel and Jeremiah.

Not far into Daniel there comes the amusing account of how Daniel, having committed himself to telling Nebuchadnezzar about his dream, then goes home to get his friends to pray that he will actually be able to do so (2:17–18). When their prayer is answered, the first thing the story relates (before telling us the content of the dream) is the way Daniel gave thanks to God for being the one who reveals mysteries and for granting their prayer. Much later, Daniel is grieved over the way God has not yet restored his people in keeping with a promise in Jeremiah (!) that he would do so after seventy years; Daniel and Jeremiah know how to grieve over their people's waywardness, chastisement, and suffering. His grief leads Daniel into a long prayer of repentance on behalf of his people in which he acknowledges their transgression and rebellion but pleads with God to have mercy (Daniel 9). In due course, God's response is another revelation. Daniel needs to know that the seventy years are going to last much longer than he thought, which would be bad news for the historical Daniel, but good news for the interpreter who is channeling Daniel four or five centuries later. In between Daniel 2 and Daniel 9, Darius bans prayer, but Daniel takes no notice of the ban (Daniel 6) and seems almost to make a point of flaunting his praying, in a nice anticipatory contrast with Matthew 5:5–6. One could certainly say that his prayers also anticipate Matthew 5:7–13 as he prays to the God of the heavens that he may implement his reign. Daniel probably didn't pray not to be brought to the time of trial because he has just knowingly walked into it, but whether or not he prayed to be delivered in the time of trial and rescued from the evil one, God did deliver and rescue him.

The strength and the frustration of such stories is that they cannot be generalized. One cannot say that God will always deliver people who stand

---

9. Fischer, "Gebete als Hermeneutischer Schlüssel," 219–37.

firm in their relationship with God even when they are forbidden to do so—as the Maccabean martyrs, who listened to these stories, found. Maybe one cannot even say that such stories imply that the faithful are always bound to obey God rather than the empire (Acts 5:29). The invitation of a story is more subtle. It is something like "Here is a story about what human beings sometimes do and what God sometimes does. Live in this world rather than a world that rules out such crazy human faithfulness and such amazing divine involvement. Let your worldview be shaped by these realities not by those non-realities."

Jeremiah, too, wants the people of Judah to live by realities rather than the apparent but actually non-realities that people were inclined to live by— the deities he referred to as nonentities, as deceptions, as hollow, as mere breath. In Jeremiah, too, prayer is a key theme. He puts prayers onto Judah's lips that he wishes they would pray. He puts prayers on their lips that they do pray, and then reveals that God despises them. He prays prayers for himself, the protests that are commonly misdescribed as his confessions; they are not confessions in the sense of confessions of sin, or confessions of faith, or autobiographical revelations like Augustine's *Confessions*. One point about them is that the recording of them is part of his prophetic work. The book of Jeremiah is not his spiritual journal. It is "YHWH's message" (e.g., 1:2).

So, the first question to ask about them is: How did these protest prayers form part of his prophesying? And the answer is, they are an aspect of the way he sought to bring home to Judah the nature of what they were doing in ignoring or opposing or seeking to silence the prophet through whom YHWH was speaking. Telling people about the way he was protesting to God was one of the ways he was seeking to get his message home—as is the case when Paul tells congregations how he is praying for them (e.g., Ephesians 1–3). The same consideration applies to Jeremiah's telling people that YHWH had told him to stop praying for them (Jer 7:16; 11:14). It should be a frightening piece of information, not least because praying for people is of the essence of being a prophet. It is the first thing we learn about prophecy in the Scriptures (Gen 20:7). I don't know how far YHWH really meant his prohibition on prayer. The stories do make clear that Jeremiah is to tell people that he meant it. They also make clear that Jeremiah himself took no notice, because he carries on praying for his people—as Daniel carried on praying when the earthly king told him to stop. Maybe YHWH was testing Jeremiah, to see if he cared enough for his prophetic responsibility to assume that YHWH didn't really mean his prohibition.

Refusing to Bow Down

What is involved in being YHWH's man or woman or in being YHWH's people, as opposed to being Nebuchadnezzar's or Bel's? The question surfaces in Daniel 3. Nebuchadnezzar erects a huge image to which people are required to fall and bow down (נפל, סגד: e.g., 3:5, 6, 7, 10, 11, 15). The verbs have similar meaning, though *fall* is a more everyday word and suggests the sudden and acute nature of the action, while *bow down* implies more an intentional and deliberate action. Both are body words; in Daniel 3, only *bow down* applies specifically to God as well as to the image (3:28). It thus commonly appears in English translations as "worship," but that translation gives a misleading impression in several respects. Bowing down is a physical act, and it doesn't imply the divinity of the thing or person one bows to (see Dan 2:46). Daniel 3 is hazy over what the image represents (e.g., a deity, or the king himself), but this vagueness points to a focus elsewhere, or to some more subtle questions about the relationship between king and deity. On one hand, either way the image has Nebuchadnezzar's authority behind it, and the falling and bowing down that directly acknowledge the image are actions that indirectly acknowledge the king. On the other hand, Nebuchadnezzar's staff associate the young men's refusal to bow down to the image with a refusal to serve Nebuchadnezzar's god (פלח: 3:12, 14), and the young men accept the association (3:17, 18). In due course, Nebuchadnezzar adds a reference to their bowing down only to their own God (3:28). Recognizing the image, recognizing Nebuchadnezzar, and recognizing Nebuchadnezzar's god are related for Nebuchadnezzar, for his staff, and for the three men.

Jeremiah speaks quite frequently about bowing down (שחה Hitpael—or חוה Eshtaphel)[10] to YHWH (e.g., 7:2; 26:2) and about not bowing down to other deities or their images (e.g., 1:16; 8:2; 13:10; 16:11; 22:9; 25:6). Like the equivalent word in Daniel, Jeremiah's word commonly appears in English translations as "worship," which again gives a misleading impression in that Jeremiah's verb refers to a physical act and need not imply the divinity of the thing or person one bows to (e.g., Isa 60:14). Alongside bowing down, like Daniel, Jeremiah speaks of serving (עבד; e.g., 8:2; 13:10; 16:11; 22:9; 25:6). More distinctive over against Daniel is his talk of "going after" YHWH or other gods (e.g., 8:2; 13:10; 16:11; 25:6). These three expressions combine to suggest that the metaphor Jeremiah is presupposing is that YHWH is king and thus leader and commander-in-chief. It is as one's king that one bows down to him, and as one's commander that one follows him or goes after him, in order to serve him. In the passages

---

10. See *HALOT*, 1457.

just noted, Jeremiah speaks also about loving in the sense of being loyal to (אהב), about listening to and therefore obeying (שמע), and about having recourse to or seeking (דרש, also elsewhere בקש).

Daniel and Jeremiah thus suggest several insights about worship. First, worship is a physical act. Human beings are bodily people and we express the significance of our actions by what we do with our bodies. When I proposed to my wife, I knelt down (with a jazz club full of people watching). When someone important comes into the room, we stand. Sitting down to worship suggests we have not understood and/or are not serious about what we are doing.

Secondly, and related, worship involves service; we still talk about church *services*. Daniel and Jeremiah are not referring to the kind of service that one gives God outside the context of worship, when they are the means of YHWH's will being implemented in the world, the kind of service prophets give or that Nebuchadnezzar unwittingly gives (Jer 7:25; 25:9). They are referring to the kind of service rendered by a king's or a president's attendants and stewards and manservants and other minions, who follow him wherever he goes. In worshipping God, we are recognizing who he is and seeking to offer something pleasing to him and something that gives worthy expression to who he is. In this sense, the etymological meaning of worship is illuminating: it means acknowledging God's worth-ship. It does not mean we are seeking to have an experience that makes us feel good.

Thirdly, worship is regularly tied up with politics. Kings and presidents are people who want to be God, which is one reason why God did not want Israel to have kings. And kings and presidents want to appropriate the power and energy of worship for themselves and their political aims. Thus, presidents have prayer breakfasts and kings get themselves installed by religious functionaries. Fourthly, worship is regularly tied up with folk religion. There are points at which the First Testament presupposes that God has not left other peoples without any awareness of who he is, but Daniel and Jeremiah focus on the implications of the fact that this awareness has been clouded over. Whereas Daniel's focus lies on its having been clouded over by politics, Jeremiah's focus lies on its having been clouded over by folk religion, which generates a concentration on the way worship can serve the reasonable human desire to be sure the crops will grow, to have children, to know what the future holds, and to stay in contact with one's family members after they have passed. Thus, fifthly, worship is intolerant. Jeremiah and Daniel know that there is one real God and that Bel or Baal are not the real thing; they are YHWH's underlings. It is YHWH who is in charge of world affairs and of the future, and worship is a context in which one expresses one's trust in him in these connections.

It expresses the fact that we love him in the sense of being loyal to him, that we listen to him, and that we have recourse to him.

Jeremiah and Daniel finished their coffee, Jeremiah slipped out to Anathoth, and Daniel packed his bags to move to Shinar.

Bibliography

Berrigan, Daniel. *Daniel*. Reprinted Eugene, OR: Wipf & Stock, 2009.
Christ in prophecy. http://christinprophecyblog.org/2016/08/brexit-and-bible-prophecy/
Fischer, Georg. "Gebete als Hermeneutischer Schlüssel zu biblischen Büchern." In *Congress Volume: Ljubljana 2007*, edited by A. Lemaire, 219–37. Leiden: Brill, 2009.
Lederach, P. M. *Daniel*. Scottdale: Herald, 1994.
Parker, Theodore. *Ten Sermons on Religion*. Boston: Crosby.
Reid, Stephen Breck. "The Theology of the Book of Daniel and the Political Theory of W. E. B. DuBois." In *The Recovery of Black Presence*, edited by R. C. Bailey and J. Grant, 37–50. Charles B. Copher Festschrift; Nashville: Abingdon, 1995.
Smith-Christopher, Daniel L. "The Book of Daniel." *NIB* 7:17–152.
Suh, David Kwang-sun. *Korean Minjung in Christ*. Kowloon: Christian Conference of Asia, 1991.

2

Job the (Im)Pious: Theological Exegesis and Ambiguity

James Harding

In te, Domine, speravi: non confundar in æternum.

I

AUTHENTICALLY CHRISTIAN EXEGESIS OF Scripture begins, ever anew, on the road to Emmaus.[1] There, having reminded his hitherto uncomprehending disciples that it had been necessary for all the things written about him in the Law of Moses, the Prophets, and the Psalms to be fulfilled, Jesus "opened their mind(s) to understand the Scriptures" (διήνοιξεν αὐτῶν τὸν νοῦν τοῦ συνιέναι τὰς γραφάς) (Luke 24:44–45). Such exegesis takes place in the light of the resurrection, as the types and shadows of Israel's Scriptures reach their fulfilment in the crucified and risen Christ, and the church, in the ancient words of the Exsultet, sings his Easter praises.

There are, however, two associated risks. The first is that, in reading Israel's Scriptures in the light of their fulfilment in the Passion of Jesus Christ,

---

1. I have explored this (scarcely novel) claim at greater length in Harding, "Road to Emmaus." That essay was also written in honor of Tim Meadowcroft, and it is a privilege to extend my thoughts, such as they are, a little further here.

Christian interpreters may—as indeed they often have—seek to close down, and thereby to control, the meaning of the Scriptures, so that not only is all potential for ambiguity ruled out, but exclusive ownership is taken of Scriptures whose home would otherwise be the synagogue, the house of study, and the living faith of Israel. The line between theology and ideology is very fine here. It is, perhaps, not helped by the fact that most Christian exegesis takes place in and through translation, beginning with the ancient Greek, Syriac, and Latin versions, each of which unavoidably alters the possibilities for meaning inherent in the Hebrew *Vorlage*, chiefly (though not solely) because one language cannot reproduce precisely the same range of meaning and connotation as another. There are, of course, ways of mitigating this,[2] some more clumsy than others, but the well-known treachery of translation (*traduttore, traditore*) needs always to be factored into the work of exegesis—even if there can sometimes be a tendency to over-exaggerate its effects—for it may have profound implications for theology and ethics, not simply for the annals of philological research.

The second risk is not unrelated to the first. That is, it may be tempting (*et ne nos inducas in tentationem*) to read the Scriptures in the light of the resurrection, while taking too little account of the darkness of the cross or of the cosmic emptiness of Holy Saturday. Here, above all, it is important to pay close attention to each of the distinctive voices of the Hebrew Bible, on their own terms, without reducing them to a simple meaning that aligns without remainder with the victory of Christ over sin and death. In spite of the cross and resurrection, there remains to our still unenlightened minds a sense of the most profound confusion before the contingencies and vicissitudes of life, a confusion that can so readily take the form of a sense of divine abandonment, even enmity and betrayal (Job 13:24). The reality of human suffering—our own suffering, the suffering of our neighbor,[3] and the suffering of the world—ought not to be too quickly

---

2. Two recent sole-authored translations of the entire Hebrew Bible have taken markedly different approaches to this sort of problem. John Goldingay has attempted to reproduce in English something of the strangeness and distinctiveness of the Hebrew text, resulting in a work that is arresting, at times unnerving, and without doubt unfamiliar (Goldingay, *First Testament*). Robert Alter, by contrast, has crowned a distinguished career as a literary scholar with a sumptuous three-volume work that seeks to render the literary qualities of the Hebrew text as faithfully as possible into literary English, thus honoring the distinctive qualities of each (Alter, *Hebrew Bible*). Both, in my view, have their place.

3. I wrote this essay during the church's season of Lent, and in the shadow of the terrible events of March 15, 2019, when worshippers fell victim to the murderous intent of a gunman at two mosques in Christchurch. Before such knowledge, perhaps the faithful response is silence—and then protest.

interpreted through the cross and resurrection, when one can so easily be seduced by the specious platitudes of familiar piety, sanctioned and sanctified by the witness of generations of the faithful: "There—we have searched this out and it is so" (הנה זאת חקרנוה כן היא) (Job 5:27a; trans. Goldingay).[4] Such platitudes are all the more troublesome precisely because, in certain circumstances, they may indeed be true. In others, however, they may be dangerously misleading.

In particular, we need to pay careful attention to passages in the Hebrew Bible where the faithful response of the devout to God is protest: at one's own suffering, at the suffering of others, or at the sheer trauma of life. For the moment, we need to suspend our knowledge of the history and shape of the scriptural canon, and of the grand narrative to which it bears witness, so that we can attend closely to the outcry of a wounded soul before her creator.[5] Although there are many passages in Scripture that could be considered here, in the psalms of lament, for example, or the book of Lamentations, or in parts of Jeremiah, I would like to focus on a short passage from the book of Job, and with only one very specific question in mind: how is the uncertainty of a wounded soul before God given voice in the poetry of the book of Job, and in particular, by means of the literary technique of ambiguity? I do not intend to engage in detail with the theoretical aspects of ambiguity in literature, nor do I intend to try and survey the range of types of ambiguity that may have been possible in ancient Hebrew poetry as it is preserved for us in the Hebrew Bible; these are tasks for another occasion. Rather, I will offer an engagement with a well-known line from the dialogue of the book of Job that is as faithful as possible both to the literary character of the text and to the lived experience of a wounded soul before God.

II

In Job 13:15, the Authorized Version famously has Job affirm that, although God may kill him, nonetheless he will trust in this God: "Though hee slay mee, yet will I trust in him: but I will maintaine[6] mine owne wayes before

---

4. See n. 2 above. It is something along these lines that I was getting at in an earlier essay, Harding, "History, Hermeneutics, and Theodicy." In what follows, I will be elaborating on just one point made there, hopefully with a little more precision and clarity.

5. By excluding masculine language here, I am not so much trying to rectify the systemic problem in English of gendered pronouns and possessive adjectives as recognizing the grammatical gender of the noun נפש (while leaving aside the difficulties with "soul" as a translation equivalent).

6. In the original 1611 edition, a marginal note *ad loc.* reads "*Heb. proue, or argue,*" referring to the verb אוכיח (יכח Hiphil).

him." This rendering gives voice to the paradox that, despite the sheer desperation in which Job finds himself, he will still trust in the God who, he believes, has caused his suffering. In his little book *Tokens of Trust*, Rowan Williams cites the first half of this verse in the context of a discussion of what makes it possible to find God believable when faced with radical evil. God may be found credible in such an extremity not by "a knockdown argument explaining why evil occurs"—not, in other words, by a theodicy in the classical sense—but by "the experience of how actual people find God real even in the midst of these terrors."[7] This is exemplified, for Williams, by the witness of Etty Hillesum, who, in the midst of the nightmare of the Nazi occupation of the Netherlands that would eventually lead to her death in Auschwitz in November 1943, was nonetheless awakened to the possibility of belief in, and dialogue with, God: "What I fear most is numbness, and all those people with whom I shall be herded together.—And yet there must be someone to live through it all and bear witness to the fact that God lived, even in these times. And why should I not be that witness?"[8]

For Williams, Job is among those in the Hebrew Bible whose witness shows that, far from being "full of comfortable and reassuring things about the life of belief and trust," the Scriptures are "often about the appalling cost of letting God come near you and of trying to trust him when all evidence seems to have gone":

> [I]f, in light of . . . the universe we're actually in, we are challenged to have confidence in its maker, it isn't because he has guaranteed our safety but because he remains there, accessible and free to move things on, even in the most desperate situations. And some of those closest to the risks are most aware of his presence. In the Old Testament, Job, who has suffered indescribable loss and anguish, says at one point, "If he kills me, I shall still trust him" (Job 13.15).[9]

It is, of course, by no means clear that Job was aware of God's presence (except as something toxic and oppressive), or that God was in any tangible sense accessible and free to move things on, at least until his appearance out of the whirlwind. Indeed, it is God's very absence that becomes a major source of anguish for Job, albeit in a somewhat paradoxical way, for Job's suffering is defined both in terms of God's absence, and in

---

7. Williams, *Tokens of Trust*, 41.

8. Smelik, *Etty*, 506 (dated July 27, 1942).

9. Williams, *Tokens of Trust*, 43. See my initial response in Harding, "History, Hermeneutics, and Theodicy," 242–44.

terms of his overbearing vigilance. God's presence is both too terrifyingly real and not real enough.

There is, though, another problem with this reading of Job 13:15. It is based on the *qeri*, which is, strictly speaking, ambiguous (in a particular sense to be clarified below), rather than on the *ketiv*, which is not[10] (this is perhaps noteworthy, as one might have expected the *qeri* to resolve the ambiguity rather than preserve it). In John Goldingay's recent translation, for example, Job 13:13–17 reads (following the *ketiv*):

> Be quiet for me and I myself will speak;
> there will befall me whatever may.
> Why do I lift my flesh between my teeth,
> put my life into the palms of my hands?
> There, though he may slay me, I will not wait,
> yet I will defend my ways to his face.

10. It is not the only problem with the KJV at this point, as Edwin Good has succinctly pointed out: "KJV's religiously splendid 'Behold though he slay me, yet will I trust in him' depends on three doubtful suppositions: (1) that one can take the imperfect *yqtlny*, 'kill me,' as a subordinate clause; (2) that Ketib *lōʾ*, 'not,' is to be abandoned in favor of Qere *lō*, 'to him'; (3) that the verb *yḥl* can mean 'trust.' Like most scholars and translators, I have taken *yqtlny* as an indicative, 'he will kill me.' With many colleagues . . . , I accept Ketib's negative. But I do not find the meaning 'hope' in *yḥl*, as many scholars do. The verb has to do with waiting, tarrying (see Job's uses of it in 6.11; 14.14; 29.21, 23; 30.26)." See Good, *In Turns of Tempest*, 84. Good's criticisms, however, raise problems of their own. In respect to point (1), a certain ambiguity is created by parataxis. In יקטלני לא איחל—to follow the *ketiv* for a moment—the words are placed together without making explicit whether יקטלני is subordinate to לא איחל (and if so, in what way), or not. As for point (2), while it is possible that an emendation from the defiant לא איחל to the devout לו איחל was the work of a "pious annotator" who thought the text needed to be corrected (thus Jacobson, "Satanic Semiotics," 67), it is also possible that a scribe replaced the aurally ambiguous לו איחל with the unambiguous לא איחל, which arguably makes slightly more sense in the immediate context, and further possible that the line was originally intended to provoke contradictory responses when read aloud. Finally, with regard to point (3), while it is true that יחל Piel would not itself generally mean "hope," it is used in Job, echoing the Psalms, in such a way as to connote a sense of hope (or the lack of it), a point to which I will return briefly below (see n. 26). Yet in any case, it is by no means clear that the difference between the *ketiv* and the *qeri* here is to be explained with reference to textual emendation at all, since this seems not to have been the purpose or intent of the work of the Masoretes (on Job 13:15, see Gordis, *Biblical Text in the Making*, 50–51; Gordis, *The Book of Job*, 144). For the view that the *qeri* represents a genuinely ancient reading tradition indispensable to the recitation of the written text, see esp. Levin, "Qeri." For a summary overview of research on *ketiv* and *qeri*, with bibliography, see Tov, *Textual Criticism*, 54–59, and see now also Fox, "The Qeré." In the case of Job 13:15, the Masorah preserves a genuine ancient variant, which is aurally ambiguous, the ambiguity being familiar already to the sages of the Mishnah (see n. 15 below). The Targum, as one might expect (see Levin, "Qeri," 196–97), follows the *qeri* in Job 13:15 (הא אין יקטלנני קדמוהי אצלי).

That, too, will be deliverance for me,
that an impious person does not come before him.
Listen attentively to my utterances,
to my declaration in your ears.[11]

Here, the notion of trust would seem to be altogether absent, and a somewhat different kind of paradox would seem to be at work. Job is now saying that he will not wait, even if God is going to kill him, which would presumably render Job's protest futile. After all, if God has resolved to kill Job no matter what, then Job's protest is surely pointless, unless God can be persuaded to relent, a hope which is at best implicit in Job 13:15, and may not be there at all, except perhaps in the mind of the reader.

The interpretation of the verse also depends somewhat on whether we understand הן as a deictic interjection ("Look . . . "), that is, a variant of הנה, or as equivalent to Aramaic הן meaning "If . . . ,"[12] and whether we understand the verb יקטלני as indicative ("he *will* kill me") or as potential subjunctive ("He *may* kill me," "If he *were* to kill me"). Whereas the Job of the Authorized Version is, at least in Job 13:15, willing to trust a hostile God no matter what, this Job is rather less submissive, and insists on protesting before God, even if God has already resolved to kill him. This is not a statement of trust, or, if it is, it is a trust not so much in God as in the justice of Job's case (thus Job 13:18; 27:5) and in God's responsibility to hear it.

The problem is that it is by no means clear what the Hebrew means. To be sure, Job will shortly elaborate somewhat on what he says here, but on a first reading at least, the meaning of Job 13:15a is not clear. The *ketiv* reads הן יקטלני לא איחל, "Look, he will kill me; I will not wait." The *qeri* is to be read *hēn yiqṭelēnî lô ăyaḥēl*, but because it would be impossible to distinguish aurally between *lô* (לו, "for him") and *lōʾ* (לא, "not"), there is an ambiguity. This ambiguity is impossible to reproduce in translation without the use of paratextual elements such as footnotes. Often, scholars note the difference between the *ketiv* and the *qeri*, but without elaborating much on the ambiguity inherent in the *qeri*. For example, in the footnotes and marginal notes to *The Jewish Study Bible*, Ed Greenstein points out that the Jewish Publication Society *Tanakh* translation—"He may well slay me; I may have no hope; Yet I will argue my case before Him"—follows the *ketiv*, whereas others follow the *qeri*, "Though He slay me, yet will I trust in Him": "The MT writes 'not' but reads 'for Him.' The sense is therefore either 'I will (no

---

11. Goldingay, *First Testament*, 504.
12. For references, see Vogt, *Lexicon of Biblical Aramaic*, 113–14.

longer) wait' or 'I will wait for Him.'"[13] Greenstein does not explicitly invoke the notion of ambiguity here, yet his interpretation does allow for the possibility that the text may be genuinely open to more than one response on the part of the reader.

Robert Alter is a little more explicit, following the *ketiv* in the translation—"Look, He slays me, I have no hope. Yet my ways I'll dispute to His face"—but noting that "the intended sense of this famous line is ambiguous ... the marginal correction (*qeri*) changes *lo'* (no) to *lo* (for him), yielding, 'though He slay me, I will hope for Him.'"[14] Alter does not, however, elaborate on what the significance of the ambiguity might be. That the ambiguity is there was recognized at least as far back as the Mishnah, well known to both Greenstein and Alter, where Job 13:15a is cited in a debate over whether Job served God out of love (אהבה), or out of fear (יראה),[15] which

---

13. Greenstein, "Job." Greenstein's own translation of Job, based on extensive philological research, has just been published (Greenstein, *Job*). Greenstein maintains that Job defied God to the end, rendering Job 42:6 unambiguously, "That is why I am fed up; I take pity on 'dust and ashes!'" (*Job*, 185; cf. 7:16; 30:19; Gen 18:27). My own view, cautiously, is that the poet's use of ambiguity throughout, including Job 13:15 and reaching a tantalizingly equivocal climax in 42:6, yields a work in which Job's submission to God in Job 42:6 is irresolvably ambiguous, and can be read as a final act of defiance without distorting the text, yet without denying that Job may in fact, in some sense, submit.

14. Alter, *Hebrew Bible*, 3:498. There exists a difference of opinion as to whether קרי ought to be vocalized *qerî*, "(it was) read" (lectum est) (thus Alter; see further Levin, "Qeri," 190 n. 13), which would strictly speaking be a *peʿîl* perfect (cf. Ezra 4:18, 23), or rather *qerê*, "what is (to be) read" (legendum), which would be a *peʿal* passive participle (thus Kautzsch, *Biblisch-Aramäischen*, 81 n., following Luzzatto, *Grammatik des biblisch-chaldäischen Sprache*, 32 n.; cf. GKC §17a n. 2). It is difficult to know how much weight to place on this distinction, and Tov, incidentally, gives both options for vocalization with a single translation, "what is read" (*Textual Criticism*, 54), but behind the disagreement lies a substantive issue: is the *qerî* preserving an ancient reading tradition (thus, e.g., Levin), or is it informing the reader how the text ought to be read, the intention being to correct how the *ketiv* might otherwise have been construed?

15. See m. Soṭ. 5:5 (cited by Gordis, *Biblical Text in the Making*, 50–51; Gordis, *Job*, 144; cf. b. Soṭ. 31a):

בו ביום דרש רבי יהושע בן הורקנוס לא עבד איוב את הקב״ה אלא מאהבה שנא׳ הן יקטלני
לו איחל ועדין הדבר שקול לו אני מצפה או איני מצפה ת״ל עד אגוע לא אסיר תומתי ממני
מלמד שמאהבה עשה א״ר יהושע מי יגלה עפר מעיניך רבן יוחנן בן זכאי שהיית דורש כל
ימיך שלא עבד איוב את המקום אלא מיראה שנאמר איש תם וישר ירא אלהים וסר מרע
והלוא יהושע תלמיד תלמידך למד שמאהבה עשה:

On that day, Rabbi Joshua ben Hyrcanus taught, "Job only served the Holy One, Blessed be He, out of love, as it is said, 'Though he will kill me, I will wait for Him.' Yet the matter is still in doubt: [does it mean] 'In him I hope' [צפה Piel] or 'I do not hope'? But there is another scriptural teaching that says, 'Until I expire, I will not put away my integrity from me' [Job 27:5b], thus teaching that he acted out of love." Rabbi Joshua said, "Who will remove the dirt from your eyes, Rabban Joḥanan ben Zakkai? For all

perhaps reflects the question posed by the Accuser (השטן) in Job 1:9 as to whether Job feared YHWH without any ulterior motive (חנם "for nothing"). If this is indeed the case, then the interpretive crux in Job 13:15a may, in fact, point to an underlying ambiguity at the heart of the work as a whole, concerning both Job's motivation for worshipping YHWH and his response when YHWH abandons him to his fate.

The recent magisterial commentary by Choon-Leong Seow on the first half of the book finds several points of ambiguity in this verse and the one following and seems unconcerned with trying to resolve them, treating them rather as integral to the poetry. The subject of יקטלני, for example, is unspecified and thus arguably ambiguous: "The attacker may be an animal or hunter about to attack the creature that has picked up its piece of meat (v. 14). Either would represent God, as all the Vrss recognize."[16] Given, however, that it is difficult to identify the subject as anyone other than God, there can only be an ambiguity if we accept that there is a metaphor implicit in the verb (at least when read in light of v. 14),[17] by means of which God is represented as a hunter or a beast of prey, though we cannot be sure which. But God can surely be said to "kill," without there being any such metaphor implied (notwithstanding the fact that God is figured by means of such metaphors elsewhere in the poem), and so I am not sure we can call this ambiguous in any really tangible sense. The *qeri* לו איחל, by contrast, can be said more meaningfully to be ambiguous:

---

your life you have been teaching that Job only served the Lord out of fear, as it is said, 'A man perfect and upright, who feared God and turned away from wickedness' [Job 1:1b]. But has not Joshua, your student's student, now taught that he acted out of love?" (my trans.)

16. Seow, *Job 1–21*, 659.

17. The point of ambiguity may, then, be in the relationship between Job 13:14 (אשא בשרי בשני ונפשי בכפי), taking על מה as dittography) and the verb יקטלני in 13:15a, rather than in the subject of יקטלני as such. There may, furthermore, be another dimension to this ambiguity. Lance R. Hawley has recently examined the use of speech and animal metaphors in the dialogue. He suggests that in Job 13:13–15, Job is potentially figured as both predatory animal (i.e., the one who takes his own flesh in his teeth in v. 14a, figuratively causing harm to himself by his act of speech) and as prey (i.e., the victim of a violent attack by a predator), but the text allows both senses to stand, as if they cannot meaningfully be separated. Eliphaz seems to take up the former in 15:6, confronting Job with the charge that it is Job's own words that have put him in the wrong (ירשיעך פיך ולא אני ושפתיך יענו בך), thereby presumably rendering him again vulnerable to divine attack. The ambiguity persists in 15:6, not only because the nature of whatever further harm Job may be to suffer is inexplicit, but because Job is presented as both the cause of his own suffering, and the victim of it. Although Hawley does not reflect on this in terms of ambiguity, his study of metaphor has incidentally shown ambiguity to be a fundamental aspect of the metaphorical language of Job. See Hawley, *Metaphor Competition*, 132–34.

One may understand that Job, believing that God is intent on killing him, is nevertheless confessing his faith in the trustworthiness of God: "yet will I trust him" (so KJV; TNIV: "yet will I hope in him"). Perhaps, however, Job is being defiant. He believes that God is trying to slay him, and he, wanting to end his misery, says he is waiting for God to do just that: "If he wants to kill me, I will wait for him!" (Malbim, Tur-Sinai, Fohrer). Job would be saying effectively, "I have no hope" (Budde, J. Gray; cf. so NRSV: "I have no hope": NJB: "I have no other hope than to justify my conduct in his eyes").

Given the poet's penchant for wordplay and parody, however, one should probably consider irony in the choice of words. And *yḥl* is used elsewhere in Job's speeches precisely for his waiting for the reprieve from suffering that death affords (6:11; 14:14). The ambiguity, *perhaps a deliberate one*, is captured by the Mishnah . . . [18]

The particle אך in Job 13:15b may also be ambiguous, according to Seow, open to being read either as emphatic ("I will *indeed* defend my ways before him") or as adversative ("*Yet* I will defend my ways before him").[19] Doubt concerning the character of Job's stance *coram Deo* is thus deepened: is Job's defense of his way of life an act of unalloyed defiance, or is he conceding that his integrity permits no other course than to defend himself before God, in spite of the danger this naturally entails?[20] Furthermore,

---

18. Seow, *Job 1–21*, 659 (emphasis mine). Seow cites *m. Soṭ.* 5:5 (cf. n. 15 above). Space does not permit a full engagement here with the various authorities cited by Seow at this point.

19. Seow, *Job 1–21*, 660.

20. I am leaving aside the question of whether we should read דרכי *dᵉrākay* (thus MT) or דרכו *dᵉrākāw*, "his ways" here, which would depend on a confusion between *w* and *y* (not uncommon in the square script) and on the 3ms pronominal suffix added to a plural noun being written *-w* rather than *-yw*. This appears to be Greenstein's view, which he substantiates by citing Job 21:31 in support (מי יגיד על פניו דרכו והוא עשה מי ישלם לו), though in 21:31 Job is referring to the wicked man whose deeds go unrequited (as the context of vv. 29–33 surely implies), contradicting his friends (v. 28) and perhaps subtly impugning the justice of God, who has permitted such a travesty. It is just possible that the implied subject of the verb in 21:31a could in fact be taken to be God, which is, it seems, how Rashi understood this verse. There may, indeed, be a deliberate ambiguity here, whereby Job is intentionally alluding to the actions of God in the subtle way he phrases a rhetorical question about the fate of the wicked. By echoing his own words in 13:15b, Job is implicitly disavowing any identification between himself and the wicked, while hinting indirectly at the injustice of God. It is also surely the case that the way the legal metaphor is developed in the poem depends on an ambiguity with respect to who, exactly, is supposed to defend his ways before whom. If so, then regardless of whether there is any ambiguity in the earliest text of Job 13:15b, there is surely a suggestive echo of its language in 21:31, an echo which points to a deeper ambiguity inherent

in 13:16a it is not clear to whom, or to what, הוא ("he," or "that") refers. Does it refer to Job's confrontation with God, which he trusts will lead to his vindication even if he cannot in the end escape death (perhaps cf. 19:25–27), or does it refer to God himself? Seow proposes that the two possibilities might be held together, with Job's claim "Yes, [even] that [*viz* my confrontation with God] will be my victory" (גם הוא לי לישועה) hinting at an ironic echo of the familiar pious affirmation that God himself is the victory of the faithful.[21] We might, however, extend the ambiguity further into Job 13:16b, where כי could perhaps be construed as "for" or "that," and "no impious man may come into his presence" (לא לפניו חנף יבוא) be taken as elaborating on the nature of Job's victory: the fact that no impious man may come into God's presence in 13:16b is thus either the referent of הוא in 13:16a (taking כי to mean "that"), with הוא perhaps even simultaneously referring back to 13:15b and forwards to 13:16b to explain what exactly Job's ישועה consists of, or (taking כי to mean "for," "because") it explains why it is that Job, who is not impious, can trust so completely that his confrontation with God will lead to his vindication (even if it were also to end in his death). Some of these options may occur more straightforwardly to the reader than others, but that need not mean that the others are not also being hinted at, and the genius of the poet is in finding precisely the words to convey all these possibilities concisely, yielding an ever deeper richness of sense the more the text is read.

It is the ambiguity between *hope* and *defiance* that is my primary interest here, an ambiguity that, it seems to me, is irresolvable and inherent in the poet's choice of words. This becomes clear when close attention is paid to the way this line fits into the poem as a whole, particularly in terms of the poet's (albeit occasional) use of יחל.[22] It is important to clarify, however, just what we mean when we use the term "ambiguity" and its cognate adjective, "ambiguous." It seems to me that these words are often used by scholars when what is actually meant is that the meaning of the text is

---

in the legal metaphor as to who, exactly, is supposed to be on trial.

21. Seow, *Job 1–21*, 660, and the translation on p. 640. Cf. הנה אל ישועתי אבטח ולא אפחד כי עזי וזמרת יה יהוה ויהי לי לישועה, "See, God is my victory, I will trust and will not fear / For Yah YHWH is my might and [my] strength (or, 'song'), and has become my victory" (Isa 12:2). Whether an allusion to an affirmation such as Isa 12:2 is intended in Job 13:16a or not, the question of whether, and in what sense, Job might be able to trust God without fear is undoubtedly what the poet is wrestling with throughout the poem.

22. See further n. 26 below. We can exclude from consideration both passages where יחל Piel refers to other people waiting for Job (Job 29:21, 23), unless they bear a faint and possibly ironic allusion to Job's own waiting for God, and passages where Elihu is said to have been waiting (יחל Hiphil) for an opportune moment to speak (Job 32:11, 16).

simply unclear. That is, the text originally bore a single meaning, perhaps intended by the author, but due to the vagaries of manuscript transmission and the limitations of our understanding of the language and literary conventions of the text, we can no longer agree what it was. I have no doubt that there are many occasions in the Scriptures where this is the case, but that is not what I mean by ambiguity in reference to the poetry of Job (nor, I think, is it what Seow means, at least in this case). My concern is with ambiguity as a literary feature, in which the conciseness of a line of poetry, its sounds, and the connotations of its words, render it open to different, perhaps contradictory, responses that can be maintained together by the reader without violating the integrity of the text. Ambiguity, in this sense, was defined thus by William Empson:

> An ambiguity, in ordinary speech, means something very pronounced, and as a rule witty or deceitful. I propose to use the word in an extended sense, and shall think relevant to my theme any verbal nuance, however slight, which gives room for alternative reactions to the same piece of language.[23]

Ambiguity is certainly used in witty and deceitful ways in the Hebrew Bible, presumably echoing such verbal cleverness in the living language to which the Hebrew Bible now bears witness only obliquely. In Job, however, ambiguity is used seriously, to convey a profound theological point. This claim will require considerable elaboration, more than can be offered here, but for now it should simply be noted that the work is replete with verbal expressions, in prose tale and poem alike, that give room for alternative reactions on the part of the reader. Empson defined seven "types" of ambiguity, but it would be both awkward and anachronistic to try and impose such a scheme without further ado on ancient Hebrew poetry, given that Empson associated his types with particular periods and genres of poetry in English. There are, nonetheless, occasional points at which Empson's study may usefully be drawn upon to illuminate what we find in Job, and Job 13:15a (*qeri*) proves, I think, to be a case in point.

In what sense, then, might Job 13:15a be regarded as ambiguous, in the context of this speech, in the context of the dialogue, and of the book as a whole? I would argue that it is precisely because, as the sages of the Mishnah saw clearly, there is a genuine uncertainty as to whether Job is affirming his trust in God or not that this verse can be said to be ambiguous, and this cannot be resolved by trying to show the priority of the *ketiv* over the *qeri*, or

---

23. Empson, *Seven Types of Ambiguity*, 19. I am indebted to Elizabeth Whitcombe for pointing out to me the relevance of Empson for the study of Job.

even its preferability,[24] because Job 13:15a is always *aurally* ambiguous. That is, the ambiguity is always there when the text is *read*, in the sense of being *read aloud*,[25] and the reading tradition cannot avoid it. The *ketiv* and *qeri* together arguably preserve both possibilities not because one is preferable to the other, but because there is really no way around an ambiguity that is inherent to the poem.

If, instead of trying to decide between them, we take the ambiguity seriously as inherent to the work, then we get something like the following. Job says that he will not wait (*ketiv*) any longer to confront God, instead defending his ways before him forthwith. Yet in the very fact of defending himself before God, there is an implicit act of waiting (*qeri*), a trust and a hope that some vindication will come, at the point of, in spite of, or even by means of death.[26] This might suggest that *lô/lō' ăyaḥēl* bears a double meaning, or it might suggest—and this, I think, is my preferred alternative—that the opposition between *lô ăyaḥēl* and *lō' ăyaḥēl* is such as "to show a fundamental division in the writer's mind,"[27] or in the mind of his character, Job. Or, just possibly, both.

---

24. *Pace* Clines, *Job 1–20*, 312–13 (also 282), which offers, nevertheless, an exceptionally thorough survey of the different possibilities for interpreting this verse, somewhat more thorough than I have managed here. For a concise and up-to-date enumeration of scholarly opinions, see now Morla, *Libro de Job*, 396–97 n. 1205.

25. This is why the particular category of Kt/Qr where לא is read for לו, or vice versa, cannot derive from oral tradition, for they are pronounced identically (Fox, "The Qeré," 170–71). Job was one of the books that was not meant for public reading (cf. Fox, "The Qeré," 161), but as Saul Levin has pointed out, "a Qeri was just as necessary if a book was read in private" ("Qeri," 191 n. 14), for the consonantal text of Scripture, replete as it was with homographs, required a tradition of oral recital in order to make sense of it (לא and לו are *homophones* rather than homographs, which suggests that this particular problem of *ketiv* and *qeri* may necessitate a qualification of Levin's general point). For an ancient reference to the book of Job being read aloud, on Yom Kippur, to a high priest who was himself unaccustomed to oral recitation, see *m. Yoma* 1:6.

26. Job has, after all, said he no longer has strength to "wait" (יחל Piel), and has surrendered any hope of a long "life" (נפש) (Job 6:11). He will shortly also, perhaps echoing Job 13:15a with more than a hint of irony, say "I will wait [יחל Piel] all the days of my service, until my relief comes" (14:14) (כל ימי צבאי איחל עד בוא חליפתי bc), perhaps alluding metaphorically to the death of the mortal in 14:14a, notwithstanding the Christian tradition of finding an allusion in the OG here to the resurrection (see Seow, *Job 1–21*, 670–71, 689). There is a darkly ironic contrast here with the "hope" (תקוה) of a tree for renewal of life (14:7), with Job waiting instead for death, which is paradoxically integral to *his* hope (cf. Job 6:8–9). When he looks back on his fate, Job says that he had "hoped [קוה Piel] for good, but evil came/waited [יחל Piel] for light, but darkness came" (30:26) (כי טוב קויתי ויבא רע ואיחלה לאור ויבא אפל), with verbs of *hope* and *waiting* in parallel (cf. Isa 51:5; Mic 5:6; Ps 130:5), and the trustworthiness of Job's hope entirely turned inside out.

27. Empson, *Seven Types of Ambiguity*, 225 (this is Empson's seventh type).

III

The importance of my argument, such as it is, for the task of theological exegesis is not only that it shows ambiguity to be integral to the literary character of the book of Job—in Job 13:14–16 at least, but this can be extended throughout the book—at which point the book could be left in the hands of literary scholars, but that it shows the literary technique of ambiguity to be *theologically* significant. It is precisely by means of ambiguity that the equivocation of a wounded soul before God can be given voice. Scripture, after all, is not simply a witness to the revealed truths of doctrine. It is also a witness to the trials and tribulations of the lived faith of Israel, and to the experience of souls wounded by the arrows of the Almighty. Job's case, in this speech, is that the consolations of his sincere friends have been found wanting precisely because their piety, and the tried and tested truths of their tradition find no room for the strange exception of Job. Nor is he an exception that proves the rule of their tradition. Rather, he is the exception that proves their rule to be inadequate to the task of addressing a suffering whose meaning is opaque, and for which no attempt at explanation could be offered that would not betray a radical failure of empathy and compassion. His only option, then, is to turn to God, but in turning to God he is taking his life in his hands,[28] and it is by no means clear—deliberately so—whether this is an act of defiance, or an act of necessity for the sake of Job's integrity, and for the sake of bearing witness to the fact that God lived, even if the divine justice that was supposed to be God's witness in the world is impossible to discern.

Bibliography

Alter, Robert. *The Hebrew Bible: A Translation with Commentary*, 3 vols. New York: W. W. Norton, 2018.

Clines, David J. A. *Job 1–20*, WBC 20. Dallas: Word, 1989.

Empson, William. *Seven Types of Ambiguity*, 3rd ed. London: Penguin, 1961.

Fox, Michael V. "The Qeré in the Context of the Masorah Parva." in *Le-ma'an Ziony: Essays in Honor of Ziony Zevit*, edited by F. E. Greenspahn and G. A. Rendsburg, 156–74. Eugene, OR: Cascade, 2017.

Goldingay, John. *The First Testament: A New Translation*. Downers Grove, IL: IVP Academic, 2018.

Good, Edwin. *In Turns of Tempest: A Reading of Job with a Translation*. Stanford: Stanford University Press, 1990.

---

28. That is, his נפשׁ. Taken as a whole, the book of Job is a profound exploration of the consequences of Job's suffering for his נפשׁ (see Job 2:6), which the poet achieves, in part, by drawing on the polyvalence of this noun.

Gordis, Robert. *The Biblical Text in the Making: A Study of the Kethib-Qere*. Philadelphia: The Dropsie College for Hebrew and Cognate Learning, 1937; repr. New York: KTAV, 1971.

———. *The Book of Job: Commentary, New Translation, and Special Studies*. Moreshet 2. New York: The Jewish Theological Seminary of America, 1978.

Greenstein, Edward L. "Job." In *The Jewish Study Bible*, edited by A. Berlin et al., 1489–1556. 2nd ed. New York: Oxford University Press, 2014.

———. *Job: A New Translation*. New Haven: Yale University Press, 2019.

Harding, James. "History, Hermeneutics, and Theodicy in Light of Israel's Tradition of Protest." In *Ears that Hear: Explorations in Theological Interpretation of the Bible*, edited by J. B. Green and T. Meadowcroft, 223–52. Sheffield: Sheffield Phoenix, 2013.

———. "Scripture on the Road to Emmaus." In *Essays in Recognition of the Retirement of Rev. Dr. Timothy Meadowcroft*, edited by Csilla Saysell and John de Jong, 25–41. *Pacific Journal of Baptist Research* 13/2 (2018).

Hawley, Lance R. *Metaphor Competition in the Book of Job*, JAJS 26. Göttingen: Vandenhoeck & Ruprecht, 2018.

Jacobson, Richard. "Satanic Semiotics, Jobian Jurisprudence." *Semeia* 19/1 (1981) 63–71.

Kautzsch, E. *Grammatik des Biblisch-Aramäischen*. Leipzig: F. C. W. Vogel, 1884.

Levin, Saul. "The 'Qeri' as the Primary Text of the Hebrew Bible." Translated and edited by J. P. Brown. *General Linguistics* 35 (1995) 181–223.

Luzzatto, Samuel David. *Grammatik des biblisch-chaldäischen Sprache und des Idioms des Thalmud Babli*. Translated and edited by M. S. Krüger. Breslau: Schletter'sche Buchhandlung, 1873.

Morla, Víctor. *Libro de Job: Recóndita Armonía*. Estella: Editorial Verbo Divino, 2017.

Seow, Choon-Leong. *Job 1–21: Interpretation and Commentary*. Illuminations. Grand Rapids: Eerdmans, 2013.

Smelik, D., ed. *Etty: The Letters and Diaries of Etty Hillesum, 1941–1943*. Translated by A. J. Pomerans. Grand Rapids: Eerdmans, 2002.

Tov, Emanuel. *Textual Criticism of the Hebrew Bible*, 3rd ed. Minneapolis: Fortress, 2012.

Vogt, Ernst. *A Lexicon of Biblical Aramaic Clarified by Ancient Documents*. Translated and revised by J. A. Fitzmyer. Rome: Gregorian and Biblical, 2011.

Williams, Rowan. *Tokens of Trust: An Introduction to Christian Belief*. Norwich: Canterbury, 2007.

3

Was Ruth a *Festschrift*?[1]

Tim Bulkeley

How are we to read Ruth, and does asking about the origins and purpose of the book throw light on its contents and teaching? Since the beginnings of the historical turn in biblical studies (in the eighteenth century at the latest), there has been considerable work attempting to ascertain or estimate the probable origins and development of biblical books.[2] At the start, the focus was on source criticism and how books might have been redacted into their present forms, but over time, alongside this, an interest in form-critical questions such as the *Sitz im Leben* and possible oral origins of the material was also explored.[3] For Ruth, the possibilities of literary source criticism were limited, usually to the two genealogies with which the book ends; although more extensive theories have been proposed, none has achieved any broad success.[4]

Yet the potential interest in the origins and development of biblical books does not end with their literary history, for it seems *a priori* that a simple and memorable tale like Ruth would have been told and retold across

1. Sadly Tim Bulkeley passed away before the publication of this volume.
2. Law, *The Historical-Critical Method*, 113–39.
3. Römer, "Form-Critical Problem," 242.
4. Something like this conclusion is now such a commonplace of scholarship that it is difficult to find it discussed in recent commentaries, but see Hubbard, *Ruth*, 8 or Bush, *Ruth/Esther*, 10–16, and the bibliography there.

years before it was fixed in writing.⁵ One of the more ambitious attempts to uncover such a history was Jacob Myers's claim to reveal an oral poetic version (a nursery tale) underlying the prose tale we possess.⁶ This claim has proved unsustainable. Myers's poetic remnants demanded (among other issues) too much textual emendation to be welcomed.⁷ Yet, the thought that this story reads like one that has been told and retold recurs. In the late 1970s, Sasson, recognizing the folktale character of the book but also the absence of evidence for such earlier oral versions, used the nomenclature "folkloristic" to describe the biblical Ruth. However, a couple of decades later Gottwald was happy to describe it simply as a "folk tale."⁸

In more recent years, especially in the light of feminist readings, it has become quite common to speak of Ruth as a tale retold time and again. In her careful exploration of the possibility of assigning female authorship in some way to Ruth, van Dijk-Hemmes explores the notion of "women's culture" to develop criteria for understanding a work as such a product. As a result of her investigation, she proposes that we see the book as the product of a guild of professional storytellers and that it reached written form from the repertory of such a female professional.⁹ I do not think that one needs to invent a profession of storyteller in ancient Israel to see this story as having been shaped by its telling by women, but in other ways my proposal follows her lead. However, my view is closer to Tischler, who wrote:

> Like Mary's story, Ruth's is the kind of "old wives' tale" kept alive by telling and retelling among families. It is a story that would have been exchanged at the many places women gather to draw water and to scrub clothes, to watch their children and to prepare their meals.¹⁰

She indeed came close to the proposal I am making in this chapter when she asserts: "[T]his story smacks of the fireplace or the kitchen table, the conversations shared when families gather on special occasions to remember who they are and where they came from."¹¹ Such claims are, of course, very difficult to substantiate by evidence or arguments, since

---

5. Gottwald, *Hebrew Bible*, 554–55 saw Ruth as a folktale, while Sasson, *Ruth*, 214–15 preferred "folkloristic," as he did not see the need to imagine an oral prehistory for the story.

6. Myers, *Ruth*.

7. E.g., S. Segert, "Vorarbeiten zur hebräischen Metrik."

8. Gottwald, *Hebrew Bible*, 554–55, Sasson, *Ruth*, 214–15.

9. van Dijk-Hemmes, "Ruth."

10. Tischler, "Ruth," 158.

11. Tischler, "Ruth," 159.

evidence of oral activity from ancient times is almost non-existent. Nielsen provides an approach that offers more hope of reasoned support when she notes that, in terms of genres present in the Bible, Ruth is perhaps most like the "family histories" of Genesis.[12]

In a period when biblical scholarship was dominated by historical questions, the presence of the two genealogical fragments that conclude the book of Ruth (4:17b and 18–22) was suggestive of an editorial process. The second fills out and completes the first, but unlike the first it also sets the story into its place in the wider tribal narrative, beginning with Perez, whose birth was earlier alluded to in 4:12 (in the conclusion to the crucial scene in which Boaz obtains the blessing of the elders of Bethlehem to marry Ruth the Moabite). In a time when history seems less solid, and therefore less weighty and significant, our interest in this doubling of the genealogical links between our narrative and David may seem more political. The story perhaps excuses David's half-blood grandfather. Politics, after all, are weighty enough to govern our daily living. We might, however, wish to return our interest to the very weightiest matters possible, existential and theological concerns, since they deal with our nature and eternal destiny. In that light, we may notice that this narrative, by its telling, reveals two of David's ancestors as thoroughly חיל (worthy).

This word is interesting; while its etymology suggests that it began by describing strength and power, connotations that it still sometimes retains in the Hebrew Bible (Num 24:18; 1 Sam 2:4; Ps 18:33, 40; Qoh 10:10; Zech 4:6), it is used there more often to ascribe wealth and property ownership (Gen 34:29; Num 31:9; Deut 8:17–18; Isa 8:4; 10:14; Jer 15:13; Job 5:5; 20:18; 2 Sam 23:20 [though here perhaps a combination of wealth with bravery]) and bravery (2 Sam 23:20; 1 Kgs 14:2). Such a breadth, together with other individual examples adding still greater range to the variety of ways someone might be חיל, suggest that the word means something like honorable or respected. In Ruth, it is first used by the narrator to describe Boaz as a thoroughly suitable relative to whom the two women might turn for assistance (2:1). It is then found on the lips of Boaz, explaining how, according to him, everyone knows that Ruth חיל (3:11). Finally (4:11), it is spoken by the elders of Bethlehem together with "all the people at the gate" as a blessing on Ruth (seen as Boaz's bride) for her reputation in Ephrathah and Bethlehem. This links her to the mothers of the people/nation of Israel. In this setting, the wish is expressed that Boaz may do חיל in Ephrathah.[13]

12. Nielsen, *Ruth*, 7.

13. KJV rendered this "may you prosper," NIV likewise has "may you have standing," while NRSV, in view of the co-text and aware of the possible dynastic implications of "Ephrathah," has "may you produce children."

The term חיל may express a rather nonspecific approval or respect. Another word, however, which appears significant for the meaning and purposes of Ruth, חסד, though similarly difficult to render consistently into English when found in different co-texts, is rather more sharply defined. It refers to the virtue that should be shown in both familial and covenant relationships. It implies the sort of faithful commitment and generous solidarity on which such relationships are founded or on which they depend. As such, it is most often ascribed to God, and is one of the commonest descriptors of YHWH in the Hebrew Bible. That this virtue is a key concept in the book of Ruth has long been recognized, and indeed Ruth's statement of her commitment to Naomi during their journey to Bethlehem is often seen as a fine exemplar of this virtue (Ruth 1:16–17).

Like חיל, חסד is only used three times in the book (1:8; 2:20; 3:10), but, as Campbell argued, several such words used only two or three times in the four chapters carry a significant freight for both the plot and the message of the book.[14] In the first usage, Naomi conventionally appeals to YHWH's חסד to bless her daughters-in-law (1:8). The second usage (2:20), also on Naomi's lips, is interestingly ambiguous. In an over-literal translation, she says: "may he be blessed by YHWH, his חסד has not left either the living or the dead!" Does this חסד belong to the God whose blessing is invoked, or to the faithful relative as the reason for the blessing? That Boaz is not merely חיל in reputation but is known to act consistently with חסד is the reason for Naomi's invocation of the חסד of God upon him. The third and final use of חסד is spoken by Boaz over Ruth (3:10). During the secretive scene at the threshing floor, he asks that YHWH may do good to her, claiming (as reason) that "her most recent חסד" is greater than her former. He then goes on to explain that her most recent חסד is choosing to request marriage from him rather than from any young man whether poor or rich. It is in this context of her staunch loyalty and love for the house of Elimelech that in the next verse he proceeds to laud her as אשת חיל ("worthy woman," NRSV).

That this book is more concerned with the loyalty and honorability of its central characters, rather than with politics, may also be suggested by the fact that the bulk of the book makes no mention of the broader dynastic context which features so prominently in the conclusion and in the coda to the book. The possible exception to the restriction of interest in political dynastic matters to the last eleven verses is the potential hint in the opening words, which stress that Elimelech is a Bethlehemite and even an Ephrathite (1:1–2).[15]

---

14. Campbell, *Ruth*, esp. 13–14.

15. Whatever was implied by this qualification, today it is unclear, and no theory seems compelling.

Otherwise, it is only at the close of the book—following the denouement in 4:10 where Boaz's declaration ends (at least potentially) the problem set up at the beginning of the book—that the speech by "all the people who were at the gate with the elders" makes the wider connection clearly. The first word of their speech, עדים (witnesses), implies their acceptance of Boaz's proposal and thereby ends the business set up in the opening verses of the book: the women have a protector and the family again has the hope of offspring. Only the birth announcement (4:13) is needed to close the narrative itself. Yet the elders' blessing (4:11–12) provides interesting cues at this point, after the closure of the story but before the genealogical coda.

Following their approval of Boaz's claim to marry Ruth, the remainder of the speech by the leaders of Bethlehem does not serve the overt narrative needs of the book. Rather, this speech serves to link this narrative into the wider narrative of Scripture. They first ask the covenant God, YHWH, to make Ruth (identified not by name, but as "the woman who is coming into your house"—the mention of בית "house" suggesting the dynastic interest of their words) "like Rachel and Leah, who together built up the house of Israel."[16] The narrative of Ruth is thus linked back to the foundation of the nation. This leads to the hope that Boaz will "act worthily (חיל) in Ephrathah" and "bestow a name/reputation in Bethlehem," which also implicitly links this narrative forward to the story of Judah's kings. For, with the exception of its use in Genesis as an earlier name for Bethlehem, the toponym Ephrathah only occurs elsewhere in two messianic contexts (Ps 132:6; Mic 5:1). The use of the gentilic Ephrathite is, however, more complex. It describes Elimelech in Ruth 1:2 and refers (also?) to David's ancestry in 1 Sam 17:12, while both the other uses are rendered by modern Bibles as "Ephraimite" for evident reasons (Judg 12:5; 1 Sam 1:1).

In their next wish, the men of Bethlehem return to the past, requesting YHWH that Boaz's house might be like the house of Perez (Ruth 4:12). This narrows the past (and therefore future) dynastic concern to one of the three strands of the tribe of Judah; the story not only belongs to Judah, but, within Judah, it focuses on the Perezites. The mention of Tamar serves at least three purposes: as a reminder of the foreign women who recur in the dynasty and the genealogy of all Judahites,[17] to highlight another example of חסד (loyalty)

---

16. Their formulation, however powerful symbolically, sadly neglected to mention Bilhah and Zilpah the slaves who also shared in "building the house of Israel" according to Genesis 30.

17. A possibility stressed by those scholars who understand the book to resist the racial purity ideas of Ezra.

beyond the ordinary in this line,[18] and to name and acknowledge women in a genealogical context that so often managed to omit them.[19]

So, the ending of the story and the various concluding elements (especially the two genealogical codas) ensure that we recognize that this seemingly simple, even pastoral, idyll concerns the worth (חיל) of these ancestors of King David. Yet the book is clearly not (directly at least) political propaganda. In those genealogies, David is not named as "king" or "messiah" (anointed). Indeed, except by being the end point of both lists, he is not distinguished from their other members. That is, the interest is in David's family as much or more than it is in David, and there is no interest expressed in his kingship. Nor is there in the body of the narrative any hint of such a political concern to justify or exalt the Judean dynasty in any way.

The book tells of the meeting and marriage of Boaz, the worthy man of Bethlehem, with Ruth, the equally worthy (חיל) woman from Moab. This telling goes out of its way to identify Ruth as a foreigner. She is called a מואביה ("Moabitess") seven times (almost half of the sixteen biblical uses of this ethnic descriptor in either gender); her place/people of origin, Moab, is also mentioned seven times in the book, making this the biblical book to use this word also the most frequently. The narrator identifies her as a Moabite (at the start and end of the first chapter, 1:4 and 22, and at the start and end of the second, 2:2 and 21), Boaz's agent so identifies her to Boaz (2:6), and Boaz himself so names her twice in his solemn declaration (4:5 and 10).

Another prominent foreign ancestress of the Judean line, Tamar, is mentioned at 4:12. On the other hand, two arguments from silence might undercut this proposal. In Matthew's genealogy, Rahab (the Canaanite) was Boaz's mother; if this is tradition rather than Matthew's own invention, it is not mentioned in Ruth. Also, if support for exogamy were the book's primary concern, the author missed a fine opportunity: the elders of Bethlehem might have objected to Boaz marrying a Moabite (a historically and socially plausible objection).

So, the book of Ruth has been claimed for two quite different political agendas, conveniently suggesting two quite different historical periods for its writing, though, sadly, the possibility of dating the text on linguistic grounds does not seem to command a sufficient consensus to decide such

---

18. The word is not used in Genesis 38 but Tamar's steadfast loyalty to her family by marriage is surely what is meant by Judah saying that she is "more righteous" than he is (Gen 38:26).

19. See, not least, the genealogies of Jesus in Luke 3:23–38 (which mentions no women) and Matt 1:1–17 (which names only Tamar, Rahab, Ruth, and "the wife of Uriah").

an issue.[20] Both suggested motives for telling this tale could work; however, neither theory seems overwhelmingly supported by the evidence of the text, as this telling does not really seem shaped to either end. Rather, the book tells an everyday tale of country folk, who are prominent (חיל) merely within their rustic setting.

The pastoral and agricultural setting of the story is indeed highlighted. The location of Elimelech's family's exile is not simply Moab, but שדי־מואב, the "pastures of Moab" (1:1, 2, 62, 22; 2:6). In Ruth, this expression is most often rendered in English as "the country of Moab." If "country" is taken to mean "countryside" then this is perhaps accurate, but if "country" means "political unit" then it is possibly misleading. The Hebrew שדה refers primarily either to open land like steppes or pasture, or to arable fields.[21] In the opening of the agricultural scene in 2:2, 32, 8, 9, 17, 22, it refers to the fields around Bethlehem. As the narrative draws towards its conclusion, the word is again used of the "field" or "land" that used to belong to Elimelech which Naomi is to sell (4:32, 5). Beyond this, the settings of chapters two and three are thoroughly and typically agricultural, the harvest field and the threshing floor. These locations are highlighted and their agricultural significance pointed up by the mention of the grains (envisaged as food) they produce, and which Boaz offers to Ruth and her mother-in-law (e.g., 2;13, 15–16, 17; 3:15, 17).

The temporal setting of the events, at harvest time, was mentioned at the close of chapter one (1:22); Ruth speaks of gleaning[22] "among the ears of grain" (2:2), and from there the whole chapter reiterates agricultural vocabulary: reapers, stalks, sheaves, harvesters, reaping. The crucial meeting with Boaz ends with Ruth not only fed (including "parched grain") until she is satisfied and has excess left over, but she also collects grain, which, after separation from the stalks, gave about an ephah of barley (a whole basketful). The last verse of chapter two moves us from the barley into the time of the wheat harvest.

Chapter three is set on the threshing floor, where the final process of the harvest takes place—that is, separating grain from chaff. The final chapter is interesting. It deals with the legal complication revealed in chapter three, and then announces the birth that resolves the storyline and the

---

20. Pace Bush, *Ruth/Esther*, 18–30.

21. There is a possible use of שדה to speak of the territory of a people, the lexicons differ in how they treat this. *HALOT*, entry "שָׂדֶה," has meanings: "pasture, territory of a tribe, or of a people"; "pasturage, territory of a city"; on the other hand, *DCH* 8:112–15 has a heading "country, territory of tribe, nation," which comes closer to thought of a political unit but does not arrive there.

22. This itself is an indirect reference to the grain being harvested, gleaning being the custom of those in need being permitted to collect spilled grain from the field.

genealogy that is thus opened up. Yet the discussion of the question of who is to marry Ruth is embroiled, by Boaz, with the question of the purchase of a portion of agricultural land (חלקת שדה). This previously unmentioned field, Boaz claims, was Elimelech's possession and is being offered for sale by Naomi (4:3). Thus, Boaz brings the rustic backcloth of the narrative to the foreground even in the crucial marriage negotiations.

Thus, this narrative shows little interest in royalty or rule, but neither does it really hammer home the point that Judah's royal lineage was replete with foreign women. Tamar is indeed mentioned (Ruth 4:12) but her foreignness is not. Rahab, according to Matthew's genealogical claims, was another foreign woman in the royal lineage. Yet though she was Boaz's mother, she is not mentioned in this book about her son's marriage! Either the author was unaware of Matthew's information, or that information is incorrect, or the writer is not interested in making a point concerning foreign marriages.

Far from having propaganda goals, whether to support the dynasty or to oppose ethnocentric marriage rules, this is (as its calm and pleasant surface suggests) the narrative of a couple who marry, and of the child born to them, who becomes grandfather of a king, indeed of "the king" to whom all later kings are compared. What is more, the focus of the telling is not on this king, but on the חיל couple and their חסד.

In the light of these things we now turn to ask to whom this story was told, and the reason or motive for its telling and recording in this manner. In other words, what were the *Sitz im Leben* and purpose of this narrative? Neither of the two proposed political purposes for telling this tale suggests any particular *Sitz*. However, thinking of the narrative as a traditional tale may be a helpful place to start. Traditional tales are retold often. The details of the telling are also not infrequently adjusted to make them more appropriate to the circumstances of particular tellings. For example, when, while preparing this essay, I was discussing the workings of narratives with a friend, and she described herself retelling the story of Goldilocks to her young nephew. "Of course," she said, "the details, particularly the setting, often get adapted, because Goldilocks is his favorite story, and Auntie Rochelle must keep it interesting." Probably anyone who has often told, or rather told and retold, stories to children (rather than reading from a static edition fixed in print) will recognize the technique. Sometimes only the names have been changed, to engage the innocent; on other occasions, details of the setting may be adapted to bring the audience's recent experiences into the tale. The element that is almost sacred, and thus stable, is the plot. In retelling history, some factual elements such as names and places are also stable, yet even the retelling of history offers many opportunities for the tale to be shaped to interest and "fit" its audiences.

With the thought of such retellings in mind, we may examine this telling of Ruth, asking what elements are made prominent. The very plot of the story, as well as its telling, stresses the need for a child to continue the line of this Bethlehemite family. Naomi articulates the young women's need of a husband (1:9), and since Naomi herself is (perhaps—1:12) too old to provide the needed child, ideally one of them will marry into Elimelech's family. That Boaz is a suitable candidate for this role is highlighted (2:1) even before we are told that Ruth will glean, let alone whose field she will stumble upon. The charming and potentially rich details of the progress of their relationship in chapters two and three are engaging and entertaining even before they lead to her proposal (for that, I think, is how we are to understand her words in 3:9) and his shocking revelation that there is another candidate for her hand (3:12), which further accentuates this interest. Despite the byplay over how the related purchase of Elimelech's field might impact the redeemer's "own" inheritance (4:3–8), and even the fascinating, if now somewhat less than clear, concern with the customs of times past (4:7), this scene too is focused on the couple's betrothal.

All of this suggests that this narration may have been shaped to fit the story to a context in which the audience's minds are on a betrothal or just possibly a marriage (though there is no wedding ceremony in this telling). I therefore propose that this telling of Ruth, however else the story may sometimes have been used (e.g., to excuse David's Moabite family, to suggest moderation of Ezra's hardline policy of endogamy), finds its home in betrothal ceremonies, and we should think of that context as its *Sitz im Leben*.

It is true that the beginning and end of the book focus on marriage and on the missing and finally present child (indeed, this is claimed as justifying the story's use as political propaganda). The heart of the story (in chapters two and three) tells of the unconventional meeting, the growth of relationship and mutual respect, and then finally the betrothal of a couple.

Their meeting at the harvest field begins by highlighting social distance, as Boaz, the owner, enquires of his manager "to whom does this young woman belong," referring to Ruth, the charity-case, gleaning in his field (2:5). Following the servant's warm reply, Boaz addresses Ruth with kindly (if a touch formal) benevolence (2:8–9). Her response (which seems overdone to many modern readers) may be no more than is due given their differences in status (2:10), though Crapon di Crapona, in the light of Bedouin cultures,[23] suggested that already here Ruth the Moabite (that

---

23. Crapon de Caprona, *Ruth La Moabite*. Although at the time of his death

is, someone originating from a semi-nomadic and therefore perforce more egalitarian and less formal society than that of Bethlehem's peasant culture) is gently parodying Boaz's stuffy formality. If so, certainly, Boaz does not notice, for he replies with another formal, kindly, though somewhat verbose speech (2:11–12). Ruth's response is again correct, but again may have a small sting in the tail. She says: "May I continue to find favor in your sight, my lord, for you have comforted me and spoken kindly to your servant, even though I am not one of your servants" (Ruth 2:13, NRSV).

Those final words, even in such a bare translation already suggest that Ruth, while using such a conventionally subservient expression "your servant," is reminding Boaz that she is not in fact a member of his entourage, but her own person (cf. his "to whom does that young woman belong" in v. 5). We can also note, as Crapon di Crapona does, that the word Ruth chooses here is different from that she will use in an otherwise similarly polite address to Boaz in the next scene. In 3:9 servant is אמה, while in 2:13 the Hebrew is שפחה. The latter may be more servile, often referring to slaves owned by the master rather than merely members of his household, servants.[24] Perhaps Ruth is ever so gently reminding Boaz that he does not own her.

The relationship between Ruth and Boaz is marked by growing mutual respect and perhaps attraction. Does Boaz, for example, go so far to protect and provide for Ruth only because he respects her work ethic, as described to him by his foreman (2:6–7)? In chapter three, this relationship is subjected to Naomi's potentially disastrous scheme that Ruth lie at the man's feet in secret in the dark and trust him to "tell her what to do." The setting is dark and secretive, and the telling is also. When in the middle of the night Boaz awakes to find a woman lying at his feet, he asks: "Who are you?" She responds politely, calling herself his "servant," yet firmly: "spread your wing over your servant, for you are the redeemer." In view of the redeemer's functions within Israelite families, and perhaps even without understanding the "wing" imagery as more than an echo of Boaz's prayer (2:12) that Ruth find protection under YHWH's wings, we surely understand this as a request

---

preparing a linguistic and social commentary on Ruth, Crapon de Crapona was an Arabist by profession. Perhaps because he was not a professional biblical scholar, or because the posthumous work is incomplete, or perhaps merely because he wrote in French not English or German, his illuminating proposals have not been widely enough (in my opinion) considered in Ruth scholarship.

24. While in some places the שפחה may be free in these they are treated or spoken of as property: Gen 12:16; 20:14; 24:35; 29:24, 29; 32:5; Deut 28:68; 2 Kgs 5:26; Est 7:4; Qoh 2:7; Jer 34:9; by contrast there are few if any places where אמה seems to intend to speak of someone as owned except perhaps in cases like Exod 21:20, 26, 27, 32. My conclusion is that while a שפחה is usually owned as a slave, an אמה is more often conceived as a free or bonded servant.

that he marry her. These hints are strengthened (though not much clarified) by association of the man's cloak "wing" with marriage in Ezekiel 16:8. Boaz responds very favorably to this proposal, making clear his view that Ruth could have "gone after" any young man in Bethlehem, both rich and poor (3:10). He says he will do as she asks, for she is known as חיל (worthy, 3:11). Thus, despite the complication of Mr. So-and-so, the carefully unnamed closer candidate as redeemer, and Naomi's reassurance that Boaz's word can be relied on, both of which follow, the betrothal is settled as far as the principals are concerned.

This core is as close as the book gets to modern ideas of a romance, but it does not contain anything like ancient Hebrew ideas of romance insofar as we can reconstruct them from the content of the Song of Songs. It is hardly needed for the political agenda, yet it provides the heartbeat of the narration. Around this heart, if we consider their content from the perspective of such a *Sitz im Leben* at a betrothal or at the negotiations leading up to the formal announcement, the outer elements also arrange themselves. Chapter one, as well as stressing the importance and dynastic significance of marriage, also provides desirable teaching on חסד—the primary virtue expected in marriage—and offers a strong female exemplar of this virtue in the character of Ruth (as well as in Orpah, a woman who shows the virtue, but is persuaded by her mother-in-law's authority to take the less risky path, and so becomes a foil to Ruth). Chapter four illustrates male חסד (also presenting the anonymous Mr. So-and-so as an ordinary point of comparison for Boaz's display of חסד) and provides the happy ending.

Further support for this claimed *Sitz im Leben* comes from Alter's recognition of the narrations of an ancestor's betrothal as a *typos* in biblical narratives. Such betrothal narratives, according to Alter, involve a man in a foreign land meeting an eligible young woman at a well and assisting her, at which she invites him for a meal with her family, and the betrothal ensues. The *typos*, while standardized in its typical elements, varies in interesting ways according to the stories and the characters of the ancestors so engaged. Isaac almost disappears from his story with Abraham's servant acting as his surrogate (Genesis 24), Jacob's tale involves trickery and multiple wives (Genesis 29), while the liberator, Moses, defends the girl against a band of shepherds, chasing them off (Exod 2:15–21).

The typical elements are found in Ruth, though with the genders reversed. The girl (in this case a mature widow after ten years of marriage to Mahlon) travels to a (to her) foreign land, Bethlehem, in chapter one.[25] There is not exactly a meeting at a well, but attention is drawn to the water that has

---

25. Cf. 2:11, which draws attention to this in the telling of the type scene itself.

been drawn for her use (2:9), and the man provides a meal (2:14), not only for her but also for what remains of her family (2:18). Given Alter's recognition of such a betrothal type scene and the presence of the necessary elements here—shaped, as always, to fit the characters and plot of this narrative—it seems reasonable to suggest that the book of Ruth as a whole might serve as a full-fledged, short-story-length example of this genre.

To what *Gattung* or *Gattungen* do such stories of an ancestor's betrothal belong? To be sure, they often form part of collected "family histories," and—perhaps inevitably in such a collection as the Hebrew Bible—these family histories are also often part of the national epic. Yet, alone out of the examples of an ancestor's betrothal that we find in Scripture, Ruth is not transmitted as part of this epic (especially not in the Hebrew Bible, where it is found among the Megilloth, either between the Song of Songs and Lamentations, or between Proverbs and the Song), but rather it is a distinct book. Perhaps this points to groups of family stories, rather than a collected "family history," as the appropriate *Gattung*. In this case, such a story would indeed be told, and retold, by family members on appropriate occasions, most notably, contemporary betrothals.

Finally, at the close of my essay I am ready to answer directly the question in my title: Was Ruth a *Festschrift* and does this *Sitz im Leben* help us understand the shape and beauty of the book? If Ruth, the book, is a written record of such a family tale told at betrothals, then it is indeed and in the most literal way a *Festschrift*, a work composed and published with some festal occasion in view! I hope that in the body of the work I have indeed demonstrated that recognizing this *Sitz im Leben* does suitably enrich and enliven our understanding and appreciation of the message and the beauty of this superb tale. I also hope that in doing so I have entertained and enlightened you, in our joint celebration of Tim Meadowcroft's *Fest*, just as over the years I was enlightened and entertained, sharing with him in teaching a postgraduate course on the arts of biblical narrative.

Bibliography

Bush, Frederick. *Ruth/Esther*. Waco: Word, 1996.
Campbell, Edward F. *Ruth*. New York: Doubleday, 1975.
Crapon de Caprona, Pierre. *Ruth La Moabite: Essai*. Genève/Paris: Labor et Fides/ Librairies protestante, 1982.
Gottwald, Norman K. *The Hebrew Bible: A Socio-Literary Introduction*. Philadelphia: Fortress, 1985.
Hubbard, Robert L. *The Book of Ruth*. Grand Rapids: Eerdmans, 1988.

Law, David R. *The Historical-Critical Method: A Guide for the Perplexed*. London: A&C Black, 2012.
Myers, Jacob Martin. *The Linguistic and Literary Form of the Book of Ruth*. Leiden: E. J. Brill, 1955.
Nielsen, Kirsten. *Ruth: A Commentary*. Louisville: Westminster John Knox, 1997.
Römer, Thomas. "The Form-Critical Problem of the So-Called Deuteronomistic History." In *The Changing Face of Form Criticism for the Twenty-First Century*, edited by Marvin Alan Sweeney and Ehud Ben Zvi, 240–52. Grand Rapids: Eerdmans, 2003.
Sasson, Jack M. *Ruth : A New Translation with a Philological Commentary and a Formalist-Folklorist Interpretation*. Sheffield: Sheffield Academic, 1995.
Segert, S. "Vorarbeiten zur hebräischen Metrik. lll: Zum Problem der metrischen Elemente im Buche Ruth." *ArOr* 25 (1957) 190–200.
Tischler, Nancy M. "Ruth." In *A Complete Literary Guide to the Bible*, edited by Leland Ryken and Tremper Longman, 151–64. Grand Rapids: Zondervan, 1993.
van Dijk-Hemmes, Fokkelien. "Ruth: A product of Women's Culture?" In *Feminist Companion to Ruth*, edited by Athalya Brenner, 134–39. London: A&C Black, 1993.

4

The Blood Manipulation of the Sin Offering and the Logic of Defilement[1]

Csilla Saysell

Last year, in a meeting of "Old Testament geeks," as Tim Meadowcroft called us, we had an animated discussion about the significance of sacrifice, driven by some of the questions I raised. Towards the end, Tim turned to me and said, "I'm not sure that we have answered your questions." While the questions do not always get answered and new ones keep coming, I am grateful for the opportunity for such conversations and offer up my reflections on the sin offering in honor of Tim.

The חטאת, usually translated "sin offering," is a key expiatory sacrifice marked out by its unique blood manipulation that forms a central part of the ritual on the Day of Atonement.[2] Understanding the significance of the prescribed actions in the חטאת, however, is fraught with difficulty. First, as with most descriptions of rituals, there is very little explanation as to the meaning, so that there is a certain amount of gap-filling involved in the process of interpretation. Since the mid-twentieth century, increasing

---

1. This chapter was first published as Saysell, "Blood Manipulation," and is reproduced here with some minor changes with permission.

2. Other sacrifices with expiatory functions (Lev 1:4; 5:16b) are the burnt offering (עלה) and the guilt offering (אשם). The former, however, does not specify any particular sins, and the latter has a narrower application for very specific sins (mainly sacrilege). It is also not performed on the Day of Atonement.

methodological doubts have been raised in anthropology regarding the interpretation of rituals, though biblical scholarship has only recently started to take on board these considerations. Essentially, given the multiplicity of interpretations around rituals in general and the paucity of explanation in the biblical material in particular, the former scholarly confidence of finding a univalent meaning in ritual action was called into question. The focus shifted from a symbolic system (what does it all mean?), interpreted either from a participant or an outsider's perspective, to a functional view (what does it do/achieve?).[3]

Secondly, the חטאת is brought to address two distinct "problem areas," namely, some sins (unintentional or committed in ignorance, e.g., Lev 4:2, 13–14, 22, 27; 5:2–3) and some ritual impurities (e.g., Lev 12:6; 14:19; 15:30). In the first case, the offerer is forgiven (e.g., Lev 4:20); in the second, he or she is pronounced clean (e.g., Lev 12:8). Thus, both the issue and the resolution are markedly different in the two cases, yet the sacrifice offered is the same. The question that springs to mind is what the exact connection is between these two seemingly disparate concerns that are united under the same remedy, as it were.

This article, then, will address two issues. Taking into consideration the methodological strictures around interpreting rituals symbolically, I nevertheless wish to reflect on the actions performed in the blood manipulation of the חטאת sacrifice, specifically the daubing of blood on the horns of the altar and sprinkling. Secondly, I shall consider the connection between ritual impurity and sin in order to understand why the same sacrifice deals with both issues.

Two Influential Interpretations

The Substitutionary Model

While a detailed history of interpretation regarding the חטאת sacrifice is outside the scope of this article, I wish to take two representative examples to set up some of the background and issues at stake. Traditional Christian interpretation has generally followed a substitutionary perspective on sacrifices focusing on the resolution to sin and primarily showing concern for the effect of the ritual on the worshipper. In this view, the sins of the person were placed on the sacrificial animal via hand-leaning, and its death was accepted in place of the person's (based on the view that sin

---

3. For some of the recent methodological issues, see Gilders, *Blood Ritual*, 1–11, and Feder, *Blood Expiation*, 147–65.

leads to death, cf. Rom 6:23).[4] The actual details of the blood manipulation were left unexplained.

Despite its prevalence, this view suffers from a number of shortcomings. First, it does not address ritual impurities (which also require the חטאת sacrifice), or it tacitly assumes that they fall under the category of sin, which is not the case. Secondly, the idea that there is a transfer of sin via the hand-leaning in the חטאת is questionable. It is based on the ceremony at the Day of Atonement (Lev 16:21) when the high priest places both hands on the head of the scapegoat and confesses Israel's sins over it. However, as Milgrom points out, the hand leaning in the regular חטאת involves only one hand not two, and there is no mention of confession or the transference of sins. Moreover, it is also performed in sacrifices that have no expiatory function ("peace offerings" שלמים—Lev 3:2).[5] Thirdly, the transfer of sins is problematic because these would defile the animal, whereas we are told that its flesh is holy (Lev 6:22).[6] Further, ritual impurities and inadvertent or ignorant sins (for which חטאת is offered) do not require the death penalty.[7] Thus the punishment (the substitutionary death of the sacrificial animal) would be disproportionate to the crime.

Although many modern commentators maintain that the חטאת purifies persons, how this is achieved if not via substitution is often sidestepped. One theory that does address the question is Gane's view that the blood of the חטאת carries the sin or impurity of people to the altar, which is removed on the Day of Atonement.[8] His meticulous analysis and insightful reflections have much to commend them, though the idea that חטאת blood carries impurities and sins into the sacred sphere seems counterintuitive. It runs into the same difficulty as the substitutionary model in that the blood would be contaminated as it reaches the altar.

Milgrom's Theory of Defilement

Perhaps the most influential alternative theory in the twentieth century has been Milgrom's construal, which proposed that the חטאת purifies sancta, not people.[9] Sancta acts as a magnet to impurity, attaching itself aerially to

---

4. E.g., Keil and Delitzsch, *The Pentateuch*, 305–7.
5. Milgrom, *Leviticus 1–16*, 150–53.
6. Dillmann, *Exodus und Leviticus*, 459.
7. Milgrom, *Leviticus 17–22*, 1475. Also e.g., Eichrodt, *Theology*, 165, n. 2.
8. Gane, *Cult and Character*, 176–81.
9. Milgrom, *Leviticus 1–16*, 253–61. Milgrom's theory has been followed by others. E.g., Hartley, *Leviticus*, 57, 70. Wenham, *Book of Leviticus*, 93–96. Throughout

the temple to be cleansed regularly, as well as thoroughly once a year on the Day of Atonement. Impurity in the holy precincts is the primary problem because its undue accumulation may lead to the deity leaving his earthly abode. Thus, according to Milgrom, once sancta is cleansed from the effects of the worshipper's offence, the person can be restored in relationship to God, declared clean or forgiven. The idea, he contends, is supported first by the observation that the חטאת blood is never applied to people, only to sancta, thus what is being affected must be sancta. Secondly, at the ordination of priests when the altar and the tabernacle are also consecrated, the daubing of the חטאת blood on the altar is followed by the statement that Moses "cleansed the altar" (ויחטא את־המזבח—Lev 8:15). Milgrom further notes the parallels with ANE practices where impurity is feared as demonic. While Israel did away with demonic connotations, Milgrom argues that impurity's dynamic power to defile sancta has been retained.

There is much to admire in Milgrom's simple scheme and in his meticulous handling of the material. By fusing the source of the problem (pollution of sancta), he is able to unite the solution and explain how the same blood manipulation resolves such seemingly diverse issues as ritual impurity and inadvertent sin. For lack of space, it is impossible to give a detailed critique of Milgrom's view here; nevertheless, I wish to make two basic points. First, his argument fundamentally depends on the fact that both ritual impurity and sin defile from a distance (which he bases on Lev 15:31; Num 19:13; Lev 20:3).[10] Admittedly, grave sins can defile without the person's physical proximity, as seen in Lev 20:3 (Molech worship pollutes the sanctuary no matter where it is performed). However, where the effects of ritual impurity are described explicitly, they always spread by contact (e.g., Lev 15:4–11; Num 19:16) or close proximity (e.g., Lev 14:46–47; Num 19:14–15). The first two references on which Milgrom bases the idea of ritual defilement by distance involves gap-filling in a way that runs counter to how ritual impurity normally behaves. The actual verses do not describe the effect of the original ritual impurity; rather, they point to the result caused by delaying purification or a refusal to do so.

There are, however, some alternative ways of understanding the issue, which are congruent with ritual impurity's general behavior of spreading by contact or proximity. One is the rabbinical view that the person goes to the sanctuary or eats sacred food in an impure state (*t. Shevu.* 1:8; *Sifra*, Hovah

---

this article I use "sancta" as the technical category for sacred objects, including the sanctuary.

10. Milgrom, *Leviticus 1–16*, 257, 310–11, 946.

13:10).¹¹ Similarly, Maccoby does not think that delaying purification is sin unless the person comes to the temple in such a state. He understands neglecting purification to include an ellipsis: "if the person enters the sanctuary."¹² Another approach, I would argue, is that it is not ritual impurity per se that causes defilement either by contact or from afar, but the defiant, rebellious attitude of the person who refuses to undergo or grossly neglects purification despite the express command of YHWH.¹³ Both of these interpretations are in line with how impurities behave in general.

Secondly, Milgrom's theory relies on etymology to support his argument that Piel כפר (usually translated as "to atone/expiate") primarily means "to purge" (from the Akkadian cognate *kupurru*, "to smear, wipe" or "wipe off").¹⁴ However, as Feder points out, this is a fallacy because the word in Hebrew is never used in this concrete sense, so "there is no reason to assume that any of these potential 'original meanings' were known to Hebrew speakers."¹⁵

The above interpretations illustrate the kind of gap-filling involved in making sense of ritual and highlight why skepticism over ritual meaning has grown in recent decades. Despite the methodological strictures, there is good reason to question these extreme positions. As Feder points out, ritual arises out of social and personal concerns (famine, illness, etc.) and it functions to alter the state of affairs that are at issue. As such, it is seen as a means of communicating with inanimate forces, and in order to be recognized as viable, it must do so in an unambiguous way.¹⁶ In Feder's construal, the reason why the original connection is obscured is because rituals undergo a development in which the original action addressing a specific need is removed from its sociohistorical context when codified and needs re-interpretation within a new framework.¹⁷ This development is rather like the way writing evolves in some cultures from pictograms that have an iconic relationship to the object they stand for (e.g., the pictogram for a house resembles a physical building). As writing becomes conventionalized, the resemblance gradually disappears

---

11. Cited in Milgrom, *Leviticus 1–16*, 257.

12. Maccoby, *Ritual and Morality*, 165–81 (esp. 170).

13. So too Gane, *Cult and Character*, 144; Kiuchi similarly posits that sancta pollution occurs because of a failure to undergo purification in Lev 15:31 and Num 19:13, 20, not because the unclean person enters the sanctuary complex. It is not clear, though, whether he thinks that it is explicitly the act of defiance that is at issue. Kiuchi, *Purification Offering*, 61–62.

14. Milgrom, *Leviticus 1–16*, 1080.

15. Feder, *Blood Expiation*, 169.

16. Feder, *Blood Expiation*, 151–52.

17. Feder, *Blood Expiation*, 164.

until the signs come to represent phonetic values and lose the connection to the original object altogether.[18]

It should be noted, however, that even though the linguistic analogy is illuminating, it does not follow that rituals are equally arbitrary once codified. To be sure, the connection is more conventionalized, but that does not make it meaningless and it may still retain aspects from its former social context such that it is possible to discern "iconic" echoes. If so, then a diachronic view may provide an extra test against which a proposal on a particular ritual's function-meaning may be evaluated. In the following, then, I shall discuss the significance of the blood manipulation in the חטאת sacrifice and put forward my own proposal regarding the blood daubed on the horns of the altar, which I shall test against Feder's diachronic reconstruction as an added check on my views.

The Blood Manipulation of the Sin Offering

Daubing Blood on the Horns of the Altar

Turning to the blood manipulation in the חטאת, the key and most constant act present in all such sacrifices and unique to it, is the daubing of blood on the horns of the altar.[19] Its function is nowhere explained in connection to the חטאת. Nevertheless, it is reminiscent of the practice of taking hold of the horns of the altar in an appeal to God's mercy and protection (Exod 21:14; 1 Kgs 1:50; 2:28). This is not a substitution of the animal's life in exchange for the worshipper. Rather, the hand-leaning ceremony expresses ownership and a symbolic identification between owner and animal.[20] As the blood of the animal is daubed on the horns of the altar, it is as if the worshipper had grasped them in a plea for mercy. While initially this may sound like an unexpected connection, a closer examination highlights some noteworthy parallels.

---

18. Feder, *Blood Expiation*, 163.

19. Likewise, the blood poured out at the base of the altar is unique to the חטאת, though less significant (שפך "to pour out"—Exod 29:12; Lev 4:7, 12, 18, 25, 30, 34 or synonymous יצק—Lev 8:15; 9:9; cf. "to dash" זרק in burnt, peace and guilt offerings—Lev 1:3; 3:2; 7:2). In the Day of Atonement ceremony, it is not even mentioned perhaps because no blood is left after all the sprinkling. This may reinforce its secondary importance.

20. A number of scholars understand hand-leaning with one hand as ownership. Wright, "The Gesture of Hand Placement"; Milgrom, *Leviticus 1–16*, 151–53; Gane, *Cult and Character*, 53–56.

The concept of criminals seeking asylum at an altar or sanctuary against prosecutors is well known in the ancient Mediterranean world (e.g., *Thucydides* 4:98).[21] In the legislation of Exod 21:13-14 the only type of crime mentioned is bloodshed, and protection is only offered if the killing is not premeditated.[22] Some biblical narratives further suggest that asylum was sought in other cases as well, though again, intentionality mattered. Thus, Adonijah seeks sanctuary after plotting to make himself king (1 Kings 1:50 cf. 1:5-8, 24-27). Given that there was a certain amount of uncertainty around the succession of David, he is at first given the benefit of the doubt but eventually executed when he continues to maneuver for power (2:13-25). A further example of asylum in cases other than bloodshed is reflected in Solomon's verdict of Shimei who, having cursed David when he fled Absalom, is now offered protection as long as he stays in Jerusalem (1 Kings 2:36-38). Although it is not the perpetrator who seeks asylum in the sacred city, but the judge who offers this alternative, it may nevertheless demonstrate the idea that asylum could cover a wider range of crimes than bloodshed.[23] Again, intentionality plays a part in the judgment of his case. Although cursing God's anointed is a weighty matter, Shimei's crime is extenuated by his later confession when David is reinstated in power (2 Sam 19:23). Solomon extends clemency with some conditions (asylum only in Jerusalem), but when these measures are flouted, protection is withdrawn. The same principle of intentionality (or lack thereof) is also evident in the law of asylum cities (Numbers 35).[24] This is paralleled by the unintentional

---

21. E.g., Propp, *Exodus 19-40*, 208. Driver, *Exodus*, 216.

22. Barmash, in her detailed study of homicide, argues that altar/sanctuary asylum was not for homicide but for political intrigue based on 1 Kings 1:51; 2:28, and that Exod 21:13-14 cannot be used as an argument for altar asylum for killers. Among other things, she finds it doubtful that a killer would be allowed to touch the altar when defiled by the blood spilled. Barmash, *Homicide*, 71-93. However, her arguments fail to convince, not least because accidental manslaughter does not create the same blood-guilt as premeditated murder. It is preferable to read the narratives recounting altar asylum as an extension on the practice described in Exod 21:13-14.

23. Milgrom observes that asylum in a city with a temple is common in the ANE extending the idea of protection from the sanctuary to the whole city unlike the Israelite cities of refuge which had no known connection to sanctuaries. Milgrom, *Numbers*, 505-6.

24. Earlier scholarship supposed that cities of refuge were developed in a later period, when altars became off-limits to the laity due to the priestly theology of holiness (e.g., Milgrom, *Numbers*, 505). Barmash, however, argues that the two developments are parallel rather than consecutive (e.g., Deut 19:1-13 does not introduce cities of refuge as an innovation and Neh 6:10-11 suggests that sanctuary asylum was still valid in the postexilic period). Barmash, *Homicide*, 73-74, 78-79. The supposed chronology of these developments does not affect my argument, though if Barmash is right and altar/sanctuary asylum is an ongoing possibility even in the postexilic period, then the blood

sins for which the חטאת is offered. To the question of how ritual impurities fit into the above scheme, I shall return later; suffice it to say here that they likewise share a lack of intentionality and mostly arise out of the human condition. Thus, the person with skin disease cannot help the outbreak, nor the one with a discharge. Although childbirth can be traced back to an intentional sexual act that triggered a chain of events leading to it, conception itself cannot be predicted or controlled. We see then that there is a reasonably good parallel between altar/sanctuary or city asylum—which encompass a wider set of sins than accidental homicide—and the unintentional sins and ritual impurities covered by the חטאת.

It is also noteworthy that Feder in his exploration of the social contexts in which the root כפר was used, traces the lexical forms back to homicide and blood feuds in which the Piel verb כפר was originally about appeasing the blood avenger or the innocent blood of the victim, which cried out for justice.[25] If he is correct, then this diachronic perspective provides further connection and support for my theory.

The one exception that does not fit comfortably with my analysis is Lev 8:15 where Moses daubs blood on the horns and thereby purifies it (ויחטא את־המזבח). The preposition את־ makes the altar the direct object of cleansing. As mentioned before, this forms the basis for Milgrom's theory that the חטאת purifies sancta, not people. It is worth noting, however, that this is a unique occasion, which is not meant to be repeated regularly and therefore not the best basis on which to build a case for the interpretation of the regular חטאת.

Moreover, Feder argues in his diachronic examination of Leviticus 8 and Exodus 29 (consecration of the altar and the priests) that the original function of the חטאת was atonement for people. The idea of purging the altar was a later development, together with the shift of expressions moving from כפר על־ "making expiation on behalf of" to כפר את־ + direct object "to purge."[26] This is a good example of the earlier point about the evolving of ritual function moving away from an iconic relationship between action and function to an increasingly conventionalized one needing explanation. Thus, the fact that an explicit statement is given regarding the function of daubing the blood on the horns of the altar suggests that the original iconic (and therefore self-evident) link between action and function has become obscured. In other words, the חטאת sacrifice in Lev 8:15 may be the

---

daubed on the altar does have a stronger iconic connection that would be recognizable and memorable.

25. Feder, *Blood Expiation*, 167–96.
26. Feder, *Blood Expiation*, 45–53.

Sprinkling the Blood

I now turn briefly to the action of sprinkling (Hiphil נזה) in the חטאת sacrifice, which is uncontroversial and fairly straightforward. While it is not unique to the חטאת, it is never practiced in the other major sacrifices (burnt, peace or guilt offerings). In the חטאת, it is only performed when the whole community is implicated in the sin. Thus, it is done in the case of the high priest whose unintentional sin brings guilt on the people (Lev 4:3, 6) and when Israel, as a whole, sins (Lev 4:13, 17). Corresponding to the above, sprinkling occurs in the Day of Atonement ceremony in connection with the high priest (Lev 16:11) and the people as a whole (v. 15), highlighting again the communal aspect. Leviticus 4 does not explain the reason for the sprinkling, and the atonement formula still points to atonement for the people involved (כפר על- in Lev 4:20 or בעד כפר in 16:11 both meaning "to atone for/on behalf of"). Nevertheless, this additional action underlines the seriousness of communal sin. In the Day of Atonement ceremony, however, sprinkling becomes a prominent element alongside daubing blood on the horns of the altar. Corresponding to it, the atonement formula for people (Lev 16:11, 17) is complemented by a second formula for sancta (כפר את- + direct object—Lev 16:16, 18–20). The former appears in every חטאת just like the daubing of blood on the horns of the altar.[27] Therefore I propose that the twofold action in the חטאת relate to the two objects the חטאת affects: the blood on the horns is linked to atonement for people and sprinkling to the same for sancta. In other texts where blood, water, or water and ashes are used in sprinkling, the action is interpreted as cleansing the person or object (Lev 14:7, 51–52; Num 8:7; 19:12, 19) and there is no reason to doubt the same function in the Day of Atonement ceremony of sprinkling the חטאת blood.[28]

From a diachronic perspective, Feder considers sprinkling a secondary development.[29] Further, in his exploration of the verb כפר, he observes that the initial nuance of the word in the context of homicide is to appease someone's/God's anger, which gradually changes to a more mechanistic view

---

27. Lev 4:20, 26, 31, 35; 5:6, 10, 13; 8:34; 9:7; 12:8; 14:19, 31; 15:15, 30; 16:11, 17.

28. When oil is used for sprinkling (occasionally mixed with blood) it functions as consecration (Exod 29:21; Lev 8:11, 30).

29. Feder, *Blood Expiation*, 38–43.

of dealing with the bloodguilt that leaves a stain or creates a debt.[30] "In other words, a dynamic that was once understood as the expression of the wills of personalized supernatural actors was ultimately treated as an embedded law of nature."[31] This coheres well with my own observations regarding the two-fold action in the חטאת. While the daubing of blood on the horns of the altar reflects a relational element between persons (humans appealing to God's mercy), the sprinkling action corresponds better with the idea that actions leave a physical mark on the environment in the form of defilement, which needs to be dealt with.

The question that remains is how these two different aspects of the חטאת and the two main actions performed in the ritual relate to the two types of issues for which חטאת is brought. At first glance, appealing to God's mercy and protection by metaphorically grabbing the horns of the altar fits better with the question of sin, while cleansing the altar seems more appropriate in the context of ritual impurities.

The Connection Between Ritual Impurity and Sin

In the following, I shall explore the connection between ritual impurity and sin in order to understand why the חטאת is offered for both ritual impurity and some sins and how the two-fold action of blood on the horns of the altar and sprinkling relate to them. To start with, it is worth reiterating the basic characteristics of ritual impurity and sin.[32] The four major groups of ritual impurity are connected to childbirth, leprosy, (genital) discharges, and corpse contamination (Leviticus 12–15; Numbers 19).[33] Ritual impurity defiles the person and is contagious. Certain forms may be contracted by touch (e.g., some genital discharges—Lev 15:4–12, 19–28), the more virulent ones pollute even by close proximity (corpse contamination—Num 19:14). It has long been noted in scholarship that these four categories that generate ritual impurity relate to sex (childbirth, genital discharge) and death (leprosy, corpse contamination).[34] While not sinful,

---

30. Feder, *Blood Expiation*, 173–86.

31. Feder, *Blood Expiation*, 183.

32. For a helpful discussion of terms and of the nature of ritual impurity in the OT see Klawans, *Impurity and Sin*, 21–42.

33. It should be noted that "leprosy" in the Bible is a reference to a variety of skin/scale diseases such as eczema or the like. I simply use the conventional term for convenience.

34. Leprosy has the least obvious connection to death, but as Milgrom points out, scaly skin is seen as a disintegration of the body (cf. Num 12:12). Milgrom, *Leviticus 1–16*, 1002. For the view that ritual impurities link in with sex and death, see

they are singled out as problematic in God's presence (symbolized by the idea of impurity) indicative of the need for the worshipper to become more god-like in order to approach the divine.[35] Sex and death are two major attributes that at present mark out humanity in contradistinction to God who neither dies nor procreates.

The dual focus on sex and death in ritual impurity is mirrored in the moral realm in the sin of sexual immorality and murder and in the religious realm in the worship of other gods (spiritual adultery) and child sacrifice (again, murder).[36] These grave sins likewise defile, though they are not contagious by touch or proximity, but have an effect even if the person does not come to the sanctuary. This may indicate that sin is always unacceptable not only when one approaches God's presence, but at all times and in all places.

There is also a certain significance discernible in the nature of the sin and the locus of its effects. Thus, sexual immorality (incest, bestiality, adultery, etc.) defiles the person (Lev 18:20, 23, 24), but also the land (v. 25), bloodshed likewise defiles the land (Num 35:30–34), and the worship of other gods defiles the sanctuary (Lev 20:3) and God's name. In Israel's legislation, both sexual immorality and murder are civil offences against other people, even if, ultimately, they are sins against YHWH. In the first instance then, defilement affects the land where the community lives, though it will eventually affect the sanctuary in the sense that it stands in polluted land. The worship of other gods most directly offends YHWH, hence it is his earthly dwelling place that is defiled. Further, it is a taint on his reputation, since such blatant unfaithfulness reflects badly on him. Most significantly, the taint that these grave sins leave cannot be removed

---

Frymer-Kensky, "Pollution, Purification, and Purgation," 401; Wright, "Unclean and Clean (OT)," 739. Milgrom subsumes the sexual aspect under the idea of death suggesting that genital discharge (blood, semen) are the loss of potential life. Milgrom, *Leviticus 1–16*, 766–68, 1000–4. For an evaluation of Milgrom and arguments for the dual rationale see also Klawans, *Purity, Sacrifice, and the Temple*, 56–58.

35. Sexual union in marriage is a gift of God and procreation a mandate (Gen 1:28; 2:24) and only inappropriate post-Eden in the context of meeting the divine (cf. the need to cover genitals in God's presence—Gen 3:7, 21; Exod 20:26; 28:42–43, to abstain from sexual activity to meet God at Sinai—Exod 19:16). Arguably, death may be seen as more negative (Gen 3:19) though recognized as part of humanity's present condition and in that sense a natural and unavoidable occurrence. For an insightful and detailed reflection on the function of *imitatio Dei* in ritual and sacrifice see esp. Klawans, *Purity, Sacrifice, and the Temple*, 58–66.

36. Molech worship is included in a list on sexual immoralities in Lev 18:21, and Israel's unfaithfulness with other gods is routinely described as spiritual adultery throughout the OT. E.g., Deut 31:16; Judg 8:27; Isa 57:3; Jer 2:20; 3:2, 6–10; 13:27 Ezek 16:15–22; 23:27; Hos 1:2, 4:12–13; Ps 106:39; 1 Chr 5:25, etc.

by sacrifice (Num 15:30–31) but only by the death of the sinner, so it is imperative that Israel avoid these.

Wright, in reflecting on the connection between ritual and moral impurity, saw the former as a first line of defense, a hedge around the more serious issues, which provides a test of one's attitude. Those who breach this outer perimeter of faithfulness will not stop there but will break the moral-religious law too.[37] Thus to ignore purity rules is in one sense a mark of arrogance, dismissing the distinction between God and humanity that separates finite human beings in their current condition from the divine. In other words, it negates the necessity for preparation in meeting God and suggests an implicit equality with him. Corresponding to the direct affront to God himself, the object of defilement is again his sanctuary (Lev 15:31; Num 19:13, 20).

Put differently, purification from ritual impurities is a constant reminder to abstain from grave sins and an index of faithfulness in the weightier moral-religious matters. Thus, there is an intrinsic connection between ritual impurities and sins in that the former provide a "preview" of the pathology of sin, which in its excessive forms can defile in a deadlier way than ritual impurities. On another level, as we have seen, both ritual impurities and inadvertent sins share a lack of intentionality and therefore present a low-grade risk, so grouping them together under the חטאת sacrifice makes sense.

Conclusion

In conclusion, given the multiplicity of connections between ritual impurity and sin on several levels, it becomes clearer how the actions performed in the חטאת sacrifice function, specifically, daubing blood on the horns of the altar and sprinkling. I proposed that the former is a symbolic expression of appealing to God's mercy that echoes the practice of altar asylum. Performed both for ritual impurities and for unintentional sins, it drives home the point that finite human beings, living in a constant cycle of birth, procreation, and death and entangled in sin, cannot approach a holy God unless he graciously accepts them. Just as Moses had to be shielded from God's glory (Exod 33:21–22) in his presence, so on a lesser scale, God's protection is needed for people to encounter him in their human condition (expressed in ritual impurity) and as sinners. This may also explain why חטאת is offered at all major festivals for the community,[38] even when there

---

37. Wright, "Spectrum of Priestly Impurity," esp. 170–80.
38. Num 28:15, 22, 30; 29:16; Lev 23:19.

is no specific sin or impurity in view, and further supports the idea that the blood on the horns of the altar expresses a humble attitude appealing to God's mercy for acceptance through ritual.

Sprinkling, which may have developed as a secondary action and is mainly performed in the Day of Atonement ceremony, cleanses the sanctuary indicating the effects of the human condition (again, both ritual impurity and sin) on God's abode. I further argued that these two actions correspond to the two-fold atonement formula (one for people and one for sancta).

Bibliography

Barmash, Pamela. *Homicide in the Biblical World*. Cambridge: Cambridge University Press, 2005.
Dillmann, August. *Die Bücher Exodus und Leviticus*. Leipzig: Hirzel, 1897.
Driver, Samuel Rolles. *The Book of Exodus*. Cambridge: Cambridge University Press, 1953.
Eichrodt, Walther. *Theology of the Old Testament*. Vol. 1. Translated by J. A. Baker. Philadelphia: Westminster, 1961.
Feder, Yitzhaq. *Blood Expiation in Hittite and Biblical Ritual: Origins, Context and Meaning*. Atlanta: SBL, 2011.
Frymer-Kensky, Tikva. "Pollution, Purification, and Purgation in Biblical Israel." In *The Word of the Lord Shall Go Forth: Essays in Honor of David Noel Freedman in Celebration of His Sixtieth Birthday*, edited by Carol L. Meyers and M. O'Connor, 391–414. Winona Lake: Eisenbrauns, 1983.
Gane, Roy E. *Cult and Character: Purification Offerings, Day of Atonement, and Theodicy*. Winona Lake: Eisenbrauns, 2005.
Gilders, William K. *Blood Ritual in the Hebrew Bible: Meaning and Power*. Baltimore: Johns Hopkins University Press, 2004.
Hartley, John E. *Leviticus*. WBC 4. Dallas: Word, 1992.
Keil, Carl Friedrich, and Franz Delitzsch. *The Pentateuch*. Vol.1 of Commentary on the Old Testament, translated by James Martin; 1866 reprint. Grand Rapids: Eerdmans, 1971.
Kiuchi, N. *The Purification Offering in the Priestly Literature: Its Meaning and Function*. JSOTSup 56. Sheffield: JSOT, 1987.
Klawans, Jonathan. *Impurity and Sin in Ancient Judaism*. New York: Oxford University Press, 2000.
———. *Purity, Sacrifice, and the Temple: Symbolism and Supersessionism in the Study of Ancient Judaism*. Oxford: Oxford University Press, 2006.
Maccoby, Hyam. *Ritual and Morality: The Ritual Purity System and its Place in Judaism*. Cambridge: Cambridge University Press, 1999.
Milgrom, Jacob. *Leviticus 1–16*. AB3. New York: Doubleday, 1991.
———. *Leviticus 17–22*. AB3A. New York: Doubleday, 2000.
———. *Numbers*. Philadelphia: Jewish Publication Society of America, 1989.
Propp, William H. C. *Exodus 19–40*. AYB. New York: Yale University Press, 2006.

Saysell, Csilla. "The Blood Manipulation of the Sin Offering and the Logic of Defilement. In *Essays in Recognition of the Retirement of Rev. Dr. Timothy Meadowcroft*, edited by Csilla Saysell and John de Jong, 61–70. *Pacific Journal of Baptist Research* 13/2 (2018).

Wenham, Gordon J. *The Book of Leviticus*. NICOT. Grand Rapids: Eerdmans, 1979.

Wright, David P. "The Gesture of Hand Placement in the Hebrew Bible and in Hittite Literature." *JAOS* 106 (1986) 433–46.

———. "The Spectrum of Priestly Impurity." In *Priesthood and Cult in Ancient Israel*, edited by. G. A. Anderson and S. M. Olyan, 150–81. JSOTSup 125. Sheffield: Sheffield Academic, 1991.

———. "Unclean and Clean (OT)." *ABD* 6:729–41.

5

Nothing Was Made without Him (John 1:3)

RICHARD NEVILLE

JOHN'S GOSPEL OPENS WITH the words "In the beginning . . ."[1] In this way, John commences his Gospel at the same point in time as the Hebrew Bible. Why does he choose to do this? Certainly, he wanted to associate the Word with the God of Genesis 1 and with his creative work. This much is clear. But is it possible to say something more particular about his choice of Genesis 1 for the starting point of his Gospel?

This investigation will argue that John's twice-repeated reference to the Word's role in creation provides an important indication of his purpose for opening his Gospel with this allusion to Genesis 1. Twice in John 1:3 the Word is credited with a role in the creation of *everything*. "Through him *everything* was made; without him *not even one thing* was made that has been made" (John 1:3).[2] In this way, John does more than claim that Jesus was involved in the work of creation. He makes the more specific and theologically significant claim that the Word, together with God, is to be credited with the creation of *everything* that exists.

The suggestion here is that, for John, the creation account in Genesis 1 emphasizes the comprehensiveness of God's work of creation. And when John wants to make the same affirmation about the Word, he does so by

---

1. I am delighted to offer this essay as a tribute to Tim Meadowcroft as a valued colleague and an able scholar.

2. Unless otherwise indicated, translations are my own.

writing the Word into the narrative of Genesis 1, "In the beginning was the Word ... Through him *everything* was made." For John, Genesis 1 is a record of the creation of *everything*. The only problem with John's choice of Genesis 1, at least for the modern reader of the text, is that Genesis 1 makes little of the comprehensiveness of God's creation. Certainly, Genesis 1 is *consistent* with the notion that God made everything, but does it explicitly affirm this comprehensiveness?

The answer is resoundingly in the affirmative, but a case needs to be made. This study argues that the first creation account has been crafted in such a manner that the comprehensiveness of God's creative work is presented as a key theological affirmation of the account. And by inserting the Word into the creation account of Genesis 1, John is able to make that same claim to comprehensiveness, this time on behalf of the Word.

But why would John wish to make such a claim for the Word? Why would John make a point of the comprehensiveness of the Word's creative activity? Far from being a trifling detail, the comprehensiveness of God's work of creation is a theological affirmation of the first order. Within the biblical canon, personal participation in the creation of everything serves as a key identifier and distinguishing mark of the one true God.

Genesis 1 and the Creation of Everything

The fact that *God made everything* is among the most important theological affirmations of the first creation account. There has been no problem recognizing the fact that God is presented as Creator in Genesis 1, and some commentators speak of God creating everything. However, the emphasis placed on the comprehensiveness of God's work of creation in the creation account has been largely overlooked in commentaries and in Old Testament works of theology. One of the reasons for this oversight is that a key indicator of this comprehensiveness has been obscured in translation. Almost all English translations of the prepositional phrase מן + ל + pronominal suffix (hereafter למנ־) render this phrase something like, "according to its kind." In Gen 1:24, for example, English translations render the phrase "according to their kinds." The Jewish Publication Society's *Tanakh* and the NRSV are exceptional when they translate the phrase "of every kind." However, the significance of this alternative rendering has not attracted the attention of commentators, who continue to speak in terms of the creation account's interest in God's *differentiation* of his creatures rather than the *comprehensiveness* of his work of creation.

When modern versions translate the phrase "according to its kind" or "according to their kinds," they treat it as an indicator of *how* God created. God created animals, birds, and sea creatures "according to their kinds," that is, "kind by kind by kind" or "one kind after the other." According to these translations, the relationship of the prepositional phrase to the verb "create" is adverbial, expressing *how* God went about creating. He created the animals in discrete categories. This is how Old Testament scholarship has understood the significance of the phrase, and this has led to the conclusion that a key feature of the creation account is its emphasis on the way God brought order to his creation by means of divisions and distinctions.[3] Just as God *separated* light from darkness (Gen 1:4) and water above from water below (Gen 1:6), so he also *differentiated* the various plants and animals, "each according to its kind."

Remarkably, the existence of two quite distinct translations of the prepositional phrase למנ has not attracted the attention of commentators. In spite of the appearance of the *Tanakh* in 1985 and the NRSV in 1989, commentators have continued to espouse the view that the text emphasizes *differentiation* without considering the possibility that the translation "of all kinds" might be saying something quite different. This may be in part due to a lack of clarity around the syntax of the prepositional phrase.[4] Any attempt to account for the syntax of the phrase immediately alerts one to the fact that the NRSV's translation "of every kind" represents a very different analysis of the syntax. Furthermore, it becomes apparent that the alternative reading has first order implications for how one understands the theology of the first creation account.

The present study maintains that the prepositional phrase למנ־ has nothing to do with the differentiation of the creatures that God made. It does not explain *how* God created. Instead, it serves to indicate *what* God created. Rather than having an adverbial relation to the verb, the phrase למנ־ has an adjectival relationship with the head noun. For example, it identifies which birds (head noun) God created. He created "birds *of every kind*."

There are a number of lines of evidence to suggest this alternative understanding of the prepositional phrase is preferable. The syntax of the prepositional phrase suggests it should be read adjectivally as an expression of what God made. This argument has been made elsewhere.[5] It is

---

3. Mathews, *Genesis 1:1—11:26*, 153; Goldingay, *Israel's Gospel*, 94; Arnold, *Genesis*, 103.

4. The syntax of the phrase has attracted little by way of focused attention (however, see n. 4). Driver suggests the noun translated "kind" is a collective noun. Driver, *Genesis*, 9. See also König, "Die Bedeutung."

5. Neville, "Differentiation in Genesis 1."

also significant that the same prepositional phrase is used in other contexts in which animals are listed, and in these other instances the prepositional phrase clearly has the meaning "of any kind" or "in all its varieties." For example, Leviticus 11 and Deuteronomy 14 use the phrase ‐למנ in their lists of clean and unclean animals.

> These you shall regard as detestable among the birds. They shall not be eaten; they are an abomination: the eagle, the vulture, the osprey, the buzzard, the kite of any kind (למינה); every raven of any kind (למינו); the ostrich, the nighthawk, the sea gull, the hawk of any kind (למינהו); the little owl, the cormorant, the great owl. (Lev 11:13–14 NRSV)

In answer to the question, "What are we to detest?" the NRSV's answer is "the kite *of any kind*." The phrase clearly does not indicate *how* the kite is to be detested or *how* it is not to be eaten. It would make no sense to say the hawk must be detested according to its kind, or that the hawk must not be eaten kind by kind by kind. Instead, it indicates *which* birds are to be detested and *which* birds must not be eaten. Israelites were not to eat hawks "of any kind." This is precisely how the phrase should be understood in Genesis 1. Not as a description of *how* God made the creatures, but *which* creatures God made.

This means that God made birds "of every kind," large aquatic creatures and fish "of every kind," cattle "of every kind," fruit "in all their varieties," and seed-bearing plants "in all their varieties." The point now becomes clear: God made *everything*. The first creation account is not concerned with how God created the seed-bearing plants, but with the fact that God made every kind of seed-bearing plant. The inference is that there was *no* seed-bearing plant that God did *not* create.

Several other features of the creation account contribute to this emphasis on God as the creator of everything:

1. The use of "all" (כל) in Genesis 1. The comprehensiveness of the first creation account is also suggested by the use of the word "all" (כל) in Gen 1:21, 25 and 2:1. For example, Gen 1:21 reads, "So God created the great sea creatures and *every* living creature that moves (כל-נפש החיה הרמשת) of every kind, with which the water teems, and *every* winged bird (כל-עוף כנף) of every kind."

2. The use of the "article of totality" to indicate all the individuals of a class or species. The article is used with the reference to the stars (הכוכבים) in Gen 1:16, indicating that *all* the stars are included.[6]

---

6. Joüon and Muraoka, *Grammar of Biblical Hebrew*, 477.

3. The use of the numbers seven and ten in the creation account. A striking feature of Genesis 1 is the number of words and phrases that occur seven or ten times.[7] In fact, the expression "of every kind" itself occurs ten times. The numbers seven and ten speak of completeness and comprehensiveness.[8] By using the numbers seven and ten throughout the creation account the emphasis of the account falls on the comprehensiveness and completeness of God's creative work. In this way the numerical patterning endorses the theological affirmation that God made everything.

4. The creation summary in Gen 2:1. The summary that comes immediately after the sixth and final day of creation also suggests God's creative work was comprehensive: "And so the heavens and earth and all their vast multitude (וכל־צבאם) were completed (ויכלו)" (2:1). This covers everything—the heavens and the earth and everything that is in them. Nothing is omitted for God's creative work; nothing came into existence except he made it.

These observations of the creation account are consistent with other biblical affirmations about the comprehensiveness of God's work of creation. For example, when the community that returned from captivity gathered to worship, the Levites opened their prayer with a reference to God's work of creating.

> You alone are YHWH. You made the heavens, the highest heavens, and all (כל) their host, the earth and all (כל) that is on it, the seas and all (כל) that is in them, and you give all of them (כלם) life, and the host of the heavens prostrate themselves before you. (Neh 9:6)

The same point features several times in the book of Psalms. "[YHWH] is the Maker of heaven and earth, the sea, and everything in them (כל־אשר־בם)—he stays faithful forever" (Ps 146:6). And in the prophets, there are texts like this one from Isaiah. "Thus says YHWH, who redeemed you, who fashioned you in the womb: I am YHWH, who made everything (כל), who alone stretched out the heavens, who spread out the earth by myself" (Isa 44:24).

Jeremiah is clear that the Lord is distinguished from all other gods by the fact that he created everything.

---

7. See Cassuto, *Genesis*, 12–15; Blocher, *In the Beginning*, 33; Wenham, *Rethinking Genesis 1–11*, 5–6.

8. Gunner, "Number," 1098; Waltke, *Genesis*, 186, 425.

Tell them this: "The gods who did not make the heavens and the earth will perish from the earth and from under these heavens" ... The portion of Jacob is not like these, for he is the one who fashioned all things (הכל), and Israel is the tribe of his inheritance—YHWH of hosts is his name. (Jer 10:11, 16, cf. 51:19)

Given the theological significance of the comprehensiveness of God's creative work evident in the Hebrew Bible, it would be passing strange if the creation account itself failed to make a point of the fact that God made everything.

Richard Bauckham has shown that the affirmation of God as the Creator of all things was also definitive for Jewish monotheism.

> The essential element in what I have called Jewish monotheism, the element that makes it a kind of monotheism, is not the denial of the existence of other "gods," but an understanding of the uniqueness of YHWH that puts him in a class of his own, a wholly different class from any other heavenly or supernatural beings, even if these are called "gods." I call this YHWH's transcendent uniqueness . . . Especially important for identifying this transcendent uniqueness are statements that distinguish YHWH by means of a unique relationship to the whole of reality: YHWH alone is Creator of *all things*, whereas all others are created by him; and Yahweh alone is the sovereign lord of all things, whereas all other things serve or are subject to his universal lordship.[9]

The affirmation of comprehensiveness is also present in New Testament descriptions of God. He is the "Sovereign Lord who made heaven and earth and sea, and everything in them (πάντα τὰ ἐν αὐτοῖς)" (Acts 4:24; 14:15), "The God who made the world and everything in it (πάντα τὰ ἐν αὐτῷ)" (Acts 17:24), the God "who created all things (τὰ πάντα)" (Eph 3:9), and "God, the Father, from whom are all things (τὰ πάντα)" (1 Cor 8:6, cf. Rom 11:36).

In summary, English translations of Genesis 1, supported by a strong tradition of identifying differentiation as a key motif of the creation account, have obscured the fact that there are clear markers in the text which suggest the first creation account was composed to emphasize a vital point for the biblical understanding of God, namely, that he made absolutely everything.

---

9. Bauckham, "Problems of Monotheism," 210–11 (emphasis mine).

John 1 and the Creation of Everything

When John opens his Gospel with words that locate the Word *in the beginning*, he places the Word in a chronological space that Gen 1:1 reserves exclusively for God and his work of creating.

בראשית ברא אלהים ... (In the beginning God created ... [Gen 1:1a])

Ἐν ἀρχῇ ἐποίησεν ὁ θεός ... (LXX) (In the beginning God created ... [Gen 1:1a])

Ἐν ἀρχῇ ἦν ὁ λόγος ... (In the beginning was the word ... [John 1:1a])

Having located the Word *in the beginning*, John proceeds to explain two things: (i) the Word's relationship to God, who was also in the beginning, and (ii) the Word's relationship to God's work of creating in the beginning. He addresses the former in John 1:1–2 and the latter in John 1:3.

The Word's relationship to God in the beginning is described in John 1:1b, c: καὶ ὁ λόγος ἦν πρὸς τὸν θεόν, καὶ θεὸς ἦν ὁ λόγος ("and the Word was with God, and the Word was God"). John asserts two things here about the presence of the Word in the beginning. First, the Word was *with* God (ἦν πρὸς τὸν θεόν). John will repeat this point in verse 2, "This one (οὗτος) was in the beginning with God (πρὸς τὸν θεόν)." In other words, the Word enjoyed a close relationship with God in the beginning.[10] Secondly, the Word *was* God (θεὸς ἦν). The use of θεὸς rather than ὁ θεὸς (with the definite article) means that the noun "is qualitative, emphasising nature rather than personal identity."[11] That is, the Word has the same essence or nature as the God of Genesis 1:1. By means of these two affirmations, John identifies the Word with God in his essence or nature ("was God"), while distinguishing the Word from God the Father in his personhood ("with God").[12]

Next, John proceeds to explain the Word's relationship to God's work of creating in the beginning. And his emphasis in making the point could not be clearer: πάντα δι' αὐτοῦ ἐγένετο, καὶ χωρὶς αὐτοῦ ἐγένετο οὐδὲ ἓν ὃ γέγονεν ("Through him everything was made; without him not even one

---

10. Cf. John 1:18. Wisdom is associated with God in the beginning, but only as a personification or hypostatization. As the prologue progresses it becomes evident that the Word is a person. Furthermore, wisdom is presented as being "set up" (נסך) and "brought forth" (חול) at that time (Prov 8:22–31), whereas the Word is not described in such terms. Instead, John says the Word *was* (ἤν) in the beginning.

11. Harris, *Jesus as God*, 67.

12. John's use of θεὸς rather than ὁ θεὸς avoids the problem of making the Word identical or co-extensive with God the Father. For discussions of the syntax here and its theological significance see Harris, *Jesus as God*, 59–67, and Wallace, 46–47 and 266–69.

thing was made which has been made"). This amounts to an emphatic statement of the comprehensiveness of the Word's creative work, affirming it both positively and negatively.[13]

Genesis 1 opens the Hebrew Bible by presenting a distinguishing feature of Israel's God. He is the creator of everything. This is a key element that sets God over and apart from all else that exists. It is significant, then, that John opens his Gospel in the same manner, identifying Jesus with the God of creation and reading the Word into the account of God's work of creation. He carefully identifies the Word with the God of Genesis 1 (identical in nature, yet a distinct person), and then attributes to Jesus a share in God's work of creating all things.

The significance of what John has done here becomes all the more apparent in the light of Bauckham's study of the Shema in the New Testament. Among the texts Bauckham investigates in his study is 1 Cor 8:1–6, which Paul concludes with his own version of the Shema: "[B]ut for us there is one God, the Father, from whom are all things and we exist for him, and one Lord, Jesus Christ, through whom are all things and we exist through him" (1 Cor 8:6). Commenting on this text, Bauckham observes,

> Paul rewrites the Shema to include both God and Jesus in the unique divine identity. But the point might not have been sufficiently clear had he not combined with the Shema itself another way of characterizing the unique identity of YHWH. Of the Jewish ways of characterizing the divine uniqueness, the most unequivocal was by reference to creation. In the uniquely divine role of creating all things it was for Jewish monotheism unthinkable that any being other than God could even assist God (Isa 44:24; 4 *Ezra* 3:4; Josephus, *C. Ap.* 2.192). But to Paul's unparalleled inclusion of Jesus in the Shema he adds the equally unparalleled inclusion of Jesus in the creative activity of God. No more unequivocal way of including Jesus in the unique divine identity is conceivable, within the framework of Second Temple Jewish monotheism.[14]

The relevance of Bauckham's comments on 1 Cor 8:6 for the present investigation is apparent. Just as Paul rewrites Jesus into the Shema, John writes the Word into the creation account of Genesis 1. Just as Paul includes Jesus Christ in God's "unique divine identity," so too John, by identifying the Word with the God of Genesis 1, includes the Word in God's "unique divine identity." And just as Paul makes his point unequivocally by including Jesus

---

13. For the translation of οὐδὲ ἕν as "not even one" see BDAG, οὐδέ 3.
14. Bauckham, "Problems of Monotheism," 224.

Christ in the work of creating all things, so too John has the Word participate in the creation of everything.[15]

Conclusion

The comprehensiveness of God's creative activity is widely cited in Scripture as a means of describing God's relationship to all else that exists, and Bauckham has shown that this affirmation was unequalled as a marker of God's unique divine identity. This study has argued that Genesis 1 is deliberate, and even emphatic, in making this same point that God made everything. By bringing these lines of argument together, it is possible to see more clearly why John chose to begin his Gospel with a retelling of Genesis 1.[16] There could be no better place to introduce the Word into the unique divine entity than *in the beginning*, a chronological locus reserved for God the Creator. And there could be no more sure way of making his point clear and unequivocal than by affirming the Word was engaged (with God and as God) in the creation of everything. Indeed, "not even one thing was made without him."

Bibliography

Arnold, Bill T. *Genesis*. Cambridge: Cambridge University Press, 2009.
Bauckham, Richard. "Biblical Theology and the Problems of Monotheism." In *Out of Egypt: Biblical Theology and Biblical Interpretation*, edited by Craig Bartholomew et al., 187–232. Grand Rapids: Zondervan, 2004.
Blocher, Henri. *In the Beginning*. Downers Grove, IL: InterVarsity, 1984.
Cassuto, Umberto. *A Commentary on the Book of Genesis*. Part 1, translated by Israel Abrahams. 1961; reprint, Jerusalem: Magnes, 1998.
Driver, Samuel R. *The Book of Genesis*. London: Methuen 1915.
Goldingay, John. *Israel's Gospel*. Vol. 1. *Old Testament Theology*. Downers Grove, IL: InterVarsity, 2003.
Gunner, R. A. H. "Number." In *Illustrated Bible Dictionary*. Edited by J. D. Douglas, 2:1096–1100. Sydney and Auckland: Inter-Varsity, 1980.

---

15. In doing so, John ascribes to the Word the same role of instrumental causation (δι' αὐτοῦ) that elsewhere is attributed to God (Rom 11:36). Bauckham points out that when describing God as the cause of all things, three forms of causation were deemed appropriate: efficient causation (ἐκ); instrumental causation (διά); and final causation (εἰς). Paul uses all three of God in Rom 11:36, whereas in 1 Cor 8:6 he applies two of them to the Father (ἐκ and εἰς) and attributes one to Jesus Christ (διά) ("Problems of Monotheism," 225).

16. It is to be expected that John 1:1–3 serves other functions and connects in various and complex ways with the rest of John's Gospel. Identifying these, however, is beyond the scope of this investigation.

Harris, Murray J. *Jesus as God. The New Testament Use of Theos in Reference to Jesus.* Grand Rapids: Baker, 1992.

Joüon, Paul, and T. Muraoka. *A Grammar of Biblical Hebrew.* 2nd ed. 2006; reprint, Rome: Pontificio Istituto Biblico, 2008.

König, Eduard. "Die Bedeutung des hebräischen מִן." *ZAW* 31 (1911) 133–46.

Mathews, Kenneth A. *Genesis 1:1—11:26.* NAC 1A. Nashville: Broadman & Holman, 1996.

Neville, Richard W. "Differentiation in Genesis 1: A Creation *ex nihilo.*" *JBL* 130 (2011) 209–26.

Wallace, Daniel B. *Greek Grammar Beyond the Basics.* Grand Rapids: Zondervan, 1996.

Waltke, Bruce K. *Genesis.* Grand Rapids: Zondervan, 2001.

Wenham, Gordon J. *Rethinking Genesis 1-11: Gateway to the Bible.* Eugene, OR: Cascade, 2015.

6

Love's Four Objects and the Pursuit of Peace[1]

Christopher D. Marshall

I FIRST MET TIM Meadowcroft when we were university students in the early 1970s and later had the pleasure of working closely with him as a colleague for some fifteen years at what is now called Laidlaw College in Auckland. What always impressed me about Tim was his equal commitment to the highest standards of biblical scholarship and to the life and mission of the church, and in both domains to remaining always open to fresh insights and perspectives, yet without losing touch with what 1 Timothy calls "the mystery of godliness" (τὸ τῆς εὐσεβείας μυστήριον) or, as the NRSV translates it, "the mystery of our religion"—the incarnation, resurrection, exaltation, and all-encompassing redemptive significance of Jesus Christ (1 Tim 3:16).

To hold fast to these profound mysteries in a world of religious difference and competing truth claims, while at the same time discharging our call as Christian disciples to be peacemakers and reconcilers (Matt 5:9, 43–48; Eph 2:14–16) is never easy. It is not easy because peacemaking, unlike mere tolerance or magnanimity on the part of majority voices, requires us to have a fundamental respect for the views of others and their right to see things differently from us. It also requires a willingness to learn from

---

1. This chapter is adapted from one of the Bechtel Lectures I delivered at the University of Waterloo, Canada, in 2013 and subsequently published in the *Conrad Grebel Review* 31, 3 (Fall 2013), 221–54.

them—the humility to receive, as well as to impart, authentic insights into the meaning of human existence in face of the incomprehensible vastness of all that exists, recognizing that all human beings are programmed to "search for God and perhaps grope for him and find him—though indeed he is not far from each one of us" (Acts 17:26–27 NRSV).

Practicing such "principled peacemaking" may not be straightforward, but it has never been more urgent than it is in today's context of mounting religious and political extremism, painfully exemplified by New Zealand's first experience of mass terrorist violence perpetrated at two Christchurch mosques on March 15, 2019, which claimed the lives of fifty worshippers. The complex challenges of learning how to live together peacefully in a multi-faith, pluralist, globalized world was thrown into stark relief two decades ago by the dreadful events of 9/11, events that dramatically altered world history. Historical change, of course, is a perpetually occurring phenomenon and there is nothing new about our human capacity for cruelty and bloodshed. But there remains a genuine sense in which history *did* change significantly on that sultry summer morning in New York City when fully laden passenger planes were flown into the Twin Towers and some 3000 innocent souls perished. Recalling that awful day, one British journalist wrote: "I was in Brussels when Armageddon arrived."[2]

As well as plunging America and her allies into an era of seemingly endless war, the religious sensibilities of the hijackers and their sponsors, as well as of many of those in America who continue to prosecute the so-called global war on terror, have heightened anxieties in the public mind about the potential—even the predisposition—of religious piety to promulgate and perpetrate acts of unspeakable horror and violence. It has also raised questions about whether it will ever be possible for the world's great religions to "dwell together in unity," to use the words of the Psalmist (Ps 133:1). It is now a commonplace to hear religion generically excoriated, especially by the so-called New Atheists, as a singular cause of the world's most entrenched hatreds and conflicts. It is much less common, but surely much more important, to hear informed discussion about how the unique power of religious belief and devotion—which is, after all, an ineradicable part of human existence and is never simply going to disappear of its own accord—can be harnessed in the cause of peace, justice, and reconciliation.

---

2. Fletcher, "Sifting Through the 9/11 Apocalypse."

A Common Word

There are some signs of hope, however. In October 2007, for example, one hundred thirty-eight Muslim leaders in America published an open letter addressed to their Christian counterparts entitled, "A Common Word Between Us and You." The letter proposed that while Islam and Christianity are obviously different religions, the scriptural commandments that true believers should love God and love their neighbors are a crucial area of agreement between the Qur'an, the Torah, and the New Testament. The unity of God, and a commitment to love this God and to love one's neighbors as oneself, forms the "common ground" on which Islam, Judaism, and Christianity are founded, and thus furnishes a constructive basis for forging interreligious understanding and peacemaking.

The following month, an appreciative response, crafted by Christian theologians at Yale University, was published in the *New York Times* under the signatures of over three hundred prominent Christian leaders. In July 2008, one hundred fifty scholars and spiritual leaders from both religious communities gathered at Yale to discuss and debate both statements. The proceedings of their conference were published in 2010 in a book entitled, *A Common Word: Muslims and Christians on Loving God and Neighbor*, and there has been a string of follow-up events as well.[3]

For a time, the Common Word initiative appeared to be one of the most successful interfaith enterprises ever attempted. It achieved unprecedented global acceptance, including endorsements by the heads of the Roman Catholic, Orthodox, Anglican, and Lutheran communions, and by over four hundred sixty Islamic organizations, as well as by some Jewish authorities. Christian theologian Miroslav Volf expressed the hope that the project could serve to redefine relations between the world's two numerically largest faiths.[4] While this is yet to eventuate, and much of the activity generated by the documents has died down over the past ten years[5]—perhaps because the ideas did not filter far enough down to the congregational level—the undergirding proposition that Muslims, Jews, and Christians should work for peace on the basis of a shared set of religious obligations remains compelling.

---

3. Volf et al., *Common Word*.
4. Volf, "God is Love."
5. See Benevento, "'A Common Word' 10 Years on."

Distinctive Frameworks

Of course, even if all three Abrahamic religions have a common emphasis on love of God and neighbor, differences of definition remain. The terms, "love," "God," and "neighbor" will mean somewhat different things to Muslims, Christians, and Jews, and there will be differences on these matters within each tradition as well. All may agree on the necessity of worshipping the one true God but will disagree on the nature and attributes of this God.

For Christians, a proper understanding of the nature of God is inextricably connected with convictions about incarnation, the crucifixion of Christ, and the doctrine of the Trinity, all of which Muslims typically deny. For many Muslims (and indeed many Jews), these classical Christian doctrines serve to imperil or impair or even contradict God's absolute unity, which lies at the basis of the great commandment. But this, of course, is not how Christians perceive it. For Christians, there is still only *one* God, one numerically identical divine essence, but one shared by *three* personal modes of subsistence, as Father, Son, and Holy Spirit. This tri-unity of God, moreover, is not some speculative or expendable detail; it is integral to appreciating what it means to *love* God. For in Christian understanding, love derives from God's interior being, so that how we understand "God" will shape how we understand "love." As 1 John 4 famously puts it, "God is love" (4:16) and "we should love one another because everyone who loves is born of God and knows God . . . for God is love" (4:7–8).

To say, "God is love" and that everyone who loves "knows God" is to say something more profound than God *has* love or *feels* love or *expresses* love for his creatures. It is to say that love is an essential attribute of God's personal being. Since love is intrinsically a *relational* reality, it requires an object toward whom it is directed and from whom, in its purest form, it may receive love in return. According to trinitarian confession, this relational give-and-take of love is present within the shared life of God's self. God is an incomparable and unique unity, to be sure, but a unity that is internally differentiated, with reciprocating love flowing endlessly between the three persons of the triune Godhead.

This love also flows outwards in historical acts of creation (cf. Psalm 145:9; John 3:16). But it manifests itself supremely in the incarnation of Christ, by which, and through whom, God graciously receives human nature into the divine experience. The ultimate demonstration of God's love, in all its unconditional, indiscriminate, sacrificial perfection, is Christ's atoning death and resurrection for the sake of our redemption. This gracious initiative of the "Son of God who loved us and gave himself up for us" (Eph 5:2, 25; cf. Gal 2:20; 1 John 4:10) serves as the supreme paradigm for what it means to love our neighbors as ourselves. "This is my commandment, that you love one another as I have loved you. No one has greater love than this, to lay down one's life for one's friends" (John 15:12–13).

So then, the Christian economy of salvation, with its undergirding apprehension of God's tri-unity, or what has been called Christianity's "complex monotheism," offers a distinctive framework for understanding the meaning and depth of the love we are summoned to show in the great commandments. Muslim and Jewish traditions will similarly have their own peculiar insights into these commandments, while demurring from certain features of Christian understanding. The challenge for all three communities is to develop not simply a tolerance for one another's idiosyncratic views, but a positive appreciation of what each brings to the table.

Such mutual appreciation will most readily arise from an open-hearted and sympathetic encounter between sincere believers of each tradition. Such interfaith engagement on the part of those who are most deeply committed to their respective faiths affords the possibility of each encountering in the religion of the "other" aspects of what is good and true and holy. And when dedicated believers of one tradition experience in the adherents of another tradition facets of truth and beauty and goodness and holiness they cannot deny, things necessarily change. When one finds God disclosed in one's neighbor, and even, perchance, in those hitherto thought to be strangers or infidels or apostates or enemies, in that discovery lies the prospect of lasting peace—a peace grounded in something far more profound than passive acquiescence and far more enduring than anything secular politics can produce.

With this background in mind, let us now turn to one of the two places in the Gospel tradition where we find the Common Word of love for God and neighbor explicitly stated, expressly endorsed by Jesus, and dramatically illustrated by a powerful story, the parable of the Good Samaritan (Luke 10:25–37). In my book, *Compassionate Justice*, I devote over one hundred seventy pages to analyzing the pertinence of this remarkable parable for modern legal theory and for the field of restorative justice in particular.[6] Drawing on that discussion, here I want to focus on the interchange between Jesus and a Jewish interlocuter about the purpose and meaning of the law that occasions in Luke the telling of the parable (vv. 25–29) and to reflect briefly on its significance for interreligious peacemaking.[7]

---

6. Marshall, *Compassionate Justice*.

7. What follows is drawn mainly from Marshall, *Compassionate Justice*, especially 55–81, where full bibliographical citations can be found in support of the exegesis proposed here. When not my own translation, Scripture citations are from the NRSV.

What Must I Do?

The passage opens with a certain "lawyer" (νομικός τις) asking Jesus what he must do "to inherit eternal life" (10:25). The lawyer would have been a Torah scholar, an expert in the texts and traditions of first-century Jewish law and custom.[8] The fact that he "stood up" to ask his question, and addressed Jesus as a "teacher," suggests he has been seated among those whom Jesus has just been instructing, thereby acknowledging Jesus' recognized authority as a rabbi.

The question he asks was probably commonplace in religious discussions of his time, and it is likely that Jesus was well known for discoursing on it (cf. 18:30; Mark 10:30; Matt 19:29; 25:46). As a specialist in the Torah, the lawyer would have naturally assumed the answer to his question resided in the Torah. But where in the Torah? How was the meaning of God's law to be rightly understood and obeyed? He was presumably hoping to elicit from Jesus a summary of the Torah's most fundamental or ineluctable requirements, perhaps captured in a single paradigmatic commandment, the fulfilment of which would comprehend all other precepts in the law and thus guarantee eternal life.

Jesus responds to his question with a counter-question that invites the lawyer to nail his own colors to the mast: "What is written in the law?" Jesus asks. "What do you read there?" (v. 26). This was a standard rabbinic formula for inviting someone to recite or expound the relevant Scriptures. What is most revealing at this point of the interchange is the extent of *common ground* between Jesus and his interlocutor. There is agreement that access to the future world is a valid concern and should not be taken for granted, that the requirements of entry are disclosed in the Torah, and that performance of the Torah is not only desirable and feasible, it is absolutely essential. There is no trace of anxiety, on either side, about the dangers of legalism or self-righteousness or earning one's own salvation through accumulating merit. The key issue is not *whether* Torah observance is necessary for salvation, but *how* the Torah is to be construed and obeyed.

In response to Jesus' question, the lawyer brings together two widely separated commandments in the Torah: the *Shema* from Deut 6:4–5, which faithful Israelites were expected to recite twice a day, and the formulation of the Golden Rule in Lev 19:18. "He answered, 'You shall love the Lord your God with all your heart, and with all your soul, and with all your strength, and with all your mind; and your neighbor as yourself.'" Here, then, we have the Common Word text. There are three striking features about this

---

8. For details, see Marshall, *Compassionate Justice*, 40–49.

interchange worth highlighting. First, it is the Jewish lawyer, not Jesus, who nominates the love commandments as the Law's center of gravity; secondly, in doing so, he conflates two distinct commandments into a single unitary obligation; and thirdly, he construes this obligation to be principally a matter of volitional obedience rather than emotional experience.

The Question of Originality

The first thing to note is that it is the lawyer who offers the twin love commandments as the heart and goal of the Law's teaching and the key to eternal life. This insight is not depicted as a hermeneutical innovation on the part of Jesus, though Christians have often regarded it as such. It comes, instead, from the cross-examining, and somewhat hostile, Jewish lawyer. Some commentators propose that the lawyer is simply echoing or reflecting back what he had first learned from Jesus' teaching.[9] That could be so, but there is absolutely no hint of it whatsoever in the text. On the contrary, Jesus expressly asks the lawyer to draw on his own existing legal knowledge to answer his question—"What do *you* read there?" he asks. The foundational importance of the love commands, in other words, is another area of commonality between Jesus and the Jewish scholar.

This may come as a surprise to many Christians, who usually credit Jesus with this original insight. Indeed, enormous scholarly effort has been expended trying to prove that Jesus' teaching on the double love commandments was innovative or unique. To be fair, the evidence is complex and difficult to assess, and there are certainly distinctive features about Jesus' teaching on the subject in the Gospels.[10] But none of the biblical accounts ever suggests that Jesus was alone in recognizing the preeminence of the twin love commandments. Certainly, Luke has absolutely nothing invested in implying that Jesus' perspective was in any way novel or original. He even places the crucial confession on the lips of an antagonistic legal opponent, who was out to test or trap (ἐκπειράζων) Jesus in his words.[11] As far as Luke, and indeed all the Gospel writers, are concerned, this truly was a "common word" shared, not only by Jesus and his supporters, but also by his critics and opponents.

---

9. For example, Manson, *Sayings of Jesus*, 260.
10. For details, see Marshall, *Compassionate Justice*, 64–67.
11. On the meaning of this verb, see Marshall, *Compassionate Justice*, 56–57.

The Conflation of the Twin Commands

This leads to the second observation on the episode: In answering Jesus' question, the lawyer conflates two distinct commandments into a single unit without differentiation, governed by a single verb, "You shall love the Lord your God with all your heart and soul and strength and mind . . . and your neighbor as yourself."

In the other, parallel story in the synoptic tradition involving the love commandments, recorded in Mark 12 and Matthew 22, the situation is different. There, love for God is identified as the "first" and "greatest" commandment, and love of neighbor as "the second" commandment, though it is "like" the first in character (Mark 12:28–31; Matt 22:38–39). This hierarchical enumeration of "first" and "second" keeps the two commandments quite distinct. Love for God is given absolute primacy; love for neighbor comes second in importance, though it remains inseparably linked with the former. But this hierarchical enumeration does not occur in Luke's episode. Here the lawyer blends the two commandments into a single obligation, controlled by a single verb. Moreover, Jesus endorses this amalgamation: "You have given the right answer," he says. "Do *this* (not, do *these*), and you will live." The two commandments are not simply juxtaposed, they are effectively combined.

What are we to infer from this? The inference seems to be that love for God includes and enables love of neighbor, while love of neighbor expresses and embodies love for God. This does not mean the two objects are considered identical or interchangeable, with "God" and "neighbor" being different words for the same reality. There are still two objects, and God is still mentioned first. But there is only *one* love. The key point is this: *There can be no love for God without love for neighbor, and no love for neighbor that does not involve obeying, pleasing, and indeed encountering God.* To love God with all of one's heart and mind and soul and strength—that is, with the totality of one's physical, moral, intellectual, and emotional capacities—as the commandment enjoins, requires loving one's neighbor as well, and loving one's neighbor is an integral part of one's total response to God. God cannot be loved in isolation but only in and through loving other people. This, once again, is something on which Jesus and the Jewish lawyer are in total agreement. Love for God and love of neighbor are inseparable obligations. Without love for neighbor, it is impossible to love or please God.

Love as Ethical Obligation

This brings us to the third observation. The "love" that Scripture speaks of in all this is primarily a volitional and moral commitment, not an emotional experience. After all, if God *commands* us to love, then love must first and foremost be a matter of formal obedience. It is not a case of having warm, fuzzy feelings towards others—which cannot be ordered into existence anyway—but rather a case of *willing* and *doing* what is necessary to secure the other's welfare.

Once more, this is something that Jesus and the lawyer agree on. The lawyer asked, "What must I *do* to inherit eternal life?" Jesus responds by prompting him to recite the love commandments, and then says, "*Do* this and you shall live." Love is something to be done, not something to be felt. Love for God is to be done by obeying God's will. Love for neighbor is to be done by acting in the neighbor's best interests. Both parties concur on this. But, for the first time in our story, a crack begins to open up between them on two other consequential matters—on the extent to which love should go on behalf of its object, and on how inclusive love's object should be. And on these two matters, Jesus appears to set a new high-water mark.

Now, remember that Jesus' interrogator is a lawyer, and a very good lawyer at that. Like all lawyers, he wants to nail down his terms, and as a good lawyer, he pays very careful attention to the actual wording and context of the relevant legislation. The Law stipulates that he must love his neighbor as himself, and Jesus confirms that it is by doing so he will gain eternal life. "But," the lawyer inquires, "Who precisely is my neighbor?"

This seems to be a perfectly reasonable question and one that close attention to the commandment's original setting and intent can easily answer. It is crystal clear in Leviticus 19 that the term "neighbor" refers to fellow members of the covenant community of Israel. It designates, not just those who live in close physical proximity to one's self, but those who share in the same full covenantal status as oneself. To "love one's neighbor," then, in Leviticus 19, does not mean to act benevolently towards all human beings in general; it means to uphold and protect the rights, dignity, and status of all those within the covenant community of Israel. In short, the neighbor of the original commandment is a fellow Israelite.

For Jesus, however, the key issue in the interpretation of Lev 19:18 is not the definition of the term neighbor; it is the meaning of the verb "love." Neighbors, according to Jesus, are not created by accident of birth or nationality or religion or law; they are discovered through love. When love is present and active, the identification of neighbors takes care of itself. According to the rule of love, we stand in neighborly relationship to every person we encounter, irrespective of any secondary status that law or religion or culture or ethnicity or nationality or creed may or may not confer upon them.

It is here, then, that Jesus differs from the lawyer. Both accept that love of neighbor sums up the Torah and is essential for eternal life. But whereas the lawyer thinks the critical issue is the scope of the term neighbor, Jesus considers it to be the breadth of the term love. The lawyer reduces love to its legal minimum by restricting the category of neighbor to fellow members of his own religious community. Jesus, however, maximizes the category of neighbor, because he refuses to limit the demands of love. Neighbors are not chosen or created by religion or by nationality. They are found and cultivated through human encounter. Moreover, because love of neighbor is inseparable from love of God, and because love of God is meant to engage the entire personality in undivided commitment, there can be no exceptions to love's attentiveness and no limits to what love requires.

How then does Jesus convey his new, radically extensive understanding of neighbor love? How does he seek to persuade the lawyer of its radical implications? Not by means of abstract philosophical reflection or by exegetical-linguistic debate, but by telling a story: the so-called parable of the Good Samaritan, an imaginary tale that operates on multiple levels and that teaches many lessons.

Here I want to focus on the parable's relevance to peacemaking. For arguably the most radical and disconcerting feature of this subversive little story is the way it elides the boundary between neighbor-love and enemy-love.

A Parable of Enemy Love

The parable tells of a man who is brutally assaulted on a trip from Jerusalem to Jericho and left for dead on the side of the road. Two passing temple officials notice the unconscious man in the ditch. But instead of stopping to help him, they cross to the other side of the road and carry on their way. Next a traveling Samaritan merchant chances upon the victim. He is "moved with compassion" (ἐσπλαγχνίσθη) at what he sees. He bandages the victim's wounds, lifts him on to his own donkey, and transports him to a nearby inn, where he takes care of him overnight. The following day, the Samaritan must resume his journey, but not before paying the innkeeper in advance to continue nursing the injured man back to health and promising to reimburse him for any other expenses he might incur. Jesus concludes the story by inviting the lawyer to nominate which of the three characters in the episode acted like a true neighbor to the man who fell into the hands of robbers, then enjoins the lawyer to "go and do likewise."

Jesus' first audience would have been taken aback at the appearance of a Samaritan in the story. After the priest and the Levite, they would have naturally expected the third character to be an Israelite layman, since the threefold division of "priests, Levites, and all the children of Israel" was a standard way of summarizing the diversity of the nation. Yet not only does Jesus use a Samaritan in place of an Israelite, he portrays him as responding in a way that puts the religious leaders of Israel to shame.

The jarring nature of this reversal of roles cannot be emphasized too strongly. All the literary and historical evidence we have suggests that relations between Jews and Samaritans in the first century were implacably hostile. Both groups viewed the other in the darkest of terms, and tensions between the two communities were widespread, deep-seated, and sometimes viciously violent.[12] It is only by appreciating the full extent of this culture of mutual loathing that we can begin to comprehend the far-reaching ramifications of Jesus' casting of a Samaritan as the savior of the Jewish stranger on the roadside.

Jesus uses the parable, we have seen, to expound the commandment, "You shall love your neighbor as yourself" (Lev 19:18). But his exposition of the commandment is stunningly subversive. Had Jesus simply wanted to emphasize the need to show charity towards those in distress, any three individuals would have sufficed as actors in the drama, as long as the third one did the right thing. Had he only wanted to take a pot shot at priestly myopia or clerical self-centeredness, the third person down the road could simply have been an Israelite layperson who showed them up by way of contrast. Had he only wanted to encourage moral concern for outsiders and opponents, he could have portrayed the victim as a Samaritan and his rescuer as a faithful Jew. But by deliberately *reversing* these roles—by portraying a despised enemy as the vehicle of compassionate, restorative love—Jesus effectively achieves two more radical outcomes: he expands the meaning of neighbor love to include enemy love, and he nullifies the identification of religious opponents with the enemies of God or the instruments of Satan.

Both moves were phenomenally daring. With few exceptions, it was taken for granted in antiquity that one should love one's friends and harm one's enemies (cf. Matt 5:43). Jesus, by startling contrast, deemed love of friends to be ethically unremarkable (Luke 6:32-34; Matt 5:46-47), while commending love for one's enemies as the true sign of fidelity to God, "for God is kind to the ungrateful and the wicked" (Luke 6:27-31, 35-36; Matt

---

12. For details, see Marshall, *Compassionate Justice*, 112-20.

5:44–45). This was shocking enough. But what is doubly shocking in the parable is that the one who displays such God-honoring enemy love was himself deemed by Jesus' hearers to be an enemy of God, a "foreigner" (Luke 17:18), who knew not the God of Israel he falsely claimed to worship (cf. John 4:22) and upon whom divine judgment could legitimately be called down (Luke 9:51–55).

Jesus could have enrolled a Samaritan as the victim and had a Jewish benefactor stop to render him assistance. That would have exemplified love for enemy well enough. But it would not have deconstructed the pervasive stereotyping of other religious groups as inherently evil adversaries and could even have reinforced his audience's sense of moral superiority towards them. To reverse the roles of hero and villain in this way was an incredibly audacious thing to do. Kenneth Bailey explains how, even after living in the Middle East for over twenty years, he never had the courage to tell Palestinians a story about a noble Israeli, or Armenians a tale about a noble Turk.

> Only one who has lived as a part of a community with a bitterly hated traditional enemy can understand fully the courage of Jesus in making the despised Samaritan appear as morally superior to the religious leadership of his audience. Thus, Jesus speaks to one of the audience's deepest hatreds and painfully exposes it.[13]

The parable of the Good Samaritan, then, is a parable of enemy love and a parable of generous religiosity. It shows how the boundaries that divide people into mutually hostile groups are relativized and destabilized when individuals choose to ascribe absolute priority to love and compassion over all other cultural and religious reservations or inhibitions. Witnessing the desperate need of the dying victim, the Samaritan is so "moved with compassion" that an erstwhile Judean enemy is transformed into a neighbor and treated as such. The Samaritan extends to an anonymous stranger the intimacy of care befitting a close friend or brother, without giving a moment's thought as to his ethnic origins or religious loyalties. It is as if the whole sorry history of hatred between these two rival groups had never existed.

The parable teaches, then, that the familiar and comforting correlation we make between friend and foe with good and evil is deceiving and dangerously unreliable. Religious enemies are capable of doing great good, and compatriots can do real evil, sometimes by doing nothing at all. It also teaches that the most powerful way to overcome such destructive dualisms is by simple acts of kindness and compassion on the part of individuals who

---

13. Bailey, *Poet and Peasant*, 48.

reach across the divisions of fear and loathing that divide hostile communities in order to treat the "other" as brother, the foreigner as friend, the enemy as neighbor, the victim as object of moral responsibility.

Love as Compassionate Action

We have seen how the love that the biblical commandments speak of is primarily a volitional and activist commitment, not an emotional experience. Commentators frequently belabor this point, with a palpable sense of relief. They note, for example, that only by understanding love in non-emotional terms is it possible to make sense of "loving your enemies." Love of enemy cannot be a feeling, because enemies, by definition, are those for whom one does not feel tenderness or affection or warmth. We love our enemies, not by feeling deeply for them, but by refraining from harming them or hurting them or killing them or perhaps by actively helping them, irrespective of our dislike of them.[14]

All this may be true insofar as it goes. Biblical love is unquestionably an action more than a sentiment, something done more than something felt. But the parable of the Good Samaritan suggests there is more to love of neighbor than benevolent activism. The Samaritan's extraordinary actions in the parable, which are recounted in exquisite detail, are the direct result of him being "moved with compassion" (ἐσπλαγχνίσθη) at what he saw (v. 33). This verb denotes a stirring in his innards, a gut-wrenching surge of emotion that propelled him into action. The love he displayed was more than a clinical, cold-hearted compliance to the dictates of moral law; it was a passionate, sympathetic sharing in the victim's personal suffering and isolation. The Samaritan did justice to his legal and moral obligation to love his neighbor as himself by *feeling* compassion *and* by acting in accordance.

For Jesus, then, neighbor-love is more than practical action. It is more than showing respect for the equal rights and freedoms of others, as it is in contemporary liberal ethics, and it is certainly more than choosing not to kill someone. It is, instead, *a love patterned after our love for God*. Just as love for God cannot be reduced to exterior actions alone but is all-encompassing in its reach—engaging the entire heart, mind, soul, and strength—love for neighbor similarly cannot be limited to external deeds alone but involves feelings, thoughts, and motivations as well. This is an important consequence of the amalgamation of the two Torah commandments into a single command, governed by a single verb. It is not uncommon in the Abrahamic traditions to see a deep affinity between one's love for God and

14. See Marshall, *Compassionate Justice*, 72.

the emotional intensity of human love, especially romantic love.[15] This is the common stuff of mysticism and worship. It is less common to reverse the relation and understand love for one's fellow human beings as demanding the same intensity and passion of love that we have for God.

But this is precisely what the parable teaches. The whole-heartedness of the covenant love for God enjoined in the Torah must also be extended to our neighbors as well. Both God and neighbor are to be loved with the whole of one's heart, mind, soul, and strength. In both cases, the love entailed is volitional, rational, practical, *and* emotional in character. Such love is *commanded*, not because it involves bloodless actions alone, but because such love begins with an intentional commitment before it is either an action or an emotion. We must *choose* to love before we do anything practical and whether or not we feel anything emotionally. But having chosen the path of love, actions *and* feelings will ensue.

The Samaritan acted with such sacrificial dedication to meeting the needs of an erstwhile enemy because he felt compassion for him. He felt compassion for him because he saw him as a fellow human being in life-threatening need. This is only explicable, in the logic of the narrative, if he had first renounced the dehumanizing stereotype that deems outsiders and religious opponents to be less than fully human—or even the embodiments of evil. For the Samaritan's actions to be explicable, he must have predetermined that he would show care to all those he directly encountered in his daily life, irrespective of race, class, religion, color, nationality, or creed. He felt compassion because he had already taught himself to put the equal humanity of others ahead of all other considerations. Then, being moved with compassion at what he encountered, he engaged all the powers of his personality—his sight, his heart, his hands, his strength, his time, his possessions, and his intelligence—to meet the needs of a collective enemy.

This is the most staggering feature of this parable. The Samaritan's display of love exceeds mere charity; it is unreserved in its passion and commitment. This leaves us, as hearers of the story, with an inescapable question: Whence comes such all-encompassing love for others? Whence comes this intensity and generosity of human love that universalizes "neighbors" and even elides the distinction between neighbors and enemies? It can only come, Christian believers would say, from the Triune God who is the source of all love. It can only come from knowing and understanding the love of God, and experiencing that love, in all its limitless depths and boundless grace.

---

15. See Marshall, *Compassionate Justice*, 73–74.

Conclusion

This, then, is perhaps the main take-home lesson of this parable for inter-religious peacemaking. If Muslims, Christians, and Jews encourage those within their respective faith traditions truly to love God with all of their hearts and minds and souls and strength, as their Scriptures all require, *and* to appreciate the extensive and self-giving nature of God's own love, *and* to model their love of neighbor on their love for God and on the love of God itself, then peace must result. "Everyone who loves," 1 John 4 says, "is born of God, and knows God, for God is love." And no one who is truly born of God or who truly knows God's love can hate or kill or demonize their enemies in the name of that God. Love of God, love of neighbor, love of self, and love of enemy are inseparable obligations.

There is a second take-home lesson for peacemaking, as well. The parable recounts a direct encounter between members of two mutually hostile religious communities and the emergence of a relationship between them. The Samaritan did not simply render emergency first aid to the victim at the roadside and then continue on his way. He committed himself to a relationship of enduring care and responsibility for the victim, both in the immediate aftermath and into the future (10:34–35). There is perhaps an important clue here for peacemaking. The deliberate fostering of interpersonal contact between individuals from opposing groups is an extremely powerful, though under-appreciated, tool for conflict transformation. Arguably the best and only lasting way to initiate change in the attitudes of mutual suspicion and hostility that divide warring groups is by building one-to-one friendships between key individuals from both sides—what Jewish conflict specialist Marc Gopin calls "civilian diplomacy."[16]

Such concrete relationships between individuals from opposite sides of the tracks, by their very existence, complexify reality and disallow the wholesale demonizing of the other group. Just as the impact of collective violence is ultimately experienced by individual actors and is disseminated through personal networks by the constant recounting of stories of suffering and injustice, so the impact of individual acts of reconciliation can spread through the relational networks that tie communities together, and gradually accumulate until a tipping-point is reached and society-wide shifts in consciousness occur. As stories of enemies acting out of character as enemies are told and retold, they erode the foundations of prejudice and stereotyping upon which historically entrenched structures of animosity rest, so that peaceful coexistence begins to be conceivable.

---

16. Gopin, *To Make the Earth Whole*.

Jesus' parable of the Good Samaritan is one such story of enemies acting out of character as enemies. It is a fictional story, to be sure, but it is still an immensely powerful story for deconstructing the comforting, yet ultimately death-dealing, distinctions we draw between "us and them," "truth and falsehood," "friends and foreigners," "believers and unbelievers," "neighbors and enemies." Certainly, it is immensely powerful for Christians, because of the unique authority of the one who tells the story. Yet it is also powerful for those outside of the Christian tradition, because of its intrinsic moral truthfulness. It is impossible to deny that the Samaritan in the story did the right thing whereas the other characters did not.

Yet, the greatest challenge of all lies not in what the Samaritan did, it lies in the closing words of Jesus (10:36–37). "Which of these three," he asks the lawyer, "do you think was a neighbor to the man who fell into the hands of robbers?" "The one who showed him mercy," the lawyer replied. Jesus said to him, "Go *you* and do likewise."

Bibliography

Bailey, Kenneth E. *Poet and Peasant, and Through Peasant Eyes: A Literary-Critical Approach to the Parables of Jesus in Luke.* Grand Rapids: Eerdmans, 1985.

Benevento, Maria. "'A Common Word' 10 Years on: Christians and Muslims Must Work Together for Peace." *National Catholic Reporter*, October 15, 2017. https://www.ncronline.org/news/world/common-word-10-years-christians-and-muslims-must-work-together-peace

Fletcher, Martin. "Sifting Through the 9/11 Apocalypse." *Dominion Post*, September 7, 2011, B5.

Gopin, Marc. *To Make the Earth Whole: The Art of Civilian Diplomacy in an Age of Religious Militancy.* Lanham: Rowman & Littlefield, 2009.

Manson, T. W. *The Sayings of Jesus.* London: SCM, 1957.

Marshall, Christopher D. *Compassionate Justice: An Interdisciplinary Dialogue with Two Gospel Parables on Law, Crime, and Restorative Justice.* Eugene, OR: Cascade, 2012.

Volf, Miroslav. "God is Love: Biblical and Theological Reflections on a Foundational Claim." In *A Common Word: Muslims and Christians on Loving God and Neighbor*, edited by Miroslav Volf et al., 88–109. Grand Rapids: Eerdmans, 2010.

Volf, Miroslav, et al., eds. *A Common Word: Muslims and Christians on Loving God and Neighbor.* Grand Rapids: Eerdmans, 2010.

7

"Saints by Calling" in Romans 1:7 and 1 Corinthians 1:2

Paul Trebilco

IT IS A GREAT pleasure to be able to contribute to this volume of essays in honor of Tim Meadowcroft. Tim has been a close and valued friend for many years. I have greatly appreciated his leadership at Laidlaw College, and within the Aotearoa New Zealand Association for Biblical Studies. He has also contributed so much to so many people and to the church through his teaching and in his own research. This is a small "thank you" for all he has done and a token of my appreciation to him.

An accurate translation of the Bible into English needs to convey not just the meaning of individual words but also the overall sense or meaning of the Hebrew or Greek sentence in question. The facets of meaning that are involved here include the theological sense. In this essay, I want to argue that the sense of both Rom 1:7 and 1 Cor 1:2 in most major translations is incorrect for a range of reasons, including the theological sense given by these translations.

Rom 1:7 in the NRSV reads: "To all God's beloved in Rome, who are *called to be saints*: Grace to you and peace from God our Father and the Lord Jesus Christ." 1 Cor 1:2 reads: "To the church of God that is in Corinth, to those who are sanctified in Christ Jesus, *called to be saints*, together with all those who in every place call on the name of our Lord Jesus Christ, both their Lord and ours" (emphasis mine).

In both cases, the expression translated "called to be saints" is κλητοῖς ἁγίοις. In English, this translation gives the strong impression that Paul's addressees are not yet "saints," but rather are called *to be* or *to become* "saints." The sense is that they are called to live out their lives as saints, to act as saints, and so to actually become in the future something that they have not yet become.[1] Comparable examples would be the phrases "called to be wise," "called to be a leader," or "called to be a disciple," where the predicate of "to be" in each case can be understood as a future state that the person "called" should aspire to; in each case it refers to something that we hope will happen. However, it will be argued here that this aspirational or hopeful future sense is not what Paul means when he uses the phrase κλητοῖς ἁγίοις, and that a much better translation is "saints by calling," or "saints by appointment."[2] This emphasizes that the readers are *already* "saints," that is, people who are currently set apart for God, as God's holy people, through God's call.

The specific issue here is that there is no verb in the Greek phrase κλητοῖς ἁγίοις. When English translators give the translation "*called to be saints*," they are supplying the verb "to be." This is the general practice of English translations with these two verses. The KJV, NKJV, RSV, NRSV, and ESV all have "called *to be* saints" in both Rom 1:7 and 1 Cor 1:2. The NIV has "called *to be* saints" in Rom 1:7 and "called *to be* his holy people" in 1 Cor 1:2. The CEV has "God . . . has chosen you *to be* his very own people" in Rom 1:7 and "Christ Jesus chose you *to be* his very own people" in 1 Cor 1:2.[3] In each case, the addition of the verb "to be" suggests that this is not a current condition which is already theirs, but a status or goal to be attained in the future. Only the Holman Christian Standard Bible has "called as saints" in both passages, while the New American Standard Bible has "called as saints" in Rom 1:7 and "saints by calling" in 1 Cor 1:2.

Literally, κλητοῖς ἁγίοις means "called saints." Are most translations correct to add the verb "to be" to the phrase? Here I will first discuss Paul's use of κλητός, and then his use of οἱ ἅγιοι, "the saints." This will then lead to a discussion of Paul's letter openings and the context of the phrase in Romans 1 and 1 Corinthians 1.

---

1. Oakes, "Made Holy," 175, notes "The 'called to be' can easily be read as an aspiration of holiness rather than a current reality." See also Garland, *1 Corinthians*, 27: "'called to be saints' may imply that this is some goal they must attain."

2. *BDAG*, 549, glosses κλητοῖς ἁγίοις in our two verses as "saints who are called (by God)."

3. The New Century Version has "To all of you in Rome whom God loves and has called *to be* his holy people" in Rom 1:7 and "You were called *to be* God's holy people" in 1 Cor 1:2.

The Meaning of κλητός

The adjective κλητός means "pert[aining] to being invited, *called, invited to a meal*."[4] Paul uses κλητός in a range of verses. Perhaps the strongest indication of the meaning of κλητοῖς ἁγίοις in Rom 1:7 and 1 Cor 1:7 comes from the fact that Paul uses a very similar expression in both passages—κλητὸς ἀπόστολος. In Rom 1:1 we read: "Paul, a servant of Jesus Christ, κλητὸς ἀπόστολος, set apart for the gospel of God."[5] Similarly, in 1 Cor 1:1 we read: "Paul, κλητὸς ἀπόστολος Χριστοῦ Ἰησοῦ[6] by the will of God, and our brother Sosthenes." How should κλητὸς ἀπόστολος be translated in each case?

It is quite clear from Paul's letters that he sees himself as currently an apostle as a result of what we have come to call the Damascus Road event. Hence in 1 Cor 9:1 we read: "Am I not free? Am I not an apostle (οὐκ εἰμὶ ἀπόστολος;)? Have I not seen Jesus our Lord?"[7] That Paul was an apostle was because of God's call, rather than any human agency.

Accordingly, in Rom 1:1 and 1 Cor 1:1 when Paul writes κλητός ἀπόστολος, he does not mean "called to be an apostle," as if this is something he currently is not. This is not an aspiration, but a reality, a position he has in the present as a result of God's call. Hence κλητός ἀπόστολος means "an apostle by calling," or "an apostle by appointment/invitation."[8] This provides a strong parallel to our very closely related expression κλητοῖς ἁγίοις, and strongly suggests a related translation "saints by [God's] call." Jewett comments:

> The appellation κλητὸς ἀπόστολος is sometimes translated "a called apostle," "called an apostle," or "called to be an apostle," which seem inexact. . . . The adjective in the expression κλητὸς ἀπόστολος in Rom 1:1 has the sense of [the] perfect passive participle (κεκλημένος), modifying "apostle," a phrase that I translate "an apostle called," implying that his office rests on divine election.[9]

---

4. See *BDAG*, 549 (emphasis original). In the LXX it means "invited, called out, chosen"; see Lust, *Greek-English Lexicon of the Septuagint*, 343. See for example Exod 12:16; Lev 23:2; Zeph 1:7.

5. The NRSV has "called to be an apostle." Quotations from Scripture are from the NRSV throughout this chapter, unless otherwise specified.

6. Here the NRSV has "called to be an apostle of Christ Jesus."

7. See also 1 Cor 15:9; Gal 1:15.

8. See Evans, "New Wine in Old Wineskins," 198.

9. Jewett, *Romans*, 101.

Jewett also comments on the translation, "called to be an apostle": "Supplying the words 'to be' seems inexact and could imply that Paul was merely called and has not yet become an apostle."[10] Hence κλητὸς ἀπόστολος refers to a *current* position.

It is noteworthy that Paul uses κλητὸς ἀπόστολος *only* in Romans and 1 Corinthians. In these two letters, he feels the need to stress his *current* apostolic status.[11] This is because he is not personally known in Rome but now wants to visit them (see Rom 1:10, 13; 15:22); to further complicate the situation he faces, they have heard slanderous talk about him and his Gospel (see Rom 3:8; 6:1).[12] In 1 Corinthians, he stresses his status because the Corinthians were currently rejecting him and his message.[13] Hence, it is important that Paul stress his *current* authoritative position using the phrase κλητὸς ἀπόστολος, rather than pointing to his future position or his aspiration. He is an "apostle by calling."

The sense of κλητός for Paul is also shown by 1 Cor 1:22-24: "For Jews demand signs and Greeks desire wisdom, but we proclaim Christ crucified, a stumbling block to Jews and foolishness to gentiles, but to those who are *the called* [τοῖς κλητοῖς], both Jews and Greeks, Christ the power of God and the wisdom of God." Those who are "the called," who are here given this self-designation through the substantival use of κλητός, are those who *in the present* know Christ as the power and wisdom of God.[14] This does not relate to an aspiration but concerns what God has already done.

This sense of "being called," "being invited," is also often found in the way Paul uses the cognate verb καλέω, which is used regularly in Romans and 1 Corinthians.[15] In using this verb, the emphasis is generally on what God has done in calling them in the past, and that they can now be regarded as those who have been called.[16]

---

10. Jewett, *Romans*, 101 n. 46.

11. This is also a concern in Galatians, but there he uses different language to emphasize his apostleship; see Gal 1:1, 11-24.

12. See Weima, *Paul the Ancient Letter Writer*, 15. Paul mentions his apostleship a second time in Rom 1:5, this is the only letter in which he mentions his apostleship twice in his description of himself; see Weima, *Paul the Ancient Letter Writer*, 18.

13. See Fee, *First Epistle to the Corinthians*, 5-16.

14. Note also Rom 1:6; 8:28.

15. For insightful discussions of Paul's use of καλέω and of "calling" language in general, see Chester, *Conversion at Corinth*, 77-112; Hussey, *Soteriological Use*, 60-88.

16. See Rom 8:30; 9:12, 24, 25, 26; 1 Cor 7:15, 17, 18, 20; 15:9. In Rom 4:17 the verb is used to say that God "calls into existence the things that do not exist"; in 1 Cor 10:27 the verb is used of an invitation to dinner.

Note, for example, 1 Cor 1:9: "God is faithful; by him you were called (δι' οὗ ἐκλήθητε) into the fellowship of his Son, Jesus Christ our Lord." This is clearly a reference to past conversion, which leads to believers now being those who have been "called" by God. Here καλέω has the sense of "appointment to salvation."[17]

1 Cor 7:21–24 is also very helpful:

> Were you a slave when *called* (δοῦλος ἐκλήθης)? Do not be concerned about it. Even if you can gain your freedom, make use of your present condition now more than ever. For whoever *was called* in the Lord as a slave (ὁ γὰρ ἐν κυρίῳ κληθεὶς δοῦλος) is a freed person belonging to the Lord, just as whoever *was free when called* (κληθείς) is a slave of Christ. You were bought with a price; do not become slaves of human masters. In whatever condition *you were called* (ἐκλήθη), brothers and sisters, there remain with God.

Here καλέω in each case has the sense of being "invited," or "summoned" in the past. Paul uses it to speak of the conversion of individual Corinthians, clearly referring to events that have happened.[18] In these passages, καλέω is not used to refer to a future "calling" or with reference to what they are called to be or to become in the future.

We see, then, that κλητός in the phrase κλητός ἅγιος does not mean "called to become something that you are not." Rather, it has the sense of being appointed, invited, or called in the past.[19]

Saints in Paul

The word translated "saints" in these two verses is the dative plural ἁγίοις, from ἅγιος, which means "dedicated to God, holy, sacred" and "that which is holy."[20] Paul uses the plural adjective ἅγιοι substantively thirty times with reference to Christ-believers, and in these cases the term is normally translated as "the saints."[21] When Paul addresses Christians as "the saints" or

---

17. Hussey, *Soteriological Use*, 85.

18. See Hussey, *Soteriological Use*, 71–73. In 1 Cor 1:26, κλῆσις is similarly used to speak of conversion. Rom 11:29 and 1 Cor 7:20 are similar.

19. Hence Procksch, "ἅγιος," 107, writes: "it is not by nature but by divine calling that Christians are ἅγιοι."

20. BDAG, 10.

21. See Rom 1:7; 8:27; 12:13; 15:25, 26, 31; 16:2, 15; 1 Cor 1:2; 6:1, 2; 14:33; 16:1, 15; 2 Cor 1:1; 8:4; 9:1, 12; 13:12; Phil 1:1; 4:21, 22; Col 1:2, 4, 12, 26; 1 Thess 3:13; 2 Thess 1:10; Phlm 5, 7. On "saints" in the New Testament, see Trebilco, *Self-Designations*

"the holy ones," he is emphasizing that they are consecrated, or set apart to God, and separated from the profane.[22] Accordingly, Fee translates οἱ ἅγιοι as "God's holy people."[23]

Paul includes all Christians in this self-designation, rather than a few particularly "holy" people. This is clear in the greetings Paul gives in Phil 1:1: "Paul and Timothy, servants of Christ Jesus, to all the saints in Christ Jesus (πᾶσιν τοῖς ἁγίοις ἐν Χριστῷ Ἰησοῦ) who are in Philippi, with the bishops and deacons." All of Paul's addressees are "in Philippi," and similarly all are "saints in Christ Jesus."[24]

Another example is Col 1:1–2: "Paul, an apostle of Christ Jesus by the will of God, and Timothy our brother, to the saints and faithful brothers and sisters in Christ (ἁγίοις καὶ πιστοῖς ἀδελφοῖς ἐν Χριστῷ) in Colossae. Grace to you and peace from God our Father." Here Paul and Timothy call all the addressees "faithful brothers and sisters in Christ," they are all "in Colossae," and similarly, they are all "the saints." Clearly, then, Paul uses οἱ ἅγιοι as a designation for all Christians.[25] Rather than using this term only for a small group of particularly holy people ("Saint Paul," "Saint Tim"), as became the custom in later church history, Paul regards *all* "Christians" as "saints." This is clearly how he uses the term in Rom 1:7 and 1 Cor 1:2. All his readers in Rome and Corinth are "saints."

It is also noteworthy that Paul uses οἱ ἅγιοι as a term of address that *currently* applies to all his readers and so he can speak of them as οἱ ἅγιοι, "God's holy people," "the saints" in the present.[26] This is clear in the letter openings in Phil 1:1 and Col 1:1–2 that I have just considered. The readers are currently "in Christ Jesus," they are currently "faithful brothers and sisters" in the present and so on.[27] Similarly, they can be called "the saints" *now in the present.*

and Group Identity, 122–63.

22. BDAG, 11. On holiness in the NT see Barton, "Dislocating and Relocating Holiness"; Dunn, "Jesus and Holiness"; Brower and Johnson, *Holiness and Ecclesiology*. On ἅγιος see Procksch, "ἅγιος"; Adewuya, *Holiness and Community*, 130–57.

23. See Fee, *First Epistle to the Corinthians*, 29; see also Fitzmyer, *Romans*, 239.

24. See Collins, *Many Faces of the Church*, 50.

25. See Fitzmyer, *Romans*, 519. Other examples are part of the letter closing (Rom 16:15; 2 Cor 13:12; Phil 4:21, 22); it is understandable that in this context, Paul would write that "all the saints greet you" or something similar. See also e.g., Rom 8:26–7; 1 Cor 14:33; Col 1:12, 26; 1 Thess 3:13.

26. See Lambrecht, *Second Corinthians*, 23; Adewuya, *Holiness and Community*, 163.

27. Paul uses a whole range of other self-designations in his letters: "believers," "assembly," "those who are being saved," and so on. See further Trebilco, *Self-Designations and Group Identity*.

That this is Paul's regular usage is also shown by his many references to "the saints in Jerusalem" in conjunction with the collection that Paul organized from his gentile churches for the Jewish Christians in Jerusalem. In Rom 15:25–26 he writes: "At present, however, I am going to Jerusalem in a ministry *to the saints* (τοῖς ἁγίοις); for Macedonia and Achaia have been pleased to share their resources with the poor *among the saints at Jerusalem* (εἰς τοὺς πτωχοὺς τῶν ἁγίων τῶν ἐν Ἰερουσαλήμ)."[28] Here he can give the Jerusalem Jesus-followers the label of "the saints" in the present. We see then that Paul's regular usage throughout his letters is to call his readers "saints" as a current and currently applicable self-designation.

All of this suggests that since they are saints *now*, a translation of κλητοῖς ἁγίοις that suggests the phrase does not currently apply to his readers but rather is something to which they must aspire is inadequate. Hence, "called to be saints" is an unhelpful translation. As Oakes comments with regard to Romans:

> In 1:7 the Roman Christians' calling makes them now holy people. The idea in the verse is not that holiness or sainthood is to be an ambition to be fulfilled. They already have this status and, given the emphatic location of ἅγιος at the end of the description of the Romans, Paul must see it as a decisive element of their identity.[29]

But it is also important to note that "the saints" as a self-designation participates in the now-and-not-yet of salvation for Paul.[30] In 1 Cor 6:11 Paul uses three metaphors for salvation: "you were washed, you were sanctified (ἡγιάσθητε), you were justified in the name of the Lord Jesus Christ and in the Spirit of our God." The aorist ἡγιάσθητε indicates an event that has occurred in the past.[31] The root meaning of ἁγιάζω is "to consecrate, . . . to dedicate to God,"[32] so Paul's language indicates that through Christ's death the Corinthian believers *have been* "consecrated" or "dedicated to God."

---

28. See also Rom 15:31; 1 Cor 16:1; 2 Cor 8:4; 9:1, 12.

29. Oakes, "Made Holy," 175.

30. On this see Dunn, *Theology of Paul the Apostle*, 317–19, 461–72. Paul can use the verb "to save" (σῴζω) to say that Christians have been saved in the past (Rom 8:24), are being saved in the present (1 Cor 15:1–2) and will be saved in the future (Rom 5:10), using all three tenses.

31. Thiselton, *First Epistle to the Corinthians*, 76, notes that in comparison to the perfect passive of ἁγιάζω in 1:2, the aorist passive here "may bring into focus more specifically the transitional and transformative event of the readers' coming to faith as an event of divine call."

32. Louw and Nida, *Greek-English Lexicon*, 53.44; see also *BDAG*, 9–10; see Exod 13:2; 28:41; 29:36; Deut 15:19; Jer 1:5.

Hence, because of the work of Christ, Paul is able to speak *in the present* of the Christians as "the holy ones," "those who are consecrated to God." This is why he can use οἱ ἅγιοι so frequently.

Yet in 1 Corinthians Paul can also berate his readers in Corinth for "un-consecrated" behavior (e.g., 1 Cor 5:1–8; 6:1–20; 10:14–22), and 1 Cor 6:7–10 shows that he saw them as in some danger of not inheriting the kingdom.[33] In a number of these passages in 1 Corinthians, Paul calls them to *live* as "God's holy people," as those who have been set apart to God, time and again calling them to abandon what he sees as "unsaintly" ways and to actually *be* "God's saints" in the present. That Paul ascribes to them the status or identity of being "saints" now does not mean that he thinks they have "arrived" and that no effort to grow in the Christian life, particularly in holiness, is required. He can ascribe holiness or saintliness to them, and *also* call on them to grow to become more holy in their day-to-day lives.[34]

However, this does not mean they cannot *now be designated or labeled as* "saints." The finished work of Christ means that they *are now* "God's holy people," "the saints" in the present, because that is what they are in the sight of God through the work of Christ. They *have been washed, justified, and sanctified* by Christ (1 Cor 6:11). But he can also call on them to change their unsainty behavior and live more and more fully as "God's holy people," and so to actually *be* "God's holy people" and to live out the ethical implications of the Gospel in the way they live. Hence, he can see becoming holy as *both* something that has *already happened* for Christians *and* as an ongoing process in their lives. They have been made "saints" through the work of Christ, and they now need to live that out. Accordingly, this self-designation participates in the classic indicative-imperative tension in Paul. What Fee notes of ἁγιάζω is also true of οἱ ἅγιοι:

> Believers are set apart for God, just as were the utensils in the Temple. But precisely because they are "set apart" for God, they must also bear the character of the God who has thus set them apart. Thus holiness forms part of God's intention in saving a people who belong to God alone (cf. 1 Thess. 4:3; 5:23). Paul's concept of holiness regularly entails observable behavior, thus "holy living." That will be particularly the case in this letter.[35]

---

33. See Fee, *First Epistle to the Corinthians*, 267.

34. See Weima, *Paul the Ancient Letter Writer*, 37–38. Oakes, "Made Holy," 175, similarly notes: "As Romans 6 shows, Paul does have aspirations for development in holiness among the Roman Christians. However, this is not conveyed by his usage of the plural adjective ἅγιοι as a noun."

35. Fee, *First Epistle to the Corinthians*, 28–29. Thiselton, *First Epistle to the Corinthians*, 77 (emphasis original) writes: "believers are *called* to a lifestyle which reflects

What this now-and-not-yet dynamic means is that we cannot object to or discount the translation of κλητοῖς ἁγίοις as "saints by calling" on theological ground. That Paul uses this phrase as something that can currently be applied to them does not mean he sees them as totally "saintly" in their lifestyle. He affirms *both* that they are "the saints," "God's holy people" because of the work of Christ, *and*, later in the letter, that they need to live in more "holy" ways. To put it another way, that they currently demonstrate "unsaintly" behavior does not mean that we should avoid the translation of κλητοῖς ἁγίοις as "saints by calling," or "the called saints." Indeed, it is vital to Paul that they *currently are* "saints by calling," since this (and not their present behavior) is at the heart of their salvation.

Paul's Descriptions of Addressees in Letter Openings

Both Rom 1:7 and 1 Cor 1:2 are found in the description of Paul's addressees in the letter openings of their respective letters.[36] Paul's practice in the descriptions of his readers in letter openings is always to state what Christ has done for his addressees, and what is currently the case. He does not exhort his readers to action in these brief descriptions of his addressees in the letter openings. Note the following descriptions of the addressees:

- 2 Cor 1:1: "To the church of God that is in Corinth, including all the saints throughout Achaia (τῇ ἐκκλησίᾳ τοῦ θεοῦ τῇ οὔσῃ ἐν Κορίνθῳ σὺν τοῖς ἁγίοις πᾶσιν τοῖς οὖσιν ἐν ὅλῃ τῇ Ἀχαΐᾳ)."

- Eph 1:1: "To the saints who are in Ephesus and are faithful in Christ Jesus (τοῖς ἁγίοις τοῖς οὖσιν [ἐν Ἐφέσῳ] καὶ πιστοῖς ἐν Χριστῷ Ἰησοῦ)."

- Phil 1:1: "To all the saints in Christ Jesus who are in Philippi, with the bishops and deacons (πᾶσιν τοῖς ἁγίοις ἐν Χριστῷ Ἰησοῦ τοῖς οὖσιν ἐν Φιλίπποις σὺν ἐπισκόποις καὶ διακόνοις)."

- Col 1:2: "To the saints and faithful brothers and sisters in Christ in Colossae (τοῖς ἐν Κολοσσαῖς ἁγίοις καὶ πιστοῖς ἀδελφοῖς ἐν Χριστῷ)."

---

their *already* given status." Similarly, Collins, *Many Faces of the Church*, 156 n. 5, writes: "The Greek phrase *klētoi hagioi* without the verb 'to be' designates a quality of the members of the community. Designated saints by God, sanctification is their vocation (see 1 Thess 4:3)." See also Gorman, "'You Shall Be Cruciform,'" 150.

36. On the letter openings of Paul's letters see Weima, *Paul the Ancient Letter Writer*, 11–50.

- 1 Thess 1:1: "To the church of the Thessalonians in God the Father and the Lord Jesus Christ (τῇ ἐκκλησίᾳ Θεσσαλονικέων ἐν θεῷ πατρὶ καὶ κυρίῳ Ἰησοῦ Χριστῷ)."[37]

Although these descriptions are brief, they are all statements of what is currently the case. They state the current location of the readers (although in Eph 1:1, ἐν Ἐφέσῳ is the less well attested reading). When there is an addition, it again relates to the present. The Ephesian addressees are "the saints" and are "faithful in Christ Jesus." The Philippian readers are "the saints in Christ Jesus." The Colossian readers are "saints and faithful brothers and sisters." The Thessalonian readers are "in God the Father and the Lord Jesus Christ." These are all current descriptors. No exhortation is found in any of these letter openings.

We also see how often Paul uses "the saints" as a designation in the openings of his letters. This is in the actual address (2 Cor 1:1; Phil 1:1; Col 1:2), or as part of the thanksgiving (Col 1:4, Phlm 5, 7). As we have seen, this is the case also in Rom 1:7 and 1 Cor 1:2. As part of the letter opening, we may suggest that "the saints" *functions* as a way for Paul to remind the readers of what he regards as the privilege of being "God's holy people," and so reminds them of a crucial dimension of their identity. This is part of his reference at the beginning of a letter to all that God has done for them.

Hence, when it comes to translating κλητοῖς ἁγίοις in Rom 1:7 and 1 Cor 1:2, it would be inexact to translate it as "called to be saints," which could be read to mean that they are not yet "saints" but rather are "called" to become saints. Rather, since all of Paul's descriptions of the addressees emphasize their current state in God's eyes, the translation of "saints by calling" is much more appropriate.[38]

---

37. In the case of Gal 1:1 we simply read "To the churches of Galatia." In this case, Paul is clearly highly concerned about the readers and rushes into the content of the letter, without even giving a thanksgiving. 2 Thess 1:1 is almost identical to 1 Thess 1:1. In Philemon, Paul uses terms of endearment when writing to Philemon, Apphia, and Archippus.

38. Hence in discussing Rom 1:7, Jewett, *Romans*, 114 (see also 95) notes that "called saints" is the preferred translation of κλητοῖς ἁγίοις, and comments that this is because "the usual translation 'called to be saints' implies a moral agenda for salvation rather than the assured status implied by the title."

The Context of the Letter Openings in Romans and 1 Corinthians

The context of the letter openings in Romans and in 1 Corinthians is relevant to our discussion of the translation of κλητοῖς ἁγίοις.

The description of the addressees in Rom 1:7 is very brief: "To all God's beloved in Rome (πᾶσιν τοῖς οὖσιν ἐν Ῥώμῃ ἀγαπητοῖς θεοῦ), κλητοῖς ἁγίοις." Clearly, they are currently "God's beloved," just as they are currently in Rome, which leads us to expect that κλητοῖς ἁγίοις is also a description of the present state of the readers.

There is an additional description of the readers in Rom 1:6, at the very end of Paul's self-introduction. Rom 1:4b–6 reads: "Jesus Christ our Lord, through whom we have received grace and apostleship to bring about the obedience of faith among all the gentiles for the sake of his name, including yourselves *who are called to belong to Jesus Christ* (ἐν οἷς ἐστε καὶ ὑμεῖς κλητοὶ Ἰησοῦ Χριστοῦ)." Here, Paul reinforces the gift of salvation that his readers, particularly his gentile readers, have received by saying that they are κλητοί of Jesus Christ. As Fitzmyer notes, in referring to them as κλητοί here, "Paul stresses the divine initiative; the Christians of Rome as 'called ones' have been the object of divine favor and grace."[39] Again, this is a *present* description of the readers. The use of κλητοί here leads us to suggest that when in the middle of the very next verse Paul writes κλητοῖς ἁγίοις, he is again referring to something they currently are through the past and effective call of Jesus Christ.

In 1 Corinthians the wider context is also particularly significant. 1 Cor 1:2 uses the participle from ἁγιάζω as well as οἱ ἅγιοι: "To the church of God that is in Corinth, to those who have been sanctified in Christ Jesus (ἡγιασμένοις ἐν Χριστῷ Ἰησοῦ), saints by calling (κλητοῖς ἁγίοις), together with all those who in every place call on the name of our Lord Jesus Christ." All of his addressees are "in Corinth," all are "sanctified in Christ Jesus," and they are together with all who are currently "calling on the name of our Lord Jesus Christ." Similarly, all are "saints by calling" in the present. We see that Paul continues the pattern of describing what is currently the case in all these clauses.

It is noteworthy that he can say they *have been* "sanctified in Christ Jesus," using ἡγιασμένοις, the perfect passive participle of ἁγιάζω.[40] Here the

---

39. Fitzmyer, *Romans*, 238.

40. The NRSV translates this as "to those who are sanctified in Christ Jesus," but this does not sufficiently express the perfect.

perfect refers to a past event with ongoing significance.[41] As Fee notes: "the emphasis lies on their becoming God's people as the result of divine activity. What God has done 'in Christ Jesus' makes them God's new people."[42] Or as Conzelmann puts it "Holiness is received, not achieved."[43] Thus, this is not a future calling, or something they must become as they live the Christian life. They are currently "sanctified in Christ Jesus," made holy through the death of Christ, as we have noted. This is elaborated on at the end of 1 Cor 1:30–31: "He [God] is the source of your life in Christ Jesus, who became for us wisdom from God, and righteousness and sanctification (ἁγιασμός) and redemption, in order that, as it is written, 'Let the one who boasts, boast in the Lord.'" Here, ἁγιασμός, a noun related to the verb ἁγιάζω and the adjective ἅγιος, is used. It refers to a current state—they are currently, through their life in Christ Jesus, made holy or sanctified, just as they are made righteous and redeemed. "Sanctification" is something that has occurred for the Christian, through the work of Christ (although of course as we have noted, they are also called to live holy lives in the present).

Also relevant here is 1 Cor 6:1–2, where Paul exhorts the addressees to take a grievance before "the saints" rather than before "the unrighteous" and then justifies this by speaking of "the saints" judging the world. In 1 Cor 6:2 the saints are identified as "you" ("and if the world is to be judged by *you* . . . "). Clearly, "the saints" is a designation for all God's people in Corinth, and it is a designation that applies *now*. They are currently sanctified, and currently "the saints."

I have also noted that in both Rom 1:1 and 1 Cor 1:1, Paul uses κλητὸς ἀπόστολος, which is best translated as "apostle by calling." Again, this very proximate use of κλητός strongly indicates that the best translation of κλητοῖς ἁγίοις is "saints by calling."

Considering Bible Translations

Why have translations regularly rendered κλητοῖς ἁγίοις as "called to be saints," particularly when a number of scholars have argued the translation is misleading? Perhaps Bible translators have taken their lead from the KJV, which translates the phrase as "called to be saints" in both our verses, and so this rendering has simply become traditional? But three further reasons for this translation may be suggested.

41. See Thiselton, *First Epistle to the Corinthians*, 76.

42. Fee, *First Epistle to the Corinthians*, 28.

43. Conzelmann, *1 Corinthians*, 21; see also Garland, *1 Corinthians*, 27–28, and Rom 6:22.

First, the term "saints" has become problematic, since in contemporary English there are a few people who are known as "saints" ("Saint Paul," "Saint Francis"), and most Christians would not think of applying this designation to themselves. Hence, a translation that regards the label of "saints" as an aspiration, not a reality, may seem more appropriate.

Secondly, in many Christian circles, "sanctification" has come to be regarded as a life-long process, rather than something that is both a gift ("you were sanctified," 1 Cor 6:11) and a vocation ("For this is the will of God, your sanctification," 1 Thess 4:3). Clearly, the translation of "called to be saints" is more in keeping with a theological position that sees sanctification primarily as an ongoing process.

Thirdly, particularly in 1 Corinthians, the translation "saints by calling" may seem inappropriate in view of the "unholy" behavior Paul tackles in the letter. It may be felt that "called to be saints" takes account of the way the Corinthians fall short in their actual lives. But this is to blunt the indicative-imperative dynamic of Paul's theology. The Corinthians *really are* "saints by calling" in God's eyes, whilst also *really needing to become* more holy in their daily lives. But this does not mean that the incredible reality of their salvation ("saints by calling") should be diminished in our translation. The translation "called to be saints" undervalues the completed work of Christ and undervalues what Christ has actually done for us.

Conclusion

Here I have argued that the best translation of κλητοῖς ἁγίοις in Rom 1:7 and 1 Cor 1:2 is "saints by calling." This is faithful to Paul's usage of both words, and to the context in Romans and 1 Corinthians, and makes it clear that being "saints" is not a goal to be attained in the future but rather a condition or status that is already given to readers. In my view, this translation also most faithfully renders the theological dynamic of Paul's understanding of salvation.

Bibliography

Adewuya, J. Ayodeji. *Holiness and Community in 2 Cor 6:14–7:1. Paul's View of Communal Holiness in the Corinthian Correspondence*. Studies in Biblical Literature 40. New York: Peter Lang, 2001.

Barton, Stephen C. "Dislocating and Relocating Holiness: A New Testament Study." In *Holiness Past and Present*, edited by Stephen C. Barton, 193–213. London: T. & T. Clark, 2003.

Brower, Kent E., and Andy Johnson, eds. *Holiness and Ecclesiology in the New Testament.* Grand Rapids: Eerdmans, 2007.

Chester, Stephen J. *Conversion at Corinth: Perspectives on Conversion in Paul's Theology and the Corinthian Church.* London: T. & T. Clark, 2003.

Collins, Raymond F. *The Many Faces of the Church: A Study in New Testament Ecclesiology.* New York: Crossroad, 2003.

Conzelmann, Hans. *1 Corinthians.* Hermeneia. Philadelphia: Fortress, 1975.

Dunn, James D. G. "Jesus and Holiness: The Challenge of Purity." In *Holiness Past and Present*, edited by Stephen C. Barton, 168–92. London: T. & T. Clark, 2003.

———. *The Theology of Paul the Apostle.* Grand Rapids: Eerdmans, 1998.

Evans, Owen E. "New Wine in Old Wineskins: XIII. The Saints." *ExpTim* 86 (1974–75) 196–200.

Fee, Gordon D. *The First Epistle to the Corinthians.* NICNT. Revised ed. Grand Rapids: Eerdmans, 2014.

Fitzmyer, Joseph A. *Romans. A New Translation with Introduction and Commentary.* Anchor Bible. New York: Doubleday, 1993.

Garland, David E. *1 Corinthians.* BECNT. Grand Rapids: Baker Academic, 2003.

Gorman, Michael J. "'You Shall Be Cruciform for I Am Cruciform': Paul's Trinitarian Reconstruction of Holiness." In *Holiness and Ecclesiology in the New Testament*, edited by Kent E. Brower and Andy Johnson, 148–66. Grand Rapids: Eerdmans, 2007.

Hussey, Ian. *The Soteriological Use of Call by Paul and Luke.* Eugene, OR: Wipf & Stock, 2018.

Jewett, Robert. *Romans: A Commentary.* Hermeneia. Minneapolis: Fortress, 2007.

Lambrecht, Jan. *Second Corinthians.* Sacra Pagina. Collegeville: The Liturgical, 1999.

Louw, Johannes P., and Eugene A. Nida, eds. *Greek-English Lexicon of the New Testament: Based on Semantic Domains.* 2nd ed. New York: United Bible Societies, 1989.

Lust, Johan et al., eds. *Greek-English Lexicon of the Septuagint.* Revised ed. Stuttgart: Deutsche Bibelgesellschaft, 2003.

Oakes, Peter. "Made Holy by the Holy Spirit: Holiness and Ecclesiology in Romans." In *Holiness and Ecclesiology in the New Testament*, edited by Kent E. Brower and Andy Johnson, 167–83. Grand Rapids: Eerdmans, 2007.

Procksch, Otto. "ἅγιος." In TDNT 1:100–10.

Thiselton, Anthony C. *The First Epistle to the Corinthians. A Commentary on the Greek Text.* NIGTC. Grand Rapids: Eerdmans, 2000.

Trebilco, Paul R. *Self-Designations and Group Identity in the New Testament.* Cambridge: Cambridge University Press, 2012.

Weima, Jeffrey A. D. *Paul the Ancient Letter Writer: An Introduction to Epistolary Analysis.* Grand Rapids: Baker Academic, 2016.

8

ΛΟΓΟΝ ΖΩΗΣ ΕΡΕΧΟΝΤΕΣ
(Holding Forth the Word of Life)

Mark Keown

For as long as I can remember, on Tim Meadowcroft's Laidlaw College office noticeboard, in bold black lettering on yellow background, stood the first three words of Philippians 2:16: λόγον ζωῆς ἐπέχοντες. With Tim's retirement, the same pin-pocked yellow paper now proudly adorns my office wall.

Meanwhile, in two publications, I have sought to defend and explicate the translation of these words, "holding *forth* the word of life," rather than the highly common "holding *fast* to the word of life."[1] The Greek of Phil 2:16a was appropriated by Bible College of New Zealand (now Laidlaw) as its defining text. It was adopted especially with the sense of "holding forth a message of life."[2] This double-passion lives on today.

In this essay, I will draw on and amplify my earlier work arguing for the centrifugal meaning and then explicate how Paul may have intended it

---

1. See Keown, *Congregational*; Keown, *Philippians*.

2. Stewart, "Editorial." See also Sanders, *Expanding Horizons*, 67–77. Sanders writes that aside from training people for Christian work, "the greatest contribution of the Institute has made to the spiritual life of New Zealand lies in the realm of evangelism." Through its work, "the Institute has kept evangelistic fires ablaze throughout the country," 67.

to be understood.³ I will posit some comments on its implications for us as a college and the wider church. I write honoring my mentor and good friend Tim, who sought to embody its ideals.

Preliminaries

The authorship of Philippians is not in dispute.⁴ Whereas some place the letter in Ephesus (AD 52–55) or Caesarea Maritima (AD 58–59), I see no reason to question the long-held unanimous tradition that it was written from Rome. Paul's situation described in Acts 28:30–31 has worsened (1:19–24),⁵ and a date of AD 62–63 seems likely. While the integrity of the letter is questioned by some, for me, the letter's integrity is not in question.

Prior to 2:12–18, Paul gives his customary greeting (1:1–2), thanks God and prays for the Philippians (1:5–11), and reports on his situation from the perspective of the progress of the gospel (1:12–26). He then directs the Philippians to live as united heavenly citizens worthy of the gospel, renouncing any false motives that could irrevocably divide them (1:27—2:4). He gives Christ as supreme example of the attitude he wants them to emulate (2:5–11). He follows this with his travel plans concerning Timothy and Epaphroditus. They are also rhetorical examples of the missional unity and passion Paul dreams of for his converts (2:19–30). He repeats earlier warnings of enemies and encourages them to emulate his determination to press on to the prize of eternal life (3:1–21). He then exhorts the evangelistic co-working women, Euodia and Syntyche, to find unity (4:1–3). After final injunctions for Christian life (4:2–9), he expresses his joy over their ongoing financial support (4:10–19). The letter ends with final greetings and grace (4:20–23). Attention will now be given to Phil 2:16a with matters of context further discussed as I elucidate its meaning.

Philippians 2:16a

While "hold fast" the word of life has merit, I will argue that it is more likely Paul is summoning all the Philippians to "hold forth the word of life."

---

3. It is my intention not to clutter this essay up with too many footnotes. The ideas are supported through my two earlier works referred to in n. 1. Where necessary, I will reference this and other works. For a similar viewpoint on Phil 2:16a see Ware, *Mission*, and Fee, *Philippians*.

4. See further Keown, *Congregational*, 37–70; Keown, *Philippians*, 1:1–93.

5. All references without abbreviated title are from Philippians.

The Participle ἐπέχοντες

The participle ἐπέχοντες is dependent on the main verb φαίνεσθε in the previous verse: "in which you *shine* as lights in the world (or stars in the universe)." There are a range of possibilities concerning the verbal relationship including: imperatival ("hold forth/fast the word of life");[6] temporal ("*as* you hold fast/forth the word of life"); a participle dependent on φαίνεσθε, "shine" ("shine as lights . . . *as* you hold forth/fast the word of life"); epexegetical ("shine as lights . . . by holding forth/fast"); a participle of means ("shine . . . *by means of* holding forth/fast the word of life");[7] causal ("*because* you hold forth/fast the word of life");[8] conditional ("*if* you hold forth/fast the word of life"); telic ("so that they hold forth/fast," or "with the result that . . . "); or of attendant circumstances ("*and* hold forth/fast the word of life").[9]

The differences are subtle and minimal with Paul's point being that they are to both shine forth their witness into the darkness of a fallen world, and they are to hold forth/fast the word of life.

The Meaning of λόγον ζωῆς

Whichever is the best rendering of the participle, ἐπέχοντες is transitive. Its object is λόγον ζωῆς. I will discuss the object and then whether ἐπέχοντες should be rendered "hold fast" or "hold forth."[10]

Λόγος features in 1:14 where it is used of the Roman Christians inspired by Paul to fearlessly preach the gospel (τὸν λόγον λαλεῖν). The term λόγος in the NT often "refers to the totality of the Christian message."[11] It evokes the Hebrew דבר (word) by which God effects his intentions in creation and history (e.g., Exod 4:28; Isa 1:10; 55:10–11). Especially in Luke and Paul, λόγος speaks of the good news of God's victory and salvation in Christ. This is the case in 1:12, where it parallels εὐαγγέλιον (1:16) and "Christ" (1:15, 17, 18).[12] Here, as is common in Paul and the NT, it is used in a genitive construction defining the λόγος.[13] A similar phrase is used of Jesus as the λόγου τῆς ζωῆς

---

6. See e.g., Meecham, "Use of the Participle"; Barrett, "The Imperatival Participle."
7. Loh and Nida, *Paul's Letter to the Philippians*, 71.
8. Meyer, *Critical and Exegetical Commentary*, 117.
9. O'Brien, *Philippians*, 297.
10. For further Keown, *Congregational*, 131–48; idem, *Philippians*, 1:486–96.
11. Hawthorne and Martin, *Philippians*, 45.
12. Fee, *Philippians*, 116.
13. "Word of God" (Rom 9:6; 1 Cor 14:36; 6:17; Col 1:25; 1 Thess 2:13; 1 Tim 4:5;

in 1 John 1:1. Here in Philippians, "word of life" can be read in that same Johannine sense (cf. John 1:1-4, further below).

Ζωή is used in 1:20-22 of earthly life and in 4:3 of "the book of life" (βίβλῳ ζωῆς) in which ζωή indicates "eternal life." Here, ζωή carries the same meaning as 4:3—eternal life. This life parallels a range of notions including:

- Σωτηρία, "salvation" (2:12, cf. 1:19, 28).
- Κέρδος, "gain" (1:21) received at the day of Christ (1:6, 10).
- Σὺν Χριστῷ εἶναι, "to be with Christ" (1:23).
- Χριστὸν κερδήσω, "to gain Christ" (3:8).
- Εὑρεθῶ ἐν αὐτῷ, "to be found in him" (3:10).
- Καταντήσω εἰς τὴν ἐξανάστασιν τὴν ἐκ νεκρῶν, "I may attain to the resurrection from the dead" (3:11).
- Μετασχηματίσει τὸ σῶμα τῆς ταπεινώσεως ἡμῶν σύμμορφον τῷ σώματι τῆς δόξης αὐτοῦ, "will transform our body of humiliation to be like his body of glory" (3:20-21).
- τὸ βραβεῖον, "the prize" that Paul presses on to gain (3:12-14).

This is the reward for those whose names are in the βίβλῳ ζωῆς (book of life, 4:3) received at the consummation when believers willingly yield to Christ (2:11) and receive their reward for which they run and labor (2:16b). Ζωή is the direct alternative to the destruction of God and the Philippians' adversaries (1:28; 3:19). This fullness of life (cf. John 10:10) begins at the moment of faith and culminates in eternal life of eternal quality and quantity with God's Son in the renewed cosmos.

The genitive ζωῆς can be attributive ("the living word"); a genitive of content ("the word full of life"); a genitive of apposition ("the word which is life"); an objective genitive ("the word concerning life"), or, as preferable, a genitive of production ("the word [gospel] that generates life").[14] The concept, then, is creational. The λόγος is God's word that generates eternal life in his people created by divine fiat (cf. Genesis 1-2). While Beare rightly recognizes that, strictly speaking, this is not the Scriptures as we have them

---

2 Tim 2:9; Tit 2:5); "word of faith" (Rom 10:8); "word of Christ" (Rom 10:17; Col 3:16); "word of the cross" (Rom 10:17; 1 Cor 1:18); "word of truth" (Eph 1:13; Col 1:5; 2 Tim 2:15); "word of the Lord" (1 Thess 1:8; 2 Thess 3:1).

14. Sumney, *Philippians*, 56. On the genitive of production: Wallace, *Greek Grammar Beyond the Basics*, 104.

today but is the active word preached and received,[15] the Scriptures inspired and illuminated have this creational power where hearts are open.

Holding Fast or Holding Forth?

The meaning of ἐπέχοντες is disputed. Aside from some ideas that have not found favor,[16] generally speaking, scholarship is divided as to whether λόγον ζωῆς ἐπέχοντες speaks of perseverance or mission (or both). Many take it of the endurance of the Philippians: "holding fast the word of life."[17] Others take it missionally and evangelistically: "holding forth the word of life."[18] Some combine both ideas, arguing that it includes both holding to and holding forth the word.[19] Earlier scholarship favored "hold forth" while mid-late twentieth-century scholars had a preference for "hold fast," with a swing back in the direction "hold forth" in recent times. Deciding between these options is one of the great NT exegetical debates. To this I now turn.

The verb is formed by a compound of ἐπί and ἔχω.[20] Ἐπί can function to intensify ἔχω, yielding the meaning "hold fast" or "hold on." Yet, ἐπί can also indicate "direction or extension toward a goal."[21] As such, the two options are both possibilities in terms of its etymology.

Background Usages

In LXX uses, ἐπέχω can mean holding or holding onto. Examples of this are "wait, stay" in a geographical setting (Gen 8:10, 12; 2 Macc 9:25); "to stop" (Job 18:2); to wait, refrain, or hold back from a military engagement (Judg 20:28; 3 Kgdms [1 Kgs] 22:6, 15; 2 Chron 18:5, 14; 2 Macc 5:25); "hold back" from going on a journey (4 Kgdms [2 Kgs] 4:24); to "hold back" speech (Job 18:2; Jer 6:11); or to "hold onto" hope (Job 27:8) or goodness

---

15. Beare, *Commentary*, 93.

16. Silva suggests the verb means "to correspond" (*Philippians*, 132). Oakes suggests it should be rendered "be" or "serve" for the life of the world ("Quelle").

17. Schenk *Die Philipperbriefe des Paulus*, 222–23; Hansen, *Philippians*, 184; Dickson, *Mission-Commitment*. See Keown, *Philippians*, 1:488 for others.

18. E.g., Bruce, *Philippians*, 85; Fee, *Philippians*, 247–48; Ware, *Mission*, 269–70; Keown, *Congregational*, 143–48; Flemming, *Philippians*, 134–35. See Keown, *Philippians*, 1:89 for others.

19. E.g., Gromacki, *Stand United in Joy*, 113.

20. In classical literature, it is also found as ἐπώχατο.

21 Ware, *Mission*, 259, notes the verb can be transitive of gripping something or intransitive where the subject of the verb pauses or ceases an action.

(Job 30:26). Jeremiah employs it of his weariness of "holding in" the message of God's wrath (Jer 6:11). Sirach uses it nine times, including to "hold onto" in the sense of "rely, trust, or seek," encompassing relying on wealth or a person of wealth (Sir 5:1, 8; 13:11) and relying or holding onto other things such as wisdom (Sir 15:4), children (Sir 16:3), dreams (Sir 34:2), the Lord (Sir 34:15), an unrighteous sacrifice (Sir 35:11), or advice from bad people (Sir 37:11). The LXX usage supports "hold fast," but never in terms of God's word. The exception is Jer 6:11, but this speaks of the prophet's constraint to preach the word.

The four NT uses are intransitive. In Luke 14:7, it carries the sense of "reaching out for" seats of honor. It is used of the disabled man in Acts 3:5, who "fixed his attention on them [Peter and John]" or "held forth his attention to them." In Acts 19:22, Paul "stayed" in Asia. The use in 1 Tim 4:16 is imperatival. Paul urges Timothy to hold fast "to yourself and the teaching." This is a possible parallel reading to "hold fast the word of life" in 2:16a.

Discussions of the use of ἐπέχω in wider Greek sources also yields possibilities either way. Others, especially Poythress, Oakes, and Dickson, have questioned whether "hold forth" is a credible translation.[22] Yet even Poythress concedes it can mean holding out a drink. Dickson, too, is prepared to concede that Ware "successfully demonstrates what scholars have long accepted, namely that the verb can convey the notion of extension."[23] Other studies have shown conclusively that "hold forth" is a very credible translation and, as will be argued in terms of context, a preferable one.[24]

Dickson's analysis concludes that outside the NT, it generally means "hold upon."[25] Yet, Dickson is prepared to concede that Ware "successfully demonstrates what scholars have long accepted, namely that the verb can convey the notion of extension."[26] James Ware rightly critiques arguments that "hold forth" is not relevant to the context, that these references are specialized

---

22. Poythress, "'Hold Fast' Versus 'Hold Out.'" He argues that "hold forth" is rare and only used in terms of holding forth drink (a clearly incorrect conclusion, as Ware and myself have argued). He takes it as "hold upon." Similarly, Dickson, *Mission-Commitment*, 108–10, notes these meanings: 1) Restrain, withhold whether speaking, judgment, passions, actions, the enemy; 2) Hold/put forth ideas or placing something on lips (playing down the idea of extension); 3) Occupy as in troops, a position; 4) Gripping, taking hold of something. He notes John Chrysostom (*Hom. Phil.* 62.244) interprets Phil 2:16 as "do the principle of life," likening it to stars retaining their light. See also Oakes, "Quelle," 266–85.

23. See Dickson, *Mission-Commitment*, 108 n. 74; Ware, *Mission*, 269.

24. See e.g., Lightfoot, *Philippians*, 118; Hendriksen and Kistemaker, *Philippians*, 126; Ware, *Mission*, 260 n. 75; Keown, *Philippians*, 1:486–96.

25. Dickson, *Mission-Commitment*, 108–10. See n. 22 for Dickson's views.

26. See Dickson, *Mission-Commitment*, 108 n .74; Ware, *Mission*, 269.

uses and of limited searches conducted in earlier studies.[27] He adds substantial detail to earlier work confirming that ἐπέχω is used of holding forth a cup for someone to drink or of a breast offered to an infant, while adding a range of other "hold forth" options (below). From the different studies, we can discern a range of uses of ἐπέχω in the sense "hold forth."

1. Offering of a cup or a drink to others (Homer, *Il.* 9.489; 22.77–83, 494; *Od.* 16.444; Aristophanes, *Nub.* 1382; Plato, *Phaed.* 117c; Lucian, *Tox.* 37).

2. Offering the breast (Homer, *Il.* 22.83; Pausanias, *Descr.* 1.33.7; Euripides, *Andr.* 225; Dio Chrysostom, *Dei cogn.* 31; Plutarch, *Quaest. rom.* 265a, 268f; *Fort. Rom.* 320d; Lucian, *Zeuxis.* 4).[28]

3. Putting forth feet (Homer, *Il.* 14.241; *Od.* 17.410; Philostratus, *Imag.* 1.5.2).[29]

4. Holding out a sword (Euripides, *Iph. taur.* 1469; Plutarch, *Caes.* 9).[30]

5. Extending a bow toward a target (Pindar, *Ol.* 2.89; Euripides, *Herc. fur.* 984; Homer, *Od.* 22.15).

6. Directing horses to a place (Homer, *Il.* 17.465; Ps. Hesiod. *Sc. Her.* 350).

7. Directing eyes to a person (Lucian, *Dial. marin.* 289).

8. An octopus extending a tentacle (Aristotle, *His. an.* 550b).

9. Holding a pitcher toward a spring (Theocritus, *Id.* 13.46).

10. Presenting an offering or a contribution (SEG 1:362).

11. The advance of ships (e.g., Thucydides, 8.105.3; Plutarch, *Tim.* 8.3).[31]

12. Enemy attack (e.g., Homer, *Od.* 19.71; Hesiod, *Theog.* 711).

---

27. Ware, *Mission*, 260–61, 62–66.

28. References from 1 and 2 from: Lightfoot, *Philippians*, 118; Hendriksen and Kistemaker, *Exposition*, 126; Ware, *Mission*, 260 n. 75; Keown, *Philippians*, 1:490–91.

29. Numbers 3–10 from Ware, *Mission*, 262.

30. See especially Euripides, *Iph. Taur.* 1455–65: "And establish this law: whenever the people keep the festival, *let a sword* (ξίφος) *be held to a man's throat and draw out blood*, in atonement for your sacrifice, so that the goddess may have her honors, and holiness is revered." See http://www.grtbooks.com/exitfram.asp?idx=0&yr=1000&aa=EU&at=j&lst=7&ref=euripides&URL=http://www.perseus.tufts.edu/cgi-bin/ptext?doc=Perseus%3Atext%3A1999.01.0112 (emphasis mine). Interestingly, *LSJ* notes that ξίφος, "sword," was a term used of the Praetorian Guard wielding swords (Philostratus, *Vit. soph.* 4.42, also Phil 1:13; see *LSJ*, 1191).

31. Numbers 11–19 come from my own research of primary sources.

13. The spread of clouds (e.g., Philo, *Abr.* 43; *Moses.* 176).
14. The spread of snow (e.g., Lucian, *Sat.* 9).
15. The spread of vegetation (e.g., Herodotus, *Hist.* 1.108; 7:19).
16. The advance of ships (e.g., Thucydides 1.50.2).
17. The spread of fire (e.g., Homer, *Il.* 23.238; 24.792).
18. The extension of darkness (e.g., Plutarch, *Mar.* 20.1; Josephus, *Ant.* 15.55).
19. The extension of light (e.g., Plato, *Resp.* 508c; Lucian, *Ver. hist.* 2.12).
20. The extension of a message, idea, or rumor (Josephus, *Ant.* 11.285; 20.145; *J.W.* 5.543; *Life* 132, 379).[32]
21. Something filling a context including a military occupation (e.g., Aristotle, *[Mund.]* 398a; Philo, *Legat.* 226; Herodotus, *Hist.* 8.32, 35; 1.104; Thucydides 7.62; 2.101).[33]

Ware goes as far as questioning whether the term has the meaning "hold fast." He notes that LSJ do not give it as an option. He writes:[34]

> It is telling that the sense "hold" or "hold fast" for the verb ἐπέχω, so popular among New Testament specialists, is virtually unknown in classical scholarship. It can be stated categorically that the verb ἐπέχω does not bear the sense "hold" or "hold fast" in any ancient passage.[35]

I conclude:

> While Ware overstates things as the work of Poythress, Dickson, the LXX, and NT usage of the term demonstrates, it is clear that on the basis of its background, that the meaning of ἐπέχω here in 2:16a cannot be decided on its use in the wider literature alone—it can go in either direction.[36]

---

32. Keown, *Congregational*, 137. See also Ware, *Mission*, 264, who includes other references. See especially Josephus, *Ant.* 20:145, where there is "a report *spreading* or *gaining* currency" (φήμης ἐπισχούσης). See also *Life* 132, where "a rumor had *now spread* through Galilee" (Ἐπισχούσης δέ φήμης).

33. Ware, *Mission*, 265, e.g., Aristotle, *[Mund.]* 398a; Philo, *Legat.* 226.

34. Including *T. Jos.* 15.3; Josephus, *J.W.* 1.230; Plutarch, *Otho.* 17; Diodorus Siculus, *Hist.* 12.27.3; Appian, *Bell. civ.* 1.1.12; 2.11.72.

35. Ware, *Mission*, 268–69.

36. Keown, *Philippians*, 1:491.

Daniel 12:3

Fee turns to the Dan 12:3 to resolve the issue in favor of "hold forth." He rightly argues that this Daniel text is alluded to in the 2:15, noting that the Old Greek Version of the LXX of Dan 12:3 reads: "and the ones who have understanding will *shine* (φανοῦσιν) as *lights* (ὡς φωστῆρες) of heaven and those having been empowered by my words as the *stars* (ἄστρα) of heaven forever."[37] In Dan 12:3 (Heb), the wise "lead many to righteousness," which adds support to seeing here an outward focus. This differs in the LXX (Old Greek Version) where it reads: "those who strengthen my words will be as the stars of heaven forever and ever." The shifts in the LXX and Hebrew readings leads Dickson to critique Fee's argument for an intertextual allusion with Dan 12:3 here.[38] However, while Dickson clearly has a case, it is certain that Paul was familiar with both the LXX and Hebrew, and his working with both cannot be ruled out.[39]

Context

The above discussion of ἐπέχω indicates that we are left to consider context in making a final assessment. It is argued by some that perseverance dominates the letter's intent.[40] Perseverance language and ideas are certainly in the letter. If we read 1:6 in soteriological terms, the verse points to God completing the good work of their salvation for Christ's return. Paul prays they will be pure and blameless to that same day (1:10–11). Paul seeks prayer that he will honored in his body whether he lives and dies (1:19–20). The military and athletic motif "standing firm in one Spirit" in 1:27c is inclusive of endurance. The passage at hand also urges the Philippians to work out their salvation by God's power (2:12–13). Paul's concern that his labor is not in vain in v. 16b speaks to some extent of perseverance. The appeal to watch out for the Judaizers in 3:2 and to take on the same mindset of Paul in 3:16–17 indicates emulating his commitment to persevere in the gospel to the end (3:10–15).

Yet, evangelism too fills the context, and in my view, more so. This includes 1:5–7 where, while the soteriological reading is popular and appealing, context suggests that the three phrases "partnership in the gospel," "a good work through you," and "partners in my grace" (συγκοινωνούς

---

37. See Ware, *Mission*, 255–56, for detail.
38. Dickson, *Mission-Commitment*, 111–13.
39. See Silva, "Old Testament in Paul."
40. E.g., Hawthorne and Martin, *Philippians*, 146.

μου τῆς χάριτος)⁴¹ should all be read missionally.⁴² The dominant theme in 1:12-26 is the progress of the gospel through Paul in Rome;⁴³ a kind of military invasion despite circumstances (esp. 1:13-18a). Although the apostle to the gentiles is imprisoned, he is a kind of trojan horse,⁴⁴ his cause well-known, soldiers influenced with some coming to Christ (cf. 4:22),⁴⁵ and members of the local church "extremely courageous to speak the word without fear."⁴⁶ While these preachers have varying motivations and are not united (1:15, 17-18), Paul is full of joy that they are inspired by his example to preach Christ.

As Paul describes their situation, he has a rhetorical eye on Philippi where two evangelists are at odds (4:2-3). His letter urges Euodia and Syntyche to be united in the gospel as they continue to share Christ in their context and beyond. This Paul is doing in Rome, despite the danger to his person and his yearning to be released to be with Christ. Yet, ongoing life means gospel-fruit for both he and the Philippians (1:22).

The appeal of Philippians 1:27-30 cannot merely be limited to perseverance, as the images of standing (στήκετε) and contending (συναθλοῦντες) call to mind the progress of the gospel in 1:13 (see 1:30) and the co-workers contending (συνήθλησάν) with Paul for the gospel (4:2-3). In the chiastic parallels between 1:27—2:4 and 2:12-18,⁴⁷ the appeal λόγον ζωῆς ἐπέχοντες takes on the notions of his earlier appeal that the Philippians "stand firm in one Spirit, contending as one for the faith of the gospel." Neither of these phrases should be read statically.⁴⁸ The ἵνα clause in 2:10 explains both the purpose and result of Christ's self-emptying mission and God's exaltation of him. The purposive aspect of this is missional: "*so that* every knee . . . every tongue confess . . . "⁴⁹

As a consequence of Christ's glorious example and Paul's appeal ("therefore," 2:12), 2:12-13 calls the Philippians individually to work out

---

41. Keown, *Congregational*, 210-37.

42. As I have argued elsewhere: Keown, *Congregational*, 207-32.

43. I am confident in the traditional view that Philippians was written from Rome ca. 62-63 rather than Caesarea Maritima or, as is more commonly argued, Ephesus. See Keown, *Philippians*, 1:2-14, 23-33.

44. Houlden, *Paul's Letters from Prison*, 58.

45. See the discussion in Keown, *Philippians*, 1:189.

46. Keown, *Philippians*, 1:193

47. On this passage as a chiasm in which 1:27—2:4 parallels 2:12-18 with the Christ-hymn at the center, see Keown, *Philippians*, 1:276. See also Fee, *Philippians* (1995), 156-57.

48. Keown, *Philippians*, 1:283.

49. Keown, *Congregational*, 306-18.

their status as God's saved people through God's power.[50] Paul then focuses on unity and holiness as they live in their fallen, dark world. Unlike Israel in the wilderness,[51] the Philippians are to "be blameless and pure, children of God without blemish in the midst of a corrupt and perverse generation, in which you shine as stars in the universe."[52] This, at first blush, speaks of ethical witness. However, this should not be read statically and defensively. Paul's speaks of the gospel as the means by which "the light of the glory of Christ" spreads forth. This usage shows that the image of light encompasses the message spread through proclaiming "Jesus Christ as Lord" (2 Cor 4:4–5). As the gospel is heard, God's light shines into people's dark hearts, illuminating them (Eph 1:18; 5:14), and from them, it radiates into the world (2 Cor 4:6; see Matt 5:14–16).

Hence, Phil 1:27–30 and 2:14–15 combine to summon the Philippians, as children of God, to live as Kingdom citizens worthy of the gospel of Christ who continue to: obey with fear and trembling, work out their status as God's saved people by God's power, stand firm unified and without complaint and argument in one Spirit, contend like athletes with unbreakable unity together for the faith of the gospel, refuse to be intimidated by unbelieving opponents, and work out their salvation status with God-generated missional engagement in unity. They are summoned to do so without complaint and argument. Living the ethic of Christ, they are to shine like lights in the world of fallen Macedonia, Achaia, the Roman Empire and beyond, much like the Thessalonian church down the Via Egnatia (1 Thess 1:8).[53]

Subsequent to this text, evangelism again dominates 2:12–18, where Paul not only gives his travel plans but presents Timothy and Epaphroditus as examples (2:19–30; 3:17). Timothy renounces self-interest, takes on Paul's mindset, and has served with Paul in the mission of the gospel "as a son with his father" (2:20–22).[54] Of the five labels attached to Epaphroditus, four have clear evangelistic nuances: brother, co-worker, fellow-soldier, and apostle.[55] The two co-workers with Paul demonstrate missional unity.

In contrast, in 3:2, 18–19, Paul will highlight the Judaizers and other enemies of the cross who are evil workers and whose end is destruction. The

---

50. On reading σωτηρία as individual salvation rather than community wholeness, see Keown, *Philippians*, 1:460–62.

51. Further, Keown, *Philippians*, 1:471.

52. Keown, *Philippians*, 1:474.

53. Ware, "Missionary Congregation"; Keown, *Congregational*, 255–64.

54. Keown, *Congregational*, 150–60.

55. Keown, *Congregational*, 161–89.

Philippians are to emulate Paul who, with all his being, seeks to know and embody Christ in his suffering and in future glory (3:10, 15–17).

The central problem of the letter is not perseverance, as the salvation of the Philippians is not really at issue (unlike the Galatians). Rather, it is the nascent conflict between two evangelistic leaders, Euodia and Syntyche. They are to be united in one mind (4:2–3). This mindset is that of Christ and others who live by his cruciform life-pattern: Paul, Timothy, Epaphroditus, and the well-motivated Romans. They are not to go the way of the gospel-corrupting Judaizers nor the falsely motivated Romans of chapter 1. Such attitudes as envy, rivalry, selfish ambition, and empty self-glorification have no place in their life and mission (1:15, 17; 2:3). In unity, emulating Christ (2:5–8), they are to be motivated by love, humility, sacrifice, suffering, service, and selflessness (1:16; 2:2–4).

Reading between the lines, their shared life and mission is being blighted by false attitudes of envy, rivalry, selfish ambition, empty pride, self-interest, complaint, and argument (1:15, 17; 2:3–4, 14). They are to hold forth the word of life without such attitudes, as did the well-motivated Romans, Christ, Paul, Timothy, and Epaphroditus. Notably, every example cited in Philippians, whether negative or positive, is evangelistic. Clearly, evangelism and unified service emulating Christ dominates the letter to a far greater degree than perseverance.[56] As I have concluded elsewhere:

> As such, there is *plenty* in the context to support an evangelistic interpretation of ἐπέχω here. That being the case, I consider it is likely that Paul is appealing for the Philippians to live the gospel, demonstrate it in their community life and individual ethics, and here, *to offer it to the people they come into contact with, particularly those of their community.*[57]

The Metaphor "Hold Forth the Word of Life"

It seems apparent then that the better reading of λόγον ζωῆς ἐπέχοντες is "hold forth the word of life." With that in view, I will now explore the delightful range of possible nuances available to readers as they read or hear Paul's words.

---

56. See Keown, *Congregational*.
57. Keown, *Philippians*, 1:494 (emphasis original).

Hold Forth the Gospel as Drink or Food

One option is that Paul is asking them "hold forth the word of life" as drink to a thirsty world.[58] This evokes thoughts of "living water" (John 4:10, 11, 14; 7:18, 37–38; Rev 7:17), new wine (Luke 5:39), Jesus as the spiritual rock from which they are to drink spiritually (1 Cor 10:4), the Spirit of which believers drink (1 Cor 12:13), healing wine,[59] and the wine of communion (1 Cor 10:21; 11:25–28; John 6:53, 55). Lightfoot suggests that "if therefore we are to look for any metaphor in ἐπέχοντες, it would most naturally be that of offering food or wine."[60]

Another possibility is holding forth food to a hungry world (see Matt 4:4) or something like the "bread of life" in John (John 6:35, 48). Paul elsewhere speaks of "solid food" (1 Cor 3:2), "spiritual food" in the wilderness which is Christ (1 Cor 10:3), the bread of communion (1 Cor 10:16–17; 11:23–28). Communion too is a proclamation of Christ's death (1 Cor 11:26).

Hold Forth the Gospel as Milk from a Woman's Breast

A second possibility is the image of the word of life as breast milk, which invokes the image of new birth and the nurturing of infants (cf. Homer, *Il.* 22.83). This is appropriate to Pauline thought. First, in Gal 4:19, a frustrated Paul addresses the Galatians as his children "for whom I am again in the anguish of childbirth until Christ is formed in you!" This indicates Paul conceived of mission from the perspective of the new birth as, more explicitly, does John (cf. John 3:3, 5). He also reminds the Thessalonians the he gently nurtured them like a "nursing mother taking care of her own children" (1 Thess 2:7–8).[61] In 1 Corinthians 3:2, Paul speaks of feeding the Corinthians milk (γάλα, cf. 1 Pet 1:23; 2:1–2).

---

58. This could potentially link to the idea of a drink offering (2:17; 2 Tim 4:6, cf. Homer, *Il.* 9.489). However, the word of life is not held forth as a sacrifice, it is the service of Paul and the Philippians that is sacrificial.

59. On the use of wine for healing see Du Toit, "Function and Value," who notes this is found in Homer. Hippocrates (460–370 BC) "praised wine as a dressing for wounds, a nutritious diet drink, an antipyretic, a purgative, and a diuretic." Wine was used to moisten wounds. See also Diocles, Asclepiades, Celsus, and Galen.

60. Lightfoot, *Philippians*, 118.

61. On the textual variant see Metzger, *Textual Commentary*, 561. They rightly state: "Despite the weight of external evidence, only ἤπιοι seems to suit the context, where the apostle's gentleness makes an appropriate sequence with the arrogance disclaimed in ver. 6."

Hold Forth the Light of the Gospel (cf. 2:15)

A third nuance is "hold forth" in the sense of the spread of light (e.g., Plato, *Resp.* 508c; Lucian, *Ver. hist.* 2.12). Critically, this angle picks up the idea of the Philippians as "lights in the universe/world" in the previous verse 2:15 and in Dan 12:3. As such, this idea has the most going for it in context, and it is appropriate to Paul's evangelistic theology (2 Cor 4:4–6; cf. 2 Tim 1:10). Believers as children of God are to hold forth the light of the gospel, the word of life, to the world.

Further, Paul elsewhere commonly speaks of the duality of darkness and light or night and day when thinking of the gospel and its power.[62] Believers are to put on the armor of light in the darkness of a fallen world (Rom 13:12; Eph 6:12–13; 1 Thess 5:7–8).[63] They are not to be unequally yoked to darkness (2 Cor 6:14) or be deceived by Satan, who masquerades as an angel of light as do false gospel preachers (2 Cor 11:12–15). Formerly children of darkness, believers are delivered from the domain of darkness (Col 1:13; cf. 1 Thess 5:4) and are now "light in the Lord" and must "walk as children of light," bear ethical "fruit of light" (cf. Col 1:10),[64] and repudiate "unfruitful works of darkness" (Eph 5:8–11, cf. 5:13–14; 1 Thess 5:5).

Beare notes the parallel with John 1:4–5 in which similar language is used: ἐν αὐτῷ ζωὴ ἦν, καὶ ἡ ζωὴ ἦν τὸ φῶς τῶν ἀνθρώπων· καὶ τὸ φῶς ἐν τῇ σκοτίᾳ φαίνει, καὶ ἡ σκοτία αὐτὸ οὐ κατέλαβεν, "in him was life, and the life was the light of humankind. And the light shines in the darkness, and the darkness has not overcome it" (translation mine).[65] Certainly, ἐπέχω is used of the extension of light and fire, darkness, or clouds (see examples above). Here then, Paul may be approaching the Johannine perspective of Christ as λόγος, with Paul urging the Philippians to hold forth Christ, the word of life, to the world. Importantly, earlier in Philippians, Christ is a synonym for the gospel and word (1:15, 17).

As noted earlier, in 1 John 1:1, Jesus is "the word of life," strengthening this Johannine idea and raising the real possibility that "the word of life" is Jesus more than it is the gospel. Like the Thessalonians from whom "the

---

62. See also Rom 2:19; 1 Cor 4:5; 2 Cor 6:15; Col 1:12; 1 Thess 5:2; 1 Tim 1:16.

63. One can note here the inclusio between 1 Thess 5:7–8 and 1 Thess 1:3 with both passages using Paul's triad faith, hope, and love. In 1 Thess 1:3, these produce work for the gospel which includes announcing the gospel into the region (1 Thess 1:8).

64. Notably the language of bearing fruit and increasing in Col 1:10 is also used of the gospel in Col 1:6, suggesting one aspect is evangelization (as did their own Epaphras, who planted the church in the city).

65 Beare, *Commentary*, 92–93.

word *of the Lord*" radiates forth (1 Thess 1:8), the Philippians are to spread the message of life into the region (cf. Josephus, *Ant.* 20:145; *Life* 132).

Hold Forth the Gospel as a Military Assault

A fourth option is the spread of the word as a military attack or invasion.[66] This is the language Paul appropriates for the effect of the gospel in Rome as it advances through the Praetorian Guard and further into the city (1:13–14).[67] There are differing possibilities in this regard. It potentially speaks of their holding forth the word of life as a sword (cf. Euripides, *Iph. taur.* 1469; Plutarch, *Caes.* 9). When writing, Paul was held captive by the Praetorian Guard, all equipped with swords (1:12–13). Elsewhere, in Eph 6:17, Paul speaks of believers equipped with the sword of the Spirit, the word of God. Also in this passage, believers are to have their feet shod with the readiness that comes from the gospel of peace (Eph 6:15, cf. Isa 52:7; Rom 10:15).[68] Arguably then, Paul here in 2:16a has in mind the wider Greek use of ἐπέχω for putting forth one's feet holding forth the word of life (Homer, *Il.* 14.241; *Od.* 17.410; Philostratus, *Imag.* 1.5.2). In Eph 6:17, believers are also to take up the sword of the Spirit, the "word of God" (ῥῆμα θεοῦ) in hand. This speaks of defending the gospel and advancing it as the army of God moves with the weapon of God's word empowered by the Spirit in hand.[69] The verb ἐπέχω is also used of the advance of military ships and of attack. This, too, sparks a range of threads.

The term "apostle," used across the NT and in Philippians of Epaphroditus (2:25), has its roots in sea-faring naval, military, and political expeditions—"it is almost a technical political term in this sense."[70] "It thus has a decisive political and military edge of those sent by the state for political or military purposes."[71] The notion of military advance is also used of the spread of the gospel in 1:13. The image of the Philippians standing firm in one Spirit, contending for the faith of the gospel as one person, refusing to be intimidated by the hordes of enemies charging at them, find their origins in military thought (1:27–30, cf. 4:2–3). Epaphroditus is not only labeled

---

66. On the military imagery see especially Krentz, "Military Language"; Geoffrion, *Rhetorical Purpose*.

67. On προκοπή in a military sense see 2 Macc 8:8; cf. *Agriculture* 160; *J.W.* 1.385; 5.446; Josephus *Ant.* 3.42 (Keown, *Philippians*, 1:185).

68. Keown, *Congregational*, 293–96.

69. See further Keown, *Congregational*, 297–300.

70. Rengstorf, "ἀπόστολος," 407.

71. See also Keown, *Philippians*, 2:39, for supporting examples.

and apostle but also is a "*fellow*-soldier" (συστρατιώτης). Paul is pointing to him as example (3:17), urging the Philippians to emulate his commitment to evangelism and hold forth the word of life to those in their "crooked and perverse generation." They are a colony of Roman citizens (1:27; 3:20) who are to offer the good news to their fellow country-folk, refusing to be intimidated by their opposition.

Hold Forth the Gospel as a Message or Idea

An even more potentially synonymous idea is Josephus's use of ἐπέχω of a message, idea, or rumor, which spreads to fill a context (Josephus, *Ant.* 11.285; 20.145; *J.W.* 5.543). The message here is the gospel. The context is the crooked and perverse Macedonian and Greco-Roman world, and the yet-unreached-lands to north, south, west, and east.

Synthesis

Paul then in 2:12–16a is exhorting the Philippians to continue in their former obedience and work out their salvation status by God's power. They are to end all grumbling and dispute and resolve their issues amicably. As God's children, in their social relationships they are to be blameless, innocent, and unblemished, while living in a wicked world.[72] In this darkness, they are to shine forth as lights, living by the ethic of the gospel as citizens worthy of it, and sharing the gospel of the life-giver Jesus to the people of the world. Their examples are Christ, Paul, and other gospel-worthy Christians. As they do this without flagging, the injunction potentially includes the notion of perseverance but is not exhausted by it—they are to do this until the end.

In what follows, Paul gives the purpose of his appeal through 2:12–16a: that he will be able to boast before God of his beloved Philippians, who show that his faithful Christian effort and work was not futile. Despite his suffering in Roman incarceration, he rejoices. He invites them to join him in the same.

As has been shown, Philippians 2:16a is nestled within an epistle that summons Christians to be gospel-worthy citizens of the Kingdom who, motivated by love, share the gospel through a posture of cruciformity. This is consistent with the wider Pauline corpus. While this gospel is an offence and foolishness to unbelievers (1 Cor 1:18–22), it is: the sword of the Spirit

---

72. As discussed in my commentary, the holiness in mind here is social holiness, love-based relationality, ethical and missio-ethical holiness (see Keown, *Philippians*, 470–79).

(Eph 6:17), the power of God for salvation (1 Cor 1:18, 24), the wisdom of God (1 Cor 1:24), and the means by which God births faith in the human heart (Rom 10:14–17; Eph 1:13–14).

Paul was passionate to proclaim the gospel (esp. Rom 1:14–15; 1 Cor 9:16). Even when imprisoned for doing so by the Romans and chained to a Roman soldier he continued to share (1:13). He asked for his congregations to pray that he would have courage and clarity of message to do so (Eph 6:19–20; Col 4:3–4). He imagined his presence catalyzing others to join him (Phil 1:18a). He raised co-workers whose core tasks were to preach the gospel and equip others for the same (Eph 4:11–12). He urged imitation of his own passion for evangelism and that of Christ who poured out his life for the purpose of people yielding to God's reign and his chosen Savior, Son, Servant, Christ, and Lord (Phil 2:6–10; 1 Cor 11:1; 1 Thess 1:6–8). Paul's *raison d'être* was evangelism and his desire that others emulate his passion to be an ambassador of Christ. It must always be ours!

In the wider NT, this passion is equally evident as the disciples were commissioned to make disciples from all nations, preaching repentance and forgiveness of sin and being Jesus' Spirit-empowered witnesses (Matt 24:14; 28:18–20; Mark 13:10; Luke 24:46–49; John 20:21; Acts 1:8). Their attitude before the Sanhedrin in the earliest days was not quietism and retreatism when threatened, but prayer for increased boldness and ongoing evangelism despite severe persecution and martyrdom (Acts 4:19–20; 5:29–32, 42; 8:4; 11:19–21; 13:49; 19:10, 20).

Concluding Reflections

As noted earlier, the motto of Laidlaw College is λόγον ζωῆς ἐπέχοντες, which adorns the College shield. When appropriated, it was understood in the missional sense: "hold forth the word of life." This was reflected in the life of the college, it being a place of evangelistic zeal. The college produced myriads of missionaries who went into God's world holding forth his life-giving word. This included Andrew M. Johnston, a blind evangelist, who traveled the country, proclaiming the gospel.[73] Evangelism and mission were the bread and butter of the college. Over time, the love for God or his God's word has not dimmed in our college, despite some critics who

---

73. Sanders, *Expanding Horizons*, 68–77. The college also hosted Rev. W. P. Nicholson, who preached through the country in a year of evangelism. As a memorial to Joseph W. Kemp, the founder and also an evangelist, the college provided caravans for evangelism through the country staffed by many graduates. They used the Lewis Eady Hall in Queen Street, Auckland, to share Christ in the city, spearheaded by Rev. John Bissett. J. O. Sanders took on the role after this and then Rev. A. J. Heffernan.

claim this very thing. However, there has been a subtle shift away from missional and evangelistic zeal to a more static focus on academic study of the word, with a diminishing of the missional edge for which we were once renowned. There is also a hesitancy that has grown due to the impacts of secularism and resistance to the gospel, along with a postmodern and postcolonial concern not to impose the gospel on other people and cultures. Such a shift is also buttressed by a lessening of the import of verses like Phil 2:16a. Rightly understood, such verses give a clarion call for believers to emulate Jesus, the apostles, and those who pioneered the churches of the world and again take up the challenge to share Christ in this context and the ends of the earth. This must come not merely through word, but in attitude, deed, and in unity, with a gospel that is as big as the world itself. Yet, it must still come by ongoing proclamation in any and every situation. The college and church in NZ must rediscover its passion, reframe the unchanging gospel, and take it again to the world.

It is time for our college, and others that teach biblical studies, theology, history, practical theology, and vocational training, to rediscover the zeal of Paul for the proclamation of the gospel. Λόγον ζωῆς ἐπέχοντες is a great place to start. It is not enough for me to have it hanging on my wall. It must become more than a decoration. It is a wonderful phrase, full of possibilities of us equipping ourselves and others to hold out to the world the word that is life, generates life, and leads to life. We are to offer it embodied with the attitude of Christ formed in us by the Spirit: a pneumatic cruciformity (Phil 2:1–11). We are to allow the gospel's light to shine as we offer the world God's water, wine, and the bread of life, and God the mother's breast milk, and the sacramental elements, and defend the gospel and advance it with the weapons of righteousness in hand (2 Cor 6:7). As we do, we will watch the gospel's inexorable advance, even if we also suffer great resistance and persecution. Indeed, the word of God cannot be chained (2 Tim 2:9). It must be passed on "in season and out of season" (2 Tim 4:2). We are to ensure God's leaders and churches are equipped for gospel proclamation and living in church and beyond (Eph 4:12). Evangelism and apologetics set within the framework of the full mission of God must be rediscovered and reframed. We are to "lift up [our] eyes and see that the fields are white for harvest" (John 4:35). The crowds are increasingly harassed and helpless sheep without shepherds, stuck in traffic, behind desks, or blundering around, eyes down, on devices. We are to have compassion for them and plead with God to raise up workers for his harvest (Matt 9:36–38). We are to pray, asking our Lord to "look upon their threats and grant your servants to continue to speak your word with all boldness" and that he would move in signs and wonders (Acts 4:29).

As David Stewart said in 1974 concerning "holding forth a message of life:"

> What a priceless gift we have to give to those dead in sins and separated from God! This speaks, too, of the aim of a Bible College. Not only to help men and women know their Bible, but to train them to be gracious and effective witnesses for Christ—a training that means not only wise methods of speaking to others about the Lord, but so to grow in the knowledge and love of God that life as well as lip will witness consistently, that the presence of Christ may become so real to them that He will radiate out through their personalities, and be seen by needy men. This is something of what a Bible College is.[74]

With the words of God's servants, the Apostle Paul and our own David Stewart, resounding in our ears, let us not be merely self-deceived hearers of the word, but doers of it (Jas 1:22), as we at Laidlaw from this time on are to train a new generation of evangelistic disciples who hold forth the word of life. This is our call.

Bibliography

Barrett, C. K. "The Imperatival Participle." *ExpTim* 59 (1948) 165–67.
Beare, Francis Wright. *A Commentary on the Epistle to the Philippians*. 3rd ed. HNTC. New York: Harper & Bros., 1976.
Bruce, F. F. *Philippians*. NIBCNT. 2nd ed. Peabody, MA: Hendrickson, 1989.
Dickson, John P. *Mission-Commitment in Ancient Judaism and in the Pauline Communities*. WUNT 2.159. Tübingen: Mohr Siebeck, 2003.
Du Toit, Andreas B. "The Function and Value of Studying the New Testament Milieu." In *Guide to the New Testament, Vol. 2: The New Testament Milieu*, edited by A. B. du Toit et al., translated by D. Roy Briggs et al., 3–31. Halfway House, SA.: Orion, 1998.
Fee, Gordon D. *Paul's Letter to the Philippians*. NICNT. Grand Rapids: Eerdmans, 1995.
Flemming, Dean. *Philippians: A Commentary in the Wesleyan Tradition*. NBBC. Kansas City: Beacon Hill, 2009.
Geoffrion, Timothy C. *The Rhetorical Purpose and the Political and Military Character of Philippians: A Call to Stand Firm*. Lewiston, NY: Mellen, 1993.
Gromacki, Robert. *Stand United in Joy: An Exposition of Philippians*. The Gromacki Expository Series. Woodlands, TX: Kress Christian, 2002.
Hansen, G. Walter. *The Letter to the Philippians*. PNTC. Grand Rapids: Eerdmans, 2009.
Hawthorne, Gerald F., and Ralph P. Martin. *Philippians*. WBC 43. Dallas: Word, 2004.
Hendriksen, William, and Simon J. Kistemaker. *Exposition of Philippians*. New Testament Commentary 5. Grand Rapids: Baker, 1953–2001.
Houlden, J. L. *Paul's Letters from Prison*. PNTC. Baltimore: Penguin, 1970.

---

74. Stewart, "Editorial."

Keown, Mark J. *Congregational Evangelism in Philippians: The Centrality of an Appeal for Gospel Proclamation to the Fabric of Philippians*. PBM. Milton Keynes: Paternoster, 2008.

———. *Philippians*. EEC. Bellingham: Lexham, 2017.

Krentz, Edgar M. "Military Language and Metaphors in Philippians." In *Origins and Method: Towards a New Understanding of Judaism and Christianity*. Festschrift for John C. Hurd. Edited by B. H. McLean, 105–27. JSNTSup 86. Sheffield: JSOT, 1993.

Lightfoot, Joseph Barber. *Saint Paul's Epistle to the Philippians*. Classic Commentaries on the Greek New Testament. London: Macmillan and Co., 1913.

Loh, I-Jin, and Eugene Albert Nida. *A Handbook on Paul's Letter to the Philippians*. UBS Handbook Series. New York: United Bible Societies, 1995.

Meecham, H. G. "The Use of the Participle for the Imperative in the New Testament." *ExpTim* 58 (1947) 207–9.

Metzger, Bruce Manning. *United Bible Societies, A Textual Commentary on the Greek New Testament, Second Edition a Companion Volume to the United Bible Societies' Greek New Testament*. 4th rev. ed. London: United Bible Societies, 1994.

Meyer, H. A. W. *Critical and Exegetical Commentary on the New Testament*. Translated by W. P. Dickson and F. Crombie. Edinburgh: T. & T. Clark, 1875.

Oakes, Peter. "Quelle devrait être l'influence des échos intertextuels sur la traduction? Le cas de l'épître aux Philippiens (2, 15–16)." In *Intertextualités: La Bible en échos*, edited by D. Marguerat and A. Curtis, 266–85. Paris: Labor et Fides, 2000.

O'Brien, Peter Thomas. *The Epistle to the Philippians: A Commentary on the Greek Text*. NIGTC. Grand Rapids: Eerdmans, 1991.

Poythress, Vern S. ""Hold Fast" Versus "Hold Out" in Philippians 2:16." *WTJ* 64/1 (2002) 45–53. http://www.frame-poythress.org/poythress_articles/2002Hold.htm.

Rengstorf, K. "ἀπόστολος." *TDNT* 1:407–45.

Sanders, J. Oswald. *Expanding Horizons: The Story of the New Zealand Bible Training Institute*. Auckland: Institute, 1971.

Schenk, Wolfgang. *Die Philipperbriefe des Paulus*. Stuttgart: Kohlhammer, 1984.

Moisés Silva, "Old Testament in Paul." In *Dictionary of Paul and His Letters*, edited by Gerald F. Hawthorne and Ralph P. Martin, 630–38. Downers Grove, IL: InterVarsity, 1993.

———. *Philippians*. 2nd ed. BECNT. Grand Rapids: Baker Academic, 2005.

Stewart, David. "Editorial: ΛΟΓΟΝ ΖΩΗΣ ΕΠΕΧΟΝΤΕΣ." *Reaper* 54/11 (1974) 402.

Sumney, J. L. *Philippians: A Greek Student's Intermediate Reader*. Peabody, MA: Hendrickson, 2007.

Wallace, Daniel B. *Greek Grammar Beyond the Basics—Exegetical Syntax of the New Testament*. Grand Rapids: Zondervan and Galaxie Software, 1996.

Ware, James. *The Mission of the Church in Paul's Letter to the Philippians in the Context of Ancient Judaism*. NovTSup 120. Leiden: Brill, 2005.

———. "The Thessalonians as a Missionary Congregation: 1Thessalonians 1:5–8." *ZNW* 83 (1992) 126–31.

9

"You Have Come to Mount Zion . . ." (Heb 12:22)

Pilgrimage to Zion and the Book of Hebrews[1]

PHILIP CHURCH

IN 2009, AFTER I took a period of study leave in Palestine, Tim Meadowcroft encouraged me to attend the 2010 Christ at the Checkpoint conference in Bethlehem. Spending ten days in the West Bank was an experience that has shaped my thinking in the years since and will continue to do so. I am grateful to Tim for his encouragement to attend, and I count it a privilege to write this essay in his honor.

Among the experiences that stand out in my memory is a visit to the Jewish settlement of אפרת (Efrat).[2] We sat in the synagogue and listened to a Jewish man with a New York accent talk about his long standing attachment to the land of Israel from when he lived in the USA, and he explained that if everybody was like "us" there would be peace. He closed his talk by quoting Isa 2:2–4, referring to that peace,

> In days to come the mountain of the LORD's house shall be established as the highest of the mountains, and shall be raised

---

1. This chapter was first published as Church, "Pilgrimage," and is reproduced here with some minor changes with permission.

2. For אפרת, see Mic 5:1. Jewish settlements frequently take on biblical place names.

above the hills; all the nations shall stream to it. Many peoples shall come and say, "Come, let us go up to the mountain of the LORD, to the house of the God of Jacob; that he may teach us his ways and that we may walk in his paths." For out of Zion shall go forth instruction, and the word of the LORD from Jerusalem. He shall judge between the nations, and shall arbitrate for many peoples; they shall beat their swords into plowshares, and their spears into pruning hooks; nation shall not lift up sword against nation, neither shall they learn war any more.[3]

He explained how the *Aliyah* was the fulfilment of that text, notwithstanding that it refers to "all the nations" streaming to Zion rather than ethnic Jews. The following day a presenter at the conference read from the same text, and interpreted it in the same way, claiming that he suspected that "all the nations . . . includes Israel."[4] It seems to me that, while the text envisages the postexilic restoration of Zion and Jerusalem, which would no doubt involve the return of the exiles, that is not the main concern. The text anticipates an eschatological pilgrimage of the nations to Zion to be instructed by and learn *halakhah* from YHWH,[5] followed by universal peace.

In this essay I am ultimately interested in understanding Heb 12:22–24, which begins, "you have come to Mount Zion, even the city of the living God, the heavenly Jerusalem . . . "[6] While the circumstances surrounding Hebrews are shrouded in mystery, it seems clear to me that it is a letter intended to be read to an ethnically Jewish group of followers of Jesus. They are probably located in Rome, while the author is located elsewhere, perhaps in Jerusalem, although this is by no means certain. The temple is still standing, but the author can see its destruction looming on the horizon. The recipients seem to be attracted to synagogue meals that other Jews, not (yet) followers of Jesus, are participating in, meals that "drew some of their significance from their dependency upon the Temple."[7] The author writes to

---

3. I have cited the NRSV. I do not recall what translation the man used.

4. See Bock, "Dispensationalist View," 117–18.

5. Sweeney, "Prophetic Torah," 50, considers that Isa 2:2–4 "is not simply a vision for the nations . . . [rather, Isa 2:5 invites] "'Israel' or 'the house of Jacob' . . . to join the nations on Zion to walk in the light of YHWH." I (a gentile) had the opportunity to visit Jerusalem one day during the conference, but thanks to Tim's prior arrangements, I spent the day in the Library at the École Biblique rather than "streaming to Zion" (the old city).

6. Unless otherwise indicated, all translations are my own.

7. Walker, "Jerusalem in Hebrews 13:9-14," 40.

warn them that if they go down that road there is no way back, and they risk losing their salvation.[8]

Zion and Jerusalem in the OT

The terms "Zion" and "Jerusalem" are relatively commonly used in the OT to refer to the dwelling place of YHWH in the temple, where he was to be worshipped, and from where he addressed his people, who were to listen to his voice.[9] This precise vocabulary is not always present, and as Isa 2:2–4 and Mic 1:1–4 demonstrate, there were a variety of designations for the location. That YHWH selected Zion/Jerusalem for his dwelling place is clear from Ps 2:6, where it is described as my holy hill; from Ps 9:11, where YHWH is said to be "seated" (ישב) in Zion;[10] and from Ps 74:2, where Mount Zion is where YHWH "dwells" (שכן). That it is where YHWH is worshipped is clear from Ps 100:1–5, where all the people of the world are called upon to enter the presence of YHWH, further described as "his gates" and "his courts," that is, the gates and courts of the temple.

One psalm where the combination of worshipping and listening to YHWH is clear is Psalm 95, partially quoted in Hebrews 3 and the subject of a midrash in Heb 3–4.[11] The first part of the psalm (vv. 1–7a) is a dual call to worship and the second part (vv. 7b–11) a prophetic announcement addressed to the gathering worshippers. The dual call to worship (vv. 1–2, 6) is followed by two reasons why YHWH should be worshipped (vv. 3–5, 7a).[12] The exhortations to come before his presence (v. 2) and to kneel before YHWH (v. 6) make it likely this psalm is part of a temple liturgy. The prophetic announcement (vv. 7b–11, quoted in Hebrews 3) is an urgent call to the gathered worshippers to listen to the voice of YHWH "today," and not to harden their hearts as did the wilderness generation at Massah and Meribah.[13] YHWH loathed that generation for forty years and swore

---

8. For argumentation supporting this paragraph see Church, *Hebrews and the Temple*, 12–18, 358–65.

9. See Thomas, "Zion," 907.

10. The verb ישב has a wide semantic range and includes the notion "sitting" as well as "dwelling," with "sitting" in this case probably including the idea of enthronement. See *DCH*, 4:318.

11. An earlier version of the following paragraphs appears in Church, *Hebrews and the Temple*, 320.

12. Goldingay, *Psalms 90–150*, 88–89.

13. The reference to the forty-year period in Ps 95:10 indicates that Massah and Meribah together probably refer to the entire wilderness journey. They occur together in Exod 17:7 (early in the wilderness period) and Deut 33:8 (near the end).

that they would not enter his "rest" (מנוחה). For the wilderness generation, the "rest" (מנוחה) is the promised land (Deut 12:9–10); for the gathering worshippers implied in the psalm it is the temple itself (2 Chron 6:41);[14] for the implied readers of Hebrews and later readers, it is their (and our) eschatological goal (Heb 4:1–11).

YHWH's selection of Zion as his dwelling place led to the belief that Zion was inviolable,[15] something that is clear in Jeremiah's temple sermon (Jeremiah 7), where, in a way reminiscent of Psalm 95, Jeremiah stands at the gate of the temple and accosts the gathering worshippers, announcing YHWH's judgment and the exile unless they amend their ways (Jer 7:4–7). At the end of the sermon, YHWH announces that he would destroy the "place" (מקום), just as he had destroyed his "place" (מקום) at Shiloh (Jer 7:12–14).[16] Soon after, with the exile of the southern kingdom, Jerusalem was sacked by Nebuchadnezzar's army and destroyed (2 Kgs 25:8–21).

However, this was not the end for Jerusalem and Zion, for Zion plays a prominent part in Israel's future in the prophetic literature.[17] The prophets predicted that the city would be cleansed, the temple rebuilt, and the people regathered. Moreover, as the text quoted by both the man in the Efrat Synagogue and by Bock at the Christ at the Checkpoint Conference shows, not only would Israel be regathered to Zion, the nations would also come to Zion to learn the ways of YHWH.

What is remarkable, however, is that Jerusalem and Zion are almost entirely absent from the NT. Apart from Heb 12:22 and Rev 14:1, Zion only appears five times—all OT quotations.[18] As for Jerusalem, while there are numerous geographical references as the backdrop for events described in the Gospels and Acts, and in discussions of Paul's collection in Romans and 1 Corinthians, the city only appears elsewhere in Gal 4:24–26 where it is displaced by the "Jerusalem above," in Heb 12:22 where it is the "heavenly Jerusalem," and three times in Revelation, where it is the "new Jerusalem" that comes down from heaven.[19] And in Heb 13:12–14, rather than moving towards Jerusalem, the followers of Jesus are called to leave the city, following Jesus to where he was executed, bearing the abuse he bore.[20]

14. The Psalms Targum at Ps 95:11 reads "the rest of my temple." In this context, מנוחה is a place of rest rather than a state of rest.

15. Thomas, "Zion," 907–8.

16. That מקום can refer to the temple is clear from a comparison of Ps 96:6 with 1 Chron 16:27. See Holladay, *Jeremiah 1*, 237.

17. Newman, "Jerusalem, Zion, Holy City," 561–62.

18. Matt 21:5; John 12:15; Rom 9:33; 11:26; 1 Pet 2:6.

19. Rev 3:12; 21:2, 10.

20. For this reading of Heb 13:12–14 see Church, *Hebrews and the Temple*, 363–65.

In what follows, I briefly examine Isa 2:2–4 along with the parallel text in Mic 4:1–4. I follow this with a glance in the direction of Isaiah 35, the subject of an allusion in Heb 12:12, and since Jeremiah plays a significant part in Hebrews,[21] I will also look at some texts from Jeremiah that discuss the return of the exiles. I follow this with a study of Heb 12:22–24 in the light of these OT texts.

Isaiah 2:2–4 and Micah 4:1–4

While the idea of an eschatological pilgrimage of the nations to Zion is found in a variety of places in the OT, I expect that Isa 2:2–4 is foundational for any discussion of the idea. Isaiah 2:2–4 is strategically located at the start of the book, perhaps heading up the collection of oracles about Judah and Jerusalem that encompass chapters 2–12.[22] The pericope also appears with minor differences in Mic 4:1–4, where it immediately follows an announcement of the devastation of Zion, Jerusalem, and "the mountain of the house" because of the sins of the leaders of the people.[23] Both texts begin with an announcement that what will happen will happen באחרית הימים ("in the future"),[24] but while the Micah text announces a reversal of the judgments of Micah 3, the Isaiah text seems to be setting out a program for the book.[25]

---

21. *NA28* (862–63) lists eleven citations of and allusions to Jeremiah in Hebrews, including Jer 31:31–34 in Heb 8, treated at length in Heb 9:1—10:18.

22. Limburg, "Swords to Ploughshares," 280.

23. It would be a diversion to enter into the debate as to whether Isaiah borrowed from Micah or vice-versa, or whether both used a preexisting oracle, which seems likely. See the discussion in Wildberger, *Isaiah 1–12*, 85–87, and Williamson, *Isaiah 1–5*, 176–79.

24. Williamson, *Isaiah 1–5*, 179–81, argues that on its own this expression is not strictly eschatological, although the LXX probably reads it that way with "in the last days" in Isa 2:2 and "at the end of days" in Mic 4:1. See Heb 1:1, "in these last days," an eschatological formula referring to the new era brought about by the exaltation of Christ. Childs, *Isaiah*, 29, reads the text as thoroughly eschatological, "It speaks of God's time, different in kind from ordinary time, and it signals immediately that there is no simple linear continuity between Israel's historical existence and the entrance of God's kingdom. Rather, into the old breaks the radical new."

25. Williamson, *Isaiah 1–5*, 172. The idea of the pilgrimage of the nations to Jerusalem pervades Isaiah and becomes more and more detailed as the book progresses. Scholars routinely relate later texts back to this programmatic statement, see e.g., Fishbane, *Biblical Interpretation*, 498; Williamson, *Isaiah 1–5*, 177–78, and Watts, *Isaiah 1–33*, 46–48. For the pilgrimage of the nations to Zion in Isaiah, see 11:10; 24:21—25:10; 45:14–17; 54:1–8; 56:1–8; 60:1–22; 66:18–24. See also Hag 2:6–9; Zech 2:10–14 (MT 2:14–17); 8:20–23; 14:16–19.

Prominent in both Isaiah 2 and Micah 4 are the words "nations" (גוים) and "peoples" (עמים), with the nations and the peoples streaming up the mountain that has been exalted as the highest of the mountains.[26] The location to which they are to ascend is variously named as "the mountain of the house of YHWH" (Isa 2:2, Mic 4:1), the "mountain of YHWH" (Isa 2:3, Mic 4:2), the "house of the God of Jacob" (Isa 2:3, Mic 4:2), "Zion" (Isa 2:3, Mic 4:2) and "Jerusalem" (Isa 2:3, Mic 4:2).[27] They encourage one another to go there so that YHWH, the God of Jacob, can teach them his ways, and they can walk in his paths. As Williamson notes, "the nations, therefore, express a desire to be taught the right way to live by God, and they demonstrate their sincerity by declaring in advance their intention to follow that out in practice."[28] This is reflected in the immediately following motive clause in both Isaiah and Micah, "For from Zion shall go forth instruction (תורה) and the word of YHWH from Jerusalem."[29] Each pericope concludes with a vision of peace among the nations.

Isaiah and Micah diverge at this point. Micah explains that the people will live securely under their own vines and fig trees, with none to make them afraid, "for the mouth of YHWH of hosts has spoken these things" (Mic 4:4), and in Isa 2:5 the people exhort one another to walk in the light of YHWH.

These parallel texts envisage the nations streaming to Zion and Jerusalem to learn the ways of YHWH, with the ultimate result being the cessation of conflict between the nations. It is not concerned with the return of the exiles of Israel and Judah, which is the way the *Aliyah* is normally understood.

---

26. Limburg, "Swords to Ploughshares," 281, notes that this description "should not be understood in terms of geological phenomena . . . but rather as an image illustrating the significance of the mountain and Jerusalem for the future community of 'all the nations' and 'many peoples.'" See also Williamson, *Isaiah 1–5*, 181–82, and Weinfeld, "Zion and Jerusalem," 108.

27. The LXX makes a second destination in Isa 2:2, reading "the mountain of the Lord and the house of God" and also inserts a copula (καί) in Isa 2:3 between "the mountain of the Lord" and (καί) "the house of the God of Jacob," which Baer, *When We All Go Home*, 267–69, also reads as two destinations. The copula is present in both the MT and the LXX of Mic 4:2, and the destination is not expanded in Mic 4:1. 1QIsaᵃ simply reads "the house of the God of Jacob" in Isa 2:3 (1QIsaᵃ II 10), omitting any reference to the mountain of YHWH.

28. Williamson, *Isaiah 1–5*, 184.

29. Willis, "Isaiah 2:2–5," 296, sees this clause as the center of the pericope on which the chiastic structure swings. Magonet, "Isaiah's Mountain," 178, finds the central affirmation in "and he will teach us his ways and we will walk in his paths." For תורה as "instruction," see Sweeney, "Prophetic Torah," 50–51.

Other Possible Texts Behind Hebrews 12:22-24

While Isa 2:2-4 and Mic 1:1-4 deal with the pilgrimage of the nations to Zion, as I suggested above, the implied readers of Hebrews are most likely ethnic Jews. There are numerous texts that refer to the return of the (Jewish) exiles to Zion, and I need to be selective. Given the allusion to Isa 35:3 in Heb 12:12 and the conclusion of that chapter with the joyful return of the exiles to Zion, and given the number of motifs in Isa 34-35 that are reflected in Hebrews,[30] Isaiah 35 warrants a brief examination. Following this, I briefly examine three texts in Jeremiah that are concerned with the return of the exiles.

Isaiah 34-35 is a separate section of Isaiah, connecting chapters 28-33 and 36-39 and probably bound together with the claim that YHWH is coming to take "vengeance" and to "vindicate the cause of Zion" (34:8; 35:4).[31] In 35:4-5, the returning exiles are encouraged to strengthen their weak hands and "wobbly knees,"[32] a text cited from the LXX in Heb 12:12, with minor differences. They are encouraged to do this because YHWH is coming to "help" them. Then in 35:10 the exiles whom YHWH has redeemed enter Zion with great rejoicing, and "grief" (cf. Heb 12:11) and suffering come to an end.

Holladay judges Jeremiah 3:16-18b to be a prose addition to Jeremiah, dated in the fifth century, during the time of Nehemiah.[33] Be that as it may, it now sits alongside Jer 3:12-14, where YHWH calls upon faithless Israel to return and announces that he will restore individuals from among the exiles and bring them to Zion and place faithful leaders over them. This announcement is followed by three oracles with an eschatological orientation,[34] concerning things that will take place (בימים ההמה) "in those days" (vv. 16, 18) and (בעת ההיא) "at that time" (v. 17). The population will increase, the ark of the covenant will be forgotten, having become redundant,[35] and YHWH will be enthroned in Jerusalem (rather than

---

30. Ellingworth, *Hebrews*, 658. Ellingworth lists the "glory" (Isa 35:2; Heb 1:3) of God; the "majesty" (Isa 35:2, cf. Heb 1:3; 7:26) of God; "encouragement" (Isa 35:4; Heb 3:13; 10:25; 13:19, 22); "cosmic disturbance" (Isa 34:4; cf. Heb 1:10-12; 12:25-29), and "judgment" (Isa 34:8; 35:4, cf. Heb 10:30; 12:26).

31. Tucker, "Isaiah 1-39," 273; Childs, *Isaiah*, 255-56.

32. Wildberger, *Isaiah 28-39*, 340.

33. Holladay, *Jeremiah 1*, 81. Craigie et al., *Jeremiah 1-25*, 60, ascribe vv. 16-17 to Jeremiah, with an early date, following Weinfeld, "Spiritual Metamorphosis," 21-24, who dates it in the time of Josiah. William McKane, *Jeremiah*, 77, is ambivalent, but seems to think the verses are exilic.

34. Holladay, *Jeremiah 1*, 1, 77; cf. Weinfeld, "Spiritual Metamorphosis," 23-26.

35. McKane, *Jeremiah*, 1: 74. See Allen, *Jeremiah*, 58, "Yahweh's ark-linked presence

between the cherubim).³⁶ "All the nations" (כל הגוים) will be gathered to Jerusalem to the name of YHWH and will no longer obey the inclinations of their stubborn hearts, and the Northern and Southern Kingdoms will be reunited. Thus, there will be a spiritual transformation, not only of the exiles from both kingdoms, but also of the nations.

Jeremiah 30–33 comprise Jeremiah's so-called "Book of Consolation."³⁷ Here YHWH promises to restore his people after the exile. Jerusalem is apparently addressed in 30:12–17, with several verbs with feminine singular suffixes, and in v. 17 YHWH promises to restore and heal Zion. In chapter 31 YHWH promises to restore the exiles, culminating in the new covenant promise of 31:31–34 and the promise of the rebuilt city. In 31:6 they encourage one another to go up to Zion, to YHWH their God, and in 31:10–14 the word of YHWH is announced to the nations, that YHWH has redeemed them and that they will come and sing for joy "on the heights of Zion" (v. 12, במרום ציון, LXX 38:12, ἐν τῷ ὄρει Σιων, "on Mount Zion") and there rejoice in the goodness of YHWH, explicated in terms of agricultural bounty.

Finally, I refer to Jer 50:4–5. Verses 1–3 of this chapter announce the fall of Babylon at the hands of a nation from the north. "In those days and at that time" (בימים ההמה ובעת ההיא) the exiles from the north and the south will come with tears of repentance to seek God. They will ask the way to Zion and turn their faces toward it and bind themselves to YHWH in an "everlasting covenant" (ברית עולם) that will not be forgotten. The everlasting covenant is another way of describing the new covenant of 31:31–34,³⁸ although the agent of the passive verb "will [not] be forgotten" is unstated. While Allen suggests that the people will not forget the covenant,³⁹ Holladay suggests that YHWH will not forget it.⁴⁰ If this is the case, then it is a promise that the rupture of exile will not happen again.⁴¹ Once again the people are reunited, and together seek Zion, acknowledging that this is the place of true worship.

---

was released to pervade the city."

36. McKane, *Jeremiah*, 1, 74. On p. 77, McKane sees this enthronement in Jerusalem as enthronement "in its common life."

37. Keown et al., *Jeremiah 26–52*, 82–84.

38. Keown et al., *Jeremiah 26–52*, 365. For the everlasting covenant see also 32:40.

39. Allen, *Jeremiah*, 512.

40. Holladay, *Jeremiah 2*, 416.

41. Brueggemann, *To Build and to Plant*, 261.

Hebrews 12:18-24

I turn now to Heb 12:18-24, which has been called the "grand finale" of Hebrews.[42] It is part of the fifth warning passage of Hebrews, extending from 12:14-29.[43] The warning begins with a positive call to pursue peace and holiness and to be on guard against any apostasy arising in the community.[44] The readers are also warned against emulating Esau, who sold his rights as a firstborn for a single meal, and later found no place for repentance. Immediately following these warnings, and logically connected to them in some way with the causal particle γάρ ("for"), is Heb 12:18-24, which comprises two contrasting sentences, the first beginning with the expression "you have not come" and the second beginning with "but you have come." Tying both sentences together is the notion of God speaking: speaking words in v. 19 that the hearers could not bear, and speaking better things than Abel in v. 24.[45] These verses are in turn followed by a warning not to disregard the one speaking (God),[46] who warned from the earth at Sinai and is now warning from heaven, with much more serious consequences.[47]

While no mountain is named as the place to which the readers have not come, it is clear from the allusions to Deut 4:11, where the same verb is used to describe the approach of the people to Horeb, that Sinai is in view. The text describes "the physical phenomena accompanying the giving of the law,"[48] followed by the reaction of the people and of Moses who trembled with fear. The overriding emotion that surfaces is terror at the presence of God.

The approach to Sinai is contrasted with the clause ἀλλὰ προσεληλύθατε Σιὼν ὄρει ("but you have come to Mount Zion"). The perfect tense indicates that the readers are to recognize that as followers of Jesus,[49] they have come

---

42. Lindars, "Rhetorical Structure," 402. See also Son, *Zion Symbolism*, 78. An earlier version of what follows appears in Church, *Hebrews and the Temple*, 343-52.

43. Bateman, "Warning Passages in Hebrews," 83.

44. O'Brien, *Hebrews*, 477.

45. For this reading see Smillie, "The One who is Speaking," 278-83.

46. Ellingworth, *Hebrews*, 683-84; Smillie, "The One who is Speaking," 283-87.

47. There is a logical connection here with the second warning passage, Hebrews 3:7—4:13, which deals with Psalm 95, mentioned above. Both are concerned with listening to God speaking, and both encourage the people to be alert, using the second person plural imperative of βλέπω (βλέπετε, "see to it"), the only instances of this form in Hebrews (3:12; 12:25).

48. Johnson, *Hebrews*, 326.

49. Several scholars use the term "conversion" in this context. See Barrett, "Eschatology," 376; Peterson, *Hebrews and Perfection*, 160; Bruce, *Hebrews*, 255. This term is anachronistic in the context, since "Jew" is an ethnic identifier and "Christ-follower"

to and are now present at Mount Zion. The two sentences contrast two covenants. The former was mediated by Moses (implied, but not stated in the first sentence) and the new covenant is mediated by Jesus (8:6; 9:15; 12:24).

Apart from the reference to a "festal gathering" (πανήγυρις) in v. 22, the positive emotions associated with Zion in Heb 12:22–24 are not explicated. The conjunction καί (and/but) appears seven times, with the eight descriptors falling into four pairs.[50] "Mount Zion" is the destination, with the first descriptor identifying Zion as the "city of the living God, the heavenly Jerusalem."[51] Given that this is the only reference to Zion in Hebrews, the readers may have inferred that the author was referring to the earthly Zion over against Sinai. However, the two additional epithets clarify that the earthly Zion is not in view.[52] The "city" (πόλις) recalls the city with foundations (11:10) that God had prepared for Abraham and the patriarchs (11:16);[53] that is, the heavenly Jerusalem.[54] The author has taken the well-known imagery of Zion/Jerusalem as the place where God is worshipped and from where God speaks and, by means of the adjective "heavenly," applied it as a metaphor for access to God under the new covenant.[55]

As elsewhere in Hebrews, "heavenly" refers to what is to come, now come into the present,[56] so that Mount Zion describes the eschatological

---

transcends ethnicity. These people remained Jews and would not have considered themselves to have "converted" from Judaism to Christianity. Nevertheless, the notion of conversion does preserve an element of truth, since it is Christ-following Jews who have come to Mount Zion, over against those who were not yet Christ-followers. For a plea to set aside the term "conversion" in discussion of Christian origins, see Fredriksen, "Mandatory Retirement," 232–37, and for the use of the term to refer to non-Jewish individuals and communities becoming Jews, see Schwartz, "How Many Judaisms," 232–37.

50. Attridge, *Hebrews*, 374; Son, *Zion Symbolism*, 87–89.

51. All these expressions are anarthrous in Greek. I have supplied a definite article in English where appropriate. Johnson, *Hebrews*, 327, translates "a city of the living God, a heavenly Jerusalem," as though there were more than one of each. He also translates the καί in the expression Σιὼν ὄρει καὶ πόλει θεοῦ ζῶντος with "and," reading "Mount Zion, and a city . . ." But surely this καί is explicative, identifying Zion with the city and Jerusalem, see Spicq, *Hébreux*, 2:405; Lane, *Hebrews 9–13*, 441; Ellingworth, *Hebrews*, 677.

52. Koester, *Hebrews*, 550; Son, *Zion Symbolism*, 89; O'Brien, *Hebrews*, 483.

53. Johnson, *Hebrews*, 331; Fuller Dow, *Images of Zion*, 173–74.

54. Attridge, *Hebrews*, 374. Buchanan, *To the Hebrews*, 222, thinks it is a reference to the restored earthly city of Jerusalem, called "heavenly" because of its divine origin. But this is to misread the eschatological orientation of Hebrews. See Gordon, *Hebrews*, 43–44.

55. DeSilva, *Perseverance in Gratitude*, 466.

56. Heb 3:1; 6:4; 8:5; 9:23; 11:16.

dwelling of God with his people.⁵⁷ Thus, temple imagery is pressed into service to symbolize the relationship between God and his people under the new covenant. The figurative language used elsewhere in Hebrews for this dwelling: "the world to come" (2:5); "God's rest" (4:1–11); "the true tent" (8:2); "within the curtain" (6:19–20; 10:19–25); "the city built by God" (11:10); "the heavenly homeland" (11:16); "the unshakeable kingdom" (12:28); and "the city to come" (13:14), is now extended to include the heavenly Jerusalem.

The next pair of descriptors refers to the inhabitants of Mount Zion, the "myriads of angels in a festal gathering" (μυριάσιν ἀγγέλων, πανηγύρει),⁵⁸ and the "assembly of the firstborn, inscribed in heaven" (ἐκκλησίᾳ πρωτοτόκων ἀπογεγραμμένων ἐν οὐρανοῖς). The presence of angels in a festal gathering is to be read in the context of the numerous references to angels in the Second Temple literature. The Qumran community seems to have envisaged that angels were present in their worship, either on earth in the life of the community, or in the heavenly temple.⁵⁹ Apocalyptic texts include the notion of a journey to heaven that is absent from Hebrews. Here, the community is pictured as having come to Mount Zion and participating in angelic worship, while still earthbound (in Rome?). Mount Zion, therefore, encompasses earth and heaven and is where the new covenant community encounters God and his heavenly entourage. The "assembly of the firstborn inscribed in heaven" comprises the firstborn ones, who belong to Jesus the firstborn one, already in the

---

57. Lane, *Hebrews 9–13*, 465; Koester, *Hebrews*, 544; Son, *Zion Symbolism*, 91; O'Brien, *Hebrews*, 483.

58. It is debated whether πανήγυρις (festal gathering) refers to what precedes (the angels) or to what follows (the assembly of the firstborn). The presence of καί after πανήγυρις suggests that is to be construed with what precedes, as a circumstantial dative qualifying the angels. If it is construed with what follows the καί functions as in v. 22, expressing the idea that the readers have come to a festal gathering, "even" (καί) the assembly of the firstborn. Apart from v. 22, καί functions elsewhere in this list to join different aspects of Mount Zion, making this latter option unlikely, although it is reflected in the punctuation of NA28. For arguments for construing it with what precedes see Attridge, *Hebrews*, 375; Lane, *Hebrews 9–13*, 441–42 (note jj); Ellingworth, *Hebrews*, 679.

59. For these connections with Qumran see Strugnell, "Angelic Liturgy at Qumran," 320; Bruce, *Hebrews*, 357–58; Lane, *Hebrews 9–13*, 468. Some of the early literature on Qumran (especially Gärtner, *The Temple*, 94–99) overstates the case for connections between Qumran and this text in Hebrews, as the differences are significant. See the judicious comments in Klinzing, *Die Umdeutung*, 201–2, who suggests the adoption of a common tradition with significant differences in the way it has been put to use. See also Jub. 31:14; T. Levi 3:5; 1 En. 5–16; Apoc. Zeph. Already in the OT numerous angels inhabit heaven and are involved in the worship of God (Ps 89:6; 103:21; 148:2), a tradition also reflected in Rev 5:11–12.

world to come (1:6). This is the "assembly" (ἐκκλησία) of Heb 2:12 that he came to sanctify: the siblings of Jesus— all the faithful, past and present, Jew and gentile, from all over the world.[60]

The next pair of descriptors describes "God the judge of all" and the "spirits of the righteous made perfect." In 10:26–31, those who persist in sin have only the fearful prospect of judgment. But the reference to God as judge, juxtaposed in this verse with the reference to the spirits of the righteous made perfect, that is, the righteous dead,[61] indicates that there is also the prospect of positive judgment for those made perfect—Christians who have died already worshipping in heaven.[62] These include those listed in Hebrews 11 (see Heb 11:40) and all who endure to the end. For these people, there is the prospect of eschatological acceptance.[63] Thus, the community of Christ-followers on earth, wherever located, is also in the heavenly temple in the presence of myriads of angels, faithful believers past and present and the righteous dead, now participating in the "Sabbath celebration" (σαββατισμός) of Heb 4:9.[64]

The final pair of descriptors, forming a climax to the entire sequence, refers to the "mediator of the new covenant, Jesus" (διαθήκης νέας μεσίτῃ Ἰησοῦ),[65] and "the blood of sprinkling, speaking in a better manner[66] than Abel" (αἵματι ῥαντισμοῦ κρεῖττον λαλοῦντι παρὰ τὸν Ἄβελ).[67] That Jesus is there indicates a reference to the heavenly temple, where he is enthroned, although not "in heaven," but wherever his people are located. The blood

60. Attridge, *Hebrews*, 23; Cockerill, *Hebrews*, 655.
61. Arowele, "Pilgrim People of God." See 1 En. 22:3–4; 41:8; 103:3–4.
62. Scholer, *Proleptic Priests*, 146.
63. O'Brien, *Hebrews*, 487.
64. Lane, *Hebrews 9–13*, 467; Koester, *Hebrews*, 545.
65. As often in Hebrews the name "Jesus" appears in an emphatic position at the end of the clause. See 2:9; 4:14; 6:20; 7:22; 12:2; 13:20.
66. κρείττων ("better") is probably best construed as an adverb (Attridge, *Hebrews*, 377) rather than a singular adjective where it would refer to "something better." P46 and 1505 read κρείττονα (plural, "better things"), but this attestation is minimal.
67. The subject of the verb to speak (λαλέω) is a complex exegetical issue. Smillie, "The One who Is Speaking," argues that God is speaking in this verse, while others argue that either Abel (see Heb 11:4) or Abel's blood (see Gen 4:10) is speaking. Ellingworth and Nida, *Handbook*, 313, note that most translations add a reference to the blood of Abel speaking (alongside the sprinkled blood of Jesus), and this reading is explicit in P46 followed by L and a few minuscules, where the definite article is neuter, governing the neuter αἷμα ("blood") rather than τόν (masculine, governing Ἄβελ), read by ℵ, A, and D and numerous minuscules. One late minuscule (1962) reads the genitive definite article. While I find Smillie's conclusion satisfying, it is somewhat difficult in that it introduces a ninth descriptor to which the readers have come (God speaking), not separated from the eighth with καί.

of sprinkling echoes Heb 9:11–22 and the inauguration of both the Sinai covenant and the new covenant, the latter enabling the promised eternal inheritance (Heb 9:22) envisaged in the present text.

This neatly balanced pericope contrasts the terrifying events surrounding the inauguration of the Sinai covenant with "the ultimate, eschatological encounter with God in the heavenly Jerusalem."[68] Considerable temple symbolism surfaces in the description, indicating that, under the new covenant, the encounter with God in Christ is the reality to which the Jerusalem temple pointed. Given the emphasis in Hebrews on the need to persevere, it seems clear that this imagery does not nullify the eschatological goal that lies ahead of the readers. Rather, it clarifies that they can now experience what is promised to them at the end of their journey. There, they will find a reality that had been experienced all along.[69] Here the faithful have access to the presence of God, yet to be consummated in the future when they attain to God's rest (4:11), as long as they remain faithful.

The Source of the Imagery in Hebrews 12:22–24

It seems clear that lying behind this text in Hebrews is the notion that Mount Zion is the place where God is encountered, where he is worshipped by the saints and the angels, where Jesus is present, and from where God addresses his people with an urgent call to listen. But Mount Zion has been translocated so that it is no longer identified with the earthly Jerusalem, but with the heavenly, where God's faithful people gather with the saints and angels. Whether the theme of the return of the exiles to Zion is present is unclear. I note that the events described in Isa 2:2–4 and Mic 4:1–4 are said to happen "in the last days" (LXX Isa 2:2, ἐν ταῖς ἐσχάταις ἡμέραις; Mic 4:1 ἐπ' ἐσχάτων τῶν ἡμερῶν) and that God's speech through an enthroned Son in Hebrews takes place "in these last days" (ἐπ' ἐσχάτου τῶν ἡμερῶν τούτων, 1:2). I note the piling up of expressions for Jerusalem and Zion in the Isaiah and Micah texts and in Heb 12:22. And I note that the word of YHWH comes from Jerusalem in Isa 2:3 and in Mic 4:2, and the claim that the mouth of YHWH has spoken (LXX λαλέω) in Mic 4:4. These compare favorably with the prominence of God's speech in Heb 12:18–25. I note the atmosphere of rejoicing in Isa 35:10 and in Heb 12:22–24 and the significance of the themes in Isa 34–35 to Hebrews overall. I note the redundancy of the ark of the covenant in Jer 3:16, something implied in the new covenant of Heb 8:13–9:14; 12:24. I note the atmosphere of joyful worship in Heb 12:23, compared with the

68. O'Brien, *Hebrews*, 491.
69. Jewett, *Letter to Pilgrims*, 223; Scholer, *Proleptic Priests*, 144.

same in Jer 31:13-14, and the everlasting covenant of Jer 50:4-5, where the returning exiles turn their faces toward Zion, compared with the everlasting covenant of Heb 13:20. These allusions are intriguing, and were no doubt ideas in the air when the author was writing his letter, but whether any of them are definitive for 12:22-24 is unclear.

What is remarkable is that while these ethnic Jews are somewhere in the Mediterranean diaspora, probably in Rome, they can be described as having come to Mount Zion. However, no journey is implied, since Zion is immediately qualified as a reference to the "heavenly Jerusalem." This expression does not appear in the OT but is found several times in Second Temple Jewish literature, in Rabbinic Judaism, and elsewhere in the NT.[70] There was a conversation about this heavenly city in the postexilic period and beyond that the author of Hebrews contributed to. So, while the OT envisaged a return to the earthly Jerusalem, this was later downplayed—and indeed in the NT, where Jerusalem is always a city under judgment, abandoned. The destination of Abraham, to which the recipients are to direct their attention is the heavenly city, whose architect and builder is God (11:10, 16). This is the "city of the living God," not the earthly Jerusalem, which is implied but not named in 13:12-14 as the place the believers are to leave, following Christ who was ejected from there.

Conclusion

I began with two ethnic Jews, one in a synagogue with a *kippah* on his head, and one a Jewish follower of Jesus,[71] both claiming that the *Aliyah* was in fulfilment of Isa 2:2-4. I am not sure that I agree with either of them, since that text implies that the nations rather than the Jews would encounter God in Zion and learn *halakhah* from God there. The author of Hebrews was an ethnic Jew writing to ethnic Jews, and whether or not the Isaiah text was in his mind when he wrote, he claimed that God's voice was to be heard not in the earthly Jerusalem but in the heavenly, in the presence of the mediator of the new covenant, Jesus. God no longer dwells exclusively in the earthly Jerusalem; he dwells in Christ and wherever his people gather in Christ's name. Fulfilment of the Isaiah text is unlikely to be found in the earthly Jerusalem; rather, it is to be found wherever Christ-followers, both Jew and gentile, gather in his name. And those who pin their hopes on an encounter

---

70. See T. Dan 5:12-13; 2 Bar. 4:2-7; 4 Ezra 7:26; 10:27, 54; 13:36; 1 En. 90:28-39; 2 En. 55:2; Tob 13:10-17; Sib. Or. 5. 250-51; Gal 4:26; Rev 3:12; 21:1-4; b. Hag 12b; B. Bat. 75b. See Barrett, "Eschatology," 374-76.

71. See Bock, "Dispensationalist View," 110-11.

with God in the earthly Jerusalem today without reference to the mediator of the new covenant, Jesus, will ultimately be disappointed.

Bibliography

Allen, Leslie C. *Jeremiah: A Commentary*. OTL. Louisville: Westminster John Knox, 2008.

Arowele, P. J. "The Pilgrim People of God (An African's Reflections on the Motif of Sojourn in the Epistle to the Hebrews)." *AJT* 4 (1990) 444–45.

Attridge, Harold W. *Hebrews*. Hermeneia. Minneapolis: Fortress, 1989.

Baer, David A. *When We All Go Home: Translation and Theology in Isaiah 56–66*. JSOTSup 318. Sheffield: Sheffield Academic, 2001.

Barrett, C. K. "The Eschatology of the Epistle to the Hebrews." In *The Background of the New Testament and its Eschatology*, edited by W. D. Davies and D. Daube, 363–93. Cambridge: Cambridge University Press, 1954.

Bateman, Herbert W., IV. "Introducing the Warning Passages in Hebrews: A Contextual Orientation." In *Four Views on the Warning Passages in Hebrews*, edited by Herbert W. Bateman IV, 23–84. Grand Rapids: Kregel, 2007.

Bock, Darrell. "The Land in the Light of the Reconciliation in Christ: A Dispensationalist View." In *Christ at the Checkpoint: Theology in the Service of Justice and Peace*, edited by Paul Alexander, 102–23. Eugene, OR: Pickwick, 2012.

Bruce, F. F. *The Epistle to the Hebrews*. Rev. ed. NICNT. Grand Rapids: Eerdmans, 1990.

Brueggemann, Walter. *To Build and to Plant: A Commentary on Jeremiah 26–52*. ITC. Grand Rapids: Eerdmans, 1991.

Buchanan, G. W. *To the Hebrews*. AB 36. New York: Doubleday, 1972.

Childs, Brevard S. *Isaiah*. OTL. Louisville: Westminster John Knox, 2001.

Church, Philip. *Hebrews and the Temple: Attitudes to the Temple in Second Temple Judaism and in Hebrews*. NovTSup 171. Leiden: Brill, 2017.

———. "'You [Jewish Christ-Followers in Rome] Have Come to Mount Zion . . .' (Heb 12:22): Pilgrimage to Zion and the Book of Hebrews." In *Essays in Recognition of the Retirement of Rev. Dr. Timothy Meadowcroft*, edited by Csilla Saysell and John de Jong, 3–14. *Pacific Journal of Baptist Research* 13/2 (2018).

Cockerill, Gareth Lee. *The Epistle to the Hebrews*. NICNT. Grand Rapids: Eerdmans, 2012.

Craigie, Peter C., et al. *Jeremiah 1–25*. WBC 26. Dallas: Word, 1994.

DeSilva, David A. *Perseverance in Gratitude: A Socio-Rhetorical Commentary on the Epistle "to the Hebrews."* Grand Rapids: Eerdmans, 2000.

Ellingworth, Paul. *The Epistle to the Hebrews*. NIGTC. Grand Rapids: Eerdmans, 1993.

Ellingworth, Paul, and Eugene A. Nida. *A Handbook on the Letter to the Hebrews*. New York: United Bible Societies, 1983.

Fishbane, M. A. *Biblical Interpretation in Ancient Israel*. Oxford: Clarendon, 1985.

Fredriksen, Paula. "Mandatory Retirement: Ideas in the Study of Christian Origins Whose Time Has Come to Go." *SR* 35 (2006) 231–46.

Fuller Dow, Lois K. *Images of Zion: Biblical Antecedents for the New Jerusalem*. New Testament Monographs 26. Sheffield: Sheffield Phoenix, 2010.

Gärtner, Bertil. *The Temple and the Community in Qumran and the New Testament: A Comparative Study in the Temple Symbolism of the Qumran Texts and the New Testament*. Cambridge: Cambridge University Press, 1965.

Goldingay, John. *Psalms Volume 3: Psalms 90–150*. BCOTWP. Grand Rapids: Baker Academic, 2008.

Gordon, Robert P. *Hebrews*. 2nd ed. Readings: A New Biblical Commentary. Sheffield: Sheffield Academic, 2008.

Holladay, William L. *Jeremiah 1*. Hermeneia. Philadelphia: Fortress, 1986.

———. *Jeremiah 2*. Hermeneia. Minneapolis: Fortress, 1989.

Jewett, R. *Letter to Pilgrims. A Commentary on the Epistle to the Hebrews*. New York: Pilgrim, 1981.

Johnson, Luke Timothy. *Hebrews: A Commentary*. NTL. Louisville: Westminster John Knox, 2006.

Keown, Gerald L., et al., eds. *Jeremiah 26–52*. WBC 27. Dallas: Word, 1995.

Klinzing, Georg. *Die Umdeutung des Kultus in der Qumrangemeinde und im NT*. SUNT 7. Göttingen: Vandenhoeck & Ruprecht, 1971.

Koester, Craig R. *Hebrews: A New Translation with Introduction and Commentary*. AB 36. New York: Doubleday, 2001.

Lane, William. *Hebrews 9-13*. WBC 47B. Grand Rapids: Zondervan, Word, 2015.

Limburg, James. "Swords to Ploughshares: Text and Contexts." In *Writing and Reading the Scroll of Isaiah: Studies of an Interpretive Tradition*, edited by Craig C. Broyles and Craig A. Evans, 279–93. Leiden: Brill, 1997.

Lindars, Barnabas. "The Rhetorical Structure of Hebrews." *NTS* 35 (1989) 382–406.

McKane, William. *A Critical and Exegetical Commentary on Jeremiah*. Vol. 1. ICC. Edinburgh: T. & T. Clark, 1986.

Magonet, Jonathan. "Isaiah's Mountain or the Shape of Things to Come." *Prooftexts* 11 (1991) 175–81.

Newman, Carey C. "Jerusalem, Zion, Holy City." In *Dictionary of the Later New Testament and its Developments*, edited by Ralph P. Martin and Peter H. Davids, 561–65. Downers Grove, IL: InterVarsity, 1997.

O'Brien, Peter T. *The Letter to the Hebrews*. PNTC. Grand Rapids: Eerdmans, 2010.

Peterson, David G. *Hebrews and Perfection: An Examination of the Concept of Perfection in "The Epistle to the Hebrews."* SNTSMS 47. Cambridge: Cambridge University Press, 1982.

Saysell, Csilla and John de Jong, eds. *Essays in Recognition of the Retirement of Rev. Dr. Timothy Meadowcroft*. Pacific Journal of Baptist Research 13/2 (2018).

Scholer, John M. *Proleptic Priests: Priesthood in the Epistle to the Hebrews*. JSNTSup 49. Sheffield: JSOT, 1991.

Schwartz, Seth. "How Many Judaisms Were There? A Critique of Neusner and Smith on Definition and Mason and Boyarin on Categorization." *JAJ* 2 (2011) 208–38.

Smillie, Gene R. "'The One who is Speaking' in Heb 12:25." *TynBul* 55 (2004) 275–94.

Son, Kiwoong. *Zion Symbolism in Hebrews: Hebrews 12:18-24 as a Hermeneutical Key to the Epistle*. PBM. Milton Keynes: Paternoster, 2005.

Spicq, Ceslas. *L'Épître aux Hébreux*. 3rd ed. 2 vols. Paris: Gabalda, 1952.

Strugnell, John. "The Angelic Liturgy at Qumran–4Q *Serek Šîrôt 'Ôlat Haššabbat*." In *Congress Volume Oxford 1959*, edited by G. W. Anderson, 318–45. VTSup 7. Leiden: Brill, 1960.

Sweeney, Marvin A. "The Book of Isaiah as Prophetic Torah." In *New Visions of Isaiah*, edited by Roy F. Melugin and Marvin A. Sweeney, 50–67. Sheffield: Sheffield Academic, 1996.

Thomas, H. A. "Zion." In *Dictionary of the Old Testament: Prophets*, edited by Mark J. Boda and J. Gordon McConville, 907–14. Downers Grove, IL: InterVarsity, 2012.

Tucker, Gene M. "The Book of Isaiah 1–39: Introduction, Commentary and Reflections." In *NIB* 6:25–305.

Walker, Peter W. L. "Jerusalem in Hebrews 13:9–14 and the Dating of the Epistle." *TynBul* 45 (1994) 39-71.

Watts, John D. W. *Isaiah 1–33*. Rev. ed. WBC 24. Nashville: Thomas Nelson, 2005.

Weinfeld, Moshe. "Jeremiah and the Spiritual Metamorphosis of Israel." *ZAW* 88 (1976) 17–56.

———. "Zion and Jerusalem as Religious and Political Capital: Ideology and Utopia." In *The Poet and the Historian: Essays in Literary and Historical Biblical Criticism*, edited by Richard Elliott Friedman, 75–115. HSS. Chico, Calif: Scholars, 1983.

Wildberger, Hans. *Isaiah 1–12*. A Continental Commentary. Minneapolis: Fortress, 1991.

———. *Isaiah 28–39*. A Continental Commentary. Minneapolis: Fortress, 2002.

Williamson, H. G. M. *A Critical and Exegetical Commentary on Isaiah 1–27. Volume 1: Commentary on Isaiah 1–5*. 3 vols. ICC. London: T. & T. Clark, 2006.

Willis, John T. "Isaiah 2:2–5 and the Psalms of Zion." In *Writing and Reading the Scroll of Isaiah: Studies of an Interpretive Tradition*, edited by Craig C. Broyles and Craig A. Evans, 295–315. Leiden: Brill, 1997.

Part II

Women, Gender, Sexuality, and the
Wider New Zealand Context

10

The Disembodied Womb and the Disappearing Mother in Hosea 13:13

Miriam Bier Hinksman

It is an honor and a privilege to offer this essay in celebration of Tim Meadowcroft's contribution to Old Testament/Hebrew Bible scholarship in New Zealand and beyond. Tim's particular brand of wit and wisdom as a teacher and supervisor has inspired and shaped my own scholarship and continues to influence my work today. In 2007 I took a class on Old Testament narrative texts with "the two Tims": Tim Meadowcroft and Tim Bulkeley. This class ignited my interest in the Old Testament and the challenges it raises for readers, especially women, in faith communities today. My first forays into academia arose from a paper on 2 Samuel 13 written for this class. That paper was subsequently developed for presentation at a colloquium on "God and Gender" held at Carey Baptist College in 2007 and published in the resulting book.[1] The essay examines the narrative perspective of the story of the rape of Tamar in 2 Sam 13:1–22. It agonizes over Tamar's fate in light of the male violence carried out against her and the male absence and silence of those who may reasonably have been expected to protect her, including God.[2] Tim Meadowcroft was kind enough

---

1. Bier, "Violence."
2. Bier, "Violence."

to respond to my fledgling efforts in a companion paper, entitled "In Whose Interests Do We Read? A Response to Miriam Bier."[3]

In his paper, Tim identifies that "all readings are personal, and hence, to a greater or lesser extent, interested."[4] And then he notes that in my reading of 2 Samuel 13, I "bring questions to this particular text that are most likely to have been posed by a woman."[5] Guilty as charged! I am a woman. But Tim also recognizes that his own questions are influenced by his particular interests and social location. And although I suspect Tim worries about many things, he acknowledges that "it would not have occurred to me to worry about Tamar after the event in the way that Bier worries about her."[6] In typical Meadowcroft style, he continues:

> Of course, I deeply regret what happens to Tamar while it is happening and I think that the men of the story are churls and I would try not to behave in the same way if my father were a king with many wives who between them had produced many half-siblings. But then I move on with the plot and immerse myself in the important masculine matter of the Davidic succession, forgetting completely about Tamar as I do so.[7]

Tim's self-deprecating comment aptly highlights the tendency of many (male) commentators to overlook elements of the biblical text that it just "would not have occurred" to them to notice. This tendency is exacerbated when male scholarship, highlighting male interests, begets male scholarship.[8] Tim also identifies my own interest in "justice and a place to stand for [my] gender."[9] And this is an interest I am happy to own, because with-

---

3. Meadowcroft, "Interests."
4. Meadowcroft, "Interests," 162.
5. Meadowcroft, "Interests," 163.
6. Meadowcroft, "Interests," 163.
7. Meadowcroft, "Interests," 163.
8. Analysis of authorship by gender across multiple disciplines highlights two key factors in this regard. First, men tend to cite their own work more than women do (King et al., "Gender and Self-Citation"; and second, men primarily cite other men, whereas women tend to cite both women and men (West et al., "The Role of Gender") While these studies do not consider theology and biblical studies specifically, analysis of gender and career progression in theology and religious studies in the UK finds broader issues in academia similar to those in other disciplines, suggesting the issue of gender difference in citation may also be similar. See Guest et al., *Gender and Career Progression*.
9. Meadowcroft, "Interests," 166.

out a woman's interest in what might be considered women's interests, half of humanity's interests are overlooked.[10]

By way of demonstration and example, in this essay I examine one verse where women's interests have perhaps been overlooked. Hosea 13:13 reads, "The pangs of childbirth come for him, but he is an unwise son; for at the proper time he does not present himself at the mouth of the womb."[11]

When I read Hos 13:13—as a woman, attuned to women's interests— the obvious question is this: If Ephraim/Israel is an unwise son, refusing to be born, then from *whose womb* does he refuse to be expelled?[12] Who is Ephraim's *mother*? In scholarly commentary, however, it seems it has not always occurred to commentators to ask this question.[13] In this essay I propose that Hos 13:13 contributes to a network of mothering metaphors for God in Hosea. These images provide an alternative way of representing the relationship between God and Israel in familial terms, beyond the portrait of God as jealous and abusive husband (Hosea 1–3) that typically dominates discussions of gendered imagery in Hosea.[14] In the first part of the essay, I

---

10. This is not to say that women are *only* interested in so-called "women's issues." Rather, it is to highlight that some women may be attuned to notice things in the biblical text that "would not have occurred" to many men to worry about. Cf. Margo G. Houts's observation that biblical feminine divine images "lay dormant until awakened by feminist scholars" (Houts, "Images").

11. All biblical citations are from the NRSV, unless otherwise indicated.

12. Hosea frequently refers to Israel with the name Ephraim and identifies Ephraim by name in verse 12.

13. Is it coincidence that there are almost no full book-length commentaries on Hosea by women? As of March 27, 2019, a search for "Hosea Commentary" on the British Library catalogue, narrowed to focus on books (rather than articles or reviews), identifies eighty-four items. Only two of those items explicitly identified as commentaries are by women. Paula Gooder's *People's Bible Commentary* takes the form of a Bible study aid for general audiences. Her two-page spread on Hos 13:9–16 does not mention verse 13 (Gooder, *Hosea to Micah*, 70–71). Carol Fry's book covers both Amos and Hosea in just 63 pages and appears to be an educational resource, perhaps for use in secondary schools. The comment on Hos 13:13 is brief: "There is a sudden change of image here to Israel as a foetus which, though the time has come for it to be born, does not recognize the signs, and so presents itself in the wrong position—the baby is therefore born dead. The blame for this is clearly placed on the child" (Fry, *Amos and Hosea*, 61). It is also instructive, perhaps, to observe the Denver Seminary OT bibliography for 2019. Of fifteen recommended authors on Hosea, none are a woman (Denver, "Old Testament Bibliography"). Gale A. Yee's commentary on Hosea in the NIB series is thus noteworthy as, to the best of my knowledge, the most extensive commentary on the whole book of Hosea by a woman (Yee, "Hosea").

14. Female and feminist attention to Hosea has predominantly focused on Hosea 1–3, where the so-called marriage metaphor is to the fore (e.g., Sherwood, *Prostitute*; Baumann, *Love and Violence*; Weems, *Battered Love*; Törnkvist, *Use and Abuse*). But Alice Keefe rightly points out that female imagery is not limited to these chapters,

survey approaches to the disembodied womb and the disappearing mother in Hosea in the literature, showing that for the most part, the mother in the metaphor is overlooked. In the second part of the essay, I identify possible images of God as mother in Hosea 13, the book of Hosea as a whole, and the Hebrew Bible more broadly, in order to suggest that the mother of Hos 13:13 may also be God.

Approaches to the Disembodied Womb in Hosea 13:13

There are, broadly speaking, two established approaches to the identity of the owner of the disembodied womb. First, there are those who identify Ephraim/Israel as the mother of the unborn child. Part of the challenge of interpreting Hos 13:13 is determining what is meant by חבלי יולדה יבאו לו (labor pains come to/for him). Typically, labor pains would come to the mother,[15] so the use of the male pronoun here is curious. In his 1905 work, William Rainey Harper addresses the curiosity by reading the birthing mother as (male) Israel. Then, he explains, "with the privilege of a Hebrew poet, the figure suddenly shifts from the mother to the child that is to be born."[16] In this reading, then, both the mother and the unborn child are read as Ephraim/Israel, with a quick change from one to the other as the metaphor proceeds through the verse.

Objecting to a change of referent part way through the verse, A. A. Macintosh determines that Ephraim/Israel is the laboring mother, but not the fetus as well. In Macintosh's reading, "He is not a clever son" is thus a parenthetical remark referring to the nation Ephraim outside the metaphor, rather than the infant within the metaphor.[17]

Both of these readings make a positive identification of the laboring mother: birth pains come "to him"; that is, to male Ephraim/Israel. And yet, by figuring the laboring mother as a male nation, the female figure of the mother within the metaphor disappears.

---

observing that throughout Hosea, "the condition and fate of the nation are figured in graphic images of maternal bereavement, the loss of female fertility, and the death of mothers with their children" (Keefe, "Family Metaphors," 125). Keefe's focus, however, is on the figuring of *Israel* as a female body rather than identifying female images for God.

15. See, e.g., Jer 6:24, 22:23, Isa 26:17–18, Isa 66:7.
16. Harper, *Amos and Hosea*, 403; cf. Landy, *Hosea*, 164.
17. MacIntosh, *Hosea*, 544.

The second, and by far the more dominant, approach is to focus solely on the fetus without making any positive identification of the mother. Like Macintosh, most commentators now agree, *pace* Harper and Landy, that the metaphor does not change its referent from Ephraim/Israel, the mother, to Ephraim/Israel, the fetus, partway through the verse. Unlike Macintosh, however, it is usually the fetus, rather than the mother, that is identified as Ephraim/Israel. The labor pains that come "to him" are understood as the pains that come "for him" or are caused "by him" when the time comes to be born.[18] In these readings, Ephraim/Israel is the unborn child, and typically there is no further comment on who his mother is.[19]

Taking this approach a step further are those who state explicitly that the identity of the mother is not relevant to the metaphor. This position is epitomized by John L. McKenzie, who states that "the mother is mentioned to complete the metaphor, and corresponds to nothing in the prophet's mind."[20] The mother is not simply overlooked or invisible, but rather explicitly dismissed.

Göran Eidevall probes the possible identity and significance of the mother in the metaphor in significantly more depth.[21] Like many commentators, Eidevall begins by observing the "unusual way" that "the

---

18. Douglas K. Stuart notes that the labor pains are used "uniquely" of the fetus here, contrasting Jer 6:24, 13:21, 22:23, Isa 13:8, 26:17–18 where "the focus is on the writhing pain of the mother" (Stuart, *Hosea-Jonah*, 207; cf. McKenzie, "Divine Passion in Osee").

19. See, for example, McKeating, *Amos, Hosea, Micah*, 150; Wolff, *Hosea*, 228; Mays, *Hosea*, 181; Smith, *Hosea, Amos, Micah*, 186; Stuart, *Hosea*, 207. Gale Yee connects verse 13 with Jacob traditions in Hosea but does not identify who the metaphorical mother might be to Ephraim the "witless fetus" in verse 13 (Yee, "Hosea," 492). M. Daniel Carroll R. identifies the unborn child as "the nation" [of Israel] and the "son of Yahweh," and argues for "continuity of reference" throughout the metaphor rather than switching from Ephraim the mother, to Ephraim the child. While he states that the child is the "son of Yahweh," however, he does not specify whether YHWH is mother or father and makes no further identification of who the mother might be (Carroll R., "Hosea"). J. Andrew Dearman notes the resonance of wisdom language in Hos 13:13 with Deuteronomy 32, an important intertext to Hos 13:13. He compares the vocabulary of Deut 32:6 (a foolish and unwise people) with Hos 13:13 (he is an unwise son), suggesting Hosea might be drawing on Deuteronomy 32 (Dearman, *Hosea*, 327–28). But he does *not* note the correspondence between the idea of the God who nurses the people in the wilderness and who gave the people birth (Deut 32:10-18) and the possibility of a God from whose womb Ephraim will not move in Hos 13:13. David Allan Hubbard does not shy away from using words related to female anatomy, describing the way labor pains would normally "cause the child to surge inch by inch through the cervix and vagina to daylight" (Hubbard, *Hosea*, 232). He does not, however, identify the owner of cervix and vagina in the context of the metaphor.

20. McKenzie, "Divine Passion," 176.

21. Eidevall, *Grapes*, 200–1.

traditional motif of 'birth pangs' is here attached to the sensory experience of the foetus" rather than the mother.[22] He notes Harper's interpretation that Ephraim/Israel is first mother then fetus,[23] but adds that the consensus is now that the nation of Ephraim/Israel is now usually "consistently" identified as the "foetus."[24] But then Eidevall goes further, observing that "the child's mother is conspicuously absent in the rest of v. 13."[25] In his concluding reflections on chapter 13, he identifies one of the themes of the chapter as "bereavement" and rereads Hos 13:13 in this context, probing the question of the "conspicuously absent" mother:

> Notice how the outlining of the vehicle field "childbirth" is remarkable in more than one respect. The most conspicuous feature is the neglect of the mother's role. She is hardly mentioned, and she cannot be identified with an agent in the topic domain.[26]

He continues:

> The mother would have felt the pain, but v. 13 states that the "birth pangs" come for the child. Further, in a situation like this, the mother's life would have been endangered, but the saying focuses entirely on the foetus, which is a metaphorical representation of the people . . . The deity seems to have the role of a passive spectator—perhaps a midwife unable (or unwilling?) to do more. It is instructive to make a comparison with 11:1, where Israel is called "my son," that is, the son of YHWH. Against this background, the following question becomes acute: Why is YHWH not assigned the role of a parent in 13:13?[27]

Eidevall teases this out further, suggesting one reason that God is not explicitly identified as parent is that this "would have opened up the possibility for divine compassion and remorse (cf. 11:8–9)."[28] That is to say, this judgment oracle excludes the possibility of salvation by intentionally avoiding identifying the mother figure with God, who is compassionate. As Eidevall observes, however, the possibility of compassion *is* immediately

---

22. Eidevall, *Grapes*, 200–1.
23. Eidevall, *Grapes*, 200.
24. Eidevall, *Grapes*, 200.
25. Eidevall, *Grapes*, 201.
26. Eidevall, *Grapes*, 205; cf. McKenzie, "Osee," 176.
27. Eidevall, *Grapes*, 205–6.
28. Eidevall, *Grapes*, 206.

raised (in 13:14) —if only to be denied.[29] And yet, even as it is being denied, Eidevall rightly identifies that "By means of the expression 'pity is hidden from my eyes' the idea of divine compassion is, paradoxically, being foregrounded. Though it is said to be 'hidden', it is made manifest in the language used."[30]

Eidevall also brings the image of God as a she-bear deprived of her young (13:8) to bear on the theme of bereavement in the chapter, along with the picture of pregnant women slashed open in 14:1. He asks:

> Denied the role of a loving parent, the deity attacks and "rips up" his/her own people, like a she-bear who has lost her young (13:8). Cannot this be seen as a distorted reflection of the deity's denied motherhood (cf. 13:13)? Is not this outburst of fury somehow related to the absence of a denunciation of the atrocities described in 14:1?[31]

Eidevall's exploration raises more questions than it answers, and in his conclusion he asks: "In my opinion, the most intriguing question raised by this discourse unit is: Why does YHWH repeatedly threaten to destroy his/her own people, when such a destruction would mean a painful bereavement also for him/herself?"[32]

In Eidevall's question the possibility that God is being figured as a mother lies latent ("his/her," "him/herself"). He asks the questions: Why does the mother disappear? Why is the deity *not* figured as the parent, as in chapter 11? While he suggests this is so that the possibility of compassion is denied, he identifies the linguistic presence of compassion in the very next verse. And he draws in the motif of the bereaved she-bear (13:8) suggesting that God, deprived of children, is expressing great sorrow at the loss of her children underneath all this rage.[33]

While Eidevall's discussion is focused around the theme of bereavement, many of the motifs he mentions are drawn from the context of mothering. In my view, rather than a denial of the mother and of the parenthood of the deity, these motifs contribute to a network of images that serves to suggest that the mother of chapter 13:13 is indeed God, even if her identity remains implicit rather than explicit. I will discuss these, and other mothering motifs, further in the second part of the essay.

---

29. Eidevall, *Grapes*, 206.
30. Eidevall, *Grapes*, 206.
31. Eidevall, *Grapes*, 206.
32. Eidevall, *Grapes*, 207.
33. Eidevall, *Grapes*, 207.

In English-language scholarship, the commentator who makes the most explicit identification of the mother figure in Hos 13:13 is H. D. Beeby.[34] In his discussion of verse 13 he states:

> Wombs can become graves and mothers executioners. The body which had chosen to give life and the cervix which exists to open wide that life might be enjoyed could also smother and strangle. God had conceived Israel (Hos 13:4). He had nurtured her (vv. 5–6). Now was the time for Israel to choose life. But evil, insane Israel had chosen death. Now "mother God" would honor the choice and be the cause of death.[35]

Beeby therefore identifies God as mother in Hos 13:13, albeit in quotation marks. In his discussion of verse 14 he goes on to state that "Ephraim has long been nurtured in the womb of God."[36] This is thus far the clearest identification of the owner of the disembodied womb: God is mother and her womb has nurtured Ephraim since she called her son out of Egypt (Hos 11:1).

The Mothering God in Hosea 13

Maternal motifs or allusions appear in almost every unit of Hosea 13. As noted, even though verse 14 denies the possibility of compassion, it is "made manifest" by the choice of vocabulary.[37] The divine voice says that נחם (pity, compassion[38]) is "hidden from my eyes" (13:14). The nominative

---

34. H. D. Beeby, *Hosea*. A significant article in German by Marie-Theres Wacker deserves a more sustained interaction than is possible within the constraints of this essay. Wacker reads Hos 13:12–14 as a unit that is determined entirely by birthing imagery (Wacker, "Gendering," 274). In her reading Ephraim the unborn child, is bound by his sins (v. 12) which is why he cannot be born (v. 13); and then in v. 14, mythic dimensions of the feminine personified as death/the destroyer come to the fore (Wacker, "Gendering," 274–76).

35. Beeby, *Hosea*, 170.

36. Beeby, *Hosea*, 171.

37. Extended discussions of the difficult syntax of verse 14 are beyond the scope of this essay. As Gale Yee puts it, "The issue is whether God is life-giver or death-dealer of a nation that refuses to leave the womb" (Yee, "Hosea," 492). Yee outlines multiple possibilities for reading v. 14 and ultimately advocates retaining the ambiguity, "since all of these possibilities are in some way true and deeply imbedded in the theological drama" (Yee, "Hosea," 493); cf. Yvonne Sherwood's assessment of the creative possibilities for interpreting the "disjunctive style" of the language of Hosea 1–3 (Sherwood, *Prostitute*, 328). By not foreclosing the meaning of the text, the possibilities of meaning remain open: God may be death dealer or life giver. Ephraim may be stillborn or may yet be delivered to new life.

38. Butterworth, "נחם"; cf. *HALOT*, 689; Wolff, *Hosea*, 222; Hubbard, *Hosea*, 234;

is a hapax legonomen, but the cognate נחמים (compassion) appears in Hos 11:8 where it is used of the parental compassion felt by God for Ephraim. While Hos 11:1–8 is often assumed to be a picture of the father-like love of God, it is written in the first person and so the gender of the parent is not evident. Further, many of the parental activities cited are arguably more likely to have been carried out by a mother.[39] Thus the compassion felt by God in 11:8; and the denial of that compassion in 13:14, may contribute to the image of God as mother.

Hosea 13:4–6 also resonates with Hosea 11, as well as with Deuteronomy 32, with the child fed and satisfied in the wilderness. While a father might feed and satisfy a child, this activity is again likely the preserve of mothers, and perhaps especially breastfeeding mothers.

Hosea 13:7–8 pictures God becoming like a wild animal, including the image of a she-bear robbed of her cubs. This mother will destroy any who deprive her of her children.[40] Hosea 13:9–11 alludes to 1 Samuel 8–12. The king given in anger and taken in wrath most likely refers to Saul, along with the very institution of the monarchy itself in Israel.[41]

The story of Saul is a tragic one.[42] In the episode detailing God's rejection of Saul as king, the prophet Samuel calls Saul to account for his unlawful sacrifice, saying: "Has the Lord as great delight in burnt offerings and sacrifices, as in obeying the voice of the Lord? Surely, to obey is better than sacrifice, and to heed than the fat of rams" (1 Sam 15:22). This is echoed in the words of Hosea 6:6: "For I desire steadfast love and not sacrifice, the knowledge of God rather than burnt offerings." Notice that there is a shift in what God requires. There is agreement that burnt offerings and sacrifice are not the crux of the matter, but somewhere along the way, the desire for obedience has transformed into the desire for steadfast love and the knowledge of God.[43] This is rather like a parent who wishes their child to obey and live the right way out of relationship and love, not out of duty and fear. Perhaps, even, this is like a mother who delights in the

---

McKeating, *Hosea*, 149; Smith, *Hosea*, 188; cf. "sympathy" (Mays, *Hosea*, 182–83). Contra "repentance" (Harper, *Hosea*, 405); "relief," (MacIntosh, *Hosea*, 546); "cause of sorrow," (Anderson and Freedman, *Hosea*, 625). Yee finds that the meaning could either be "revenge" or "compassion," and advocates leaving the ambiguity unresolved (Yee, "Hosea" 492).

39. Bulkeley, "Motherly God"; cf. Keefe, *Woman's Body*, 17; Morrell and Clark Kroeger, "Hosea," 441.

40. Cf. Houts, "Images," 357; Morrell and Kroeger, "Hosea," 441.

41. Cf. Landy, *Hosea*, 162.

42. See further Exum, *Tragedy*, 16–44.

43 Cf. Landy, *Hosea*, 82.

knowledge of her child, their mutual love, and the strength of their relationship, which grounds any behavioral expectations, rather than a father who expects unquestioned obedience.

The graphic image of pregnant mothers being split open in Samaria in 13:6 [Heb 14:1] must also be mentioned in connection with mothering imagery in Hosea 13.[44] The verb בקע (Pual, "be ripped up") is the same as that used of the wild animal who tears Ephraim to pieces in v. 8. The wild animal of the field is the God who tears unborn children from the womb, in a reversal of God's maternal compassion on the mothers of Samaria. There is hardly an episode in this entire chapter, then, that has nothing to do with mothering.

The Mothering God in Hosea

The book of Hosea is ripe with maternal images.[45] The image of God as mother in Hos 11:1–8 has already been mentioned. Jennifer Davidson highlights a number of other possible appearances of the mothering God in Hosea. Her argument hinges on her translation of Hos 14:3 as "In you the orphan is wombed," on the basis of the linguistic connection between "womb" and "compassion/pity" (רחם).[46]

Davidson identifies the "same linguistic play" in the name of Gomer's daughter Lo-ruhamah in Hos 1:6 and 2:23.[47] Alice Laffey makes explicit the implicit connection between womb/compassion in her name, stating that "Wherever God is described as compassionate, as acting with compassion (and the texts are not infrequent; e.g., Isa 49:10; 54:10; Jer 31:20), the reader should hear echoes of God's maternal concern."[48]

The linguistic link between womb and compassion is also present in Hosea 9. In a judgment rich with maternal imagery (no birth, no pregnancy,

---

44. Cf. Landy, *Hosea*, 164.

45. While the so-called marriage metaphor of chapters 1–3 has attracted much attention as regards the female body in Hosea, Alice Keefe rightly demonstrates that there are myriad other maternal images in chapters 4–14 (Keefe, *Woman's Body*, 17). Keefe also points out that the so-called marriage metaphor of chapters 1–3 is also a maternal metaphor, as the woman is not only wife, but also mother (Keefe, "Family Metaphors," 125 and throughout). Keefe's work makes an invaluable contribution to illuminating maternal imagery in Hosea but primarily focuses on the female body as a cipher for the Israelite social body, rather than examining maternal imagery used of God.

46. Davidson, "The Womb of God," 17. See further Trible, *Rhetoric of Sexuality*, 31–34.

47. Davidson, "Womb," 17–18.

48. Laffey, *Introduction*, 171; cf. Morrell and Kroeger, "Hosea," 436.

no conception, v. 11), the women of Israel will have a miscarrying womb (רחם, v. 14) and the cherished offspring of their womb (בטן, v. 16) will be killed by God. This word of judgment, like the name Lo-ruhamah, indicates a reversal of God's mother-like compassion on the mothers of Ephraim.

But for Davidson, the key to the maternal image of God in Hosea is found in 14:3, in the "the subtle, delicate shift of 'finds mercy' to 'is wombed.'"[49] This, for Davidson, indicates a "divine identification with female sexuality."[50] She states:

> As the God who wombs the orphan, God identifies with the most vulnerable of creation. It is out of this agony that God, sounding much like a mother, asks, "How can I give you up, Ephraim? How can I *deliver* you, O Israel? How can I destroy you . . . ? My heart recoils within me; my compassion grows warm and tender" (11:8).[51]

Davidson does not discuss Hosea 13 in her essay, but the identification of God as en-wombing mother in Hos 13:13 would seem to chime with her broader analysis.

The Mothering God in the Hebrew Bible

The full range of female images for God in the Hebrew Bible cannot be examined in detail in the context of this essay, but Margo Houts provides an excellent succinct survey.[52] In terms of maternal imagery for God, Houts identifies God as a mother breastfeeding and caring for children (Num 11:12); a mother giving birth to the Israelites (Deut 32:18; to which we could add nurturing them in the wilderness, Deut 32:10–18); a laboring mother (Isa 42:14); a "mother who births and protects Israel" and who "carries Israel in the womb"[53] (Isa 46:3–4); a mother who cannot forget her nursing child (Isa 49:14–15); a mother comforting her children (Isa 66:12–13); and a "mother who calls, teaches, holds, heals and feeds her young"[54] (Hos 11: 1–4). She identifies "other maternal images" for God in Job 38:8, 29, Ps 90:2, 131:2, Prov 8:22 25; Isa 45:9–11; Acts 17:28; and 1 Pet 2:2–3.[55]

49. Davidson, "Womb," 18.
50. Davidson, "Womb," 18.
51. Davidson, "Womb," 18 (emphasis original).
52. Houts, "Images," 356–57.
53. Houts, "Images," 356.
54. Houts, "Images," 357.
55. Houts, "Images," 357. Cf. Morrell and Kroeger, who highlight Deut 32:11, 18;

Conclusions

Perhaps I am pushing the metaphor too far. After all, it is imperative to recognize that there is always an "is" and an "is not" in a metaphor. There are limits to interpretation, as M. Daniel Carroll R. insists in his critique of feminist readings of Hosea that, in his view, too strongly identify the abusive husband of Hosea with abusive husbands today:

> It is clear that all metaphors have limitations and finally break down. For example, in Hosea Yahweh is portrayed as a moth, a wild beast, a farmer, a parent, morning dew, and a tree, as well as a husband. This wide repertoire of tropes serves to illuminate different things about God, each of which, however, can only be taken so far. A comprehensive picture of Yahweh requires a judicious appreciation of what each word picture can offer and discernment about when certain aspects of a metaphor just do not apply.[56]

Conversely, it is important to note that any metaphors/images for God in the Hebrew Bible are *necessarily* metaphorical, given the prophetic anathema for idols.[57]

I cannot be exhaustive in an essay of this length, but I have sought to be representative. And in this representative survey, by far the dominant approach to Hosea 13:13 is to discuss the son's reluctance to leave the womb without any identification of whose womb that might be. Where the womb's owner has been identified, it has primarily been as the nation Israel, before he becomes at the next moment the child refusing to leave. It is entirely possible I am pushing the metaphor too far, such that McKenzie is correct in his assessment that the mother means "nothing."[58] But by asking the questions "Whose womb?" and "Who is Ephraim's mother?" I am trying to make a broader interpretive point. In Tim Meadowcroft's words, in whose interests do we read? Does the figure of a woman gasping in pain to birth a baby that does not want to be born get overlooked or dismissed because it is not relevant to the metaphor, or because it is not of interest to Hosea's (primarily male) interpreters?

Ps 131:2–3; Isa 42:13–14; 49:15; 66:9–13; Hos 13:8 as "significant points in the Hebrew Scriptures" in which "God is portrayed in feminine imagery" (Morrell and Kroeger, "Hosea," 441). Davidson identifies verses in Isaiah where womb and compassion are linked: 13:18; 49:13b,15; 54:1, 7 (Davidson, "Womb," 18); cf. Bulkeley, who identifies the motherly love of God in Isa 49; 44; 46; 66 (Bulkeley, "Motherly God," 127–29).

56. Carroll R., "Hosea," 223.
57. See further Bulkeley, "God as Mother?"; cf. Houts, "Images," 356.
58. McKenzie, "Osee," 176.

In this essay I have explored the question of to "whose womb" Ephraim clings in Hosea 13:13 and proposed that the verse contributes to maternal imagery for God in the Hebrew Bible. It would be nonsensical to speak of a literal womb and cervix of God, just as it would be idolatrous to speak of the phallus and testes of God. The God of Israel is not a man or a woman who can be cast in physical form (Hos 11:9).[59] And yet the metaphor of God as mother, which perhaps "would not have occurred" to Tim Meadowcroft and others to notice in Hos 13:13, is present in point-counterpoint fashion throughout the book of Hosea. Maternal images for God thus have their place in the language and liturgy of the church alongside other metaphors highlighting the various attributes and characters of God.

Bibliography

Anderson, Francis I., and David Noel Freedman. *Hosea*. ABC 24. New Haven: Yale University Press, 1996.

Baumann, Gerlinde. *Love and Violence: Marriage as Metaphor for the Relationship between YHWH and Israel in the Prophetic Books*. Translated by Linda M. Maloney. Collegeville: Liturgical, 2003.

Beeby, H. D. *Hosea: Grace Abounding*. International Theological Commentary. Grand Rapids: Eerdmans, 1989.

Bier, Miriam. "Is There a God in This Text? Violence, Absence, and Silence in 2 Samuel 13:1–22." In *Reconsidering Gender: Evangelical Perspectives*, edited by Myk Habets and Beulah Wood, 148–60. Eugene, OR: Pickwick, 2010.

Bulkeley, Tim. "Biblical Talk of the Motherly God." *Asian Journal of Pentecostal Studies* 17 (2014) 119–37.

———. "God as Mother? Some Ideas to Clarify before We Start." *Asian Journal of Pentecostal Studies* 17 (2014) 107–18.

Butterworth, Mike. "נחם." In *NIDOTTE* 3:81–83.

Carroll R., M. Daniel. "Hosea." In *The Expositor's Bible Commentary Revised Edition*, edited by T. Longman and D. E. Garland, 213–305. Grand Rapids: Zondervan, 2008.

Davidson, Jennifer W. "The Womb of God." *The Other Side* 40/5 (2004) 16–18.

Dearman, J. Andrew. *The Book of Hosea*. New International Commentary on the Old Testament. Cambridge: Eerdmans, 2010.

Denver Seminary. "Annotated Old Testament Bibliography—2019." https://denverseminary.edu/resources/news-and-articles/annotated-old-testament-bibliography-2019/

Eidevall, Göran. *Grapes in the Desert: Metaphors, Models, and Themes in Hosea 4–14*. Coniectanea Biblica Old Testament Series 43. Stockholm: Almqvist & Wiksell International, 1996.

Exum, J. Cheryl. *Tragedy and Biblical Narrative: Arrows of the Almighty*. Cambridge: Cambridge University Press, 1992.

---

59. Cf. Bulkeley, "Motherly God," 119 and throughout.

Fry, Carol. *Amos and Hosea*. Prophets Series. Exeter: Religious and Moral Education, 1986.

Gooder, Paula. *Hosea to Micah: A Bible Commentary for Every Day*. People's Bible Commentary. Oxford: Bible Reading Fellowship, 2005.

Guest, Mathew, et al. *Gender and Career Progression in Theology and Religious Studies*. Durham: Durham University, 2013.

Harper, William Rainey. *Amos and Hosea*. International Critical Commentary. Edinburgh: T. & T. Clark, 1905.

Hubbard, David Allan. *Hosea*. Tyndale Old Testament Commentaries. Downers Grove, IL: IVP Academic, 2009.

Houts, Margo G. "Images of God as Female." In *The IVP Women's Bible Commentary*, edited by Catherine Clark Kroeger and Mary J. Evans, 356–58. Downers Grove, IL: InterVarsity, 2002.

Keefe, Alice A. "Family Metaphors and Social Conflict in Hosea." In *Writing and Reading War: Rhetoric, Gender, and Ethics in Biblical and Modern Contexts*, edited by Brad E. Kelle and Frank Ritchel Ames, 113–27. Atlanta: SBL, 2008.

———. *Woman's Body and the Social Body in Hosea*. JSOTSup 338. Sheffield: Sheffield Academic, 2001.

King, Molly M., et al. "Men Set Their Own Cites High: Gender and Self-Citation across Fields and over Time." *Socius* 3 (2017) 1–22. https://doi.org/10.1177/2378023117738903

Laffey, Alice L. *An Introduction to the Old Testament: A Feminist Perspective*. Philadelphia: Fortress, 1988.

Landy, Francis. *Hosea*. Readings: A New Biblical Commentary. Sheffield: Sheffield Academic, 1995.

McKeating, Henry. *Amos, Hosea, Micah*. The Cambridge Bible Commentary. Cambridge: Cambridge University Press, 1971.

McKenzie, John L. "Divine Passion in Osee." *The Catholic Biblical Quarterly* 17 (1955) 287–99.

MacIntosh, A. A. *Hosea*. International Critical Commentary. Edinburgh: T. & T. Clark, 1997.

Mays, James Luther. *Hosea*. Old Testament Library. London: SCM, 1969.

Meadowcroft, Tim. "In Whose Interests Do We Read? A Response to Miriam Bier." In *Reconsidering Gender: Evangelical Perspectives*, edited by Myk Habets and Beulah Wood, 161–70. Eugene, OR: Pickwick, 2010.

Morrell, Keren E. and Catherine Clark Kroeger. "Hosea." In *The IVP Women's Bible Commentary*, edited by Catherine Clark Kroeger and Mary J. Evans, 432–42. Downers Grove, IL: InterVarsity, 2002.

Trible, Phyllis. *God and the Rhetoric of Sexuality*. Overtures to Biblical Theology. Philadelphia: Fortress, 1978.

Sherwood, Yvonne. *The Prostitute and the Prophet: Hosea's Marriage in Literary-Theoretical Perspective*. London: T &T Clark, 2004.

Smith, Gary V. *Hosea, Amos, Micah*. NIV Application Commentary. Grand Rapids: Zondervan, 2001.

Stuart, Douglas K. *Hosea-Jonah*. WBC 31. Grand Rapids: Zondervan, 1987.

Törnkvist, Rut. *The Use and Abuse of Female Sexual Imagery in the Book of Hosea*. Uppsala Women's Studies A7. Uppsala: Acta Universitatis Upsaliensis, 1998.

Wacker, Marie-Theres. "Gendering Hosea 13." In *On Reading Prophetic Texts: Gender-Specific and Related Studies in Memory of Fokkelien van Dijk-Hemmes*, edited by Bob Becking and Meindert Dijkstra, 265–82. Leiden: Brill, 1996.

Weems, Renita J. *Battered Love: Marriage, Sex, and Violence in the Hebrew Prophets*. Overtures to Biblical Theology. Minneapolis: Fortress, 1995.

West, Jevin D., et al. "The Role of Gender in Scholarly Authorship." *PLoS ONE* 8/7 (2013) 1–6. https://doi.org/10.1371/journal.pone.0066212

Wolff, Hans Walter. *Hosea: A Commentary on the Book of the Prophet Hosea*. Translated by Gary Stansell, edited by Paul D. Hanson. Hermeneia. Philadelphia: Fortress, 1982.

Yee, Gale A. "The Book of Hosea: Introduction, Commentary, and Reflections." In *NIB* 5:422–97.

11

What About the Women of *Ḥesed*?

A Reaction to the Honors Gallery in Sir 44:1—50:24

Karen Nelson

In Sir 44:1—50:24,[1] Ben Sira honors particular men featured in the law, the prophets, and other writings, along with the more recently deceased high priest, Simeon.[2] He describes them as "men of חסד."[3] However, there is some discrepancy between those explicitly named as possessors, agents, or patients of חסד in the Hebrew Scriptures,[4] and those named in Ben Sira's honors list. Most obviously, no "women of חסד" are honored in

---

1. Scholars differ in their opinions about where the section ends. I adopt Lee's conclusion that it extends through to 50:24, in light of the evidence he presents: the form-critical connection (doxologies in chs. 45 and 50), the priestly emphasis, and "the parallels between the engineering feats of Simon and Hezekiah, Nehemiah, et al." Lee, *Form of Sirach 44-50*,10-21. Corley labels 44:16—49:16, "ancestry of Simeon." It precedes 50:1-21, "deeds of Simeon." Corley, "Numerical Structure," 45.

2. Simeon's activities are described in the past tense (e.g., 50:1 [B]; Simeon II died 196 BC), but issues associated with the Maccabean revolt against Antiochus IV Epiphanes (167 BC) are not reflected. Eisenbaum, "Sirach," 298-99; Mack, "Sirach (Ecclesiasticus)," 66; Wright, "Sirach (Ecclesiasticus)," 412.

3. Parker and Abegg, "Ben Sira," use "devout men" (Sir 44:1, 10). Other scholars use various English words to translate חסד (e.g., devotion, steadfast love, loyalty, mercy), but I have chosen to leave it untranslated throughout this article.

4. I.e., those to whom חסד belongs, those who demonstrate or promise חסד, and those who receive or are promised חסד respectively.

his list. By tracing the process through which women are "displaced" from Ben Sira's "hymn to the fathers," Claudia Camp seeks to "return women to th[is] scene of glory."[5] By presenting women named as possessors, agents, or patients of חסד in the Hebrew Bible, who could have been candidates for Ben Sira's list if he had honored people of either gender, I attempt to return women to that scene in a different way.[6] I also consider whether there is evidence within these חסד scenarios that the Hebrew Bible portrays women as "valued for more than their role as wives and mothers."[7]

Ben Sira and the People of חסד

Evidently, I am not the first to notice the absence of women among those honored in Sirach 44–50. Some scholars consider Ben Sira's choice to include men only as typical of his time and role, or the genre in which he writes.[8] For example, Pamela Eisenbaum describes the function of women in the worldview of ancient Mediterranean society (their behavior aids or damages men's honor) and claims that the absence of women in the "catalogue of heroes" is "typical of ancient Jewish hero lists."[9] Similarly, after noting that no woman appears in Ben Sira's final hymn and then asserting that the ideal

---

5. Camp, "Honor and Shame," 178.

6. I acknowledge that the Hebrew Bible canon was not finalized when Ben Sira wrote. Nevertheless, I compare his list to all the people of חסד named in the Hebrew Bible, including those in Ruth and Esther, two of the books to which Ben Sira "does not refer at all." Skehan and Di Lella, *Wisdom of Ben Sira*, 41.

7. This clause from Roger Tomes, "A Father's Anxieties," 91, but used out of context here.

8. I note, with deSilva, however, that Ben Sira does nothing to critique attitudes toward women prevalent in his world. David A. deSilva, *Introducing the Apocrypha*, 184.

9. Eisenbaum, "Sirach," 299, 301. Indeed, from the historical surveys listed by Di Lella ("Ezek 20:4–44; Neh 9:6–37; Psalms 78; 105; 106; 135; 136; Jdt 5:5–21; Wis 10:1—12:27; 1 Macc 2:51–64; Acts 7:2–53; Jas 5:10–11; and Heb 11:2–39"), only Heb 11:2-39 honors a woman by name—Rahab; v. 31 (Skehan and Di Lella, *Wisdom of Ben Sira*, 499–500). However, Camp shows how Ben Sira's "masculinization of glory/honor in Ch. 44," can be viewed in light of an earlier description. Having indicated that "failure to control the sexual behavior of his wife" is "[t]he primary way [in which] a man can be shamed," Camp explains, "By reproducing the language of the adulteress pericope [23:22–27], while eliminating the adulteress, Ch. 44 in effect rhetorically guarantees the seed of the pious from all potential shame." (Note, however, that Sir 23:22–27 is not available among the Hebrew texts. See Blachorsky, "Index of Passages," 15.) Camp continues, "The process by which women and their shame are erased and replaced by an ideal cosmos constituted entirely of men finds completion in the depiction of Simon's glory in Ch. 50" ("Honor and Shame," 185–86).

he desires is "an all-male space," Stacy Davis explains that "Ben Sira is a man of his time" with respect to words of praise that do not "fit comfortably in today's time."[10] In addition, Mark Sneed asserts that the sages were "typically chauvinistic, with wisdom literature being composed by males and for males,"[11] and Teresa Ann Ellis points out that "[t]he Greek genre of *praise* disallows a mixed group of female and male subjects.[12]

On the other hand, I noticed the absence of women in Ben Sira's list by comparing the possessors, agents, and patients of חסד in the Hebrew Bible with the names listed in Sir 44–50. In the introduction to this hymn (44:1–15), Ben Sira indicates that those worthy of praise were "men of חסד":

Sir 44:1 (B, M):[13]	Literal translation:[14]
אהללה נא אנשי חסד [ ]א אנֹ[ ] חסד	Let me praise now the men of חסד
Sir 44:10 (B, M):	Literal translation:
ואולם אלה אנשי חסד אולם אלה אנשי חסד	But these were men of חסד

While it is unclear whether the "categories of heroes" listed in 44:3–6 are meant to correspond to those in the "portrait gallery" that follows,[15] there are certainly individuals listed in the gallery who fit those descriptions (e.g.,

10. Stacy Davis, "Sirach," 1021.

11. Sneed, *Social World of the Sages*, 296.

12. Emphasis original. Ellis, *Gender*, 72–73.

13. Hebrew texts from Sirach are as recorded on bensira.org.

14. Translations mine, unless stated otherwise, but with reference to https://www.bensira.org; NRSV; ESV; *HALOT*.

15. Referring to Sir 44:3–6, Raymond writes, "some [critics] have suggested that the passage refers to the non-Jewish population, others have asserted that it refers to the heroes of the following hymn, and still others have argued that it pertains to certain Jews who have won fame in their life, . . . " Raymond, "Prelude," 1. The labels "portrait gallery" and "categories of heroes," are used by Skehan and Di Lella, *Wisdom of Ben Sira*, 500. According to MS B (https://www.bensira.org), the gallery includes Adam, Seth, and Enosh (49:16), Enoch (44:16), [No]ah (44:17), Shem (49:16), Abraham (44:19), Isaac (44:22), and Jacob/Israel (44:23; 45:5), Joseph (49:15), Moses (45:1), Aaron (45:6), Phinehas son of Eleazar (45:23), Joshua son of Nun (46:1), Caleb son of Jephunneh (46:7), the Judges (46:11), Samuel (46:13), Nathan (47:1), David (45:25), Solomon (47:13), Elijah and [E]l[isha] (48:4, 12), Hezekiah and Josiah (48:17; 49:1, 4), Isaiah (48:20), Jeremiah (49:7), Ezekiel (49:8), Job (49:9), the Twelve Prophets (49:10), [Zerubbabe]l (49:11), and Nehemiah (49:13). Dathan, Abiram, Korah (45:18), Rehoboam, and Jeroboam (47:23) are probably mentioned for contrast.

David and Solomon are among "those who ruled the earth in their kingdoms"; Samuel and Elijah "perceived everything by prophecy"[16]). Some of these ancestors are also explicitly identified as possessors, agents, or patients of חסד within the Hebrew Bible (e.g., Hezekiah and Josiah in 2 Chr 32:32; 35:26; cf. Sir 48:22; 49:1–4 [B]);[17] others are not (e.g., Elijah, Elisha, Ezekiel, and those who lived prior to Abraham).[18] Repetition of the word חסד elsewhere in the hymn indicates that a man's demonstration of חסד (Joshua and Caleb, Sir 46:6–7 [B]; Josiah, 49:3 [B]) and God's maintenance of חסד relationship (47:22 [B]) are key issues for Ben Sira.[19] Indeed, in keeping with John Collins's assertion that the passage on Sim[e]on is "the culmination of all that has gone before,"[20] I note that the last verse of this hymn (50:24 [B]) begins with the clause, יאמן עם שמעון חסדו ("Let his חסד be established with Simeon"; cf. 1 Chr 17:23). This repetition and the additional emphasis on covenants in the descriptions of Abraham (Sir 44:19–20 [B]), Israel (44:22–23 [B]), Aaron/David (45:15, 25 [B]), and Phinehas (45:23–24 [B]), suggest that Ben Sira wants his hearers also to demonstrate חסד/covenant loyalty.[21]

Nevertheless, there are several men and women explicitly identified in Hebrew Bible texts as possessors, agents, or patients of חסד, to whom Ben Sira does not give honor (e.g., Jehoiada [2 Chr 24:22]; Rahab [Josh 2:12]). In the remainder of this article, I focus on the women among them, and discuss ways in which each earns the title, "woman of חסד."

Women of חסד in the Hebrew Bible

Given that women's involvement in חסד activities, as recorded in the Hebrew Bible, mostly reflects what Katharine Doob Sakenfeld calls either "secular" or "divine" uses of חסד, I adopt here Sakenfeld's descriptions of

16. 44:3 [B, M]. This phrase translated by Parker and Abegg, B XIII Verso, https://www.bensira.org.

17. Given that Hezekiah and Josiah were honored specifically for their חסדים in Chronicles, it is not surprising that Ben Sira skips from Hezekiah to Josiah with respect to kings of Judah. Ben Sira's selectivity is noted by Snaith, "Sirach," 797.

18. It could be said, however, that most come under the general label of חסידים, as it refers to YHWH's covenant people (Ps 50:5).

19. Also note the recommendation to regard one's name, for "a name of חסד will not be cut off" (Sir 41:11–12; cf. 44:8–9 [B, M]), and the repetition of "For his חסד is forever," as a reason for thanksgiving (51:12a–n [B]).

20. Collins, *Jewish Wisdom*, 106.

21. DeSilva writes, "The encomium on the Jewish heroes . . . serves to focus the hearers on their particular Jewish heritage, encouraging them . . . to see the loyalty to the ancient covenant as the path to their own honorable remembrance in the future." *Introducing the Apocrypha*, 187.

the features of חסד in such contexts, as follows: For secular uses, "the human actor always has some recognizable responsibility for the person who is to receive *ḥesed*, either because of an obvious personal relationship or because of some previous action"; "situationally the actor is always quite free not to perform the act of *ḥesed* "; "the act of *ḥesed* usually fulfills an important need for the recipient"; and "it is something which he cannot possibly do for himself and often is something which no one but the actor can do for him."[22] Regarding YHWH's חסד to an individual/various individuals within the contexts identified in this article, either "God responds to a specific personal need of the individual which might not otherwise be met," or a blessing is directed toward that individual/s.[23]

I deal first with Sarah, Rahab, Ruth, Orpah, Naomi, and Esther, who are named in the Hebrew Bible as direct participants in relationships involving חסד ("secular" or "divine" uses of חסד, as outlined above). To these women, I give the label "women of חסד." In addition, I consider Hannah and the worthy woman described in Proverbs, who are perceivers of either חסד or חסידים,[24] but their perceptions indicate that they might also be considered as parties in חסד relationships.

Sarah

In Gen 20:13, Abraham recalls before Abimelech, king of Gerar, what he had previously said to his wife, Sarah, when God caused him to wander from his father's house:

---

22. Sakenfeld, *Meaning of* Hesed, 24.

23. Sakenfeld, *Meaning of* Hesed, 93.

24. I.e. those who observe, predict, or appreciate the presence/treatment of חסד or חסיד. חסיד is the adjective of חסד. It often refers to a person in covenant relationship with YHWH. Sakenfeld treats חסיד as "a religious technical term." *Meaning of* Hesed, 242.

For other female/feminine associations with חסד, see Gen 24:15, 24–27, 45–49 (Rebekah becomes involved in a חסד event, but not as a possessor, agent, or patient of חסד); Isa 54:8–10 (the barren one becomes a patient of חסד); Hos 2:21[Eng. 19] (חסד is part of the gift for Israel's betrothal); and Ps 132:16 (Zion is a possessor of חסידים).

Gen 20:13:	Literal translation:
זה חסדך אשר תעשי עמדי אל כל המקום אשר נבוא שמה אמרי לי [25]אחי הוא	"This is your חסד which you will do with me: At every place to which we come, (there) say of me, 'He is my brother.'"

Abraham calls this instance of חסד, "your חסד, which you will do with me." Thus, according to Abraham, Sarah will be both possessor ("your חסד") and agent of חסד ("which you will do with me") in the scenario he describes. From Abraham's perspective, this is a potential act of חסד because Sarah would be doing her part to keep him from being killed in a place where there is no fear of God (v. 11).[26] To the degree that (a) Sarah has responsibility toward Abraham by virtue of being his "wife-sister"; (b) she may or may not choose to comply with Abraham's request; (c) her compliance would fulfil Abraham's need for protection from death; and (d) "there is no other person who can perform this particular act," the requested activity fits Sakenfeld's description of a "secular" act of חסד.[27] Nevertheless, doing what Abraham requested put Sarah and their marital relationship at risk.[28] As a result of Abraham's partially deceitful scheme, Abimelech "took" Sarah (v. 2). Consequently, God closed the wombs of all the women in Abimelech's house and told Abimelech that he would die (vv. 3, 18).

Rahab

Prior to letting two Israelite spies escape from her city by descending a rope dangled from her window, the Canaanite prostitute, Rahab, told the spies

25. Hebrew Bible texts included in this article are from *BHS*.

26. According to Gen 12:11–13, Abraham considers Sarah to be a beautiful woman, one for whom the Egyptians will kill him, and instructs her to say that she is his sister so that his life will be spared. Wenham observes that Abraham's instruction to Sarah in Egypt is the only recorded use of this misleading device prior to the scenario in Gerar (ch. 20), despite Abraham's claim that this was "his general policy." Wenham, *Genesis 16–50*, 73. Furthermore, as Westermann points out, that which was said on the Egyptian border "is here transposed to the beginning of Abraham's travels," and Abraham's concern that there was no fear of God "in this place" (20:11) does not make sense/fit with the generalization (Westermann, *Genesis 12–36*, 326).

27. Sakenfeld, *Meaning of* Hesed, 26–27.

28. Sakenfeld, *Meaning of* Hesed, 27. According to Glueck, Abraham pleads with Sarah on the basis of her familial obligation to him; however, this puts Sarah in danger. Glueck, *Das Wort Ḥesed*, 5; trans. Gottschalk, Ḥesed, 40.

that the inhabitants of Jericho feared the Israelites because of what YHWH had already done for them. Then she proposed a deal, as follows:[29]

Josh 2:12–13:	Literal translation:
ועתה השבעו נא לי ביהוה כי עשיתי עמכם חסד ועשיתם גם אתם עם בית אבי חסד ונתתם לי אות אמת והחיתם את אבי ואת אמי ואת אחי ואת אחותי[30] ואת כל אשר להם והצלתם את נפשתינו ממות	"And now, please swear to me by YHWH, that, [as] I have done חסד with you, you also will do חסד with my father's house, and give (to) me a sign of faithfulness that you will spare my father and my mother and my brothers and my sisters[31] and all who [belong] to them, and deliver our lives from death."

In this statement, Rahab presents herself as both agent and potential patient of חסד. Rahab believes that she has already "done חסד" with the spies (Josh 2:12; i.e., she is an agent of חסד), presumably by hiding them on her roof when they were being pursued (2:4, 6; cf. 6:17, 25; Heb 11:31). Thus, when in a "situationally superior" position,[32] Rahab chose to demonstrate חסד by protecting the lives of the spies who sought shelter under her roof.[33] She was the only person who could provide that protection under the circumstances.

Rahab's subsequent request indicates that, owing to her prior demonstration of חסד, the spies now have a moral responsibility to do חסד with members of her father's house, in *their* imminent time of dire need. Should the spies agree to her request, Rahab would become a patient of חסד by virtue of being a member of her father's house. However, in their reply, the spies indicate that this חסד arrangement exists between Rahab herself (patient) and them. These Israelite men agree to Rahab's deal, on the condition that she does not speak of their "business" in the city:[34]

---

29. Butler refers to this proposed agreement as "tantamount to a covenant treaty." He points out that such agreements with the Canaanites are forbidden, but the spies must accept Rahab's terms and enter into this treaty "to save their own lives." Butler, *Joshua 1–12*, 262.

30. Qere: אחיותי.

31. The Masoretic pointing suggests this plural. Butler, *Joshua 1–12*, 240 n. 13.b.

32. Sakenfeld, *Meaning of* Hesed, 69, 234.

33. Glueck views this as one of Rahab's obligations of hospitality as the host in the situation. *Das Wort Ḥesed*, 10; trans. Gottschalk, Ḥesed, 44.

34. This translation ("business") from NRSV.

Josh 2:14:	Literal translation:
ויאמרו לה האנשים נפשנו תחתיכם למות אם לא תגידו[35] את דברנו זה והיה בתת יהוה לנו את הארץ ועשינו עמך חסד ואמת	And the men said to her, "Our lives in place of yours to death! If you do not tell this business of ours, then (it shall be), when YHWH gives the land to us, we will do with you חסד and faithfulness."

According to the agreement, when Rahab is in a "situationally inferior" position,[36] she will receive חסד, because the spies will provide a way for her life and the lives of all the members of her household to be protected. The spies are the only ones who know how to identify her household under the circumstances.

On Joshua's instruction (6:17, 22, 25), the spies eventually carry out the promised חסד by bringing out Rahab, her family, and all who belonged to her, and setting them outside Israel's camp. After the destruction of Jericho, Rahab is permitted to live permanently in the midst of Israel as a reward for her demonstration of חסד (6:25). Recalling that "the divine law of the ban" (חרם) calls for total destruction, Thomas Dozeman points out the central role that חסד plays "in fashioning an exemption" to this law.[37]

Ruth, Orpah, and Naomi

There are three occurrences of the word חסד and three named women of חסד in the book of Ruth. In 1:8, Naomi is preparing to part from her two widowed daughters-in-law, Ruth and Orpah, and to continue on to Bethlehem on the route between Moab and Judah. Naomi says to them,

---

35. Some MSS: די-. However, as Thomas B. Dozeman puts it, "The second masculine plural of the Hebrew *taggîdû* suggests that the condition of secrecy is placed on the entire family of Rahab." Dozeman, *Joshua 1–12*, 232.

36. Sakenfeld, *Meaning of* Hesed, 69, 234.

37. Dozeman, *Joshua 1–12*, 246–47. Butler suggests that, although "God has forbidden agreements with the Canaanites (Exod 23:32–33; Deut 7:2–5; 20:16–18)," the spies "are apparently willing to enter into a treaty with a Canaanite if it proves the way to save their own lives" (*Joshua 1–12*, 262).

Ruth 1:8:	Literal translation:
לכנה שבנה אשה לבית אמה יעשה[38] יהוה עמכם חסד כאשר עשיתם עם המתים ועמדי	"Go, return, [each] woman to the house of her mother! May YHWH do[39] חסד with you, as you have done with the dead and with me."

Assuming that she is not able to do anything more for Ruth and Orpah,[40] Naomi's parting blessing calls for YHWH to be an agent of חסד with Ruth and Orpah (patients) as they have been agents of חסד with "the dead" (presumably Elimelech, Mahlon, and Chilion) and with Naomi (patients). Sakenfeld's suggestion about the content of Ruth's and Orpah's "kindness" (i.e., חסד) seems appropriate for the circumstances: "Presumably it consisted of many individual acts that could be summarized as their loyal state of being with regard to this family of foreigners in the midst of the Moabite community."[41] As wives and daughters-in-law, Ruth and Orpah have acted responsibly toward their family members in times of need. As for the content of YHWH's חסד, I refer to 1:9, where Naomi calls upon YHWH to ensure that each daughter-in-law finds rest in the house of a new husband—an important means of provision and protection for a woman in a patriarchal society.

Ruth, however, decides to continue on the journey with Naomi. Arriving in Bethlehem at harvest time, Ruth takes the initiative to provide for Naomi and herself by gleaning grain. It so happens that Boaz, a near-relative, owns the part of the field to which Ruth goes. When Ruth tells Naomi the name of the man with whom she has worked during the day, Naomi recognizes the family connection and declares (2:20),

Ruth 2:20:	Literal translation:
ברוך הוא ליהוה אשר לא עזב חסדו את החיים ואת המתים	"Blessed be he by YHWH who has not forsaken his חסד to the living or to the dead."

---

38. Qere: עשו.

39. Schipper writes, "Rather than the modal ya'aseh (ketib), the qere has a jussive ya'aś (. . .). Yet the ketib could also be translated as a jussive (. . .)" (Ruth, 91).

40. Sakenfeld, Ruth, 24.

41. Sakenfeld, Ruth, 25.

Either YHWH or "he" (i.e., Boaz) could be the antecedent of אשר ("who") in this sentence,[42] and therefore, the possessor and agent of חסד.[43] The more relevant issue for this discussion, however, is the position of the women in relation to "his חסד." Naomi and Ruth are among the "living" patients of חסד in this context. Naomi perceives that "his חסד" has not forsaken them, because Ruth happened to work in the field of someone with the potential and responsibility to provide for the women's present and future needs in ways that they are unable to do.

The third occurrence of חסד in Ruth is recorded in 3:10. After finding Ruth lying at his feet as part of a symbolic request for marriage, Boaz says to her,

Ruth 3:10:	Literal translation:
ברוכה את ליהוה בתי היטבת חסדך האחרון מן הראשין לבלתי לכת אחרי הבחורים אם דל ואם עשיר	"May you be blessed by YHWH, my daughter; your latter חסד is better than the first, for you have not gone after young men, whether poor or rich."

Boaz identifies two specific demonstrations of חסד that belong to Ruth (possessor/agent). The latter concerns Ruth "going after" Boaz instead of younger men. In so doing, Ruth continues to take her responsibility in providing for her mother-in-law in ways that Naomi cannot. In keeping with this responsibility, the former demonstration of חסד is probably that to which Boaz referred during his previous encounter with Ruth: that which she had already done for her mother-in-law since the death of Ruth's husband.

Esther

An expression involving חסד that is unique to the book of Esther indicates that the Jewess Esther (Hadassah) possesses or demonstrates חסד in some

---

42. Some scholars favor Boaz as the agent of חסד in Naomi's blessing. For example, Kim argues this in light of the incidental nature of the praise of YHWH, the results of syntactic analysis, congruence with the theme of human חסד in the book, and Boaz's actions perpetuating the name of "the dead." Kim, "Agent of Ḥesed," 595–601. Others think that the ambiguity is intentional. For example, for Hawk, it suggests that "Naomi sees Boaz and Yahweh acting in concert as agents of blessing." Hawk, *Ruth*, 86. I favor YHWH as the antecedent of אשר, because Naomi seems to be correcting her previous perceptions, as recorded in 1:13, 20–21.

43. "His חסד" could also be the subject of "forsaken" and agent of the action. But either YHWH or Boaz remains the possessor of חסד.

way. Esther 2:9 records the reaction of the eunuch Hegai to Esther when she and many other women are taken into the palace of King Ahasuerus and put in Hegai's custody:

Esth 2:9:	Literal translation:
ותיטב הנערה בעיניו ותשא חסד לפניו	And the young woman was pleasing in his eyes; and she lifted up חסד before him

Similarly, 2:17 records the reaction of King Ahasuerus to Esther when it is her turn to go to him.

Esth 2:17:	Literal translation:
ויאהב המלך את אסתר מכל הנשים ותשא חן וחסד לפניו מכל הבתולת	And the king loved Esther more than all the women, and she lifted up grace and חסד before him more than all the virgins

In each case, Esther stands out from the other young women, she "lifts up" (נשא) חסד before the man who observes her, and she is rewarded accordingly. Hegai gives Esther cosmetic treatments, food, and advancement to the best place in the harem. The king sets a crown on her head and makes her queen instead of Vashti.

Thus, Esther's חסד is viewed favorably. But just what it means for Esther to "lift up" (נשא) חסד is debatable. Sakenfeld writes,

> The idiom with nś' is used in comparing Esther to the other virgins (2:17), in describing the reaction of people who "see" her (2:15), in describing the response of the head of the harem (2:9). In each of these cases, one would expect her physical appearance to be the primary object of attention. Only the response of the king upon seeing his queen unbidden (5:2) might be ambiguous, but even here it is possible that her beauty caused the king to grant clemency. Hence for the idiom nś' ḥn/ḥsd a translation such as "appeared beautiful" may be preferable.[44]

On the other hand, I consider the active nature of the expression, תשא חסד. In 3:1 and 5:11, King Ahasuerus "lifts up" (Piel of נשא) Haman in the sense of promoting him, and, in 9:3, the royal officials "lift up" (Piel of נשא)

---

44. Sakenfeld, *Meaning of* Hesed, 160.

the Jews in the sense of supporting them.[45] However, in 2:15 and 5:2, it is Esther who "lifts up" (Qal of נשא) חן (also an active expression) in the eyes of those who observe her.[46] In so doing, Esther may be admired for her appearance or win favor,[47] but I suggest the alternative that, at least in 2:15, Esther emanates grace before her observers.[48] It is also conceivable that in 2:9, 17, the expressions תשא חסד and תשא חן וחסד indicate that Esther exhibits grace and חסד, and the men notice her doing so. In any case, the active expression suggests that Esther possesses and/or demonstrates חסד, not her observers. As a result, she becomes the new Queen in Persia, a position that eventually proves pivotal to the deliverance of her people.

Hannah and the Worthy Woman

When YHWH remembers Hannah and she bears a son, Hannah takes the child Samuel to the house of YHWH at Shiloh (1 Sam 1:19–28). Hannah, the implied author of the prayer response (2:1–10), exults YHWH for reversing various circumstances, and then says concerning YHWH, ישמר[49] רגלי חסידו ("he will keep/guard the feet of his חסידים"). She predicts that YHWH will treat his חסידים in this manner, which makes her a perceiver of חסידים (2:9). In the antithetical parallel statement that follows, the wicked are contrasted with YHWH's חסידים. However, within this narrative framework, the implied author of the prayer might be considered among the חסידים,[50] and her rival, among the "the wicked" who will be silenced/perish in darkness.[51] Neither group prevails by power/might. Rather, as Ralph Klein puts it, "The devout will prevail by God's power alone (cf. Zech 4:6). That too could be the only claim to power by those who stumble or starve, who are barren or near death."[52] As a previously barren woman who has now borne a child, Hannah would appreciate this principle.

---

45. HALOT 726–27.

46. For an explanation about the active and passive senses of expressions associated with Esther and חסד or חן, see Bush, Ruth, Esther, 364, 404.

47. Cf. NRSV translations.

48. חן is usually "found" (מצא; see Esth 5:8; 7:3; 8:5) and sometimes "given" (נתן), but rarely "lifted up" (נשא).

49. Qere: חסידיו.

50. Cf. the use of חסיד in Ps 16:10, where the psalmist may be referring generally to any person in covenant relationship with YHWH and/or, in particular, to the psalmist himself.

51. Brueggemann writes, "The wicked are those who rely on their own strength–people like Peninnah or the Philistines." Brueggemann, First and Second Samuel, 20.

52. Klein, 1 Samuel, 19.

One description of "a worthy woman" recorded in the Proverbs 31 list (vv. 10–29) is תורת חסד על לשונה ("teaching of חסד is on her tongue"; v. 26). Roland Murphy interprets "'torah of kindness'" as "either the teaching about kindness or kindness with which she gives instruction."[53] Bruce Waltke speaks of the woman's teaching as "informed by her own lovingkindness," "a reference to a particular body of teaching about kindness," or "a metonymy of adjunct for all her speech."[54] However, Tremper Longman III's emphasis on the connection between חסד and covenant relationship is valid: The "noble" woman's words flow "from the covenant between God and his people." Thus, he translates תורת חסד, "covenantal instruction."[55] Given that תורת חסד is parallel to חכמה ("wisdom") and, elsewhere, God does/keeps חסד with those who keep God's commandments (e.g., Exod 20:6; Deut 5:10; 7:9), I suggest that this woman speaks of devotion to the covenant; that is, sustaining a way of life in which keeping God's commandments is the priority.[56] In any case, by virtue of having teaching of חסד "on her tongue," this woman can be considered either a possessor or a perceiver of חסד.

Honoring the Biblical Women of חסד

Seeking to return women to the place of honor from which Ben Sira and other writers of ancient hero lists have excluded them, I have identified Sarah,[57] Rahab,[58] Orpah,[59] Ruth,[60] Naomi,[61] and Esther[62] as possessors, agents, and/or patients of חסד. In addition, Hannah may include herself when she observes the way that YHWH treats his חסידים, and the worthy woman of Prov 31 has the teaching of חסד on her tongue. Does this suggest, however, that the Hebrew Bible portrays women as "valued for more than their role as wives and mothers"?[63]

---

53. Murphy, *Proverbs*, 248.
54. Waltke, *Proverbs Chapters 15–31*, 532.
55. Longman, *Proverbs*, 542, 546–47.
56. If Ben Sira had included the achievements of women in his hymn, Prov 31:26 would have been relevant to the emphasis on covenant faithfulness there as well.
57. Possessor and agent.
58. Agent and patient.
59. Agent and patient.
60. Possessor, agent, and patient.
61. Patient.
62. Possessor and/or agent.
63. As for n. 7.

In keeping with the cultural pattern, what Abraham considers Sarah's responsibility toward him relates to her role as a wife-sister. Similarly, Orpah and Ruth are loyal wives and daughters-in-law. In return, their mother-in-law prays that they will each find rest in the house of a new husband. Orpah is content with that scenario. But Ruth's subsequent demonstrations of חסד go beyond the call of duty. She accompanies her mother-in-law to a land yet unknown to herself, provides for their sustenance there, and eventually carries out Naomi's plan to ensure provision for their ongoing needs. In doing so, Ruth earns the label "worthy woman" from Boaz (Ruth 3:11), the neighborhood women tell Naomi that Ruth is better to her than seven sons (4:15), and she becomes an ancestor of King David (4:17). Furthermore, despite their difficult circumstances, YHWH/Boaz does not forsake his חסד to Naomi, Ruth, or their family.

It is difficult to determine the extent to which Hannah, Esther, and the Proverbs 31 "worthy woman" demonstrate or experience חסד according to the expectations of women in their day. The worthy woman probably instructs her children or maidservants in the covenant.[64] Hannah is blessed to bear a child (a future judge and prophet) after some time waiting for one, but her observation actually concerns the general protection of YHWH's חסידים. Likewise, we are not told exactly how Esther "lifts up" חסד. But we do know that she wins the favor of a Persian king as a result, and later demonstrates outstanding loyalty to her own people, by helping to save them from total destruction. Events associated with her courageous act are commemorated each year during the days of Purim (Esth 9:26–28). Then again, Rahab's noteworthy act of חסד is clearly articulated. She protects Israelite spies from being caught by the king of Jericho. Thus, while Rahab is performing her duty as a host, the act for which she is remembered seems to exceed expectations. Rahab also challenges the Israelites to reciprocate חסד by delivering her household from death under the ban. After being rescued, she lives among the Israelites (Josh 6:25).

Despite Ben Sira's exclusion of women from his honors gallery, there are several women of חסד named in the Hebrew Scriptures. Some of their demonstrations and experiences of חסד reflect the typical roles of women in ancient society. Others demand extraordinary courage, determination, and initiative. Either way, these women are worthy of at least as much honor as the men in Ben Sira's list.

---

64. Murphy, *Proverbs*, 248.

Bibliography

Blachorsky, Joshua A. "The Book of Ben Sira Index of Passages," 1–35. https://www.bensira.org

Brueggemann, Walter. *First and Second Samuel*. Interpretation. Louisville: John Knox, 1990.

Bush, Frederic. *Ruth, Esther*. WBC 9. Dallas: Word, 1996.

Butler, Trent C. *Joshua 1–12*. 2nd ed. WBC 7A. Grand Rapids: Zondervan, 2014.

Camp, Claudia V. "Honor and Shame in Ben Sira: Anthropological and Theological Reflections." In *The Book of Ben Sira in Modern Research: Proceedings of the First International Ben Sira Conference, 28-31 July 1996, Soesterberg, Netherlands*, edited by Pancratius C. Beentjes, 171–87. BZAW 255. Berlin: de Gruyter, 1997.

Collins, John J. *Jewish Wisdom in the Hellenistic Age*. Louisville: Westminster John Knox, 1997.

Corley, Jeremy. "A Numerical Structure in Sirach 44:1—50:24." *CBQ* 69 (2007) 43–63.

Davis, Stacy. "Sirach." In *Fortress Commentary on the Bible: The Old Testament and Apocrypha*, edited by Gale A. Yee at al., 999–1025. Minneapolis: Fortress, 2014.

deSilva, David A. *Introducing the Apocrypha: Message, Context, and Significance*. Grand Rapids: Baker Academic, 2002.

Dozeman, Thomas B. *Joshua 1–12: A New Translation with Introduction and Commentary*. AYB 1. New Haven: Yale University Press, 2015.

Eisenbaum, Pamela M. "Sirach." In *Women's Bible Commentary*, edited by Carol A. Newsom and Sharon H. Ringe, 298–304. Expanded ed. Louisville: Westminster John Knox, 1998.

Ellis, Teresa Ann. *Gender in the Book of Ben Sira: Divine Wisdom, Erotic Poetry, and the Garden of Eden*. BZAW 453. Berlin: de Gruyter, 2013.

Glueck, Nelson. *Das Wort Ḥesed im Alttestamentlichen Sprachgebrauche als Menschliche und Göttliche Gemeinschaftgemässe Verhaltungsweise*. BZAW 47. Berlin: Alfred Töpelmann, 1961. Translated by Alfred Gottschalk. In *Ḥesed in the Bible*, edited by Elias L. Epstein. Eugene, OR: Wipf & Stock, 2011.

Hawk, L. Daniel. *Ruth*, AOTC 7B. Nottingham: Apollos; Downers Grove, IL: InterVarsity, 2015.

Kim, Yoo-ki. "The Agent of Ḥesed in Naomi's Blessing (Ruth 2,20)." *Biblica* 95 (2014) 589–601.

Klein, Ralph W. *1 Samuel*. 2nd ed. WBC 10. Nashville: Thomas Nelson, 2008.

Lee, Thomas R. *Studies in the Form of Sirach 44–50*. SBLDS 75. Atlanta: Scholars, 1986.

Longman, Tremper, III. *Proverbs*. BCOTWP. Grand Rapids: Baker Academic, 2006.

Mack, Burton L. "Sirach (Ecclesiasticus)." In *The Books of the Bible 2: The Apocrypha and the New Testament*, edited by Bernhard W. Anderson, 65–86. New York: Charles Scribner's Sons, 1989.

Murphy, Roland E. *Proverbs*. WBC 22. Nashville: Thomas Nelson, 1998.

Parker, Benjamin H., and Martin G. Abegg. "The Book of Ben Sira." https://www.bensira.org

Raymond, Eric D. "Prelude to the Praise of the Ancestors, Sirach 44:1–15." *HUCA* 72 (2001) 1–14.

Sakenfeld, Katharine Doob. *Ruth*. IBC. Louisville: John Knox, 1999.

———. *The Meaning of* Ḥesed *in the Hebrew Bible: A New Inquiry*. Eugene, OR: Wipf & Stock, 1978.

Schipper, Jeremy. *Ruth: A New Translation with Introduction and Commentary.* AYB 7D. New Haven: Yale University Press, 2016.

Skehan, Patrick W., and Alexander A. Di Lella. *The Wisdom of Ben Sira.* AB 39. New York: Doubleday, 1987.

Snaith, John. "Sirach." In *Eerdmans Commentary on the Bible*, edited by James D. G. Dunn and John W. Rogerson, 779–98. Grand Rapids: Eerdmans, 2003.

Sneed, Mark R. *The Social World of the Sages: An Introduction to Israelite and Jewish Wisdom Literature.* Minneapolis: Fortress, 2015.

Tomes, Roger. "A Father's Anxieties (Sirach 42:9–11)." In *Women in the Biblical Tradition*, edited by George J. Brooke, 71–91. Studies in Women and Religion 31. Lewiston, NY: Mellen, 1992.

Waltke, Bruce K. *The Book of Proverbs Chapters 15–31.* NICOT. Grand Rapids: Eerdmans, 2005.

Wenham, Gordon. *Genesis 16–50.* WBC 2. Dallas: Word, 1994.

Westermann, Claus. *Genesis 12–36: A Commentary.* Translated by John J. Scullion. Minneapolis: Augsburg, 1985.

Wright, Benjamin G. "Sirach (Ecclesiasticus)." In *T. & T. Clark Companion to the Septuagint*, edited by James K. Aitken, 410–24. London: Bloomsbury T. & T. Clark, 2015.

12

Tiptoe through the Minefields
Navigating Gender, Sexuality, and the Bible in Aotearoa New Zealand

CAROLINE BLYTH AND EMILY COLGAN

WE LIVE IN A world where many people regard gender violence as an inevitable, even acceptable, fact of life—a "normalized expectation" that arises from mainstream gender discourses pervading our cultural and social landscapes.[1] Gender violence wears multiple guises, including the subjective violence of sexual and physical assault, the symbolic violence of misogynistic, homophobic, and transphobic language, and the structural violence of cisheteropatriarchal[2] power structures.[3] These various forms of gender violence affect multiple intersecting identities, including those re-

---

1. Burnett, "Rape Culture," 1.

2. This rather wordy word sums up quite neatly the dominant discourses within Western cultures that normalize cisgendered, heterosexual, and hegemonic masculine identities while simultaneously othering or delegitimizing anyone who does not fit into these categories, be they transgender or gender diverse, other-than-heterosexual, female, and/or non-compliant with traditional masculine ideals.

3. We draw on Slavoj Žižek's categories of objective and subjective violence here: subjective violence relates to the physical violence of crime and terror; objective violence includes the symbolic violence of hate speech and discriminatory language and the structural (or systemic) violence inherent within political and economic systems of power. See Slavoj Žižek, *Violence*.

lating to race, class, ability, sexuality, gender identity, and ethnicity. Within many cultures and communities around the world, occurrences of gender violence have reached epidemic proportions, with rape, sexual abuse, family violence, homophobia, biphobia, and transphobia becoming lived realities for a great many people.[4]

Within this wider discourse of gender violence and the inequities that sustain it, Aotearoa New Zealand has often prided itself as a nation committed both to gender equality and to protecting the rights of lesbian, gay, bisexual, and transgender (LGBT) communities. After all, it was the first country to extend suffrage to women in 1883 and, to date, has had a total of three women prime ministers.[5] New Zealand was also a forerunner in abolishing certain discriminations on the basis of sexual orientation, introducing civil unions in 2004, followed by legalizing same-sex marriage in 2013. These examples are often used to affirm the nation's self-identification as a paradigm of social equality and progressive politics in the Western world.[6] In reality, though, there is a sharp disconnect between this cultural projection and the lived experience of many New Zealanders, particularly those caught in the crosshairs of violence, poverty, and discrimination wrought by the legacy of colonization.[7] As feminist historian Harriet Winn notes ruefully, rather than being a "frontrunner in the worldwide race towards gender equality," Aotearoa New Zealand "is stumbling behind on the fringes."[8]

Winn's observation here is particularly pertinent when we consider recent national statistics around gender violence. Aotearoa New Zealand has one of the highest rates of gender violence among developed countries in the Organization for Economic Co-operation and Development (OECD).[9] This was confirmed in a recent report by the New Zealand Human Rights Commission, which identified gender-based violence as the country's "most significant human rights issue affecting women," with around half a million people—about a fifth of the New Zealand population—impacted by it.[10]

---

4. See, e.g., Human Rights Campaign, "Transgender Community"; UN Women, "Facts and Figures"; United Nations General Assembly, "Discriminatory Laws"; United Nations Population Fund, *UNFPA Engagement*.

5. Jenny Shipley was New Zealand's first woman prime minister (1997–1999) and was succeeded by Helen Clark, whose nine-year tenure (1999–2008) makes her one of the longest-serving women leaders in the world. Jacinda Ardern became the country's third woman prime minister in 2017.

6. Anand, "Unsafe Haven."

7. Tuhiwai Smith, *Decolonizing Methodologies*, 33–34.

8. Winn, "Thursdays in Black," 52.

9. See OECD, "Violence against Women."

10. New Zealand Human Rights Commission, "Women's Rights," 3.

Moreover, according to Ministry of Justice statistics, 24 percent of women and 6 percent of men in Aotearoa New Zealand report having experienced at least one incident of sexual violence during their lifetime, while 20 percent of girls and 9 percent of boys report unwanted sexual touching or being forced to do sexual things.[11] These statistics are even more disturbing when one considers that only 9 percent of rape cases and around 20 percent of domestic violence episodes are reported to the New Zealand police, suggesting that the actual rates of such violence are considerably higher than those commonly recorded. Additionally, ethnic identities, (dis)abilities, age, and sexual orientations intersect with gender identities to make certain communities in Aotearoa even more vulnerable to gender violence. Māori and Pasifika women, migrant women, women with disabilities, queer people, transgender and gender-diverse people, and young women aged between seventeen and twenty-four all experience disproportionately high levels of sexual violence, sexual abuse, and intimate-partner violence.[12] Aotearoa New Zealand, it seems, is a society within which gender-based violence remains scandalously pervasive.

Located within this global and national crisis, Christianity continues to play a significant and often contentious role in shaping the social imaginary—or collective consciousness—relating to gender violence. Within Christian interpretative traditions, certain biblical texts have been used uncritically to support patriarchal gender hierarchies and cisheteronormative discourses, which work to sustain and sanctify multiple forms of gender violence.[13] Church teachings (and church leaders) have counseled women to remain within violent marriages and forgive their abusers,[14] promoted intolerance towards and negated the full humanity of people in LGBT communities,[15] and sustained chronic levels of sexism and heteropatriarchy within institutional

---

11. Te Ohaakii a Hine—National Network Ending Sexual Violence Together (TOAH-NNEST), "What Is Sexual Violence: He Aha Tēnei," accessed January 31, 2019, http://toah-nnest.org.nz/what-is-sexual-violence/prevalence; cited in New Zealand Human Rights Commission, "Women's Rights," 4.

12. Māori girls and women are nearly twice as likely to experience sexual violence as the general population in Aotearoa New Zealand. The rates of Māori women who report child sexual abuse are also considerably higher than European women and those from other ethnic groups. Pasifika and migrant women are at a statistically greater risk of being victims of sexual violence. For further information, see Rape Prevention Education, "Statistics." For data and reports on violence against lesbian, gay, bisexual, transgender and gender-diverse people, see Hohou, "Reports and Findings."

13. See Nason-Clark, *The Battered Wife*; Haddad, "Dr. Catherine Clark Kroeger"; Vorster, "Queering of Biblical Discourse."

14. See Adams, "I just raped my wife!"; Marsden, "The Church's Contribution."

15. See Hare, "LGBT Affirmation"; Henderson-Merrygold, "Queer(y)ing."

hierarchies,[16] all in the name of the Christian faith. Equally problematic, in the past few decades, are the horrific levels of child abuse perpetrated by Christian individuals and institutions that have come to light, despite systemic and self-preservatory attempts by these institutions to cover up this abuse.[17] While the relationships between Christianity and gender violence are complex and multifaceted, they *are* undeniably problematic, encompassing both subjective and objective forms of violence.

To be sure, a number of Christian theologians have responded to these issues by critiquing the complicity of the church and the Christian faith in perpetuating inequalities that sustain gender violence.[18] Moreover, Christian theologians, communities, and organizations, both at local and global levels, have worked to develop educational resources on gender violence prevention, as well as providing pastoral care and support services for those impacted by such violence.[19] These efforts are laudable, yet they do little to challenge the deeply-entrenched structures, ideologies, and traditions within Christianity that play an undeniable role in sustaining multiple forms of gender violence. It is therefore high time that the church and wider Christian community recognize the crucial role they can play in tackling the cultural ideologies that perpetuate such violence, acknowledge the church's responsibility to help survivors seek justice and healing, and admit that the voices of these survivors have been (and continue to be) ignored or even silenced by centuries of Christian teachings and traditions.[20]

The endemic levels of gender violence in Aotearoa New Zealand—including sexual violence, family violence, homophobia, transphobia, and sexual abuse—surely make this issue a priority for theological studies generally, and for biblical studies specifically, within our country's seminaries, universities, and churches. There is a critical need for scholars to disrupt the misogynistic, homophobic, and transphobic discourses that still exist at a symbolic and semantic level within the Christian tradition, as these discourses sustain contemporary, cisheteropatriarchal ideologies and create an environment in which gender violence in *all* its forms can flourish.

16. Daly, *Beyond God the Father*.

17. McPhillips, "Royal Commission"; Alvear and Tombs, *Listening to Male Survivors*.

18. See, for example, Adams and Fortune, *Violence Against Women and Children*; Althaus-Reid, *Indecent Theology*; Fortune, *Sexual Violence*; Nason-Clark, "Shattered Silence or Holy Hush"; Sneed, *Representations of Homosexuality*.

19. For example, Tearfund, a Christian international relief and development agency, has created resources and projects that tackle sexual and gender-based violence in a number of countries around the world. For further details, see their web page, "Sexual and Gender Based Violence."

20. Fortune, "Faith Is Fundamental," esp. 469–70.

Given Tim's involvement in theological education and church leadership over the years, and given his own willingness, more recently, to tackle some of the difficult conversations around the symbolic violence of cisheteropatriarchal discourses within Christianity, we felt it fitting to include this conversation in his *Festschrift*. Our hope is that the discussions laid out in this chapter will inspire him, as well as his colleagues, students, and congregants, to continue addressing this urgent issue. In the following discussion, we therefore reflect upon some of the themes and practices that theological educators need to consider when teaching, writing, and preaching about biblical "texts of terror"—texts that relate, condone, or even inspire episodes of gender violence in all its forms. Within classrooms, conference rooms, and places of worship, we navigate a minefield peppered with resistance, where there are ever-present possibilities to engage with others about gender violence in ways that are either damaging *or* healing. Reflecting on our own attempts to journey through some of these hazardous spaces, we share our thoughts, learning opportunities, and experiences of engaging with biblical texts of terror. Particularly, we contemplate how to engage with these texts responsibly, given our own cultural location within (post)colonial Aotearoa New Zealand. As we tiptoe through this minefield, we invite readers (including theological educators, academics, pastors, and students) to think about their *own* engagements with biblical texts of terror in light of our discussion. We also offer a summons to those engaged in theological education (be it in church, seminary, or university) to persist in these tough conversations and thereby commit to challenging gender violence within both the pages of the Bible *and* our own communities and cultural contexts.

Creating Safe Spaces to Talk About and Challenge Gender Violence

The first step in addressing gender violence within classrooms and churches is a practical one—that of ensuring our institutions are safe spaces for people to engage with these issues. This process begins with an appeal for all universities, churches, and seminaries to undergo a comprehensive review of their existing policies regarding sexual and gender-based harassment, checking that these policies are in line with what is currently considered "good practice." This includes the provision of care for survivors that is accessible, culturally aware, and community focused and that prioritizes their wellbeing and empowerment in accordance with their ethnic, gender, and sexual identity.[21]

21. TOAH-NNEST, "Crisis Support Services."

Nevertheless, creating safe spaces involves more than just adopting a well-written policy or responding to episodes of gender violence as and when they occur. It is also about direct education and ongoing conversation with the church or teaching community, including, for example, workshops and resources that educate congregants and students about how to recognize different forms of gender violence, the significance of consent, and the right of every individual, whatever their gender or sexual orientation, *not* to be assaulted or harassed.[22] This educational approach might also include training around power and gender violence for those currently in (or going into) positions of leadership within the church and wider community. For it is only by acknowledging the realities of gender violence in all its forms that intervention becomes possible, enabling substantial improvements to systems and institutions that sustain the normalization and pervasiveness of such violence.[23]

These initial steps of providing education and conversation about gender violence are crucial; they are, however, only the start of what will inevitably be a much larger and more complex project. In order to take gender violence prevention seriously, we need to consider critically the ways that Christianity intersects with contemporary cultural discourses around gender violence, specifically examining the roles that Christian texts, traditions, practices, and belief systems can play in perpetuating *or* disrupting these discourses. We need to interrogate the extent to which our churches and classrooms articulate and enact gendered ideologies that normalize male leadership and female subordination. We need to ask if church leaders and educators are (knowingly or not) perpetuating commonly held rape-supportive ideologies, including slut shaming and victim blaming, female sexualization and objectification, the normalization of "naturally" aggressive (cishetero)masculinity, and the belittlement of rape victims as "damaged goods." We need to inquire how church leaders and congregations meet the spiritual needs of their LGBT Christian members. We need to investigate whether or not our churches and teaching institutions are drawing on Christian texts and teachings to denigrate and dehumanize members of queer communities and to promote homophobic, biphobic, and transphobic discourses. These can be difficult and unpopular questions to ask, but they are *essential* if we are serious about learning how our own Christian communities might be complicit in sustaining gender violence.

---

22. Winn, "Thursdays in Black," 57.
23. Winn, "Thursdays in Black," 57.

Interrogating Biblical Texts of Terror

The Bible is a violent book, its pages filled with traditions attesting to the ubiquity of gendered aggression and abuse within biblical Israel. Its narratives confirm the commonality of wartime rape (e.g., Judg 21), forced marriage (e.g., Deut 21:10–4), and sex slavery (e.g., Genesis 16). We read stories of stranger rape (e.g., Genesis 34), acquaintance rape (e.g., 2 Samuel 13), and gang rape (both threatened and actualized; e.g., Genesis 19; Judges 19). Turn to the prophetic texts and we are offered numerous metaphorical renditions of spousal abuse and intimate partner violence, perpetrated (or at least sanctioned) by Israel's jealous deity (e.g., Hosea 1–3; Ezekiel 16, 23). Meanwhile, biblical laws uphold the structural violence of patriarchal power, which grants divine mandate to the rigidly prescriptive and proscriptive control of women's (and sometimes vulnerable men's) bodies, while normalizing their social, sexual, and religious subjugation (e.g., Lev 20:13, 18; 21:9; Num 5:11–31).

Given their placement within the pages of sacred Scripture, these articulations of gender violence have amassed significant authority and power over the centuries. This power remains undiminished today, not only through the religious teachings and traditions of Judaism and Christianity but also by way of contemporary social discourses that (implicitly or explicitly) draw upon the ideologies inherent within biblical texts to justify multiple forms of gender violence. While the origins of gender violence by no means lie *exclusively* (or even predominantly) within the biblical traditions, these texts are not blameless. For no literature (particularly sacred literature) is ever value neutral, nor does it leave the reader unchanged by the reading process. Rather, all texts invite their audience to embrace certain discourses, values, and belief systems, expressed through their authors' rhetorical strategies. As Elisabeth Schüssler Fiorenza notes, "Stories are never just descriptive but always also prescriptive."[24] In other words, biblical texts may reflect the ideologies of the ancient communities in which they are written, but they also have the potential to validate and sanction similar ideologies within communities in which they are read today. And when these ideologies endorse the structural violence of gender inequality and cisheteropatriarchal hegemony, their power to impact contemporary readers' lives, worldviews, and behaviors cannot be underestimated. As Patrocinio Schweickart insists, "We cannot afford to ignore the activity of reading, for it is here that literature is realized in *praxis*. Literature acts on the world

---

24. Schüssler Fiorenza, *Wisdom Ways*, 136.

by acting on its readers."[25] Interrogating biblical texts of terror and exposing their harmful discourses is therefore a crucial task for biblical scholars, teachers, and preachers.

Some scholars and readers of the Bible may, however, contend that it is anachronistic to use contemporary definitions of gender violence to make sense of violent events evoked in biblical texts. To do so, they argue, is to impose conceptualizations of gender and sexuality upon the biblical traditions that bear little or no relevance to those held by their ancient authors.[26] Nevertheless, while some of the gender discourses articulated in the Bible may differ to those we encounter in our own cultural contexts, the gendered violence evoked therein remains all too familiar.[27] Our ability to recognize episodes of coercive sexual behavior, sex slavery, or brutal gang rape in the biblical texts need not be hindered by our acknowledgment that Israelite women appeared to have no legally cognizable right of consent. The fact that the abduction and rape of female prisoners of war is mandated in the legal codes (Deut 21:10–14) ought not stop us from seeing the horrific abuse inherent within this law. When we read that God mandates the stripping, slashing, starving, and stoning of his adulterous "wife" in Hosea 2 and Ezekiel 16, we are no less aghast when we acknowledge the metaphorical nature of these sadistic assaults. Gender violence is undeniably evoked within these texts. If we refuse to recognize this, we simply become complicit in its erasure, allowing it to remain accepted and unchallenged by contemporary readers.[28] Our task, then, is to contest this complicity, and to name (and shame) the multiple forms of gender violence presented unproblematically (or even positively) in the biblical traditions. By doing so, we can begin to undermine the potentially harmful influence that biblical texts of terror still have within contemporary culture.

How, then, do we engage biblical studies students, pastors, and church congregants in discussions about biblical texts of terror?[29] This is not a step to be taken lightly, or a means of raising church and lecture attendance through the scholarly equivalent of clickbait. But it is a crucial step to take

---

25. Schweickart, "Reading Ourselves," 615 (emphasis original).

26. For further discussion of this interpretive approach, and examples of biblical scholars who appear to endorse it, see Scholz, "Back Then."

27. Scholz, "Back Then," 2.

28. See Scott, "The Bible's #MeToo Problem"; Blyth, *The Narrative of Rape*, 8–12.

29. Some of the courses we teach focus on a biblical text that happens to contain narratives of gender violence (e.g., Genesis, Judges, 1 and 2 Samuel). Other courses consider the Bible more thematically, and our explorations of biblical "texts of terror" form part of wider discussions around the Bible in relation to contemporary understandings of gender, sexuality, violence, (post)colonialism, and popular culture.

because, like it or not, these texts are *in* the Bible. It is therefore imperative to draw readers' attention to this fact if we are serious about improving their biblical knowledge. For some Christians, these texts of terror will come as a surprise, as they are typically omitted from church lectionaries and are rarely the focus of sermons or Bible study groups. Other readers may be familiar with them but are happier to leave them *un*studied in either their classrooms or their church. Yet to exclude these texts from course syllabi and church lectionaries is to do students and congregants a huge disservice; for, to properly understand the Bible, Christian readers must have the integrity to confront it in its entirety, regardless of how tough the ensuing conversations might prove.[30]

So how does our location of Aotearoa New Zealand—where gender violence is so pervasive—inform the ways we teach and preach about these troubling texts? As biblical scholars and educators, we are not claiming that the Bible (or Christianity more broadly) is the sole source of the incredibly high rates of gender violence in Aotearoa New Zealand; we do contend, however, that it must be interrogated as a text that both supports and perpetuates such violence, particularly given the Bible's colonial legacy. We cannot afford to ignore the potential for biblical traditions to contribute to the harm experienced by countless victims of gender violence who live with us upon this land. This conviction has informed our scholarly engagement with biblical texts of terror in three ways, which are important to remember wherever the conversation occurs, whether in a classroom, at a conference, or in a church setting.

First, when talking to people about biblical texts of terror, we must always be sensitive to the very real possibility that some of our audience may be affected personally by gender violence. With this in mind, we always ensure some basic steps are taken to minimize our own potential to further the harm they may already have experienced. We take time at the beginning of lectures and presentations to remind our audience that we will be talking about gender violence, acknowledging to them that we are aware some people might find this topic especially confronting. We also invite anyone who does feel distressed by the content of our discussion to talk to us directly, or to contact appropriate support services (the details of which we provide at the start of our presentation). Equally important, we remind everyone how important it is that the space we are in (be it a lecture theatre, conference room, or church) remains a safe space for *everyone*; discussions must therefore be carried out with a sensitivity to others' diverse perspectives and

---

30. Day, "Teaching," 176.

experiences, and a commitment to hold each other's words and testimonies in confidence. What we say in that room stays in that room.

Secondly, we acknowledge that among our audiences, there may also be those who participate in the social structures that sustain gender violence. This can be incredibly challenging, particularly when members of the audience voice rape-supportive or homophobic and transphobic opinions or try to downplay the seriousness of gender violence within both the biblical texts and their own contemporary cultures. We have had people tell us that biblical rape victims must have "deserved" their assault or that the perpetrator of gender violence was somehow "justified" in their actions. This is particularly common when the perpetrator is a biblical "hero" (like David) or even the biblical God himself. Moreover, we have both sat in a biblical studies conference in Aotearoa New Zealand when the mere mention of "same-sex marriage" in the context of biblical theology provoked an outburst of disdainful laughter. At a similar conference, we listened as a colleague began his presentation with a joke about physically assaulting his wife, much to the amusement of many attendees. Trying to retain a level of professionalism while maintaining the safety of our discussion spaces is a fine line to walk. We are committed to calling out cisheteropatriarchal discourses expressed by members of our audience, be they students, colleagues, or members of faith communities. This is surely our responsibility as academic role models and, let's face it, as decent human beings. We feel compelled to remind our audiences that language has enormous power to sustain these violent discourses and to negatively impact the lives of gender violence victims and survivors. These conversations can be difficult, but they are also a learning opportunity, where we remind ourselves and others that the gendered violence evoked in the biblical texts can still have consequences within our own contemporary contexts and communities.

Thirdly, the practices we outlined in our last two points reflect our commitment to our role as critic and conscience—in classrooms, conference rooms, and churches. We need to stress to our audiences that the issue of biblical gender violence *matters*, particularly because ancient sacred texts continue to have power in contemporary communities to sustain violent discourses. We live in a cisnormative, heteronormative, and patriarchal culture and read the Bible within this culture. We want to remind our audiences of this fact and invite them to stand alongside us as critic and conscience within their own academic, cultural, and faith communities. Some of the people we engage with will take what they learn from our discussions back to others—congregants, Bible study groups, youth groups, or simply family and friends. We remind them that their own engagement with biblical texts of terror have the potential to impact other people's views of gender and gender violence.

As Linda Day notes, the students in our classrooms "will be responsible to a wider public, and hence must learn to be aware of how they are either serving or harming others through their methods and results when interpreting the Bible."[31] This is similarly true when it comes to the academic colleagues we encounter in our institutions and at conferences, as well as the congregants in our churches and other faith-based institutions.

Yet, within the classrooms, conference rooms, and churches in Aotearoa New Zealand, conversations about the Bible and gender violence are not always easy to negotiate. We engage with biblical scholarship in a bicultural country, and, situated in Auckland, we are located in one of the most ethnically diverse cities within that country. Our classrooms and conferences reflect this diversity, containing students and colleagues who identify as Māori, Pākehā,[32] Pasifika, and Asian. Some of the people we talk to about biblical texts of terror belong to cultures that embrace traditional gender roles and hierarchies, which normalize and sustain various forms of gender violence. How do we critique such gender violence when these are recognized by some of our students and colleagues as being so closely woven together with their own cultural identities? How do we challenge the unacceptable violence of patriarchy, misogyny, and all forms of intolerance to LGBT communities, while still being sensitive to others' investment in their cultural traditions? To what extent can we invite our audiences to critique the traditional underpinnings of their own cultures, particularly when we ourselves do not belong to these cultures? These are thorny questions, which highlight that issues of colonization and marginalization constantly intersect with discourses of gender violence. We are conscious of the fact that, as educators who self-identify as Pākehā, we always run the risk of "colonizing" our students' and colleagues' own cultural contexts, of prioritizing our Western value systems and ideologies over their own diverse worldviews. At the same time, however, we must always invite them to join us in our quest to each scrutinize our own cultural traditions with integrity and to acknowledge that *all* of our cultures and communities are, to some extent at least, complicit in sustaining the discourses that enable gender violence to flourish.

Another thorny issue we are often confronted with is not unique to Aotearoa New Zealand but is encountered by biblical scholars teaching and researching biblical texts of terror throughout the world. For many of

---

31. Day, "Teaching," 174.

32. We recognize that the term Pākehā conveys a range of meanings for different communities and is used to signify both political and ethnic identities. In this chapter, we draw on one of its more common usages: to refer to inhabitants of New Zealand who are of European descent.

our colleagues and students, the Bible is not only their course "textbook"; it is also their sacred Scripture. This is also true for those we address in church congregations, Bible study groups, and other faith-based organizations. When we invite Christian members of our audience to interrogate its texts and identify the problematic ideologies around gender violence voiced within them, we often encounter resistance or even a refusal to do so. Some find it too threatening to engage with any reading of a text that (in their eyes) challenges its authority or appears to undermine its message of "Good News." They may refuse to discuss, or even consider, the potential for biblical texts of terror to convey "Bad News" to people who have themselves been impacted by gender violence. Instead, they suspend their critical faculties, unwilling to recognize the violence within the text, despite the fact that they would likely acknowledge and condemn the same violence were it to appear in other literary (non-biblical) forms.[33]

Moreover, Christian readers of the Bible (be they students, academics, or otherwise) often resort to performing an impressive display of interpretive gymnastics to sanitize the text and preserve its sacred reputation in which they are so heavily invested. Prophetic re-enactments of spousal abuse are dismissed as "harmless metaphors"; biblical laws that sanction wartime rape are justified as "relatively humanitarian" compared to other ancient Near Eastern legal codes; and biblical heroes such as Abraham and David, who perpetrate unequivocal acts of gendered violence, are excused because they are "doing God's work," playing a vital role in Israel's (and ultimately Christianity's) wider redemptive narrative. Meanwhile, biblical texts that offer a potentially subversive alternative to cisheteronormative discourses—such as the David and Jonathan narratives (1 Sam 19–20; 2 Samuel 1), the book of Ruth, the Samson and Delilah saga (Judges 16), the Judas kiss (Mark 14:43–45), and the eunuch traditions (Isa 56:3–5; Acts 8:27–39)—are typically given very "straight" readings, with their queer potentialities either ignored, ridiculed, or denied.[34]

Yet such exegetical contortions only serve to sustain a vicious cycle of interpretation and affirmation that protects the destructive power of biblical texts of terror. As critic and conscience both in and beyond the biblical studies academy, we therefore have to equip our audiences to consider the capacity of the text to perpetuate gender violence in all its forms. While affirming our respect for *everyone's* faith traditions, we nevertheless reiterate to them the responsibility we all have to ask searching questions about biblical texts. We

---

33. Day, "Teaching," 176.

34. Queer readings of the Bible, however, are certainly possible *and* valuable. For some recent examples, see the various chapters in Hornsby Stone, *Bible Trouble*.

remind them of the power that language—particularly sacred language—has to impact the lives of real people and their experiences of violence. And, most importantly, we offer them a safe and non-judgmental space within which they can interrogate and explore their sacred texts.

In all honesty, sometimes this works and sometimes it doesn't. Some of our students (and the occasional colleague) have told us that they truly appreciate the opportunity to discuss gender violence, which remains such a taboo topic within their own cultures and communities. When they encounter such violence in the biblical narrative, they feel empowered to talk openly about these issues within church and family contexts. As sacred Scripture, the Bible can mitigate strict cultural taboos, offering a point of entry for discussions around contemporary instances of gender violence. The Bible ceases to be an "otherworldly" text that has little relevance to everyday life and becomes instead a means by which social praxis is fostered and enacted. For those who may themselves have been impacted by gender violence, reading texts that evoke the trauma of biblical rape victims like Tamar (2 Samuel 13) and Dinah (Genesis 34) has the potential to be both healing and affirming, as it allows survivors to see something of themselves within these texts—a verification that *their* experiences and narratives ought to be heard and taken seriously within their faith communities. Meanwhile, other readers may be struck afresh by the gendered injustices evoked in some of the biblical traditions. This, in turn, encourages them to think about these injustices in their own culture, to understand gender violence from the victim's perspective, and to critique their own complicity in the perpetuation of a culture where such violence continues to flourish.

Yet at other times, our experiences of talking about biblical gender violence are far less well received. We still encounter those who disengage (be it in the classroom, conference room, or church setting) or become frustrated with the subject matter. Some even project their frustrations against *us*—the bearers of "Bad News"—articulating their hostility in discussions, emails, and their written work (not to mention on social media). We have been accused of "misreading" the biblical texts, of having a "feminist agenda," or being "biased towards LGBTI concerns" in our research and teaching, and of being "anti-Christian" in our approach to scriptural traditions. Such encounters can be demoralizing, distressing, and exhausting—both for ourselves and for those students and colleagues who feel as passionate as we do about our academic responsibilities as critic and conscience. At the end of the day, though, these criticisms only serve to reinforce for us the importance of persisting—and persisting and persisting—with these tough conversations in Aotearoa New Zealand and beyond.

Bibliography

Adams, Carol J. "'I Just Raped My Wife! What Are You Going to Do About It, Pastor?' The Church and Sexual Violence." In *Transforming A Rape Culture*, edited by Emilie Buchwald et al., 57–86. Minneapolis: Milkweed, 1993.

Adams, Carol J., and Marie M. Fortune, eds. *Violence Against Women and Children: A Christian Theological Sourcebook*. New York: Continuum, 1998.

Althaus-Reid, Marcella. *Indecent Theology: Theological Perversions in Sex, Gender and Politics*. London: Routledge, 2000.

Alvear, Rocío Figueroa, and David Tombs. *Listening to Male Survivors of Church Sexual Abuse: Voices from Survivors of Sodalicio Abuses in Peru*. Dunedin: Centre for Theology and Public Issues, University of Otago, 2016.

Anand, Sangeeta. "Unsafe Haven." *Ms. Magazine*, Spring Issue 2009.

Blyth, Caroline. *The Narrative of Rape in Genesis 34: Interpreting Dinah's Silence*. Oxford: Oxford University Press, 2010.

Burnett, Ann. "Rape Culture." In *Wiley Blackwell Encyclopedia of Gender and Sexuality Studies*, edited by Angela Wong et al., 1–5. Singapore: John Wiley & Sons, 2016.

Daly, Mary. *Beyond God the Father: Toward a Philosophy of Women's Liberation*. Boston: Beacon, 1973.

Day, Linda. "Teaching the Prophetic Marriage Metaphor Texts." *Teaching Theology and Religion* 2/3 (1999) 173–79.

Fortune, Marie M. "Faith Is Fundamental to Ending Domestic Terror." *Women's Rights Law Reporter* 33 (2012) 463–70.

———. *Sexual Violence: The Unmentionable Sin*. Cleveland: Pilgrim, 1983.

Haddad, Mimi. "Dr. Catherine Clark Kroeger: An Evangelical Legacy." *Priscilla Papers* 25/3 (2011) 4–9.

Hare, David. "LGBT Affirmation and Identity in Christian Teachings and Church Communities." In *Rape Culture, Gender Violence, and Religion: Interdisciplinary Perspectives*, edited by Caroline Blyth et al., 135–44. New York: Palgrave Macmillan, 2018.

Henderson-Merrygold, Jo. "Queer(y)ing the Epistemic Violence of Christian Gender Discourses." In *Rape Culture, Gender Violence, and Religion: Christian Perspectives*, edited by Caroline Blyth, 97–117. New York: Palgrave Macmillan, 2018.

Hohou Te Rongo Kahukura—Outing Violence. "Reports and Findings." Accessed January 31, 2019, http://www.kahukura.co.nz/uncategorized/reportandfindings/

Hornsby, Teresa J., and Ken Stone, eds. *Bible Trouble: Queer Reading at the Boundaries of Biblical Scholarship*. Atlanta: Society of Biblical Literature, 2011.

Human Rights Campaign. "Violence Against the Transgender Community in 2017." Accessed January 23, 2019, https://www.hrc.org/resources/violence-against-the-transgender-community-in-2017

McPhillips, Kathleen. "The Royal Commission Investigates Child Sexual Abuse: Uncovering Cultures of Sexual Violence in the Catholic Church." In *Rape Culture, Gender Violence, and Religion: Interdisciplinary Perspectives*, edited by Caroline Blyth et al., 53–71. New York: Palgrave Macmillan, 2018.

Marsden, Daphne. "The Church's Contribution to Domestic Violence: Submission, Headship, and Patriarchy." In *Rape Culture, Gender Violence, and Religion: Christian Perspectives*, edited by Caroline Blyth et al., 73–95. New York: Palgrave Macmillan, 2018.

Nason-Clark, Nancy. "Shattered Silence or Holy Hush: Emerging Definitions of Violence Against Women," *Journal of Family Ministry* 13/1 (1999) 39–56.

———. *The Battered Wife: How Christians Confront Family Violence*. Louisville: Westminster John Knox, 1997.

New Zealand Human Rights Commission. "Women's Rights in New Zealand." June 11, 2018, 3. https://tbinternet.ohchr.org/Treaties/CEDAW/Shared%20Documents/NZL/INT_CEDAW_IFN_NZL_31478_E.pdf

OECD. "Violence against Women." Accessed January 11, 2019. https://data.oecd.org/inequality/violence-against-women.htm.

Rape Prevention Education. "Statistics: Sexual Violence in Aotearoa New Zealand." Accessed January 31, 2019. http://rpe.co.nz/information/statistics/

Scholz, Susanne. "'Back Then It Was Legal': The Epistemological Imbalance in Readings of Biblical and Ancient Near Eastern Rape Legislation." *Bible and Critical Theory* 1/4 (2005) 1–22.

Schüssler Fiorenza, Elisabeth. *Wisdom Ways: Introducing Feminist Biblical Interpretation*. Maryknoll, NY: Orbis, 2001.

Schweickart, Patrocinio P. "Reading Ourselves: Toward a Feminist Theory of Reading." In *Feminisms: An Anthology of Literary Theory and Criticism*, edited by Robyn R. Warhol and Diane Price Herndl, 609–34. New Brunswick: Rutgers University Press, 1993.

Scott, Emily M. D. "The Bible's #MeToo Problem." *New York Times*. June 16, 2018. https://www.nytimes.com/2018/06/16/opinion/sunday/women-the-bible-metoo.html

Sneed, Roger A. *Representations of Homosexuality: Black Liberation Theology and Cultural Criticism. Black Religion/Womanist Thought/Social Justice*. New York: Palgrave Macmillan, 2010.

Tearfund. "Sexual and Gender Based Violence." https://learn.tearfund.org/en/themes/sexual_and_gender-based_violence/

TOAH-NNEST Good Practice. "Crisis Support Services for Survivors (Mainstream Services)." Accessed January 31, 2019. http://www.communityresearch.org.nz/wp-content/uploads/formidable/Good-Practice-Responding-to-Sexual-Violence-Crisis-Support-Services-2016-with-Reports.pdf

Tuhiwai Smith, Linda. *Decolonizing Methodologies: Research and Indigenous Peoples*. Dunedin: University of Otago Press, 1999.

United Nations General Assembly. "Discriminatory Laws and Practices and Acts of Violence against Individuals Based on Their Sexual Orientation and Gender Identity." HRC Res 17/19, 19th sess., Agenda Items 2, 8, UN Doc A/HRC19/41, November 17, 2011. http://www2.ohchr.org/english/bodies/hrcouncil/docs/19session/A.HRC.19.41_English.pdf

United Nations Population Fund. *UNFPA Engagement in Ending Gender-Based Violence*. New York: United Nations Population Fund, 2016. http://www.unfpa.org/sites/default/files/resource-pdf/UNFPA_Brochures_on_GBV_Prevention_and_response.pdf

UN Women. "Facts and Figures: Ending Violence against Women." Accessed January 11, 2017. http://www.unwomen.org/en/what-we-do/ending-violence-against-women/facts-and-figures

Vorster, Johannes N. "The Queering of Biblical Discourse." *Scriptura* 111, no. 3 (2012) 602–20.

Winn, Harriet. "Thursdays in Black: Localized Responses to Rape Culture and Gender Violence in Aotearoa New Zealand." In *Rape Culture, Gender Violence, and Religion: Interdisciplinary Perspectives*, edited by Caroline Blyth et al., 51–70. New York: Palgrave Macmillan, 2018.

Žižek, Slavoj. *Violence: Six Sideways Reflections*. London: Profile, 2008.

13

Holy Love: Seeking a Unified Theology in a Divided Church

Peter Carrell

I FIRST MET TIM when I was about twelve years old and he was about eighteen years old. Our paths did not cross much for the eighteen years that followed, until we were both working on doctorates, Tim in Edinburgh and me in Durham, and reconnected through our mutual friends, Derek and Lea Tovey, who lived in Durham. Subsequently, back in Aotearoa New Zealand, our paths have crossed many times, most often in relation to academic and ecclesiastical adventures. One of these, the General Synod of the Anglican Church in Aotearoa, New Zealand, and Polynesia (ACANZP), which met in May 2018 in New Plymouth, is the genesis of this essay.

In summary, at our General Synod we legislated for permission to be given for blessing same-sex civil marriages or civil unions and for tolerance for those who would teach for or against such blessings being permitted.[1] One general observation before, during, and after the Synod concerned an alleged lack of theological work underpinning these legislative changes to the polity of ACANZP. In the course of the Synod, both Tim and I spoke to this charge, offering, albeit briefly and extempore, two theological approaches to the changes being debated.

---

1. A report on the actual legislative changes made (five in total) is Anglican Taonga, "Yes to Blessings."

I observed that those seeking permissive change and those seeking to prohibit change were both reading Scripture. Focusing on Johannine theologies of love, on one side was a reading that proceeded from 1 John with its talk of God's love in relation to human love (especially in chapter 4). This, I said, could be summed up as "where love is, there is God."[2] Such love, so this side argues, may be blessed. On the other side were the words, "If you love me, you will keep my commandments" (John 14:15). Understanding "commandments" to include the commandments of Moses not set aside by Jesus, keeping the commandments of Jesus does not permit same-sex sexual intercourse, in any context or era; thus, logically, so this side argues, no blessings can be permitted.[3] Crudely put, there is a tension between "love" and "holiness." We had not yet found, I proposed to the synod, a unifying theology of "holy love."[4] We may never find such a unifying theology, but that should not be for want of trying. Here I offer some possibilities for how such a theology might develop through recognition of the role justice plays in the way we interpret holy commandments.

Holy Commandments?

The law of Moses sets out the permissions and prohibitions which constrain Israel in the direction of holiness, of being a holy nation. As a holy nation, Israel demonstrates both that she is not like other nations and that the character of YHWH as the holy God of Israel is not like the gods of other nations (e.g., Exod 19:1–6; Lev 11:44–45; 18:1–5; 19:2; 20:7) . Not least, the Mosaic law is concerned with sexual holiness (e.g., Leviticus 18). On some matters what the law says has (more or less) held sway in Judaism, in Christianity, and in cultures whose foundations have strong Judeo-Christian influence. Leviticus 18:6–18, for example, setting out prohibitions of kinship relationships, remains applicable today. Bestiality (Lev 18:23) remains prohibited. That is, the requirements for Israel to be sexually holy (i.e., distinguished from the nations roundabout them (18:24) with respect to, for instance,

---

2. These words are not found in any Johannine writing. They are the title of a short story by Leo Tolstoy and the first line of the famous hymn, *Ubi Caritas: Ubi caritas et amor, Deus ibi est* (Where charity and love are, there is God).

3. A longer explanation could note that the teaching of Jesus, while never specifically citing same-sex questions and issues, intensified the teaching of Moses on marriage and divorce, upheld the Law of Moses (except with respect to food and hand-washing rules), and is consistent with the Pauline approach to matters of same-sex relationships found in Romans 1 and 1 Corinthians 6.

4. Carrell, "Slow start. Big finish."

incest and bestiality, is, thousands of years later, a requirement across many nations and cultures for good behavior by citizens.

But there are other matters where Mosaic law no longer has sway. The well-known prohibition in Lev 18:22 concerning sexual intercourse between men is increasingly not upheld in legal jurisdictions in the Western world. The law of Moses permits (or at least tolerates) polygamy (e.g., Deut 21:15–17). In all cultures founded on Judeo-Christianity (with a few notable exceptions such as an extreme form of Mormonism and a bizarre commendation by Luther and Melanchthon to Philip of Hesse that he could take a second wife),[5] monogamy is normative, and that normativity is upheld by church and state in the Judeo-Christian world.

In that same chapter of Deuteronomy, 21:10–14, rules are set down for conduct when captives are taken in the midst of war and an attractive captive woman catches the eye of an Israelite man. First, the man is permitted to "take her as your wife" (v. 11). Secondly, the husband-to-be must provide for the new wife to be cleaned up and to have a statutory period of mourning for her parents (vv. 12–13a). Then, thirdly, the new marriage may be consummated (v. 13b). There is no indication whether this is with or without the consent of the woman. Finally, if the new wife is subsequently found to be unsatisfactory, she is to be let go of, but in a respectful manner, and treating her as a slave able to be sold as a commodity is expressly forbidden (v. 14). Terrible treatment of women in wars continues to be a tragic feature of human history, but no culture founded on Judeo-Christianity maintains these rules.

We may also note, relevant to the matter of the Mosaic law holding sway or not among twenty-first-century readers of the Scriptures, that even where we accept the ongoing relevance and applicability of the law, we do not accept what the law prescribes for punishments. Our abhorrence of bestiality is no longer accompanied by the desire to put offenders to death (Lev 20:15). There is no debate about why we apply Lev 18:23 but not Lev 20:15.

In these kinds of instances, we recognize that the teaching of Jesus that the Mosaic law is to be upheld (Matt 5:17–20) cannot be taken as a straightforward endorsement of everything in that law. Indeed, we note that when pressed by a specific issue being raised, Jesus set aside some laws, notably with respect to food (Mark 7:1–23), but also with respect to punishment for adultery (John 7:53—8:11). By extension, we are likely to conclude that if Jesus had been asked about stoning a rebellious son (Deut 21:18–21) he would have sided with the son and not the judicial community that those verses charge with carrying out the punishment. Yet this kind of presumptive reading is at variance with Matt 5:17–20 in its plain sense.

---

5. Massing, *Fatal Discord*, 763.

For the present enquiry, seeking a unifying theology of holy love, these kinds of considerations, along with investigation of a passage such as Deut 21:10–21, highlight problems with any simple notion of holy commandments (for instance, that we know what they are and we need have no debates about what they are). Might such investigation yield a way forward towards a theology of holy love that unifies a church torn with tension between holiness and love? Before we turn to that question, I make a general observation about the regulation of sexual desire.

On the Regulation of Sexual Desire and its Fulfilment

The general, consistent approach of Scripture towards sexual desire and its fulfilment is to regulate. Moses lays down general, abiding rules which we follow today in all situations (e.g., prohibiting adultery) or specific, situation-bound rules (such as our example above regarding an attractive captive woman). Proverbs strenuously warns, with great wisdom, against dallying in the company of wayward women. Prophets readily invoke adultery as a metaphor for wayward Israel. Jesus sternly and intensively equates lust with adultery. This regulatory approach occurred in contexts in which surrounding nations and cultures were more tolerant, at least with respect to male sexual desire, accepting that its fulfilment could take place inside and outside of marriage, both legally and religiously, offering temple prostitution as a no-fault zone for indulgence. That is, according to Scripture, both Israel and the early church shared common ground in, first, advancing rules and guidance that confined sexual intercourse to marriage between a man and a woman, and, secondly, eschewing any form of temple prostitution. The latter was especially forbidden because it involved idolatry.[6]

With respect to the decision of the ACANZP General Synod in 2018 to permit blessings of civil marriages and civil unions, I observe that this was a regulatory decision with respect to sexual desire and its fulfilment. What may be blessed is not "relationships" or "lifestyle" in some general sense but regulated relationships, bound by the rule of civic law.

---

6. Pertinent are Mark 7:17–23; Rom 1:18–32; 1 Cor 5:1–13; 6:9–20; 10:1–9.

Deuteronomy 21:10–14; 15–17; 18–21: Ancient and Modern Approaches to Holy Commandments

Deuteronomy presents commandments of God that continue to set out how Israel is to live in a holy manner. The seriousness of the commandments is in no doubt by the time we get to Deuteronomy 28: obedience leads to blessing, disobedience yields curses. Obeying holy commandments is not optional for Israel. Yet the three topics dealt with by 21:10–21, captive women, polygamy, and rebellious sons, do not sit easily in modern Christian contexts. The commandments permit forced marriage (i.e., rape), polygamy, and execution of a rebellious son. Yet we can also recognize that these commandments represent a community, in its ancient context, addressing certain issues in a responsible manner that invokes an understanding of justice according to its time and context.[7]

Captive Women (Deut 21:10–14)

Rather than a free-for-all approach by Israelite men to women captured in war, this law constrains men to offer a captive woman dignity (vv. 12–13), including respect for her mourning (or for the possibility that she might be pregnant, though we observe that she mourns her parents and not her husband) before she becomes his wife (v. 13). Then, if the captive wife is unsatisfactory, she is not to be enslaved (v. 14). Thus, a captured non-Israelite woman is provided with legal status via Israelite law.[8]

Well over two millennia later, our reading of this law cannot avoid noting that it nevertheless offers no opportunity for consent by the woman and thus is a law supporting rape (since consummation is the means by which the new marriage is established). Nevertheless, we can also read this law as establishing a tendency in which Israel's holy commandments include laws which address contemporary issues. In this tendency, Israel is constrained in the

---

7. Levinson, *Legal Innovation*, 3, engages with the relationship between Deuteronomy 12–26 and the Covenant Code (Exod 20:22—23:33) and argues that "Deuteronomy represents a radical revision of the Covenant Code. The authors of Deuteronomy sought to implement a far-reaching transformation of religion, law and social structure that was essentially without cultural precedent. They therefore turned to the earlier code in order to anchor their departure from legal convention in the very textual heritage from which they cut themselves free in substantive terms." That is, what is going on in Deuteronomy is both subtle and complicated in respect to Israel's prior Scriptures and its contemporary situation. This is not without analogy to the situation of churches in the twenty-first century innovating with the aid of ancient Scriptures.

8. See, for instance, Bernard M. Levinson's notes on Deuteronomy in Coogan et al., *The New Oxford Annotated Bible*, 284–85.

direction of respect for outsiders, expressed through provision of legal status for such persons. Thus, Israel shows a degree of recognition of the importance of just treatment for people who previously had no legal rights.

We can further argue that today's refusal to follow this commandment, because of new, relatively recent reappraisal of the rights of women, even when captured in battle, is an extension of a trajectory inherent within Deut 21:10–14. Today, justice requires consent by a woman before she becomes a wife, and it requires that a woman has the same opportunity to be dissatisfied with her husband and to let him go free as he has according to v. 14. To treat a captive wife justly is an intention of the ancient text, but this understanding of justice for women leaves much to be desired in our modern age. To refuse to follow the ancient text in the modern world is to share with the text an intention to act justly, while bringing to the text a fuller understanding of justice for women as well as men.[9]

That we might approach the text in such a manner today also involves acknowledgment of the voice of the outsider to the community. The Israelite man is addressed in the text and the non-Israelite captive woman is granted a degree of legal respect, but her voice is not asked for. Neither the voice of her consent to be married nor the voice of her contribution to the enactment of this law is heard. Today we accept that justice—a fuller understanding of justice than that held by those who composed and edited Deuteronomy—extends not only to seeking the voice of consent but also to seeking the view of the outsider in the formation of law which applies to the outsider.

Finally, I observe that this law acknowledges the reality of physical attraction and sexual desire. The law seeks to regulate what happens when an Israelite man is captured by desire for a beautiful woman. The law does not counsel celibacy or repression of the desire. Noting the treatment of polygamy that follows in 21:15–17, we observe that the law does not constrain such desire in the case of a man who is already married. It offers no prohibition of taking the captive woman as a new, additional wife. This law

9. MacIntyre, *Whose Justice?*, argues from historical examples such as Aristotle, Augustine, Aquinas, and Hume, that our understanding of justice draws on our prior understanding of practical reason, that is, our underlying philosophy or worldview. Here I suggest that an enlarged understanding of justice today indeed draws on aspects of modern life in which (say) men and women are understood to have equal rights. But similar considerations arise when we go back to foundational parts of Scripture, for example, back to understanding that when God made humanity, God made us male and female without predetermined inferiority of one to the other. Similarly, an approach to the justice of punishment that is extremely diffident about corporal let alone capital punishment for wrongdoing is coherent with a so-called progressive approach to education, parenting, and crime but it is also an approach consistent with respecting human dignity because each person is made in the image of God, to say nothing of an approach that asks what a merciful God might do in given situations.

sees marriage—the consummation of desire—as the way to deal with the desire, albeit via an understanding of marriage in which the husband fulfils his desire whether or not the wife desires him, and a marriage in which, when he loses desire, the husband may jettison the wife.

Polygamy (Deut 21:15–19)

Here there is an intention to also deal, to a degree, with potential injustice in a polygamous marriage, while failing to deal with the injustice of polygamy itself. The injustice, on the face of it, is that a son might be disinherited on the basis of prejudice against his mother as the unloved of two wives. But a woman who can be divorced (Deut 24:1–2) and who has a son with no inheritance is a woman potentially bound into poverty for the remainder of her life. The law here offers the prospect of twofold justice: the firstborn son of the husband of the unloved and loved wives is treated properly, and his mother is protected, should being unloved translate into being divorced.

Again, we see a community through its teaching of the law engaging with a contemporary issue, bringing to bear on it an understanding of justice. If today we eschew the possibility of polygamy being legalized, we are extending the application of a fuller understanding of justice to polygamy, but this time denying that polygamy itself can be just.

Rebellious Sons (21:18–21)

If we accept that rebellion is a terrible thing, and the rebellion of a gluttonous and drunkard son a greater degree of terribleness, under what circumstances would parents in the twenty-first century commit such a son to trial, knowing that their own evidence would be sufficient to convict and for the death penalty to be automatically invoked? It is difficult to think of those circumstances. Actually, we cannot find any such circumstance in the Old Testament.[10]

As modern readers, why do we not promote this "holy commandment"? Is the instruction to stone such a son not a holy commandment from God and should we not obey it?[11] Again, it looks like modern readers

---

10. McConville, *Deuteronomy*, 331, "there is no evidence of such measures actually having been taken in the OT." So also Christensen, who likewise notes that "it is safe to conclude that the primary purpose of this law was pedagogical—that 'all Israel shall hear and fear' (v21)." Christensen, *Deuteronomy 21:10—34:12*, 484.

11. There is an interesting reflection to be made if a response were advanced such as "this was not enacted then and so need not be enacted now." There is no instance in the

have brought considerations of justice to the text and allowed those considerations to override the text. Such considerations, unlike our first two passages, are not extensions of an application of justice within the text itself. These considerations include whether the punishment fits the crime and whether the community can find another, less drastic way to purge itself of such evil.

In short, considering three instances of holy commandments in Deut 21:1–21, we have found none of the three is obeyed in today's world, and the reason why this is so lies in considerations of a fuller understanding of justice being brought to the situations in life which these commandments address.

Thus, Christian communities of faith today are taking a different approach to matters addressed by some ancient holy commandments. In doing so, they are treating holy commandments as commandments that are nevertheless subject to considerations of justice—where justice is understood in an enlarged manner compared with ancient times.

The vexed question, then and now, of divorce and remarriage also involves Christian communities addressing contemporary matters for which there are ancient holy commandments. Considerations of justice attend these discussions also. We begin with Christian communities in the time of Jesus and Paul.

Accommodation: Addressing Community Issues with Respect to Marriage and Divorce

When Jesus responded to questions about divorce and remarriage with an invocation of relevant passages from the first chapter of Israel's Scriptures, he left his followers in no doubt that God's enduring intention and ideal for the sexual life, building on narratives of creation in Genesis 1–2, was that a man and a woman should enter into marriage as a consummated ("one flesh"), permanent, exclusive, monogamous covenant. Jesus underlined what Israel's story of the creation of man and woman itself said. An alternative ideal was celibacy (Matt 19:10–12; cf. 1 Corinthians 7, which, among other things, comments favorably on celibacy).[12]

Further, there is also no doubt that Jesus' response sets out the standard for the kingdom of God—for followers of Jesus not only to aspire to but also to achieve. On this standard, Matt 19:5 agrees with Mark 10:6–9 that marriage is a unity not to be divided. On the matter that divorce followed

---

OT of any same-sex couple being punished for disobedience of Lev 18:22.

12. See, e.g., Morris, *Matthew*, 478–86.

by remarriage is adultery, Matt 5:32/19:9 agrees with Mark 10:11–12, which agrees with Luke 16:18. Paul, in 1 Cor 7:10–11, does not talk about remarriage being adultery, but reports the Lord's command on divorce being a prohibition of divorce.

Yet we can talk about the "Matthean exception" (Matt 5:32/19:9) and the "Pauline exception" (1 Cor 7:12–16). In the former, some kind of sexual infidelity—adultery or entering into a forbidden marriage—may be reason for divorce, and for remarriage after divorce, not being reckoned as adultery. In the latter, a believer divorced by an unbelieving spouse may be free to remarry.

One observation we can make about Jesus' general antipathy to divorce and remarriage (whether we deem that he himself gave the Matthean exception or whether its origins lies in the Matthean community) is that he was shifting the context for divorce away from male domination. Divorce in the Judaism of Jesus' day was a male privilege to initiate. By speaking against divorce, Jesus was speaking up for dignity and just treatment for females.

In a different context, one where women could initiate divorce, according to Roman law, Paul offers another exception which, in its own way, involves considerations of justice. Is it fair that a spouse divorced solely on the grounds of their faith in Christ is then bound never to enjoy marriage again? Paul thinks not and proposes that such a spouse is "not bound," i.e., is free to remarry (1 Cor 7:15).[13]

Christian churches remain divided on the matter of divorce and remarriage, with different approaches found across Roman, Eastern, and Protestant/Pentecostal churches, but with all churches facing issues concerning marriage that are not neatly covered by the Matthean and Pauline exceptions. May a woman divorce her unrepentant abusive husband? (Should she trust her abusive husband when he says he repents?) Is an addiction by a spouse to pornography or to gambling an "exception" similar to the two biblical exceptions? May we talk about the "death" of a marriage and thus proceed to accept divorce as a complete end of a marriage so that a new marriage does not invoke talk of "adultery" relative to a still-living former spouse? Such issues raise searching questions about what the church

---

13. Thiselton, *Corinthians*, 523, "in Jewish, Greek and Roman law a husband could divorce his wife for a variety of reasons, and in Greek and Roman law divorce could be initiated freely from either side." Whether "not bound" = "free to remarry" is a matter of contention among commentators, but here I am simply giving the general sense of the Pauline exception, that divorce is generally not permitted because marriage is indissoluble (so Christians ought not to divorce each other, 1 Cor 7:10–11), but there is an exception to the general rule when an unbelieving spouse initiates divorce. Instone-Brewer, *Divorce and Remarriage*, 201, argues that "not bound" does mean freedom to remarry.

understands to be God's justice and mercy in situations that involve pain, loss, and distress. Where churches find a way to affirm through liturgy a new marriage after divorce, there is a recognition, shared by both Deut 21:11 and 1 Cor 7:9, that sexual attraction and sexual desire is a basic, common, motivating human experience towards forming companionship and relationships of mutual support (cf. Gen 2:18–20).

1 Corinthians 7:9 is a blunt, carnally respectful acknowledgement that the strength of sexual desire is better met through marriage (and thus fulfilment of that desire) than "burning", which equates to failed (at worst) or deeply frustrating (at best) attempts at self-control. The general "desire" or ambition of Paul for his Corinthian readers is that they should be like him—a self-controlled, celibate, mission-focused, freed-from-the-cares-of-the-world servant of Christ (7:7, 8, 40). That is the better way. But the lesser way, marriage, is no sin (7:8–9, 28, 36–38). Giving way to sexual desire by marrying is clearly the right thing to do, and giving way to it by indulging in "sexual immorality" is the wrong thing (7:1–2; also chapters 5–6).

That is, the church, from the first century AD Matthean and Pauline exceptions through to the exceptions of our day, has engaged the challenge of accommodating the ideal of marriage in the teaching of Jesus with the reality of human desire to love and to be loved.

Addressing a Community Issue in the Twenty-First Century: Homosexuality and Formal Unions of Same-Sex Couples

When Paul wrote about homosexuality in Romans 1, and referenced homosexuality in 1 Cor 6:9–10 and 1 Tim 1:10, he wrote in a milieu in which men consorting sexually with men and women with women was well-known, and within Greco-Roman communities, tolerated.[14] Thus the few texts in the New Testament that address homosexuality address a contemporary issue. In 1 Cor 6:11, Paul can talk about those who have escaped the grip of behavior that prohibited entry to the kingdom of God. There is no reason to exclude some form of homosexual activity from the implied list of things from which some of Paul's readers have been set free.[15]

---

14. See, e.g., Plato's *Symposium*.

15. There is much debate over the precise meaning of the Greek words μαλακοὶ and ἀρσενοκοῖται in 1 Cor. 6:9 (amply covered in Thiselton, *Corinthians*, 440–54), but it is beyond debate that some form of same-sex sexual activity between men is condemned here.

But the address of Paul does not encompass two aspects of homosexuality that modern life is engaged with. And by "modern life" I mean to include people talking openly and frankly about their sexual orientation and families lovingly accepting sons and daughters, nephews and nieces as gay or lesbian—that is, families lovingly accepting that some members of their family are incapable of loving a person of the opposite sex deeply, sexually, committedly in the usual way of marriage between a man and a woman. Whatever the science of homosexuality says, wherever certain contemporary cultural tides are flowing, the openness and frankness of modern life mean that people are able to be honest to themselves as well as to those whom they love and trust and make no pretense that their own sexual desire can be fulfilled through marrying a person of the opposite sex.

The first aspect of homosexuality not addressed by Paul is recognition that homosexual orientation (sexual desire for a person of the same sex, not for a person of the opposite sex) is permanent, stable, and dominant in gay and lesbian persons. There is no discussion anywhere within Scripture whether this makes any difference to how we read texts such as Lev 18:22, Rom 1:18–32, or 1 Cor 6:9–10. While we may have significant amounts of scriptural presumption that gay and lesbian persons, because constitutionally unable to marry in the usual way, must therefore be permanently celibate, there nevertheless is zero address in Scripture of what is reasonable expectation of a gay or lesbian person with respect to fulfilment of sexual desire.

The second aspect of homosexuality not addressed by Paul is the situation in which an increasing number of countries around the world are making legal provision for same-sex couples to marry.[16] Thus, churches in these countries are finding within their congregations that they have couples who are legally married yet uncertain in what "state" they are viewed by the church with which they associate. Are they sinners? Are they blessed by God for making the commitment they have made to each other? Is their state somewhat indeterminate because no one wishes to condemn them and no one is available to bless them (i.e., declare God's blessing on them)? What does it mean for the congregation to love and to accept this couple? Notably, some congregations are in "crisis" over such questions, because it turns out that congregations cannot agree on answers to them.

While some in a congregation may understand Paul to provide ample guidance on these two aspects, others may wonder what a modern-day Paul, offering a 1 Corinthians 7 style and length of exposition on the matter, would have to say. In particular, what would Paul's "better to marry than burn"

16. Note, incidentally, that ACANZP covers multiple jurisdictions across the South Pacific, only one of which, New Zealand, has approved civil marriage of same-sex couples.

response to homosexual sexual desire be? And, what would Paul say to Christian families who accept their partnered gay or lesbian family members and wonder why the church cannot also accept them? Would Paul—sophisticated, sensitive, realistic about sexual desire in 1 Corinthians 7—simply condemn these Christian families because they are (frankly) wrong, and, worse, spiritually dangerous (because misleading their loved ones)?

Critical in such consideration is the question whether or not churches accept that homosexuality is intrinsic to human life through all human history, from the creation itself. This question is a matter for another essay, but it would be unfair not to make reference to it here. As long as homosexuality is understood as a result of the fall of humanity into sin (Genesis 3), it is inherently likely that Christian thinking on homosexuality will understand it through a lens of "sin." In turn, it is likely that application of that lens to texts that prohibit or condemn sexual activity between men or between women will be in a manner that conserves prohibitions and condemnations (albeit modified by removal of any talk of capital punishment).[17] In application of such a lens, it is likely that such texts will be read straightforwardly in their plain sense rather than read with the possibility that a new understanding of homosexuality raises the question of an enlarged understanding of justice (what is fair for persons relative to their life circumstances) and thus a different lens to "sin"—a lens of justice.

The discussion above, on Deut 21:10–21 and on NT texts concerning divorce, remarriage, and sexual desire, points towards the possibility of re-reading prohibitive texts concerning homosexuality with a lens of justice. The larger ecclesiastical question is whether a new reading with respect to justice could unite congregations; the narrower exegetical question is whether a new reading of, for instance, Lev 18:22 or 1 Cor 6:9–10, is plausible, offering some consistency with readings proposed above for Deut 21:10–21.

First, is it fair to expect celibacy of a minority of persons (who are otherwise capable of entering into a civil marriage, that is, into a permanent, covenanted, exclusive, loving partnership) when that is not expected of the majority of persons? Conversely, note that raising such a question of fairness need not imply any diminishment of respect and honor for those who choose celibacy, in line with what both Jesus and Paul commended, in the latter case, as a "better way."

Secondly, is it just to re-read Jesus and Paul on divorce and remarriage in modern times, extending the list of "exceptions," while refusing to reread Moses and Paul on same-sex sexual relationships? Note that both re-readings

17. In the week in which I am completing writing of this chapter, news has been broadcast of Brunei, a state not far from New Zealand, instituting the death penalty, according to Sharia Law, for homosexuality and for adultery.

can be driven by similar concerns to determine appropriate Christian regulation of sexual desire. Neither re-reading has anything to do with justifying current Western tolerance for casual sexual relationships.

Thirdly, is it just to reject commandments such as found in Deut 21:10–21 in favor of an enlarged understanding of justice while continuing to resist applying an enlarged understanding of justice to a text such as Lev 18:22? If some holy commandments may be questioned without fear of diminishing our general commitment to live holy lives (so that Israel is a holy nation, so that the kingdom of God is populated by God's holy people), might we not question all holy commandments through the lens of justice? One role of all commandments of God is to enable just dealings between people.

Fourthly, there is a further aspect of Lev 18:22 we could consider. Milgrom, in his commentary, argues that the theme of the prohibitions in Leviticus 18 is "procreation" and this is why, contrary to surrounding cultures, Lev 18:22, prohibits "all acts of sodomy . . . whether performed by richer or poorer, higher or lower stations, citizen or alien."[18] No such act can lead to progeny. Milgrom's thesis is arguable; for instance, is Molek sacrifice forbidden simply because it is destruction of progeny? But it does make a point that if the purpose of sex in biblical discourse is primarily procreation, then in an age in which procreation is both constrained in most marriages through regular use of contraception,[19] and not uniformly required of all marriages in a massively populated world, is it just to maintain this ancient prohibition?

Finally, fifthly, taking up an observation made above about a fuller understanding of justice with respect to the captive woman in Deut 21:10–14, will consideration of justice grant a role to the voice of lesbian and gay Christians within their congregations? Are they to be silent (like the captive woman), or is their voice a welcome contribution to the enactment of congregational determination of what might be affirmed and blessed within its life? Determination, for instance, as the situation of members is considered, whether in a situation of divorce and anticipation of a new marriage or of civil marriage and seeking the blessing of the presbyter/minister.

---

18. Milgrom, *Leviticus*, 1566 (citation), 1567 (argument from procreation).

19. I include both natural and artificial methods of contraception in this assessment of a world in which many families find ways and means to have far fewer children than our great grandparents managed to have!

Conclusion

In other words, considerations of how justice influences our reading of texts such as Deut 21:10–21, and familiar texts in the NT on divorce and remarriage, raises the question whether we might draw on conceptions of fairness and on precedents for finding accommodations to offer a way for congregations to relate with similar fairness and accommodation to their gay and lesbian members.

The key to unity in such congregations could then turn on a shared recognition of the importance of extending fairness to all church members and on a common commitment to finding accommodation for all. That this might not be a pragmatic exercise but a genuine working out of a theology of holy love would then draw on recognition that holy commandments may be subject to considerations of justice, and that affirmation of love, including sexual love, in Christian contexts informed by Holy Scripture, includes determining appropriate regulation of sexual desire, both heterosexual and homosexual desire.

There would be much to work out about our shared understanding of Scripture. Would such a congregation be open to recognizing, with Levinson, that innovation anchored in Scripture is possible, because such innovation is itself a feature of Scripture?[20] Could such a congregation recognize ways in which, within both Old and New Testament, innovation anchored in Scripture occurs?[21]

Bibliography

Anglican Taonga. "Yes to Blessings." Accessed April 1, 2019. http://www.anglicantaonga.org.nz/news/general_synod/yes

Carrell, Peter. "Slow start. Big finish." Anglican Taonga. Accessed December 26, 2018, http://www.anglicantaonga.org.nz/news/general_synod/tuesday

Christensen, Duane. *Deuteronomy 21:10—34:12*. WBC 6B. Nashville: Thomas Nelson, 2002.

---

20. See n. 7 above.

21. I am thinking, for example, of the relationship of John's Gospel to the Synoptic Gospels, to say nothing of the Matthean and Pauline exceptions in relation to Jesus' own teaching. The former is relevant here because, intriguingly, John's Gospel has no teaching on divorce and remarriage but does include the enigmatic story of the Samaritan woman Jesus encounters at a well. This woman has had five husbands, lives with a sixth, and becomes an apostle of the gospel (John 4:16–42). Does John, very late in the first century AD, shift debate over divorce and possible exceptions towards God's pneumatic affirmation of a believer, expressed through that Spirit-empowered believer's availability for gospel ministry?

Coogan, Michael D., et al., eds. *The New Oxford Annotated Bible: New Revised Standard Version.* 5th ed., fully revised and expanded. New York: Oxford University Press, 2018.

Instone-Brewer, David. *Divorce and Remarriage in the Bible: The Social and Literary Context.* Grand Rapids: Eerdmans, 2002.

Levinson, Bernard M. *Deuteronomy and the Hermeneutics of Legal Innovation.* New York: Oxford University Press, 1997.

McConville, J. Gordon. *Deuteronomy.* AOTC 5. Leicester: Apollos, 2002.

MacIntyre, Alasdair. *Whose Justice? Which Rationality?* London: Duckworth, 1988.

Massing, Michael. *Fatal Discord: Erasmus, Luther and the Fight for the Western Mind.* New York: HarperCollins, 2018.

Milgrom, Jacob. *Leviticus 17–22: A New Translation with Introduction and Commentary.* AB 3A. New York: Doubleday, 2000.

Morris, Leon. *The Gospel According to Matthew.* Grand Rapids: Eerdmans; Leicester: Inter-Varsity, 1992.

Thiselton, Anthony C. *The First Epistle to the Corinthians: A Commentary on the Greek Text.* NIGTC. Grand Rapids: Eerdmans, 2000.

14

The Gospel of John as a Defense of Jesus' Honor?

Some Reflections out of Intercontextual Analysis with the Māori Concept of Mana[1]

Derek Tovey

It is a privilege to provide this contribution in honor of Tim Meadowcroft whose *mana* as a biblical scholar is well established. Here I examine the concept of δόξα (or "glory") by drawing analogically upon the Māori concept *mana*. I make a case for the use in John's Gospel of this "glory" concept and language to establish the status and honor of Jesus (both as a character in the story and as portrayed in the dynamics of the implied author's narrative). Thus readers, by understanding Jesus' honor and status as both ascribed and achieved, may accept the Gospel's claim for Jesus as God's Son.

In an article that relates the concepts of glory and glorification to the value of honor and the dynamics of patron-client relations, Ronald Piper notes that "the concepts of 'glory' and 'glorification' have long been considered themes of major *theological* significance within that work."[2] By correlating

---

1. Some content has previously appeared on pp. 288–290 of Roncace, Mark; Weaver, Joseph, *Global Perspectives on the Bible*. 1st ed., © 2014. Reprinted by permission of Pearson Education, Inc, New York, New York.

2. Piper, "Glory," 281. A prime example of an exponent of the view that the "glory" of Jesus denotes the "heavenly glory" that Jesus wears throughout his sojourn on

δόξα with *mana*, I aim to moderate what I think is sometimes an overly severe divide between a "theological understanding" of Jesus' glory, which emphasizes his divine status, over against a "view from below," which sees that δόξα, or "glory," as manifest in and through a human character.

Δόξα is used eighteen times in John's Gospel, while the verbal form, δοξάζω (appearing, of course, in a variety of cases and tenses) is used twenty-two times. This use of the noun "glory" (δόξα) and a range of uses of the verb "to glorify" (δοξάζω) requires an examination of the connotations of these words for, as a number of commentators have noted, the concepts contained within these words are varied and not easy to capture.[3]

In ancient secular Greek, the word δόξα had two basic meanings. One was "opinion" in the sense of one's own perspective, or thoughts on a matter; as Aalen puts it, it refers to "the opinion about a person or thing that I am prepared to defend";[4] while Ramsey correlates this with the Latin word *opinio*.[5]

It was also used in an objective sense to refer to one's standing or repute in the eyes of others. Thus, it was used for "reputation" and "renown" or to denote the "honor" in which one was held. For this sense, Ramsey offers the Latin *gloria* and speaks of it meaning as "distinction" or "fame."[6] It is this latter sense that contributed, most likely, to the translators' choice of δόξα for usage in the Septuagint to translate כבוד. כבוד derives from the verb כבד, "to be heavy, weighty," and from this developed its use to denote someone who is a "weighty" person in society, "someone who is honorable, impressive, worthy of respect"[7]; or, as G. B. Caird puts it, כבוד "is always used metaphorically to connote the weight a person carries, his status, importance, worth, impressiveness, majesty."[8] It referred to the esteem and respect that

---

earth, and, as such, is an indication of the Gospel's high Christology, is Käsemann, *The Testament of Jesus*. Lee sees glory as a central Johannine theme and states that is it "a theological term that is fundamentally concerned with God and only in a secondary sense applies to human beings." She goes on to say, drawing upon Witherington, that it expresses "the splendour or majesty of overwhelming weightiness of the divine presence"; see Lee, *Flesh and Glory*, 34. See also Brown, *John I-XII*, 503; and Witherington, *John's Wisdom*, 55.

3. Ramsey, *Glory*. Translators attest to the difficulty of understanding both the Greek and the English; see Fry, "Translating 'Glory,'" 422. Also Bratcher, "What Does 'Glory' Mean."

4. Aalen, "Glory, Honor."

5. Ramsey, *Glory*, 23.

6. Ramsey, *Glory*, 23.

7. Oswalt, "*kabod, kabed.*"

8. Caird, "Glory of God," 267.

one might receive on account of one's power or wealth;[9] or one's rank as a king (hence it could mean "majesty").[10] Hegermann states that

> [i]t can be used fundamentally of every person, probably with respect to his or her position within the creation (Ps 8:6) or within the community of mankind, where *kābôd* is manifest in a graduated way as rank, dignity, and position of power.[11]

Dale Patrick states that "glory" "denotes admiration won by doing something significant or by possessing attributes held in high esteem. It is more than fame, because it is experienced as a quality of something or someone, the aura emanating from the person or being."[12] We might use here the Latin word, *gravitas*.[13] With this word, the idea of "authority" is introduced—though, of course, a given position or rank within society carries its own inherent authority.

The use of δόξα in the Septuagint to translate כבוד led to an important extension of the meaning of the word when used in contexts to do with God and the presence of God. Partly, I suspect, because it is used in contexts where the presence of God is marked by theophanic images where the radiance or brightness of God, the splendor of God, is in view, the word itself has come to connote "divine radiance" or "brightness"—a sense that "glory" conveys strongly.[14] Thus, the word δόξα, especially in its association with the concept of the "glory of the Lord" (δόξα κυρίου; cf. כבוד יהוה) comes to refer to a divine mode of being.[15]

Like δόξα, *mana* is a big concept: it is one, says Rangimarie Pere, that is "beyond translation from the Māori language,"[16] while Joan Metge states that it has "not one clear-cut meaning but a range of related meanings with many ramifications."[17] Pere says that "its meaning is multiform and includes

9. Spicq, "*Doxa*."
10. Hegermann, "*Doxa, doxazo*."
11. Hegermann, "*Doxa*," 345.
12. Patrick, "Glory, Glorious, Glorify."
13. See Kittel, "δοκέω, δόξα κτλ."
14. See, for instance, Exodus 33:18; 34:29–31; 40:34.

15. Weinfeld, "*Kabod*," see especially 27–31; also Renn, "Glory." Note the important point made by John Collins regarding the range of words that contributed to the use of δόξα, see Collins, "*kbd*," esp. 586. Newman discusses the term in relation to כבוד as denoting the divine presence, or even "God's visible appearing"; see Newman, *Paul's Glory-Christology*, 133, see also 152.

16. Pere, *Ako*, 36. See also Mataira, "*Mana and Tapu*," 101.

17. Metge, *Touch*, 62. One of the difficulties in defining *mana*, as Metge points out, is that the word has become common currency in New Zealand English and is used in a broad sense and even loosely to refer to something that has "dignity" or is worthy of

psychic influence, control, prestige, power, vested and acquired authority and influence, being influential or binding over others, and that quality of the person that others know he or she has!"[18] Interestingly, Metge draws a subtle distinction between a Pākehā (European/non- Māori) understanding of *mana* and a Māori perspective. When asked about its meaning, Pākehā tend to "suggest 'prestige' or 'standing' first, then 'power' and 'authority'" and "interpret it in personal and social terms." Further, she writes,

> Māori, give the same answers as Pākehā when questioned about the meaning of mana, but listening carefully to the way they use the word, in Māori and English, we find that they place the primary stress on "power" and "authority," see "prestige" and "standing" as derived from the demonstrable possession of power and authority, and in many cases identify the power involved as being of a spiritual, supernatural kind.[19]

We shall return to this last aspect presently, but here we may say that in secular, worldly terms to have *mana* is to have authority and the power of control (or sovereignty) over some people or something, or in given contexts.[20] In personal terms, to have *mana* is to be a person who has prestige, status, charisma, dignity, and influence. *Mana* is, however, something that every person is born with, inherited from one's parents. The degree of *mana* inherited depends upon the parents' achievements, their social position, the regard in which they are held by others, and their contribution to the well-being of the tribal group.[21]

It should be noted that *mana* is closely associated with *tapu*. Indeed, there are tribal differences in the use of the words so that, as Shirres points out, "where some tribes speak of *tapu*, others speak of *mana*,"[22] and in some instances the terms are used interchangeably.[23] *Tapu* is a difficult concept

---

admiration.

18. Pere, *Ako*, 36.

19. Metge, *Touch*, 62.

20. For example, Mason Durie uses it to denote (political) authority and control in a variety of contexts as, for instance, Māori self-determination (Mana Māori), or over economic and social aspects of Māori life: Mana Whenua = control, rights over, ownership of land; Mana Moana = control, authority, rights over, ownership of fisheries (*moana* = lit. "sea," "lake"); Mana Tiriti = rights deriving from the Treaty of Waitangi, see Durie, *Te Mana*, esp. 2.

21. See Mead, *Tikanga Maori*, 51. Though Margaret Orbell states that *mana* "was not something that tūtūā [low-born people] could possess," see Orbell, *Concise Encyclopedia*, 71.

22. Shirres, *Te Tangata*, 33.

23. Shirres, *Te Tangata*, 36.

to render in English; it can mean "sacred," but this appears to be a modern sense of the word.[24] When someone or something is *tapu*, he, she, or it is placed under "a religious or spiritual restriction."[25] This can mean either that the person or thing that is *tapu* is "holy," or one might even say "consecrated, set apart";[26] or that the person or thing is off-limits as "polluting" or unclean, depending on the context. Though a person had an intrinsic *tapu* from birth, the *mana* which derived from this was not intrinsic to the person but was an endowment from the gods.[27]

Individuals of high rank in Māori society inherited an initial store of *mana*, but they could increase or decrease their *mana* by their own actions.[28] It was something not only built up by the individual but also "given" by the community. *Mana* derives from the recognition and respect given by others.[29] It is interesting to note that a Māori scholar, Professor Hugh Kawharu, writing about *rangatiratanga* (or "chieftainship"; more broadly, "sovereignty"), and quoting an important dictionary of the Māori language, where the meaning of the word is given as "evidence of breeding and greatness," writes as follows:

> Here, "breeding and greatness" allude to the two main criteria for leadership: primogeniture (generally male) and proven ability. "Evidence," for its part, turns on the concept of "mana." Mana is that power and authority that is endowed by the gods to human beings to enable them to achieve their potential, indeed, to excel, and, where appropriate, to lead . . . What is looked for, then, in a rangatira [chief, leader] is evidence of a high order of spiritually sanctioned power and authority. Primogeniture, in so far as it refers to proximity by way of a line through the ancestors to the supernatural source of such power and authority, may thus be called the prescribed factor in rangatiratanga, and ability the achieved factor.[30]

---

24. See Williams, *Dictionary*, 385.
25. Indeed, this phrase, or something like it, is given as a definition of *tapu*, by several writers, see e.g., Williams, *Dictionary*, 385. Also, Metge, *Touch*, 158. This definition is included in both Kawharu, *Waitangi*, 314, and its successor volume, Belgrave et al., *Waitangi Revisited*, 396.
26. Compare Mead's glossary definition of *tapu*, in Mead, *Tikanga Maori*, 367.
27. See Shirres, *Te Tangata*, 34, 36–37. See also Best, *The Maori*, 1:251, 258.
28. Joan Metge, *The Maoris*, 8. See also Buck, *Coming of Maori*, 346.
29. Metge, *Touch*, 68–73. See also Pere, *Ako*, 36.
30. Kawharu, ed. *Waitangi*, xix. See also Williams, *Dictionary*, 323.

Associated with this is the fact that *mana* is not simply something which someone has, but one is also granted *mana* by others, so that we might also speak of "honor" as an aspect of *mana*.

Mana also has spiritual connotations, though it is a stretch to relate the word to the sense of "glory" that we have been speaking about earlier in connection with δόξα. *Mana* is, according to Māori Marsden, "spiritual power and authority," a charisma that is greater than the "vital force or personal magnetism" which may be an inherent, intrinsic quality in a human being. *Mana* is given by the gods, or God; it is a gift—an endowed authority or power.[31] *Mana* "is divine power made manifest in the world of human experience," writes Joan Metge.[32]

> Mana as spiritual power is closely linked with tapu. People and things which "have" mana "are" tapu, and vice versa. While mana is a moving force, tapu is a state of being—the state of being which results from the indwelling of mana . . . When the indwelling of mana comes from God . . ., tapu is virtually identical with the Christian concept of sacred as set apart under the care and for the service of God . . .[33]

The spiritual aspect of *mana*, though in effect all *mana* has its origin in the endowment of God, or in traditional Māori thought, "the gods,"[34] enables a person to do great deeds and perform healings. This sort of *mana*, according to Metge, is accompanied by signs. Margaret Orbell writes of how

> [i]n many circumstances, mana had to be protected by being entrusted to a guardian. A powerful rangatira [chief] might possess (and be responsible for) the mana of his people, and the mana of their land as well; his mana would ensure the safety of these other mana.[35]

One thinks of Jesus stating how he has protected his disciples while he was with them in the world in John 17:12.

The pertinence of drawing an analogy between *mana* and the use of the δόξα concept and language in John's Gospel lies precisely in the way in which *mana* sees a nexus between the divine and the human. This draws together what might be described as a more "theological" understanding of

---

31. Marsden, "God, Man and Universe," 193–94.
32. Metge, *Touch*, 63.
33. Metge, *Touch*, 65–66; cf. Jesus' statement in John 17:19.
34. On this, and the close relation of *tapu* and *mana* in the endowment of *mana*, see Best, *The Maori*, 1:251, 258. Also Shirres, *Te Tangata*, 33, 57–60; Metge, *Touch*, 67.
35. Orbell, *Concise Encyclopedia*, 72.

δόξα in relation to Jesus, that is, the aspect that points up his divine status and identity, with what might be called a more "sociological" descriptor, that is, his bearing of δόξα as a human character in the world of the story. This means that, in the rhetoric of the implied author, the δόξα, or *mana* (if you will) of Jesus is seen "from below" (through his works, or "signs," for instance), as much as it is portrayed "from above" through the implied author's narrative and the discourse of Jesus.

The way in which *mana*, in the literature I have surveyed, may be understood as being both ascribed and achieved coheres well with the way in which these sociological categories are discussed in the literature on the value of honor in ancient Mediterranean societies. In the first place, primogeniture was important in both ancient Māori and in Mediterranean—specifically Israelite—societies.[36] In reference to Israelite society, Matthews and Benjamin state that "[f]athers used primogeniture or birth order to designate an heir in order to achieve stability for their household."[37] This reduced competition among other males and females within the household. Similarly, succession in Māori chiefly families was decided by primogeniture, the eldest son inheriting the *mana* of the chiefly position.[38] Birth, then, was the primary way in which honor was ascribed.[39] One might also have honor ascribed by someone else, through say, adoption into a well-born family, or the gift of an inheritance of wealth.

On the other hand, honor was also achieved and could be built up or broken down by one's actions. Buck writes:

> Besides the inherited *mana*, a new *ariki* [paramount chief, eldest son] could acquire additional *mana* by the wise administration of his tribe at home and by the successful conduct of military campaigns abroad ... On the other hand, poor administration and defeats in war might lead to loss of power and prestige. The *mana* of a chief was integrated with the strength of the tribe. It was not a mysterious, indefinable quality flowing from supernatural sources; it was basically the result of successive and successful human achievements.[40]

---

36. Malina, *New Testament World*, 29.
37. Matthews and Benjamin, *Social World*, 110.
38. Buck, *Coming of Maori*, 343–44, 46.
39. See Malina and Rohrbaugh, *Social-Science Commentary*, 123. Also Best, *The Maori*, 1:347–48, 352.
40. Buck, *Coming of Maori*, 346.

Joan Metge includes proficiency in Māori speech-making, genealogy, history and ceremonial alongside "seniority of descent" as sources of honor and respect.[41]

In a discussion on the place of grace in gaining honor, Julian Pitt-Rivers makes the point that when honor has been achieved through a competition for precedence, the victor must convert honor gained by striving into honor validated by others (especially the defeated or subjugated parties) by displays of magnanimity and moderation.[42]

Elsdon Best makes it clear that misfortune, lack of courage, lack of skill in administration, or lack of the necessary intelligence and grace might deprive a son of his status as a *rangatira* (chief).[43] Younger brothers sometimes attained the role of the chief if the first-born male could not fulfil his role "through physical or mental incapacity."[44] "The *mana* of a chief would be hereditary, but he would need to carefully uphold it, otherwise he might weaken it by ill-advised behavior, or actions."[45] "A *rangatira*, to preserve his *mana* and position, must act in a *rangatira* like manner."[46] *Mana* might be lost by a tribe when defeated in warfare; or an individual would lose *mana* if he contravened the stipulations surrounding *tapu* (such as restrictions on foods, certain locations such as the women's quarters, and so forth).[47]

Honor (or *mana*) in both types of ancient societies (Māori and Mediterranean) was dependent upon the estimation of others.[48] Public opinion was a strong social force among Māori.[49] Malina and Rohrbaugh discuss how honor can be gained or lost, particularly through "the never-ending game of challenge-response that characterized nearly all social interaction."[50] This ranged from the verbal—positively, a compliment, or, negatively, a hostile question or insult requiring a clever reply or an insult returned—through to the physical: an exchange of gifts, or physical assault. Challenges, whether positive or negative, could not be ignored or left unanswered without loss of honor: and, in a collectivist society, loss of honor to an individual also

41. Metge, *Maoris*, 201.
42. Pitt-Rivers, "Postscript," 242–43.
43. Best, *The Maori*, 1:347–50
44. Buck, *Coming of Maori*, 345. See also, Best, *The Maori*, 1:350. Cf. Matthews and Benjamin, *Social World*, 111.
45. Best, *The Maori*, 1:387.
46. Best, *The Maori*, 1:347
47. Best, *The Maori*, 1:389.
48. See Best *The Maori*, 1:350–51. Also, Metge, *Maoris*, 64.
49. Best, *The Maori*, 1:356; Cf. here Malina and Rohrbaugh, *Social-Science*, 121.
50. Malina and Rohrbaugh, *Social-Science*, 147; cf. 123. "Challenge-response" is also termed "challenge-riposte."

betokened dishonor upon the individual's family, tribe, or group.[51] Two physical affronts to honor that are important for a reading of John's Gospel are the dishonoring of the head or face,[52] and the defilement of a dead body (by mutilation) or the denial of burial.[53] We shall return to these later.

Now I will briefly sketch how I see the narrative dynamics of John's Gospel present a defense of Jesus' honor in the way in which the plot is developed. The narrative dynamics, both in what the narrator asserts about Jesus and in the words and actions of Jesus, function to convey to the reader an understanding of the true status, or honor, or *mana* of Jesus. This is done by both portraying the honor ascribed to Jesus and showing how Jesus achieves honor.

The prologue, John 1:1–18, is, *par excellence*, an example of how the narrator outlines Jesus' ascribed honor—indeed, his status—as the Word who is the same as God who is, in fact, God's only begotten. Is it too much to say that this is the narrator's way of establishing Jesus' "primogeniture"? Indeed, I would argue that the implied author begins the Gospel in this fashion precisely in order to establish that Jesus' status as God's Son is ascribed.

When the narrator says of the Word who has "lived among us," in v. 14, that "we have seen his glory, glory as of a father's only son" (NRSV), he does not mean, or he does not *just* mean, "we have seen in him the divine splendor of God shining forth," but "we have seen and come to understand his true status; we have recognized his *mana* as the one who is one with the Father."[54] This "oneness" with the Father is, of course, something that the implied author will go on to have Jesus assert again and again, in different ways and contexts. In John 17:5 we have an instance where Jesus directly claims this honor: "So now, Father, honor me in your own presence with that status/honor/*mana* that I had in your presence before the world existed" (NRSV, adapted).

Naturally, this claim to "divine primogeniture" is challenged when, in response to Jesus' claim to be "bread" that has come from heaven, "the Jews" say, "Is not this Jesus, the son of Joseph, whose father and mother we know? How can he now say, 'I have come down from heaven'?" (John 6:42). And on

---

51. Malina and Rohrbaugh, *Social-Science*, 123–24. See also Malina, *New Testament World*, 38: and on the social dynamics of honor as a whole, 29–39.

52. See Malina, *New Testament World*, 35. See also Pitt-Rivers, *Fate of Shechem*, 4–5. On the importance of the head in Māori culture, see Buck, *Coming of Maori*, 347. Also, Mead, *Tikanga Maori*, 49; Pere, *Ako*, 41.

53. Campbell, "The Greek Hero," 132.

54. In support of this, see Newman and Nida, *Handbook*, 23–24. "[G]lory combines the components of prestige and importance, almost equivalent to 'we saw how great he is,'" (24). See also Malina and Rohrbaugh, *Social-Science*, 33.

two occasions they are specifically shown to attempt to kill Jesus on account of the fact that they perceive him to be blaspheming (8:59; 10:31–33).

As Malina and Rohrbaugh say in their *Social-Science Commentary on the Gospel of John*, honor "must be publicly acknowledged."[55] So it is the achieved/acquired status, or honor, of Jesus that the implied author is particularly interested in getting across to the reader. The signs, those miraculous deeds that Jesus does, are supposed to make clear for all who have eyes to see what Jesus' true status is, the real *mana* that he has. This, I suggest, is made explicit in the very first sign Jesus performs (2:1–11). At the conclusion of this event, when Jesus has turned the water into wine, the narrator comments that in this first sign Jesus revealed his "glory" (his honor, status, *mana*) and his disciples believed in him.

In John 11:4, at the outset of what may be taken as the last miraculous sign, Jesus intimates that the raising of Lazarus will function to bring "glory"/honor both to God, and "the Son of God" who will be "glorified"/honored through it.[56] Thus it is that in his narrative, the implied author has the "glory" of Jesus revealed in his actions as a human being: σαρχ ("flesh") and δόξα combine, just as the two words lie "side-by-side," as it were, in John 1:14.

This narrative strategy has Jesus engaging in what may be called situations of "challenge and riposte," to use the language of scholars who apply social-scientific analysis to the issue of honor.[57] In other words, Jesus engages in a verbal defense of his honor by claiming that those who are truly alive to the import of his actions would recognize the "honor" that he is due, and the honor (status/*mana*) that he shares with God.

So, for example, in John 5:39–47 he says that, although his interlocutors search the Scriptures, because they refuse to come to Jesus or accept him because they will not attribute honor to him, they will stand accused by the very Moses whose Scriptures they treasure. In fact, the root problem is that they are prepared to accept honor from one another but are not prepared to seek the honor that comes from the one God (v. 44). And earlier Jesus has drawn explicit correlation between the honor given to the Son and that given

---

55. Malina and Rohrbaugh, *Social-Science*, 33.

56. This is reiterated at 11:40 (the believing mentioned here is also tied up with believing in Jesus as "the resurrection and the life"; v. 25). In v. 26, Martha makes a christological affirmation such as should flow from understanding Jesus' true *mana*.

57. On challenge and riposte, see Malina, *Insights from Cultural Anthropology*, chapter 2. Also, Malina and Rohrbaugh, *Social-Science*, 147–48, and Neyrey, *John*, 65–67, 136–37, 164–67.

to the Father (5:22, 23), although in this case the Greek words used are various forms of the verb τιμάω ("to estimate, value, honor, revere").[58]

John 10:31–39 is an especially good example of a challenge/riposte situation where Jesus refers his opponents ("the Jews") to his works as guarantors of his status as God's "Son," and as sharing the same honor as the Father. Even if they do not believe what Jesus has to say about himself, then they should at least be prepared to accept who he is on account of the works he is doing. This, by the way, is the same challenge Jesus gives his disciples in 14:11.

John 8:31–59 contains a particularly striking, and disturbing, instance of challenge and riposte as both "the Jews" and Jesus exchange insults, with Jesus accusing his opponents of being children of their "father," the devil (and "the father of lies"), and "the Jews" accusing Jesus of being "a Samaritan" who has a demon (8:44; 48). It is worth noting that here Jesus bases part of his response on the assertion that he does not seek his own honor, but rather receives his honor from his Father, the God whom the Jews claim as their God (8:50, 54, 55). It is the mark of a truly honorable man not to seek to promote his own honor.[59]

Finally, we may note in this all too brief survey on the theme of honor in the Gospel, that rhetoric about Jesus' honor particularly coheres around "his hour," the narrative leading up to his crucifixion. We find that Jesus uses the language of "glorification" in John 12 after an embassy of Greeks has come to request an audience, a request that prompts Jesus to speak of his impending "hour of suffering" (see John 12: 20–28; especially vv. 23, 28). Again, after Judas departs into the night to set in train his act of betrayal, Jesus speaks of the revelation of the Son of Man's "glory." Both in discourse, and in narrative action, this is linked with Jesus' "exaltation" or "lifting up," so that there is much ironic play on the fact that Jesus achieves his *mana* as the risen Christ through dishonor (see e.g., 19:1–3, 5, 16–25).[60]

We may select two instances from the Johannine Passion narrative that are informed by cultural mores to do with honor. The first example has to do with the dishonor done to Jesus by what is done to his body, particularly his head. When Jesus is hauled before Annas for questioning (John 18:19–24) he responds to Annas's questioning about his teaching by referring Annas

---

58. These include the masculine singular present participle forming a gerund, "the [one] (not) honoring."

59. See Malina and Rohrbaugh, *Social-Science*, 121–22.

60. "Jesus' 'glory' is oxymoronic because it is attached to his shame, namely his crucifixion," Neyrey, *John*, 45. For treatments of Jesus' death that handle it in terms of honor/shame dynamics, see Neyrey, "Despising the Shame." Also, Massyngbaerde Ford, "Jesus as Sovereign."

to those who have heard his teaching. This response earns Jesus a stinging blow to the face by one of the temple police. To this physical put-down Jesus calmly replies by asking why he has been struck as he is only making a quite reasonable statement. The implication is that Jesus maintains his honor in the face of an insincere interrogation.[61]

Later, when on trial before Pilate, Jesus is sent off to be flogged (19:1–5). Here the aim to dishonor Jesus is more intentional and overt. The soldiers mock Jesus as "King of the Jews" by dressing him in a purple robe, forcing a crown of thorns onto his head, and striking him in the face. Though Pilate feels that the charges against Jesus are a charade, and that there is no case against him, he nevertheless does not attempt to spare Jesus from humiliation, and contemptuously says "Here is the man" as he parades a battered Jesus before his Jewish opponents. No doubt, his references to Jesus as the Jews' "King" is also contemptuous and an attempt to humiliate them.

The other instance occurs after Jesus has died, when Jesus' body is mutilated by the thrust of a soldier's spear. But here the implied author works hard to preserve Jesus' honor in death, first in the fact that the soldiers do not break his legs as they find him already dead (19:32–33). Furthermore, the narrator states that Jesus' body is removed for burial by Joseph of Arimathea who lays Jesus in a new tomb. He is accompanied by Nicodemus, who is bearing a huge amount of burial spices. This description, the great weight of spices and the new tomb, ensure that the reader knows that, after all the humiliation of the trials and the crucifixion, Jesus will get an honorable burial.[62] It is, of course, the resurrection of Jesus that will finally and decisively demonstrate his true honor and his status as the Son of the Father. This is a status and an honor in which those who believe in Jesus' name (belong to his group) may share (20:17; 1:12, 13, 16; 14:18–24).

The Gospel's presentation of Jesus' honor is such that it subverts and challenges the conceptions of honor held by both Māori and Mediterranean societies and, indeed, conceptions of honor as a contemporary social value. The honor that Jesus achieves is gained not by striving for domination over others but by the seeming weakness of a humiliating death upon a cross. While Jesus is presented as engaging in robust episodes of challenge and riposte, he never resorts to physical violence against other humans.[63] Though his opponents and interlocutors are several times driven to attempt violence against him (see e.g., 8:59; 10:31, 39), and, at the

---

61 See Malina and Rohrbaugh, *Social-Science*, 253. Also Neyrey, *John*, 293.

62. See Neyrey, "Despising the Shame," 132.

63. The one episode where Jesus uses physical violence is when he uses a whip to drive the traders' animals out of the temple precincts (2:14–16).

end, both the Jewish and the Roman authorities subject him to violence, Jesus himself eschews such actions. Indeed, when Simon Peter attempts to prevent Jesus' arrest by attacking Malchus's ear with a sword, Jesus instructs him to re-sheath his weapon (18:10–11). He will follow his Father's program even if it means he must "drink the cup" of death. If his kingship was based on the values of this world, Jesus later tells Pilate, then his followers would indeed fight to prevent him being handed over (18:36). The basis of Jesus' honor is a "glory" that is ascribed to him by God, his Father, and his whole aim is to bring "glory" to God (17:1–5). Jesus will trust in no human systems of gaining honor but trust completely in "power from above" (19:9–11; cf. 5:36–38; 8:28–29, 54–55).[64]

In summary, in his Gospel the implied author presents the human character, Jesus, who attains honor by his actions. But these actions bespeak a *mana* that is more than merely human: this true, divine status of Jesus is reinforced by the narrator, who refers to Jesus' ascribed honor in the Prologue; and by the discourse of Jesus in which Jesus also makes claims for his divine status, and challenges his interlocutors to accept this on the evidence of his works. In the end, this is a *mana*, and a style of seeking honor, that subverts human conceptions of honor.

Bibliography

Aalen, S. "Glory, Honor." *NIDNTT* 2:44–52.
Belgrave, Michael, et al., eds. *Waitangi Revisited: Perspectives of the Treaty of Waitangi*. Oxford: Oxford University Press, 2005.
Best, Elsdon. *The Maori*. Memoirs of the Polynesian Society 5; 2 vols. Wellington: The Polynesian Society, 1924.
Bratcher, Robert G. "What Does 'Glory' Mean in Relation to Jesus? Translating *doxa* and *doxazo* in John." *TBT* 42 (1991) 401–8.
Brown, Raymond E. *The Gospel According to John I–XII*. New York: Doubleday, 1966.
Buck, Peter [Te Rangi Hiroa]. *The Coming of the Maori*. Wellington: Maori Purposes Fund Board and Whitcombe & Tombs, 1950.
Caird, G. B. "The Glory of God in the Fourth Gospel: An Exercise in Biblical Semantics." *NTS* 15 (1968–69) 265–77.
Campbell, John. "The Greek Hero." In *Honor and Grace in Anthropology*, edited by J. G. Peristiany and Pitt-Rivers, 129–49. Cambridge Studies in Social and Cultural Anthropology 76. Cambridge: Cambridge University Press, 1992.
Collins, John. "*kbd*." *NIDOTTE* 2:577–87.
Durie, M. H. *Te Mana, Te Kawanatanga. The Politics of Maori Self-Determination*. Auckland: Oxford University Press, 1998.
Fry, Euan. "Translating 'Glory' in the New Testament." *TBT* 27 (1976) 422–27.
Hegermann, H. "*Doxa, doxazo*." *EDNT* 1:344–49.

64. On the exchange with Pilate, see also Neyrey, "Despising the Shame," 127–28.

Käsemann, Ernst. *The Testament of Jesus: A Study of the Gospel of John in the Light of Chapter 17.* Translated by Gerhard Krodel. Philadelphia: Fortress, 1968.

Kawharu, I.H., ed. *Waitangi: Maori and Pakeha Perspectives on the Treaty of Waitangi.* Oxford: Oxford University Press, 1989.

Kittel, G. "δοκέω, δόξα κτλ." *TDNT* 2:232–55.

Lee, Dorothy. *Flesh and Glory: Symbolism, Gender and Theology in the Gospel of John.* New York: Crossroad, 2002.

Malina, Bruce J., and Richard L. Rohrbaugh. *Social-Science Commentary on the Gospel of John.* Minneapolis: Fortress, 1998.

Malina, Bruce J. *The New Testament World: Insights from Cultural Anthropology.* London: SCM, 1983.

Marsden, Maori. "God, Man and Universe: A Maori View." In *Te Ao Hurihuri, The World Moves On: Aspects of Maoritanga,* edited by Michael King, 193–94. Wellington: Hicks Smith & Sons, 1975.

Massyngbaerde Ford, Josephine. "Jesus as Sovereign in the Passion according to John." *BTB* 25 (1995) 110–17.

Mataira, Peter J. "*Mana* and *Tapu*: Sacred Knowledge, Sacred Boundaries." In *Indigenous Religions: A Companion,* edited by Graham Harvey, 99–112. London: Cassell, 2000.

Matthews, Victor H., and Don C. Benjamin. *Social World of Ancient Israel 1250–587 BCE.* Peabody, MA: Hendrickson, 1993.

Mead, Hirini Moko. *Tikanga Maori: Living by Maori Values.* Wellington: Huia, 2003.

Shirres, Michael P. *Te Tangata: the Human Person.* Auckland: Accent, 1997.

Metge, Joan. *In and Out of Touch: Whakamaa in Cross Cultural Context.* Wellington: Victoria University Press, 1986.

———. *The Maoris of New Zealand Rautahi.* London: Routledge & Kegan Paul, 1976.

Newman, Barclay M., and Eugene A. Nida. *A Translator's Handbook on the Gospel of John.* London: United Bible Societies, 1980.

Newman, Carey C. *Paul's Glory-Christology: Tradition and Rhetoric.* NovTSup 69. Leiden: Brill, 1992.

Neyrey, Jerome H. "Despising the Shame of the Cross: Honor and Shame in the Johannine Passion Narrative." *Semeia* 68 (1994) 113–37.

———. *The Gospel of John.* NCBC. Cambridge: Cambridge University Press, 2007.

Orbell, Margaret. *A Concise Encyclopedia of Maori Myth and Legend.* Christchurch: Canterbury University Press, 1998.

Oswalt, John N. "*kabod, kabed.*" *TWOT* 1:426–27.

Patrick, Dale. "Glory, Glorious, Glorify." In *The Westminster Theological Wordbook of the Bible,* edited by Donald E. McGowan, 161–64. Louisville: John Knox, 2003.

Pere, Rangimarie Rose. *Ako: Concepts and Learning in Maori Tradition.* Wellington: Te Kohanga Reo National Trust Board, 1982.

Piper, Ronald. "Glory, Honor and Patronage in the Fourth Gospel: Understanding the *Doxa* Given to the Disciples in John 17." In *Social Scientific Models for Interpreting the Bible: Essays by the Context Group in Honor of Bruce J. Malina,* edited by John J. Pilch, 281–309. Biblical Interpretation 53. Leiden: Brill, 2001.

Pitt-Rivers, Julian. "Postscript: The Place of Grace in Anthropology." In *Honor and Grace in Anthropology.* Edited by J.G. Peristiany and Julian Pitt-Rivers, 215–46. Cambridge Studies in Social and Cultural Anthropology 76. Cambridge: Cambridge University Press, 1992.

———. *The Fate of Shechem, or The Politics of Sex: Essays in the Anthropology of the Mediterranean*. Cambridge Studies in Social Anthropology 19. Cambridge: Cambridge University Press, 1977.

Ramsey, A.M. *The Glory of God and the Transfiguration of Christ*. London: Longmans, Green & Co., 1949.

Renn, Stephen D. "Glory." In *Expository Dictionary of Bible Words*, edited by Stephen D. Renn, 435–37. Peabody, MA: Hendrickson, 2005.

Spicq, Ceslas. "*Doxa*." *TLNT* 1:362–79.

Weinfeld, M. "*Kabod*." *TDOT* 7:22–38.

Williams, H. W. *Dictionary of the Maori Language*. Wellington: GP Publications, 1971.

Witherington, Ben, III. *John's Wisdom: A Commentary on the Fourth Gospel*. Louisville: Westminster John Knox, 1995.

15

Whakawhiti Kōrero: Theology and Social Vocation[1]

Mark G. Brett

THE REFLECTIONS IN THIS essay build on many conversations with Tim Meadowcroft over the years as we have sought to respond to our own regional context. I am pleased to offer this essay in honor of the countless contributions that Tim has made to the communities of learning in Aotearoa New Zealand, Australia, Papua New Guinea, and further abroad. As he reaches this point of retirement from formal teaching responsibilities, we can only hope that the years to come will be full of renewed energy for research and engagement in our region.

The scope of my topic is very broad, and there are many places where we could begin.[2] One might arbitrarily nominate a few months in 1769, when an English ship called *Endeavour* sailed around Aotearoa bearing a copy of the King James Version, published "by His Majesty's Special Command." This was no ordinary book. It had shaped an entire world, which was held to be created in 4004 BC and more recently divided among

---

1. This chapter was first published as Brett, "Theology and Social Vocation," and is reproduced here with some minor changes with permission.

2. This paper was first presented at a conference at Laidlaw College, "Whakawhiti Kōrero: Conversations between Theology and Social Vocation," October 1–2, 2018. I am grateful to the organizers of the conference for the opportunity to participate in such a rich, interdisciplinary conversation.

Christian monarchs. In Cook's Bible, the patronage of King James reflected the sacred alliance between church and state in seventeenth century England, an alliance that could continue to underwrite not just a Bible translation but also the colonial Doctrine of Discovery and the patterns of sociality within settler colonialism.

This unholy alliance of Bible, culture, and law may seem a very unpromising starting point to begin a conversation about relational theology, but it is part of the colonial story that is shared between Aotearoa New Zealand and Australia, and critical reflection on it will be revealing in several ways. The story provokes some fundamental questions about the conditions that may allow for any genuine conversation, which will in turn yield some implications for a theology of sociality. In this essay I want to show how a critique of coloniality helps us to think afresh about the relationship between creation theology and the love of neighbor.

First, we may remember that the King James Version points to the tribal politics of Christianity. The *Endeavour* did not set sail under the authority of a papal bull or a Catholic version of the Doctrine of Discovery. Protestant imperial competition unfolded within a revised version of international legal imagination, which presented itself as more humanitarian and more respectful of Indigenous natural rights.[3] In the 1830s, mission societies leveled some strong critique against colonial abuses of power,[4] but by the end of the nineteenth century these critiques had subsided, along with the very idea of natural rights. The earlier anxieties about colonialism on the Pākehā side seem to have been steadily overwhelmed by economic interests, but with an exquisite irony, some of the Māori resistance in the second half of the nineteenth century began to draw on the Bible and theology. Theology offered the possibility of mediation between Māori and Pākehā, but there were still a number of impediments to genuine conversation. I will not pretend to know all the details of nineteenth century history in Aotearoa, but I offer some suggestions here for conversation.

The collaboration of the northern chiefs in their Declaration of Independence in 1835 (*He Whakaputanga o te Rangatiratanga*) forged a new kind of collaboration on the Māori side, and in the Treaty of Waitangi in 1840, the chiefs did not yield sovereignty to the English Crown.[5] This became clear in the 1850s in a new way when Chief Wiremu Tāmihana advocated for an alliance of Māori iwi under a king, and his reasoning was in some respects comparable with what we find in the books of Samuel. In the

---

3. Brett, *Political Trauma*, 36–54.
4. Carey, *God's Empire*, 322–28.
5. Waitangi Tribunal, *Te Paparahi o te Raki*, xxii.

biblical narrative, the elders of Israel introduce the novel idea of a king in order to unite their tribes mainly because the Philistines were advancing from the west. Similarly, the Māori of the nineteenth century were experiencing a threat to their own tribal sovereignty with Pākehā advancing from the west. But Tāmihana's argument attempted a more subtle compromise than we find in Samuel, which could better express the implications of the Treaty of Waitangi: a new *Kingitanga*, supported by local Māori councils, could relate directly to the English version of sovereignty.[6] The suggestion was, in effect, an adaptive vision of political theology that could hold together the various parties in a new complex society.

Tāmihana's remarkable biblical arguments were advanced in a famous speech in 1861. The Crown had suggested to the Waikato Māori that they could keep their land "so long only as they are strong enough to keep it; might and not right will become their sole title."[7] Tāmihana's response is recorded in the British Parliamentary Papers at the time.[8] He begins with traditional *waiata* as lament,[9] and moves on to a poetic critique of the colonial administration. If the British were to take to heart their own Bible, they should acknowledge the law of the monarchy stipulated in Deut 17:15, "Thou shalt in any wise set him king over thee, whom the LORD thy God shall choose: one from among thy brethren shalt thou set king over thee: thou mayest not set a stranger over thee, which is not thy brother" (KJV). The English who had been "far away" had now drawn near (invoking Eph 2:13), but in this expanded sociality, only a Māori brother could exercise *rangatiratanga*, whatever the shared arrangements under the Treaty of Waitangi might suggest. England had its monarch, and so did Māori : "leave this King to stand upon his own place, and let it rest with our Maker."[10] This political claim sits within a larger theology of creation: "God did not make night and day for you only. No, summer and winter are for all, the rain and the wind, food and life, are for all of us."[11]

Chief Tāmihana's argument was extraordinary in many respects, but I want to take it as an example of the kind of theology that can build a more complex society within which it is possible to live with multiple sovereignties. This kind of theology was much needed in settler societies, but the

---

6. Hill and O'Malley, *Māori Quest*, 2–5.

7. O'Malley, *The Great War*, 141. I am indebted to Steve Taylor for his presentation on Wiremu Tāmihana, delivered at Whitley College for the "Reimagining Home" conference, July 2–5, 2017. See Taylor, "Indigenous Home-Making."

8. Tāmihana, "Reply to the Declaration."

9. On the *waiata* as lament see McKenzie, "Learning to Lament."

10. Tāmihana, "Reply to the Declaration."

11. Tāmihana, "Reply to the Declaration."

theologians at the time seem to have had their energies diverted by other issues, and the social vocation of Christianity was embedded, in large measure, within an ideology of a civilizing mission.[12]

Tāmihana's theology set a different agenda. He conceived of a world structured with multiple social identities and loyalties, covenanted together in such a way that those identities could also find common ground. The Treaty of Waitangi did not need to be seen as the submission of one group to another, or as a legal sanction for unequal distributions of power. Rather, it provided a set of principles which fostered new relationships, which were themselves ultimately grounded in the divine gifts of the created order. This theology implicitly affirmed the possibility of expanding a social identity while recognizing the validity of other ways of imagining connections to God. And this points us to one of the key questions for any political theology: how do people hold together the particularity of their own distinctive commitments while, at the same time, seeking to form a common life with those who have a different vision of the world? Or to put that in more personal terms, how do we love our neighbor without imposing our own expectations on them?

Mindful of these questions of power and culture in the formation of a common good, how is a social vocation to be conceived in theological terms? I want to explore some of the contours of Old Testament theology before turning to the radical demands that are implied in the call to love our neighbor.

Beginning with Creation Theology

We have begun by acknowledging Tāmihana's grounding of sociality in a creation theology. A number of the Old Testament writers also begin with creation and only then move to sociality. The creation theology in Psalm 104, for example, has deep resonances with Indigenous spiritualities. Instead of seeing God's dwelling in heaven, with divine sovereignty being exercised at a lofty distance, this psalmist finds a sacral presence throughout the cosmos. All of creation becomes, in effect, a temple.[13] The spirit of God pulses with an intimate power through every living creature.

---

12. As already noted, however, problems with colonialism were clearly articulated already in the 1830s and '40s. See, e.g., Chamerovzow, *The New Zealand*.

13. Krüger, "Kosmo-theologies." A comparable view is suggested in Amos 9:6 and Isa 66:1–2. Amos 9:6 is distinctive insofar as this cosmic hymn is immediately followed by a dramatic critique of Israel's election. Strawn, "What is Cush Doing." Schmid, "Himmelsgott."

> [All creatures] all look to you
>> to give them their food in due season;
> when you give to them, they gather it up;
>> when you open your hand, they are filled with good things.
> When you hide your face, they are dismayed;
>> when you take away their breath, they die
>> and return to their dust.
> When you send forth your spirit, they are created;
>> and you renew the face of the ground. (Ps 104:27–30)

This immanent conception of divine presence is comparable in some respects with the first creation narrative in the book of Genesis, even if these texts come from quite different theological schools. In Genesis 1, for example, it is not simply that the Creator lives in the heavens,[14] but rather that the heavens themselves are the created "firmament" (Gen 1:7–8). They are the hard dome that holds back the primeval waters above the sky. This implies an ancient cosmic geography, which we cannot take literally anymore, but the theological emphasis of Genesis 1 is not found in its cosmic dividing of the waters above the dome and the waters below that earth; that conception was an intercultural commonplace. The theological proposal in this representation of the world's beginning was that God is qualitatively different from the world, and as a consequence God is free to appear anywhere.[15] We can view this as the common ground between Psalm 104 and the first creation narrative, since they both find God at work throughout the whole earth, and not just in Israel, and not just in in a temple. Accordingly, Genesis 1 consistently refuses to name God using Israel's national name, YHWH. God is consistently named "Elohim" in the first creation narrative (without a definite article), and this is not so much a name as a tantalizing abstraction, like "divinity" in English, which leaves open the naming of God.

Genesis 1 begins a larger composition that is woven throughout the first few books of the Bible, and in contrast with the national tradition, this composition insists that the ancestors only knew the Creator under the name El Shaddai (Exod 6:2–3). The abstract non-naming of God in Genesis 1 expresses an inclusive monotheism, in principle shared by all humankind.[16] Most importantly, all human beings—both men and women—were made in the image of Elohim, and not in the image of a national god. The

---

14. In some traditions, God's dwelling may be located "above" the heavens, as in Ezekiel 1 and Ps 29:10. Cf. Uehlinger and Müller Trufaut, "Ezekiel 1."

15. Schmid, "Himmelsgott," 135–36.

16. See especially de Pury, "Gottesname." Regarding the Yahwistic traditions in Genesis, see now Brett, "YHWH among the Nations."

basic assertion was that the one Creator had many names, and by implication, each people group could find their own way to God. In contrast with the national denomination in Deuteronomy, which calls for a uniformity of religion, this is a more ecumenical social vision, which biblical scholarship has dubbed the "Priestly" tradition.

The genius of Wiremu Tāmihana's theology is that he proposed, in effect, a combination of the national and the creation traditions. In order to grasp this paradoxical combination, I have been suggesting that we also need to appreciate the diversity of creation traditions in the Hebrew Bible, which stretch from the Priestly creation story to the wisdom literature. While Priestly denomination in the Torah is often seen as diametrically opposed to the wisdom traditions, I would argue that there are some very substantial agreements between them. The Priestly and the wisdom traditions both addressed the question of how to relate to God outside of Israel's own peculiar covenant traditions. Similarly, the understanding of a universal divine presence in Psalm 104 is linked to the presence of wisdom in all of creation and not just within the land of Israel. Accordingly, in the wisdom traditions like Proverbs and Job, we find a way of understanding the traces of God in the world through the experience of creation rather than through the peculiar story of Israel.[17]

Let's consider the book of Job for a moment. In this book, ethics are clearly grounded in creation rather than in the law of Moses, but Job's understanding of social vocation also overlaps with what we find in Mosaic law. Especially in chapter 31, Job claims that he has defended the rights of slaves, widows, orphans, and aliens, subscribing precisely to the social norms that we find in Israel's national laws, without agreeing that these norms are based on a Yahwistic faith.[18] Job sees himself as answerable before El, rather than YHWH:

> If I have rejected the rights [מִשְׁפַּט] of my male or female slaves,
> when they brought a complaint against me,
> what then should I do when El arises?
> When he investigates, how shall I respond?
> Did not He who made me in the belly make them,
> and form me in the one womb?
> If I have withheld anything that the poor desired,
> or brought resignation to the eyes of the widow,

---

17. Human wisdom is localized, whereas divine wisdom encompasses the whole world and all its creatures, but this is more a difference of scope and extent. See especially Fiddes, *Seeing the World*.

18. E.g., Deut 14:28–29; 16:11–14; 24:19–22.

> eaten my morsel alone, and the orphan has not eaten from it . . .
> then let my shoulder blade fall from my shoulder,
> and let my arm be broken from its socket . . .
> No stranger (גר) spent the night outside;
> I have opened my doors in their path. (Job 31:13–17, 22, 32)

This social vision is law-observant without the need of positive law, and Job is engaged in an argument with El rather than YHWH. In this respect, the name of Job's divinity coincides with the "Elohim" and "El" of the Priestly denomination in the Pentateuch.

In developing his theology of protest, Job shifts attention from torah observance to world observance. Having established the ethical foundations in creation, he urges his friends to learn from nature:

> But ask the wild beast, and *she will instruct you*;
> the birds of the air, and they will declare to you;
> speak to the earth, and *she will instruct you*;
> and the fish of the sea will relate to you.
> Who among all these does not know
> that the hand of YHWH has done this?
> In his hand is the life of every living thing
> and the spirit of all human flesh. (Job 12:7–10)

This passage is dense with allusions to the creation narratives in Genesis, but most striking is the two-fold choice of the verb form ותרך (literally "and she will instruct you"). This wording is related to the familiar noun for law and instruction in the legal tradition: תורה (torah). The semantic play is too significant to pass over, and we must therefore conclude that the earth has, according to Job, its own forms of instruction for those who are willing to listen. This where we might find Job in fundamental agreement with Indigenous spiritualities.

At this point, then, we can draw some preliminary conclusions about the value of the Priestly and wisdom traditions for intercultural theology. Rather than Deuteronomy, which tends to promote a uniformity of national religion, the Priestly and wisdom traditions in the Hebrew Bible are ready to engage in a different way with the nations. It is no accident, then, that when the Apostle Paul comes to reflect the Old Testament covenants, he concludes that the gentiles can enter into the story and blessings of Abraham, the founding ancestor of the international Priestly tradition, but not into the national covenant. The followers of Jesus are not baptized into Moses.

The theological proposal that came from Wiremu Tāmihana in 1861 fits together very well with the social visions of the Priestly and wisdom traditions, and it is a great tragedy that the dominant theology of settler colonialism did not take this road.[19] It is especially in the Priestly and wisdom traditions that we find the universality of creation theology, which can then shape the character of engagement with the neighbors who share our common life. With this creational approach, we can conclude with Luke Bretherton that

> As creatures, situated in various covenantal relations . . . we are always already in relationship with others. Our personhood is the fruit of a social and wider ecological womb as much as a single physical one; that is, we come to be in and through others not like us, including non-human others. This means we cannot exist without some kind of common life with a plurality of human and non-human ways of being alive.[20]

Love of Neighbor as Social Vocation

Some Christian theologians tend to ground all talk of social vocation in a doctrine of the Trinity. Perhaps because I am a Hebrew Bible scholar, I am reluctant to do so. But as I have already suggested, it is actually the Apostle Paul who, already in his first-century gospel for the gentiles, orientates his scriptural interpretation around Abraham rather than Moses. Abraham, not Moses, is the ecumenical ancestor, and the Priestly tradition can point us down the road towards an intercultural theology without at the same time sacrificing any of the particularity of a faith in YHWH. Accordingly, I am more inclined to pursue Luke Bretherton's theology of the neighbor rather than conceptions of trinitarian theology that may inadvertently convey a lack of hospitality in the very peculiarity of Christian language.

In his book *Christ and the Common Life*, Bretherton examines the spectrum of relational practices through which human solidarity may be built, ranging from personal and ecclesial interactions to more broadly political constructions of the common good. At each layer of social interaction, we may encounter power imbalances and exploitation and, by implication, the need for reconciliation if a common life is to be created or sustained. And this raises a fundamental question of motivation: what are the most

---

19. See especially Paulson and Brett, "Five Smooth Stones"; Havea, *Postcolonial Voices*; Habel, *Acknowledgement*.

20. Bretherton, *Christ and the Common Life*, 22.

compelling reasons for creating and sustaining a shared world of meaning in human relationships?

In many respects, the easiest and most natural way to answer this question is with a "ripple" theory of sociality, which suggests that our strongest solidarities begin with one's central point of connection within a family, but in addition, that solidarity may flow outwards like ripples in a pond to tribes and nations—with the strength of the social bonds steadily weakening as they move further and further from the ego's own family. Within Indigenous cultures, these ripples would include the wider ecological relationships with one's own traditional country. Even as an account of natural affections, however, there are limitations to ripple theories, not least because violence and abuse can arise even within a single family, and unexpected friendships can form across the most formidable of social distances.

If we conceive of the love of neighbor as a vocation, as Bretherton argues, then the crossing of social boundaries could become a practice that may be exercised on a daily basis. Neighbor love does not cease at the border of a nation state, because literally anyone can become a neighbor, even an enemy. Some have suggested that a love of enemies may be regarded as utopian practice, and not a political one, but this response simply points us to the distinctive difference between national loyalties and a Christian love of neighbor. The *institutionalizing* of boundaries between friends and enemies is inherently problematic from a Christian point of view.

Bretherton argues that political arrangements should always be seen as contingent and open to revision. We should be ready to relinquish them into the hands of the Creator. Letting go of these "contingent" social arrangements is a lot easier said than done, since they are often constructed and maintained over generations, if not centuries. But suspending our prejudices is a necessary condition for the love of neighbor. A neighbor does not arrive in our lives with a preassigned social category (like an ethnic label or a gender), or a legal status (like a citizen or a refugee), or a role (like a business client or a soldier), all of which can conveniently structure our social expectations. The neighbor arrives in one's world simply as a person, or, more broadly, as a creature of God, and loving them might well call us across great social distances—whether economic, cultural, or even geographical distances. Ironically, this suspension of conventional identity formations is precisely what allows us to love a person in all their particularity.

While at first glance this account of neighbor love might indeed appear utopian, it is better described as a vocation. Betherton puts it this way:

> Being a neighbor is a vocation that does not depend on liking, having a rapport with, or being equal to others . . . Indeed, the

encounter with a neighbor confronts us with a need to interrogate our own settled identities, roles, and habits and the ways these inhibit our ability to love our neighbor. Neighbor love therefore disrupts hierarchal, institutional, and identity-based ways of structuring status.[21]

If we can relate this argument back to the Priestly imagination in the Hebrew Bible, it is the fundamental recognition that human beings are made in the image of Elohim that allows this paradigm of biblical theology to suggest that natives and immigrants should be embraced by a single law (notably in Exod 12:49; Lev 24:22).[22] To update that daring vision for our present discussion, we might say that it is necessary to reach through the many layers of social descriptors and categories in order to welcome the person beyond any categories into our own social world. In order to discover a common good, it will be necessary to cut across established patterns of meaning.

This account of neighbor love sharpens some of the key issues for us, but it also reveals that this kind of love differs markedly from our conventional attachments. We might need to conclude, in fact, that this is not an everyday vocation, but one which calls us into liminal experiences. Acknowledging this liminality might also help to explain why, in the famous parable of the sheep and the goats in Matthew 25, the love of the poor and the stranger is performed in a kind of cloud of unknowing.

> Then the righteous will answer him, "Lord, when was it that we saw you hungry and gave you food, or thirsty and gave you something to drink? And when was it that we saw you a stranger and welcomed you, or naked and gave you clothing?" (Matt 25:37–38)

It is not that the righteous in this parable have special spiritual powers that allow them to discriminate between those who belong to the body of Christ and those who do not. Quite the contrary, it is clear that the righteous do not have such powers of discrimination, and this points to the kind of unknowing that can provide for the love of enemies. Here we encounter a paradoxical Christology without Christ—or at least, a Christ who is hidden.[23]

---

21. Bretherton, *Christ and the Common Life*, 41.
22. Brett, "Natives and Immigrants."
23. Cf. Paul's comment in 1 Cor 10:4 on the desert rock as a "hidden Christ" in Israel's journey from Egypt. Similarly, the theme of hiddenness arguably belongs to cosmic Christology. See especially Balabanski, "Hellenistic Cosmology."

While I would not want to base any procedures for professional social practice directly on this parable in Matthew 25, I do want to suggest that we should find a remarkable analogy between the righteous who cannot identify Christ in the stranger and the Priestly Abraham who does not yet know the name of YHWH. The love of a neighbor whose humanity lies beyond any categorization intersects with the love of a God whose name is not yet known. Both of these theological perspectives in Scripture urge us into a liminal space beyond conventional attachments to family, culture, and religious denomination. Both neighbor love and Priestly theology provoke us to suspend our prejudices in order to listen again, and to embrace the other simply because they are made in the image of Elohim, or more broadly, because they are creatures who are enlivened with the spirit of Elohim. In this liminal space, we do not rest on conventional understandings or preconceived generalities; instead, we learn to pay attention at a much more basic level.

It is not that we can remain transfixed in this liminal state, in a cloud of unknowing, because this is not how we live our everyday lives. There are other kinds of love that certainly require enduring attachments, especially the range of relationships that have a covenantal value—including the more explicitly named relationships within the body of Christ. But a radical love of neighbor provides the conditions under which we might delight in the particularities of others, and not impose our preconceptions upon them. This is the kind of social vocation that allows our world to expand, much in the way that Wiremu Tāmihana suggested long ago when he invoked Ephesians 2:13 in his speech of 1861, when he saw that the English who had been "far away" were now drawn near. This new proximity called for a new set of covenant relationships, expressed in *te Tiriti o Waitangi*.[24] The idea that the Treaty might be a new sacred covenant between multiple communities seems to have been shared by many of those who signed the Treaty in 1840.[25]

Conclusion

In some respects, it might be very difficult to think of a political process like the Treaty of Waitangi as an expression of social vocation, but that is precisely what I want to suggest. It presents a model for a society within which multiple communities maintain a continuity of identity while risking new relational practices and covenantal connections.[26] Misunderstandings will

---

24. Picard, "Treaty People."
25. Picard, "Treaty People," 52, citing Cadogan, "Three-Way Relationship," 31.
26. See further, Fiddes, "Covenant."

be inevitable, and for that very reason, it will often be necessary to enter the liminal space of neighbor love in order to practice the suspension of prior judgments. The relational processes are made all the more difficult when power and resources are distributed unequally, but then, inequalities of power are often characteristic even of the most intimate relationships within a family. Whether we are paying attention to individuals or to groups, the vocation of neighbor love calls us to expand our social imagination and to recognize our common creaturely dependence on God. The love of neighbor provides the conditions that enable us to love all of God's creatures in the way that they are created to be loved.

Bibliography

Balabanski, Vicky S. "Hellenistic Cosmology and the Letter to the Colossians: Towards an Ecological Hermeneutic." In *Ecological Hermeneutics: Biblical, Historical and Theological Perspectives*, edited by David G. Horrell, et al., 94–107. London: T. & T. Clark, 2010.

Bretherton, Luke. *Christ and the Common Life: A Guide to Political Theology*. Grand Rapids: Eerdmans, 2019.

Brett, Mark G. "Natives and Immigrants in the Social Imagination of the Holiness School." In *Imagining the Other and Constructing Israelite Identity in the Early Second Temple Period*, edited by Ehud Ben Zvi and Diana Edelman, 89–104. New York: T. & T. Clark, 2014.

———. *Political Trauma and Healing: Biblical Ethics for a Postcolonial World*. Grand Rapids: Eerdmans, 2016.

———. "Whakawhiti Kōrero: Theology and Social Vocation." In *Essays in Recognition of the Retirement of Rev. Dr. Timothy Meadowcroft*, edited by Csilla Saysell and John de Jong, 15–24. *Pacific Journal of Baptist Research* 13/2 (2018).

———. "YHWH among the Nations: The Politics of Divine Names in Genesis." In *The Politics of the Ancestors: Exegetical and Historical Perspectives on Genesis 12–36*, edited by Mark G. Brett and Jakob Wöhrle, 113–30. FAT 124. Tübingen: Mohr Siebeck, 2018.

Cadogan, Tui. "A Three-Way Relationship: God, Land, People. A Māori Woman Reflects." In *Land and Place, He Whenua, He Wāhi: Spiritualities for Aotearoa New Zealand*, edited by Helen Bergin and Susan Smith, 27–44. Auckland: Accent, 2004.

Carey, Hilary. *God's Empire: Religion and Colonialism in the British World, c. 1801–1908*. Cambridge: Cambridge University Press, 2011.

Chamerovzow, Louis A. *The New Zealand Question and the Rights of Aborigines*. London: T.C. Newby, 1848.

de Pury, Albert. "Gottesname, Gottesbezeichnung und Gottesbegriff: 'Elohim' als Indiz zur Entstehungsgeschichte des Pentateuch." In *Abschied vom Jahwisten: Die Komposition des Hexateuch in der jüngsten Diskussion*, edited by Jan C. Gertz, et al., 25–47. BZAW 315. Berlin: de Gruyter, 2002.

Fiddes, Paul S. "Covenant: A Basis for Inter-Faith Dialogue in Scripture and Baptist Thinking." Unpublished paper given at the Commission on Interfaith Relations of the Baptist World Alliance, Vancouver, July 5, 2016.

———. *Seeing the World and Knowing the World: Hebrew Wisdom and Christian Doctrine in a Late-Modern Context*. Oxford: Oxford University Press, 2013.

Habel, Norman. *Acknowledgement of the Land and Faith of Aboriginal Custodians*. Melbourne: Morning Star, 2018.

Havea, Jione, ed. *Postcolonial Voices from Downunder: Indigenous Matters, Confronting Readings*. Eugene, OR: Pickwick, 2017.

Hill, Richard S., and Vincent O'Malley. *The Māori quest for Rangatiratanga /Autonomy, 1840–2000*. Occasional Papers 4. Wellington: Treaty of Waitangi Research Unit, Stout Research Centre, Victoria University of Wellington, 2000.

Krüger, Thomas. "'Kosmo-theologies' zwischen Mythos und Erfahrung: Psalm 104 im Horizont altororietalischer 'Schöpfungs' Konzepte." *BN* 68 (1993) 49–74.

McKenzie, Alistair. "Learning to Lament in Aotearoa." In *Spiritual Complaint: The Theology and Practice of Lament*, edited by Miriam J. Bier and Tim Bulkeley, 173–86. Eugene, OR: Pickwick, 2013.

O'Malley, Vincent. *The Great War for New Zealand: Waikato 1800–2000*. Wellington: Bridget Williams, 2016).

Paulson, Graham, and Mark Brett. "Five Smooth Stones: Reading the Bible through Aboriginal Eyes." In *Voices from the Margin: 25th Anniversary Edition*, edited by R. S. Sugirtharajah, 61–76. Maryknoll: Orbis, 2016.

Picard, Andrew. "'On the Way', and 'In the Fray' in Aotearoa: A Pākehā's Covenantal Reflections from the Context of a Treaty People." *Pacific Journal of Baptist Research* 11/1 (2016) 44–58.

Schmid, Konrad. "Himmelsgott, Weltgott und Schöpfer; 'Gott' und der 'Himmel' in der Literatur der Zeit des Zweiten Tempels." In *Der Himmel*, edited by Dorothea Sattler and Samuel Vollenweider, 111–148. Neukirchen-Vluyn: Neukirchener, 2006.

Strawn, Brent. "What is Cush Doing in Amos 9:7? The Poetics of Exodus in the Plural." *VT* 63 (2013) 99–123.

Tāmihana, Wiremu. "Reply to the Declaration Addressed by the Governor to the Natives Assembled at Ngaruawaha." *Great Britain Parliamentary Papers*, 1862 [3040], 73.

Taylor, Steve. "Indigenous home-making as public theology in the words and deeds of Māori leader, Wiremu Tāmihana." In *Re-Imagining Home: Understanding, Reconciling and Engaging with God's Stories Together*, edited by Darren Cronshaw, et al., 188–207. Sydney: Morling, 2019.

Uehlinger, Christoph, and Susan Müller Trufaut. "Ezekiel 1, Babylonian Cosmological Scholarship and Iconography: Attempts at Further Refinement." *ThZ* 57 (2001) 140–71.

Waitangi Tribunal. *Te Paparahi o te Raki: Northland Inquiry, Part One*. Wellington: Waitangi Tribunal, 2014.

Part III

Language, Linguistics, and Hermeneutics

16

The Early Greek-Language Tradition behind the Gospels

ALLAN BELL

THIS ESSAY IS AN attempt to cross disciplines, to bring to the study of the biblical text insights that may be gained from another discipline, namely sociolinguistics. Sociolinguistics is the field that occupies itself with all manner of interrelations between language and society and, in particular for the topic of this chapter, with bilingualism and its operation among individuals and society. Crossing disciplines entails both opportunities and hazards. In my pursuit of this interest over the past decade, Tim Meadowcroft has been my main guide and mentor, repository of knowledge, and target of endless questions. My intent here is to see if the field from which I come can add to our understanding of the biblical record, in this instance the origins of the canonical Gospels.

What was the sociolinguistic situation in the Palestine of Jesus' day? In a much-quoted dictum from the third century AD, Rabbi Jonathan of Eleutheropolis said: "Four languages are appropriately used in the world. And these are: Greek for song, Latin for war, Aramaic for mourning, Hebrew for speaking."[1]

Not all these sociolinguistic associations are self-evident. The link of war with Latin, the language of the imperial conqueror, is not surprising.

---

1. Quoted in Hezser, *Jewish Literacy*, 250.

Nor is Greek for poetry, as an emblem of its culture. Aramaic was felt suitable for mourning, presumably because it had become the vernacular of the suppressed people (even though it was itself the imposed language of an earlier empire). Hebrew for "speaking" is the least transparent: Hezser suggests that this may have referenced the reading-aloud of the Torah.[2]

One question has dominated New Testament scholars' consideration of language issues in first-century Palestine, and that is: What language did Jesus speak? More specifically: What language did Jesus teach in? I will suggest below that those questions could be better framed, and I will have something to say about them later in this chapter, but they are not my primary focus here, for two reasons.

First, in our current state of knowledge, questions about Jesus' language capability and usage are simply not answerable. Neither the biblical record nor other writings nor archaeology offer us adequate evidence of the kind needed to make any definitive call on Jesus' language. I endorse Bird's conclusion: "We simply lack the evidence to prove *that* he spoke Greek let alone *when* he spoke Greek, *how* well he spoke Greek, *who* he spoke Greek to, and *what* exactly he said."[3] Short of startling fresh manuscript or archaeological finds that bring new and appropriate evidence to the table, our best deductions concerning Jesus' language usage remain speculations, not sureties.

Secondly, the question of Jesus' own language knowledge and usage is also not, in my view, the most important sociolinguistic issue in the Gospels, even though it may arouse the most fascination. What is more important is the language history of the Gospel tradition. What language/s did the tradition originate in, and what language/s was it transmitted in?

It can be easy for biblical scholars to forget that what we have in the Gospels is something linguistically odd, as James Barr pointed out fifty years ago:[4] the tradition has been communicated in a language other than the one it is assumed to have originated in. If our only evidence for the language of Jesus was the four canonical Gospels, we would have to conclude that he conversed and taught in Greek, with occasional switches into Aramaic; that he used a few Latin words for things associated with the Roman occupiers; and that he could read Hebrew. But the consensus for more than a century is that Jesus taught in Aramaic: How and when did that become the Greek of the Gospels that we know? That is the question this chapter addresses.

---

2. Hezser, *Jewish Literacy*, 250.
3. Bird, "The Criterion," 63.
4. Barr, "Which Language."

Existing Scholarship on Language in the Gospels

Language issues are heavily canvassed in NT scholarship. This is natural; the study of the New Testament (as of the Hebrew Scriptures, or of any founding religious text such as the Qur'an) is fundamentally textual analysis and interpretation. Language and linguistic analysis is therefore unavoidable. Much of the biblical text has been worked over in mind-boggling grammatical detail and debated by Christian and Jewish scholars for millennia.

Interest in the languages as such and the issues they raise goes back to the time of the Renaissance.[5] But with few exceptions, contemporary linguistics—as initiated by Saussure in the early twentieth century[6]—its theories and analytical tools, are unrepresented, and apparently unknown in NT studies.[7] NT language analysis is largely of the traditional philological type that has been used in the study of classical languages over many centuries. With even fewer exceptions, contemporary sociolinguistics and its methods for understanding the use and relationship of languages in a society is absent, even though since the late nineteenth century NT scholars have been addressing sociolinguistic questions—mostly without knowing that that was what they were doing.

Biblical scholars' interest has been in particular to describe the language situation in first-century Palestine that Jesus and his followers operated in, and to deduce what the language repertoire and usage of Jesus may have been. A great deal has been written on this over the past century and beyond, positions have been taken, schools established, oppositions drawn.[8] Through a sociolinguistic lens, I see this scholarship as falling into four categories:

1. The majority shows little sense of the sociolinguistic nuances of, for example, multilinguals' language usage. Its assumptions are monolingualist: the question asked is "What language did Jesus speak?" without recognition that multilingualism does not consist of multiple monolingualisms. Bilingual speakers mix their languages as they talk. My preference for framing the questions would be: What languages did Jesus know? What languages did Jesus use? When and how?

2. A minority of Gospels scholarship, however, shows an instinctive grasp of the fluidity of multilingual situations and what they mean for

---

5. Fitzmyer, *Aramean*.
6. de Saussure, *Cours de linguistique générale*.
7. Porter, *Linguistic Analysis*, 83.
8. For an overview of the positions, see Fitzmyer, *Aramean*; Stuckenbruck, "Aramaic Sources."

NT studies. In particular, some writings of J. N. Sevenster, James Barr, and Joseph Fitzmyer evidence this kind of understanding. Most of this work is not recent, but it has much to offer.[9] See, for example, the probing questions with which Sevenster begins his book on the place of Greek among the early Christians:

- What language did the first Christians speak and write?
- Did they know only one language, or were they bilingual?
- Did only a few know Greek?
- Was Greek the language of trade and communication, or was it exclusive to higher social circles?
- Was Aramaic used only in villages, in the country, in the lowest social circles?
- Is it certain that someone from the Galilee countryside couldn't speak Greek?
- Did Palestinian Christians' contact with others from outside or from Jerusalem increase their knowledge of Greek, or their opportunities to use it?[10]

Leading Aramaicists of an earlier generation such as Barr and Fitzmyer have noted the need for careful use of comparative evidence, which has often been adduced from another place, e.g., from Egypt rather than Palestine, or from another time, e.g., two centuries after Jesus.[11] The use of such evidence is understandable, since it is often the best that exists, there being nothing directly from first-century Palestine itself. However, as scholars develop their analyses, they tend to forget their own caveats on how such comparisons should be applied. Barr also notes the need to understand the nuances of social variation of language in Palestine.[12] Among Gospels scholars, Betz, Hengel, and Bird take positions on the origins and transmission of the Jesus tradition that are similar to the one I shall reach below.[13]

1. A handful of NT scholars have explicitly taken up and applied sociolinguistic concepts and tools in their work—Stanley Porter's large oeuvre

---

9. Sevenster, *Do You Know Greek?*; Barr, "Which Language"; Fitzmyer, "Did Jesus Speak Greek?"
10. Sevenster, *Do You Know Greek?* 1.
11. Fitzmyer, *Aramean*.
12. Barr, "Which Language," 26.
13. Betz, "Wellhausen's Dictum"; Hengel, *Hellenization*; Bird, *The Gospel of the Lord*.

is the leading example.[14] The publications of Jonathan Watt bring a sharp sensibility to understanding multilingual repertoires and usages.[15] Sociolinguistic research is also incorporated into the work of Ong, Silva, Lee, and Stuckenbruck.[16] Perhaps inevitably when crossing disciplines, there is a tendency to transfer sociolinguistic concepts that are now quite dated in the field itself (such as *diglossia*),[17] and there is some over-reliance on introductory texts.[18] I also note that the most eminent Gospels scholar New Zealand has produced, Graham Stanton, discovered and engaged with sociolinguistic concepts in the last years of his working life and recommended their potential to other scholars.[19]

2. From the other disciplinary end, only a couple of sociolinguists that I know of have addressed themselves in print to issues of biblical languages. The Jewish scholar Bernard Spolsky is primary among these and has dealt with Jewish languages of the first century, though his interest is of course not with the New Testament as such but with the Jewish situation.[20] Spolsky stresses the paucity of the data about this sociolinguistic scenario and the poverty of the kind of data that we do have (e.g., inscriptions on ossuaries). Christina Bratt Paulston engaged with NT scholars in a workshop on *diglossia*, from which Porter published a collection of essays.[21] She also makes the same point on the lack of data: to a field where audio recordings are the basis of most research, the smattering of written records that we have here is perturbingly slight evidence. Paulston also questions whether the concept of *diglossia* offers much explanatory power for sociolinguistic questions in NT studies, with which I would concur.

---

14. E.g., Porter, "Greek in Galilee"; Porter, "Functional Distribution"; Porter, "Criterion of Greek"; Porter, "Greek of the Jews."

15. E.g., Watt, "Gutturals and Galileans"; Watt, "Implications of Bilingualism"; Watt, "Living Language Environment."

16. Ong, "Language Choice"; Silva, "Bilingualism"; Lee, "Some Features." Stuckenbruck, "Semitic Influence."

17. Ferguson, "Diglossia."

18. I can sympathize, since I am crossing between these fields from the other direction.

19. Stanton, *Jesus and Gospel*.

20. Spolsky, *Languages of the Jews*.

21. Bratt Paulston, "Language Repertoire."

Languages in the Gospels Tradition

So, to my primary question in this chapter: what were the languages of origination and transmission of the Gospel traditions? The candidates are those listed in the quote from Rabbi Jonathan at the start. There is not space here to lay out the detailed issues and evidence on the situation of the languages in first-century Palestine, that is a task for another essay. But to briefly summarize the majority view on the relative situations of the four languages:

- Aramaic was the first language and the general spoken language of the people of Palestine, and was therefore Jesus' first language, and the language in which he conversed and taught.
- Greek was quite widespread, including in Galilee. Jesus probably knew some Greek as a second language. He may have conversed in it, but probably would not have taught in Greek.
- Hebrew was much attenuated as an everyday language. It was possibly used by the educated elite, and in some remote rural areas. It was the language of religion, including of religious discussion. Jesus may have been able to read Hebrew.
- Latin was a marginal language for the Jewish population, serving some official purposes. Jesus knew only the few regular borrowings of terms from the Romans.

In this multilingual situation, the only conclusion we can draw with any great certainty is the relatively uninteresting one that Latin had a marginal status and was not spoken as such by Jesus or other Jews. The situation of the other three languages remains highly contestable and contested.

The general answer to the question of the languages of the Gospel tradition is that Jesus talked in Aramaic, therefore the tradition was preserved and passed on in Aramaic. The narrative runs that there then followed a long, possibly semi-formal, and probably quite late process of translation into Greek, either by the evangelists themselves, or by other hands in the years before the evangelists did their redaction work. The translation was probably undertaken a generation or more after Jesus and after the founding of the church.

However, what we know about the operation of bilingualism makes the above process and timeline highly unlikely. Scholars agree that there were Greek speakers among Jesus' twelve disciples—Philip and Andrew have purely Greek names, Peter had a Greek name as well as Aramaic, and both he and his brother Andrew came from Bethsaida, noted as a Hellenistic town.[22] The wider circle of disciples—including for example the seventy (or seventy-two) sent out by Jesus in Luke 10—will have included more who were also Greek speakers, being Aramaic-Greek bilinguals.

Now, bilinguals do not sit down and translate between their languages when they want to discuss something with other people. They hear something in one language and can then reproduce it in their other language.[23] That is, bilingual disciples of Jesus were quite capable of hearing his teaching in Aramaic and then passing it on in Greek to Greek speakers. I believe this process will have operated in two stages:

1. Bilingual disciples will have heard Jesus' teaching in Aramaic and then naturally verbalized it themselves in Greek when talking to Greek-dominant hearers. The bilingual mind does not require a process of translation. On this view, during Jesus' lifetime, his bilingual followers will have already been transmitting and conserving his tradition in Greek. Two examples of this process: John 12 tells the incident of the Greek speakers who approached Philip for an introduction to Jesus, and Philip in turn approached Andrew. The Gospel adds the information (otherwise superfluous) that Philip was from Bethsaida, in apparent explanation of why he was the one approached. This appears to be because of the known Hellenistic nature of that settlement, which made him a likely fluent Greek speaker.[24] Secondly, the seventy/seventy-two disciples sent out by Jesus in Luke 10 will have, on sheer probability of numbers, included a significant cohort who were bilingual in Greek as well as Aramaic. It seems likely they will have used some Greek to appropriate listeners during their ministry.

2. A similar process will have operated in the early church after Jesus' death. It seems that the church consisted of a majority who could speak Greek possibly from the very start—Acts 2 stresses the presence of diaspora Jews on the day of Pentecost, for whom Greek will have been the lingua franca (alongside the "home languages" listed there as the spoken tongues). Certainly from soon afterwards, there was a strong Greek component to the church. The cultural/linguistic difference between "Hebraists" and "Hellenists" became a point of tension in the early years of the church's expansion (Acts 6).[25] That is, the linguistic demographics of the early church made a Greek as well as an

22. E.g., Croy, "Translating"; Bauckham, *Eyewitnesses*, 205.
23. Baker, *Foundations*.
24. Croy, "Translating," 158.
25. Fitzmyer, "Did Jesus Speak Greek?"

Aramaic tradition unavoidable. These new disciples will have spoken on the Jesus tradition in Greek, having heard it in Aramaic if they were bilinguals, or already in Greek if that was their sole language. Therefore, even if there had been no Greek-language tradition during Jesus' lifetime, bilingual disciples will necessarily have begun formulating one very soon after.

Clearly then, no translation process was required in order to originate and transmit the Gospel tradition in koine Greek within the earliest church. Therefore, a statement such as Black's on the translation process behind the Gospels is unfounded: "The Greek Evangelists or the first Greek translators of the Gospels . . . have interpreted a tradition originally circulating in one language, Aramaic, and composed in more or less literary Greek the results of their interpretation."[26]

My argument is then that what we know about how bilinguals operate in their two languages leaves no doubt that there will have been a very early Greek-language tradition about Jesus. This probably began already within his lifetime, but certainly established quite quickly within the infant church. We are, I believe, on quite firm ground deducing the presence of such a tradition on the basis of the known characteristics of bilinguals. This conclusion concerning the Greek-language tradition is quite independent of whether Jesus himself knew or ever used Greek, since it relies only on something that we know well from the record in Acts: that there were large numbers of Greek speakers in the early church.

An Excursus on Jesus and Greek

Although Jesus' own language usage is indeterminate and not a precondition for the production of an early Greek-language tradition, there are some aspects of the language repertoire of Jesus and his immediate disciples that are worth our consideration. On the basis of the slight available evidence, biblical scholars have worked through the following chain of deduction:

1. Establish what the sociolinguistic situation in first-century Palestine was—that is, what languages were used, by whom, in what situations;

2. Take those findings to represent Jesus' potential linguistic repertoire and behavior;

---

26. Black, *Aramaic Approach*, 275.

3. Analyze Jesus' interactions as narrated in the Gospels to deduce what language he may have used in specific situations where contextual detail is given.

Sociolinguistically, this is to draw a very long bow. It is risky to deduce actual language choices in a given situation only on the basis of a speaker's presumed repertoire and the nature of the situation. Unfortunately, by the time they come to draw their conclusions, some scholars have forgotten how speculative their chain of deduction is. Ong, for example, claims to be able to determine which language Jesus will have used in specific encounters,[27] which reaches well beyond what the evidence of the Gospels will bear. We cannot escape being in the realm of speculation here, and those speculations must remain inconclusive. I believe we are on much more solid ground in examining the language of the tradition's transmission, because there we are able to appeal to known universal patterns of bilingual behavior.

The Aramaic Substrate

When speakers of one language learn another, their first language routinely influences the pronunciation and grammar of the second language. Such effects can be embedded across generations to create an "ethnolect"—that is, the dialect of a particular group (usually ethnic) which has been influenced by a heritage language. All scholars agree that the Greek of the Gospels is influenced in this way by an Aramaic substrate, that is, that Jews in first-century Palestine spoke an aramaicized ethnolect of Greek.

Some NT scholars have deduced that there is therefore an underlay of gospels written in Aramaic behind the Greek canonical Gospels. Aramaic originals of some kind have been suggested by a long line of scholars: Dalman, Torrey, Burney, Black, Casey.[28] Some have attempted to back-translate from the Greek to an original Aramaic text. Sociolinguistically, that is an extremely hazardous enterprise—there are many potential sources of Aramaic influence, and it is impossible to isolate and tease out particular effects and attribute them to a written Aramaic gospel. The aramaicization could result from at least the following causes:

- Written Aramaic gospels (or parts of),
- Aramaic oral tradition,
- The Aramaic-influenced Jewish-Greek ethnolect, and

27. Ong, "Linguistic Analysis."
28. E.g., Black, *Aramaic Approach*; Casey, *Aramaic Sources*.

- Idiolectal L1-Aramaic effects on the Greek of individual Aramaic writers.

Overall, although absence of evidence does not constitute evidence of absence, it is notable that among the thousands of documents and fragments discovered particularly over the past sixty years, my understanding is that no trace of a written Aramaic gospel has yet been found.

Genre: Teaching Versus Conversing

NT researchers have tended to make a distinction between Jesus' potential ability to converse in Greek and an assumed inability to deliver his teaching in Greek. Even such a careful scholar as Fitzmyer endorses such a conclusion.[29] But this is a highly problematic assumption. Speakers do not put up such walls between the genres they use such as conversation, or argumentation, or teaching. And in particular in the case of Jesus, if we are to give any credence to the contexts described in the Gospels in which his teaching occurred, his was a highly interactive teaching style, particularly in question-and-answer format. There was clearly no generic distinction for him between conversation and some of his teaching. Therefore, if we conclude—with most NT scholars—that Jesus would in fact have been able to converse in Greek, we must also allow the equal possibility that he taught in Greek too.[30]

Jesus' Code-Switching

Code-switching is the process by which bilingual speakers mix their languages for longer or shorter stretches.[31] They may insert a single word or phrase from one language into the flow of another, or alternate their languages in alternate sentences, or speak for a stretch in one language, and then in the other. This is what bilinguals do, to the point that it is almost a test of bilingual capability that speakers can mix their languages unreflectingly in this way.

I have already noted that it is an oddity that the Gospels are written in a language other than the original. In fact, if we had only the text of the Gospels to inform us, we would conclude that Jesus had spoken Greek with occasional code-switches into Aramaic. That is the opposite of what is

---

29. Fitzmyer, "Did Jesus Speak Greek?"
30. Cf. Porter, "Response to Maurice Casey."
31. See for example, Heller, *Code-Switching*.

assumed to be the case: these code-switches in the Gospel texts are taken not to reflect original switches made by Jesus. Rather, they presumably reflect brief excerpts from Jesus' original Aramaic discourse, which are included in the flow of Greek text for verisimilitude, or for narrative color, or because the Aramaic wording was particularly striking or significant (as Jesus' words from the cross, for example). The Gospels are written in Greek not because that was the language that had been used in the events they cover but because that was the lingua franca of their readership throughout the eastern Mediterranean Roman empire.

The code-switches in the Gospels therefore do not represent code-switches by Jesus. If he did any code-switching it will have been from Aramaic into Greek, not vice versa. And one thing we can be sure of as an entailment: if Jesus did indeed have a fair level of productive competence in Greek: he will have at times code-switched from Aramaic into Greek, especially if conversing with interlocutors who were dominant in Greek (see the encounters studied by Porter),[32] because that is what bilinguals do. While the premise that Jesus spoke Greek remains speculative, there can be little doubt about the deduction that, *if* he had a fair level of Greek competence, he will have code-switched.

Again, to draw out more of the sociolinguistic implications if Jesus did speak Greek: if he was teaching an audience with an observable proportion of Greek speakers, it seems likely that he may have switched into Greek for a number of purposes, for example to give crucial terms in Greek, or to summarize his Aramaic story or argument in Greek. A fact that surfaces surprisingly little in NT scholars' discussion of Jesus' itinerant ministry is that he necessarily will have delivered similar material multiple times to different audiences in different locations. He would have told the same stories, used the same aphorisms, etc. Except that no one tells the same story in precisely the same words, and this may well be the source of different versions of a parable coming down to us in different canonical Gospels. As part of his self-repetition, Greek-language competence would likely entail that Jesus would repeat in Greek a form of what he had said in Aramaic if his audience contained Greek speakers.

Code-switches of this kind seem to me to be likely candidates to be remembered and transmitted as part of the Greek-language tradition. It is possible that Jesus might have identified and used Greek equivalents of key terms from his Aramaic teaching. This would have required no great level of Greek competence on his own part, since he could presumably rely on linguistic help from his Greek-speaking disciples. Equally plausibly, when

---

32. E.g., Porter, "Greek in Galilee."

sending out his followers, he could have endorsed, for those who were fluent bilinguals, some key Greek terms to be used when they encountered Greek audiences. More broadly, it will have been self-evident—requiring no kind of divine foreknowledge—for Jesus to see that if his message was to receive circulation beyond Palestine, that would have to be in Greek not Aramaic. That scenario would also have been an incentive to provide at least key words or phrases in Greek. Jesus showed a clear concern in the way he worded his teaching to ensure it would be in a memorable form for his disciples, and a concern to embed key Greek terms fits with that orientation. Such terms would be prime candidates for preservation by Greek-speaking disciples and for feeding into the Gospel tradition. Given the known ability of oral tradition to preserve key spoken material over long periods of time,[33] it seems quite possible that Greek originals of some of Jesus' words were maintained throughout the Gospel tradition.

Conclusion

My argument here, then, can be summarized as follows.

It remains speculative and ultimately unprovable whether Jesus himself knew or used Greek. But what we can say is that *if* he did, he could and probably did teach in the language, certainly would have code-switched into Greek on occasion, and possibly produced key terms in Greek which his disciples could use and remember.

Even if Aramaic was Jesus' main teaching language, it is probable that during his lifetime bilinguals recounted his deeds and sayings in Greek.

Given the prevalence of Greek speakers within the early church, it is inescapable that they will have formulated a Greek-language tradition very soon after the death of Jesus and the founding of the church.

A process of translation was then superfluous in the generation of a Greek-language Gospel tradition, which drew on the language facility of early Christian bilinguals.

Therefore, the oral tradition on which the written Gospels are based could in large measure have been drawn directly from this early Greek-language tradition.

This is not to deny that the evangelists may have had multiple strands of tradition available to them: some in Greek, some in Aramaic; some oral, some written; some translated, some not.

I believe that scholars should therefore approach the Gospel texts with a default assumption that these originated primarily in an early

---

33. Bailey, *Poet and Peasant*; Lord, *Singer of Tales*; Bauckham, *Eyewitnesses*.

Greek-language tradition and that there is therefore a much more direct line than is usually credited leading back from the canonical Gospels to the originating traditions.

Bibliography

Bailey, Kenneth E. *Poet and Peasant*. Grand Rapids: Eerdmans, 1976.
Baker, Colin. *Foundations of Bilingual Education and Bilingualism*. 5th ed. Clevedon: Multilingual Matters, 2011.
Barr, James. "Which Language Did Jesus Speak?—Some Remarks of a Semitist." *BJRL* 53 (1970) 9–29.
Bauckham, Richard. *Jesus and the Eyewitnesses: The Gospels as Eyewitness Testimony*. Grand Rapids: Eerdmans, 2006.
Betz, Hans Dieter. "Wellhausen's Dictum 'Jesus Was Not a Christian, But a Jew' in Light of Present Scholarship." *ST* 45/2 (1991) 83–110.
Bird, Michael F. "The Criterion of Greek Language and Context: A Response to Stanley E. Porter." *Journal for the Study of the Historical Jesus* 4 (2006) 55–67.
———. *The Gospel of the Lord: How the Early Church Wrote the Story of Jesus*. Grand Rapids: Eerdmans, 2014.
Black, Matthew. *An Aramaic Approach to the Gospels and Acts*. 3rd ed. Peabody, MA: Hendrickson, 1967.
Bratt Paulston, Christina. "Language Repertoire and Diglossia in First-Century Palestine: Some Comments." In *Diglossia and Other Topics in New Testament Linguistics*, edited by Stanley E Porter, 79–89. JSNTSup 193, Studies in New Testament Greek 6. Sheffield: Sheffield Academic, 2000.
Casey, Maurice. *Aramaic Sources of Mark's Gospel*. Cambridge: Cambridge University Press, 1998.
Croy, Clayton N. "Translating for Jesus: Philip and Andrew in John 12: 20–22," *Neot* 49/1 (2015) 145–74.
de Saussure, Ferdinand. *Cours de linguistique générale*, edited by C. Bally and A. Sechehaye. Lausanne & Paris: Payot, 1916.
Ferguson, Charles A. "Diglossia." *Word* 15 (1959) 325–40.
Fitzmyer, Joseph A. *A Wandering Aramean: Collected Aramaic Essays*. Atlanta: Scholars, 1979.
———. "Did Jesus Speak Greek?" *BAR* 18/5 (1992) 58–63, 76–77.
Heller, Monica. *Code-Switching: Anthropological and Sociolinguistic Perspectives*. Berlin: de Gruyter, 1988.
Hengel, Martin. *The "Hellenization" of Judaea in the First Century after Christ*. Translated by John Bowden. London/Philadelphia: SCM/Trinity International, 1989.
Hezser, Catherine. *Jewish Literacy in Roman Palestine*. Tübingen: Mohr Siebeck, 2001.
Lee, J. A. L. "Some Features of the Speech of Jesus in Mark's Gospel." *NovT* 27/1 (1985) 1–26.
Lord, Albert B. *The Singer of Tales*. Cambridge, MA: Harvard University Press, 1960.
Ong, Hughson. "Can Linguistic Analysis in Historical Jesus Research Stand on Its Own? A Sociolinguistic Analysis of Matthew 26:36—27:26." *Biblical and Ancient Greek Linguistics* 2 (2013) 109–38.

———. "Language Choice in Ancient Palestine: A Sociolinguistic Study of Jesus' Language Use Based on Four 'I Have Come' Sayings." *Biblical and Ancient Greek Linguistics* 1 (2012) 63–101.

Porter, Stanley E. "Jesus and the Use of Greek: A Response to Maurice Casey." *BBR* 10 (2000) 71–87.

———. "Jesus and the Use of Greek in Galilee." In *Studying the Historical Jesus: Evaluations of the State of Current Research*, edited by Bruce Chilton and Craig A. Evans, 123–54. New Testament Tools and Studies 19. Leiden: Brill, 1994.

———. *Linguistic Analysis of the Greek New Testament: Studies in Tools, Methods, and Practice*. Grand Rapids: Baker Academic, 2015.

———. "The Criterion of Greek Language and Its Context: A Further Response," *Journal for the Study of the Historical Jesus* 4 (2006) 69–74.

———. "The Functional Distribution of Koine Greek in First-Century Palestine." In *Diglossia and Other Topics in New Testament Linguistics*, edited by Stanley E. Porter, 53–78. JSNTSup 193, Studies in New Testament Greek 6. Sheffield: Sheffield Academic, 2000.

———. "The Greek of the Jews and Early Christians: The Language of the People from a Historical Sociolinguistic Perspective." In *Far from Minimal: Celebrating the Work and Influence of Philip R. Davies*, edited by Duncan Burns and J. W. Rogerson, 350–64. Library of Hebrew Bible/Old Testament Studies 484. London & New York: T. & T. Clark, 2012.

Silva, Moises. "Bilingualism and the Character of Palestinian Greek." In *The Language of the New Testament: Classic Essays*, edited by Stanley E. Porter, 204–26. JSNTSup 60. Sheffield: Sheffield Academic, 1991.

Spolsky, Bernard. *The Languages of the Jews*. Cambridge University Press: Cambridge, 2014.

Stanton, Graham N. *Jesus and Gospel*. Cambridge: Cambridge University Press, 2004.

Stuckenbruck, Loren T. "An Approach to the New Testament through Aramaic Sources: The Recent Methodological Debate." *JSP* 8 (1991) 3–29.

———. "'Semitic Influence on Greek:' An Authenticating Criterion in Jesus Research?" In *Jesus, Criteria, and the Demise of Authenticity*, edited by Chris Keith and Anthony Le Donne, 73–94. New York: T. & T. Clark, 2012.

Sevenster, J. N. *Do You Know Greek? How Much Greek Could the First Jewish Christians Have Known?* NovTSup 19. Leiden: Brill, 1968.

Watt, Jonathan M. "Of Gutturals and Galileans: The Two Slurs of Matthew 26:73." In *Diglossia and Other Topics in New Testament Linguistics*, edited by Stanley E. Porter, 107-20. JSNTSup 193, Studies in New Testament Greek 6. Sheffield: Sheffield Academic, 2000.

———. "Some Implications of Bilingualism for New Testament Exegesis." In *The Language of the New Testament: Context, History, and Development*, edited by Stanley E. Porter and Andrew W. Pitts, 9–27. Leiden & Boston: Brill, 2013.

———. "The Living Language Environment of Acts 21:27–40." *Biblical and Ancient Greek Linguistics* 4 (2015) 30–48.

17

Textual Criticism, the Textus Receptus, and Adoniram Judson's Burmese New Testaments[1]

John de Jong

Tim Meadowcroft was one of my doctoral supervisors, forming a great team with Allan Bell. For the entire duration of my doctoral candidacy I was living in Yangon, Myanmar, visiting New Zealand once a year for supervision meetings. In one of these early meetings, Tim said to me, "I finally understand you! You just love beavering away at this technical work." With a nod in that direction, it is a privilege to offer this article in honor of Tim on his retirement. It is serendipitous that this collection of articles for Tim is in a Baptist publication, for mine concerns that most celebrated of Baptists, Adoniram Judson, the pioneering missionary to Myanmar (Burma). Judson's translation of the entire Bible into Burmese, completed in 1840, remains the most widely used version in modern day Myanmar, a veritable "textus receptus." This article will look at Judson's translation of the NT into Burmese and consider its relationship with *the* Textus Receptus.

When Adoniram Judson had finished his translation of the entire Bible into Burmese, a project which had taken from 1816 to 1840, he sent some copies to the USA with a covering letter that included these words:

1. This chapter was first published as de Jong, "Textual Criticism," and is reproduced here with some minor changes with permission.

> In my first attempts at translating portions of the New Testament, above twenty years ago, I followed Griesbach, as all the world then did; and though, from year to year, I have found reason to distrust his authority, still not wishing to be ever changing, I deviated but little from his text, in subsequent editions, until the last; in preparing which I have followed the text of Knapp, (though not implicitly,) as upon the whole the safest and best extant; in consequence of which, the present Burmese version of the New Testament accords more nearly with the received English.[2]

In his analysis of the Judson Bible, James W. Khong independently concluded that Judson's NT variant choices "go together with (the) KJV."[3] My previous research on the Judson Bible focused on his OT translation and textual criticism, demonstrating that Judson exploited the best international scholarship of his time to produce a sophisticated version of the OT in Burmese. His reading of Ps 92:10b, "you (God) have poured over me fresh oil" (NRSV), for example, only entered English versions with the RSV in 1952.[4] Yet, by his own testimony, Judson moved away from the best available scholarship for his final NT translation. This article will pursue three questions in relation to the issues raised above:

1. What are the differences between the final and earlier editions of Judson's Burmese NT?
2. How do Judson's earlier and final NT editions compare with modern English versions as opposed to the KJV ("the received English" in the letter above)?
3. Finally, and most difficult to answer, why was Judson suspicious of Griesbach's critical editions of the Greek NT?

To answer these questions, I have compared Judson's 1832 NT edition with his final 1840 NT edition.[5] The 1840 NT translation is still the most commonly used Burmese version to this day, although spelling was standardized in subsequent editions. For this research I have used an 1866 publication.[6] Griesbach's critical Greek NT is available on BibleWorks

---

2. Judson. "Letter, Dec. 28, 1840."

3. Khong, "Gospel Message," 87. Khong's thesis is a valuable analysis of three Burmese Bible translations by a native Myanmar speaker with reference to modern translation theory.

4. See de Jong, "New England Exegete."

5. *The New Testament, in Burmese.*

6. *New Testament of Our Lord.*

10.[7] Unfortunately I have not had access to "Knapp's text" in order to see to what extent the changes in the 1840 edition, from the 1832 edition, were based on Knapp, but this does not hinder my analysis.

Methodology

To get a comprehensive answer to the differences between the 1832 and 1840 Burmese NT editions would require line by line analysis of both texts. But this demands too much effort and time, certainly more than my present questions require. Instead, I have made use of the NRSV's text critical notes, which are more generous than most modern English versions. I have gone through the NRSV NT and compared the variant readings it highlights with the KJV, the Judson 1832, and the Judson 1840 editions, all the time keeping an eye on Griesbach's critical Greek NT. This methodology cannot claim to give a comprehensive analysis of the two Judson NT editions, and there are almost certainly other differences between the two versions, based on text critical decisions, beyond those I have identified. Nevertheless, my methodology is sufficient to answer the questions, and has also shed light upon why Judson was suspicious of Griesbach's critical NT texts.

Any hope I might have had that the earlier version of Judson's NT would resemble our modern versions was quickly dashed. The 1832 edition is more similar to the KJV than to modern NT versions. This is because Griesbach's critical Greek NT was still largely similar to the Textus Receptus. The breakthroughs in NT textual criticism that produced our modern NT versions were to come in the late nineteenth century, and Griesbach was yet a child of the late eighteenth century. Nevertheless, he was a seminal figure, and those later breakthroughs built upon his thorough ground-breaking work.

The Textus Receptus and Griesbach's Greek NT

In 1516, Desiderus Erasmus of Rotterdam published the first edition of his Greek NT.[8] After the invention of the printing press, Erasmus's Greek NT was not the first to be printed, an honor which went to the Complutensian

---

7. Griesbach. *Manual Edition*.

8. The following account draws heavily on Metzger and Ehrman, *Text of the New Testament*, chapter 3, "The Pre-critical Period: The Origin and Dominance of the Textus Receptus," 137–64; and chapter 4, "The Modern Period: From Griesbach to the Present," 165–94. I will, however, refer to Metzger in the body of the essay, as these historical sections have been largely reproduced from Metzger, *Text of the New Testament*.

Polyglot (1514).⁹ The Complutensian Polyglot was a better critical Greek NT than that of Erasmus, but it was Erasmus's text that became the standard Greek NT for Reformation and Protestant scholarship, the "Textus Receptus." Bruce Metzger paints Erasmus's NT in the worst possible terms. It was hurriedly put together, was based upon inferior Greek texts, and constitutes a "debased form of the Greek Testament."¹⁰ While not disputing the substandard character of Erasmus's NT, Robert Hull gives some mitigating factors:

> Had he [Erasmus] been given more time and expended more effort to gather manuscripts, he could have produced a better text (by today's standards) than what he did produce—but only marginally so, for the science of textual criticism was not far enough advanced to prepare him to make the judgments needed, even if he had been able to acquire many more ancient manuscripts.¹¹

Erasmus's NT was reproduced in influential editions in the sixteenth century by Robert Estienne, known as Stephanus (1546, 1549, 1550, 1551), and Théodore de Bèza (Beza), Calvin's successor at Geneva, who reproduced Erasmus's NT in ten editions from 1565 to 1611 (one posthumous). Both of these scholars engaged in textual analysis, but they only made annotations to Erasmus's text rather than producing their own, in this way bolstering the authority of Erasmus's NT.¹² Its authoritative status as the "received text," Textus Receptus, came from the preface to the second edition published by Abraham and Bonaventure Elzevir in Leiden (1633), claiming that "[the reader has] the text which is now received by all, in which we give nothing changed or corrupted."¹³ This marketing strategy has had far-reaching effects, with the status of Erasmus's NT as the Textus Receptus evoking powerful religious convictions, even to the present era.¹⁴

In the seventeenth and eighteenth centuries, scholars made great progress in collecting variant readings from the NT manuscripts, but these efforts were routinely condemned as attacks on the sacred text. John Mill's collection

---

9. The Complutensian Polyglot was not published, however, until 1522, after it received the papal imprimatur in 1520, "by which time it had been 'scooped' by the edition of Erasmus." Hull, *New Testament Text*, 36.

10. Metzger and Ehrman, *Text of the New Testament*, 149.

11. Hull, *New Testament Text*, 37–38.

12. Metzger and Ehrman, *Text of the New Testament*, 149–52.

13. Metzger and Ehrman, *Text of the New Testament*, 152.

14. See, e.g., the YouTube video entitled, "The NIV is a fake Bible" https://www.youtube.com/watch?v=dS-tIgZoPvI accessed 11/09/18. Similarly, https://www.youtube.com/watch?v=Lr-onxCHaLE "NIV (do you use the New International Version NIV?)," accessed September 11, 2018. These video presentations condemn the NIV because it departs from the Textus Receptus.

of 30,000 variant readings, for example, was attacked by Daniel Whitby as undermining the authority of Scripture and "tantamount to tampering with the text."[15] A new stage in NT textual criticism began with Johann Albrecht Bengel (1687–1752), who established that the reliability of manuscripts lies not in how many there are, but in the quality of the manuscript. He assessed the reliability of NT manuscripts by distinguishing two groups of texts: Asiatic, from Constantinople and its environs, and African—divided into two, represented by codex Alexandrinus and the Old Latin. Bengel also formulated the idea that the difficult reading is preferred to the easy reading. For his pioneering work he was attacked as an enemy of the faith.[16] Johann Salomo Semler (1725–91) further refined Bengel's methodology, classifying NT manuscripts into three major groups.[17]

Johann Griesbach (1745–1812) built upon this work, and Metzger credits him with having "laid foundations for all subsequent work on the Greek text of the New Testament."[18] Griesbach further refined both the groups of texts—Alexandrian, Western, and Byzantine—and text-critical theory with his fifteen canons of textual criticism.[19] In addition to Griesbach's contribution to the development of NT textual criticism, he was the first to change the text itself, rather than making annotations to the Textus Receptus, as previous textual critics had done.[20] His Greek NT editions were published at Halle (1775–77), Halle and London (1796–1806); Leipzig (1803–07), and editions were also published in England, Scotland and America.[21]

The first Greek NT to be printed in the USA was the Textus Receptus, in Massachusetts in 1800.[22] Griesbach's critical Greek NT, however, was not far behind, being introduced to a burgeoning American biblical scholarship by the forerunner of the New England biblical studies movement, Joseph

---

15. Metzger and Ehrman, *Text of the New Testament*, 152–58. Quotation, 155. Consider also the title of Dr. Leonard Twell's response to Daniel Mace's NT, which had extensive text-critical annotations: *A Critical Examination of the last New Testament and Version of the New Testament: wherein the Editor's Corrupt Text, False Version, and fallacious Notes are Detected and Censur'd* (London, 1731–32). Cited in Metzger and Ehrman, *Text of the New Testament*, 158.

16. Metzger and Ehrman, *Text of the New Testament*, 158–160.

17. Metzger and Ehrman, *Text of the New Testament*, 161–162.

18. Metzger and Ehrman, *Text of the New Testament*, 165.

19. Metzger and Ehrman, *Text of the New Testament*, 165–67. See further, Hull, *New Testament Text*, 72–75.

20. Hull, *New Testament Text*, 74.

21. Hull, *New Testament Text*, 167.

22. Hull, *New Testament Text*, 164.

Stevens Buckminster. Amongst a library of three thousand volumes that he brought back from Europe were Griesbach's works on New Testament textual criticism. Buckminster had Griesbach's 1794 "manual" edition of the Greek NT printed in New England, under the auspices of Harvard University, in 1809.[23] Such was their commitment to rigorous scholarship that Griesbach's text was accepted above the Textus Receptus by the New England scholars, who formed the heart of the nineteenth-century American biblical studies movement. It was Griesbach's NT text that Adoniram Judson pored over for many years as he translated the NT into Burmese. But, as his letter reveals, Judson harbored suspicions over Griesbach's text and eventually abandoned it in favor of George Christian Knapp's critical Greek NT.

Comparing Judson's 1832, 1840, and Modern New Testaments

Analysis of Judson's 1832 and 1840 editions is presented in four categories. It must be noted, however, that compared with the thirty-six instances discussed below, I observed a further two-hundred twenty-seven times in which both the 1832 and 1840 editions agree with the KJV, over and against the NRSV. This shows how similar Griesbach's NT is to the Textus Receptus.

1. Variants Followed in the 1832 Edition but Not the 1840 Edition, Based on Griesbach's Text, Adopted in Most Modern New Testaments

This first section identifies passages in the 1832 edition where Judson followed Griesbach over and against the Textus Receptus, decisions that have stood the test of time and are followed by most modern versions. Judson then rejected these variant readings and followed the readings found in the Textus Receptus for his final 1840 edition.

- *Matthew 6:13* "For the kingdom and the power and the glory are yours forever. Amen." Like the NRSV and most modern English versions, the concluding doxology to the Lord's Prayer is omitted from the 1832 edition but reappears in the 1840 edition.

---

23. Brown, *Rise of Biblical Criticism*, 23–24. The "manual" edition was Griesbach's Greek NT with abridged text-critical notes.

- *Matthew 6:18* "... your Father who sees you in secret will reward you (openly)." Most modern NTs omit "openly," as does the 1832 edition, but it reappears in the 1840 edition.

- *Matthew 20:22* "But Jesus answered and said, 'Ye know not what ye ask. Are ye able to drink of the cup that I shall drink of, <u>and to be baptized with the baptism that I am baptized with</u>?' They say unto him, 'We are able'" (KJV). The underlined section is omitted from most modern versions, and from the 1832 edition, but included in the 1840 edition.

- *Matthew 24:13* "Watch therefore, for ye know neither the day nor the hour <u>wherein the Son of man cometh</u>" (KJV). The underlined section is omitted from most modern versions and the 1832 edition but included in the 1840 edition.

- *Mark 9:38* "And John answered him, saying, Master, we saw one casting out devils in thy name, <u>and he followeth not us</u>: and we forbad him, because he followeth not us" (KJV). The underlined phrase, "who does not follow us," is omitted from most modern versions and the 1832 edition but included in the 1840 edition.

- *Luke 9:56* "<u>For the Son of man is not come to destroy men's lives, but to save *them*</u>. And they went to another village" (Luke 9:56 KJV). Most modern versions and the 1832 edition omit the underlined sentence, but it reappears in the 1840 edition.

- *Luke 11:2* "And he said unto them, 'When ye pray, say, <u>Our</u> Father which art in heaven, Hallowed be thy name. Thy kingdom come. <u>Thy will be done, as in heaven, so in earth</u>'" (KJV). "Our" is omitted from most modern versions, and from the 1832 edition, as is the clause, "Your will be done, on earth as in heaven." Both return in the 1840 edition.

- *Luke 11:4* "And forgive us our sins; for we also forgive every one that is indebted to us. And lead us not into temptation; <u>but deliver us from evil</u> (KJV)." The underlined clause is omitted from most modern versions and the 1832 edition but included in the 1840 edition.

- *Luke 17:36* "There will be two women grinding meal together; one will be taken and the other left" (NRSV). This entire verse is omitted in most modern versions and the 1832 edition but included in the 1840 edition.

- *Acts 8:37* "And Philip said, If thou believest with all thine heart, thou mayest. And he answered and said, I believe that Jesus Christ is the Son of God" (KJV). This verse is omitted from most modern versions and from the 1832 edition but included in the 1840 edition.

- *Acts 15:18* "Known to God from eternity are all His works" (NKJV). The underlined words are omitted from most modern versions and the 1832 edition but included in the 1840 edition. The omitted words constitute what is judged an addition (underlined): Γνωστὰ ἀπ᾽ αἰῶνός ἐστιν τῷ θεῷ πάντα τὰ ἔργα αὐτοῦ. Thus, NRSV, "Known from long ago."
- *Colossians 1:14* "In whom we have redemption through his blood, even the forgiveness of sins" (KJV). "Through his blood" is omitted in most modern versions and the 1832 edition but reappears in the 1840 edition.
- *Hebrews 2:7* "Thou madest him a little lower than the angels; thou crownedst him with glory and honor, and didst set him over the works of thy hands" (KJV). The underlined clause is omitted in most modern versions and the 1832 edition but reappears in the 1840 edition.

These thirteen instances show Judson's 1832 Burmese NT, like many parts of his OT translation, utilized the cutting edge of biblical scholarship, enabling him to make text-critical decisions that are accepted today. Unlike his OT translation, Judson subsequently rejected these decisions and reverted to the traditional readings of the Textus Receptus for his final edition of the Burmese NT.

2. Places Where Both the 1832 and 1840 Editions Agree, Against the Textus Receptus

This second section analyses eleven places where Judson's 1832 and 1840 editions of the NT both disagree with the Textus Receptus and follow textual variants which have been accepted by most modern NT versions. Without access to Knapp's text, it is not possible to see whether Knapp also followed these variants, although it seems likely that he would have, or at least could have, as his was also a critical Greek NT, although inferior to Griesbach's.[24] There may also have been places where Judson has continued to follow Griesbach against Knapp.

- *Matthew 16:20* "Then charged he his disciples that they should tell no man that he was Jesus the Christ" (KJV). Most modern versions omit "Jesus" from this verse, as does both the 1832 and the 1840 editions.

---

24. See the contemporary comparative review, Gray and Bowen, "Griesbach's Standard Greek Text."

- *Matthew 27:35* "And they crucified him, and parted his garments, casting lots: that it might be fulfilled which was spoken by the prophet, They parted my garments among them, and upon my vesture did they cast lots" (KJV). The underlined section, not included in most modern versions, is omitted from both the 1832 and 1840 editions.
- *Matthew 28:20; Mark 16:20; Luke 24:53* The concluding "Amen" to the gospel is omitted from both the 1832 and 1840 editions, as it is in most modern versions.
- *John 3:25* "Then there arose a question between *some* of John's disciples and the Jews about purifying" (KJV). Most modern versions and both the 1832 and 1840 editions have "a Jew."
- *Acts 17:27* "That they should seek the Lord . . . " (KJV). Most modern versions have "God" instead of "The Lord," as do both the 1832 and the 1840 editions.
- *1 Thessalonians 2:15* "Who both killed the Lord Jesus, and their own prophets, and have persecuted us; and they please not God, and are contrary to all men:" (KJV). Most modern versions have "the prophets," as also in both the 1832 and 1840 editions.
- *2 Thessalonians 2:8* "And then shall that Wicked be revealed, whom the Lord shall consume with the spirit of his mouth, and shall destroy with the brightness of his coming" (KJV). Most modern versions and both the 1832 and 1840 editions have "the Lord Jesus."
- *1 Timothy 2:7* "Whereunto I am ordained a preacher, and an apostle, (I speak the truth in Christ, *and* lie not;) a teacher of the Gentiles in faith and verity" (KJV). "In Christ" is omitted in most modern versions and both the 1832 and 1840 editions.
- *1 John 5:21* The final "Amen" is omitted in most modern versions and both the 1832 and 1840 editions.

This section shows that Judson did not reject the discipline of textual criticism for the NT, nor did he have an unconditional commitment to the Textus Receptus.

3. Variants That Are Different from Both the Textus Receptus and Modern Versions, Based on Griesbach

The third section of analysis shows two cases where the 1832 edition followed Griesbach's text critical decisions, which have not stood the test of time.

- *John 6:69* The 1832 edition, following Griesbach, has "The Christ, the Son of God," omitting the "living" from the KJV and the 1840 edition, "The Christ, the Son of the living God." Both are quite different from most modern versions, "The Holy One of God" (NRSV). This modern reading was followed by the New England scholar George Noyes, a contemporary of Judson, who translated Tischendorf's Greek NT in 1869.[25]

- *Romans 16:25-27* In the 1832 edition, the conclusion to Romans, 16:25-27, is transposed to immediately after Rom 14:23, becoming Rom 14:24-27. The 1840 edition repositioned it back to 16:25-27. History has proven that in this case Judson made the right decision in following the Textus Receptus in the final 1840 edition.

4. Places Where the 1832 Edition Follows the Textus Receptus Against Griesbach

The following ten cases show Judson rejecting Griesbach's decisions and following the Textus Receptus in the 1832 edition, decisions which were retained in the 1840 edition.

- *Romans 15:29* "And I am sure that, when I come unto you, I shall come in the fulness of the blessing of the gospel of Christ" (KJV). The underlined phrase is different than most modern versions which omit "of the gospel," e.g., "and I know that when I come to you, I will come in the fullness of the blessing of Christ" (NRSV). Griesbach also omits this phrase (τοῦ εὐαγγελίου). Judson, however, included it in both the 1832 and 1840 editions.

- *Galatians 4:6* "And because ye are sons, God hath sent forth the Spirit of his Son into your hearts, crying, Abba, Father" (KJV). In most modern versions and Griesbach, the underlined "your" is "our." In both the 1832 and 1840 NTs Judson follows the Textus Receptus.

---

25. See BibleWorks—Version 10.0.8.498. For Lobegott Friedrich Constantin von Tischendorf (1815–1874), see Hull, *Story of the New Testament Text*, 78–79.

- *Ephesians 4:9* "Now that he ascended, what is it but that he also descended <u>first</u> into the lower parts of the earth?" (KJV). Although "first" is omitted in most modern versions and Griesbach, Judson includes it in both the 1832 and 1840 NTs.

- *Ephesians 6:24; 1 Timothy 6:21; Titus 3:15; Philemon 25* Judson includes the final "Amen" in both editions of his NT, although most modern versions and Griesbach omit it.

- *Colossians 2:2* "That their hearts might be comforted, being knit together in love, and unto all riches of the full assurance of understanding, to the acknowledgement of <u>the mystery of God, and of the Father, and of Christ</u>;" (KJV). In place of the underlined text, the NRSV has, "God's mystery, that is, Christ himself" (τοῦ μυστηρίου τοῦ θεοῦ, Χριστου), which (in Greek) is close to Griesbach: "God's mystery" (τοῦ μυστηρίου τοῦ θεου). Judson, however, follows the Textus Receptus in both the 1832 and 1840 editions.

- *1 Timothy 3:16* "And without controversy great is the mystery of godliness: <u>God</u> was manifest in the flesh, justified in the Spirit, seen of angels, preached unto the Gentiles, believed on in the world, received up into glory" (KJV). Most modern versions and Griesbach read "he" or "who" instead of "God," i.e., "He (ὅς "who") was revealed in the flesh" (NRSV).[26] Judson follows the Textus Receptus in both the 1832 and 1840 editions.

- *1 John 5:7–8* "For there are three that bear record in heaven, the Father, the Word, and the Holy Ghost: and these three are one. And there are three that bear witness in earth, the Spirit, and the water, and the blood: and these three agree in one" (KJV). The underlined section is omitted in most modern versions and Griesbach but included in both the 1832 and 1840 editions. This variant, the so-called *Comma Johanneum*, is so weakly attested that even Erasmus omitted it at first, not inserting until the third edition of his Greek NT in 1522.[27] [/BL 1–7]

This fourth section gives insight into why Judson was suspicious of Griesbach. Judson was, on the one hand, a meticulous scholar, but on the other he was an orthodox Calvinistic evangelist and church planter. He may have been uncomfortable removing "of the gospel" in Rom 15:29, but more tellingly Col 2:2, 1 Tim 3:16 and 1 John 5:7–8 all have christological and trinitarian elements that Judson has retained. It must also be remembered

---

26. See Hull, *Story of the New Testament Text*, 63, for how *hos* became *theos* (God).

27. Hull, *Story of the New Testament Text*, 37; Metzger and Ehrman, *Text of the New Testament*, 146–48.

that in Judson's base, New England, orthodox Calvinists were locked into an intractable battle with the Unitarian movement.[28] It is evident that Judson was unwilling to follow Griesbach in these cases on theological grounds.

Conclusion: Why Judson Was Suspicious of Griesbach

If Judson was suspicious of Griesbach's critical NT text, why did he use his text for so many years before abandoning it? The answer is clear. Griesbach's critical NT text was considered the gold standard within the New England biblical studies movement, the movement which produced Judson.[29] As the committed biblical scholar that Judson was, there was probably never any question about whether he would use Griesbach's Greek NT as the basis of his translation. Yet he was suspicious of Griesbach's text and eventually abandoned it in favor of George Christian Knapp's Greek NT. What led to this decision?

Judging from a review article in *The North American Review*, a Boston publication, Griesbach's reputation had not diminished in New England by 1830.[30] Gray and Bowen (first names unknown) compared Griesbach's Greek NT with Knapp's. They were unequivocal that Griesbach's NT was a ground-breaking new recension whereas Knapp's was a much inferior work. Of Knapp's NT, Gray and Bowen wrote,

> The language of the preface throughout leads the reader to anticipate a sort of halting compromise between critical accuracy, which had made some of its claims heard, and a lingering popular attachment to some vitiated passages, which have now, with a remarkable unanimity of sects, been condemned, as not entitled to a place in Scripture.[31]

This resonates with the changes that Judson made in his final 1840 edition of the NT. The analysis of Judson's 1832 and 1840 editions above shows that significant textual decisions in the 1832 edition, which have carried the day in modern versions, were rejected in the 1840 edition, where he turned back to the Textus Receptus. It seems that the power of the Textus Receptus had a hold on Judson. This becomes evident in the fourth section of the textual analysis where even in the 1832 edition Judson did not follow Griesbach, particularly 1 Tim 3:16 and 1 John 5:7–8. These passages

---

28. See Brown, *Rise of Biblical Criticism*, especially 10–26; 125–39.

29. About this movement see Brown, *Rise of Biblical Criticism*; Giltner, *Moses Stuart*; Williams, *Edward Robinson*. For Judson as a product of this movement, see de Jong, "New England Exegete."

30. Gray and Bowen, "Griesbach's Standard Greek Text."

31. Gray and Bowen, "Griesbach's Standard Greek Text," 271.

explicitly confirm Christ's divinity and the doctrine of the Trinity, respectively. Although Judson was, apparently grudgingly, committed to following Griesbach's text, he would not follow him there. Here, two different sides of Judson appear. On the one hand he was an accomplished and meticulous scholar, but on the other he was a committed believer and a church-planting evangelist. It seems these two sides were in some tension when it came to translating the NT. In the final analysis, tension between scholarship and faith played a role in Judson's translation of the NT into Burmese.

Bibliography

Brown, Jerry Wayne. *The Rise of Biblical Criticism in American, 1800–1870: The New England Scholars*. Connecticut: Wesleyan University Press, 1969.

de Jong, John. "A Nineteenth-Century New England Exegete Abroad: Adoniram Judson and the Burmese Bible." *HTR* 112/3 (2019) 319–39.

———. "Textual Criticism, the Textus Receptus, and Adoniram Judson's Burmese New Testaments." In *Essays in Recognition of the Retirement of Rev. Dr. Timothy Meadowcroft*, edited by Csilla Saysell and John de Jong, 51–60. *Pacific Journal of Baptist Research* 13/2 (2018).

Giltner, John H. *Moses Stuart: The Father of Biblical Science in America*. Atlanta: SBL, 1988.

Gray and Bowen. "The New Testament in the Common Version, Conformed to Griesbach's Standard Greek Text." *The North American Review* 31 (1830) 267–75.

Griesbach, Johann Jakob. *Novum Testamentum Graece: Manual Edition*. 1805. On BibleWorks—Version 10.0.8.498.

Hull, Robert F., Jr. *The Story of the New Testament Text: Movers, Materials, Motives, Methods, and Models*. Leiden: Brill, 2011.

Judson, Adoniram. "Letter, Dec. 28, 1840." *The Baptist Missionary Magazine* 21/6 (1841) 186.

Khong, James W. "Presenting the Gospel Message to the Modern Burmans: Through Scriptural Translations." MA diss., Fuller Theological Seminary School of World Mission, 1992.

Metzger, Bruce M. *The Text of the New Testament: Its Transmission, Corruption, and Restoration*. 2nd ed. Oxford: Clarendon, 1968.

Metzger, Bruce M., and Bart D. Ehrman. *The Text of the New Testament: Its Transmission, Corruption, and Restoration*. 4th ed. New York; Oxford: Oxford University Press, 2005.

The New Testament, in Burmese. Maulmein, 1832. https://books.google.co.nz/books?id=UylKAAAAMAAJ&printsec=frontcover&source=gbs_ge_summary_r&cad=0#v=onepage&q&f=false

The New Testament of Our Lord and Saviour Jesus Christ; Translated into the Burmese from the Original Greek. Rangoon: American Baptist Mission, 1866. https://books.google.com.mm/books?id=y2lpAAAAcAAJ

Williams, Jay G. *The Times and Life of Edward Robinson: Connecticut Yankee in King Solomon's Court*. Atlanta: SBL, 1999.

18

Reception History: Signaling Change in Biblical Studies[1]

Donald P. Moffat

It is a pleasure to offer this article in recognition of Tim Meadowcroft, who has contributed so significantly to biblical scholarship and biblical scholars in this part of the world. This tribute contains three themes that reflect Tim's scholarship: his hermeneutical depth, his passion for the Old Testament, and his role as a teacher and encourager of biblical scholars.

Biblical scholars have an increasingly diverse and complex set of interpretive tools with which to examine the text in the effort to understand it well. Yet this burgeoning group of newer interpretive approaches also signals a sea change in the academic discipline that is biblical studies. The ideas that underpin a number of these interpretive approaches demand a change in some of the foundational assumptions about what the Bible is and what the task of the interpreter is. These are issues that bubble under the surface of biblical studies, occasionally rising to the surface but so far not broadly affecting the discipline. More needs to happen because the newer critical methods are growing, and the landscape is changing incrementally. Students entering the field need help to orientate, and the discipline needs to handle the transition from a modernist world to a postmodern one.

1. This chapter was first published as Moffat, "Reception History," and is reproduced here with some minor changes with permission.

Reception History

Reception history is a parade example of a new critical method that is increasingly popular. It is also an approach to biblical studies that is highlighting, and to an extent magnifying, fault lines within biblical studies. The discussion that follows is largely taken from a Hebrew Bible/Old Testament perspective, but writings of New Testament scholars indicate the same issues are true in the discipline generally.

Reception history, as the title implies, focuses on the history of how the text has been understood. That is not a simply a history of scholarly interpretation but also a history of the effects of a wide variety of interpretations. The German *Wirkungsgeschichte,* sometimes translated "history of effects," emphasizes that the impact of the text is the key focus of reception history. Choon-Leong Seow comments that he prefers to call the approach "History of Consequences," which for him encapsulates all the influences of the text, from exegesis and scholarly interpretation to "application, use, influence, and impact" along with the ethical implications of interpretation and use of the text.[2] In his introduction to *The Oxford Handbook of the Reception of the Bible,* Jonathan Roberts writes:

> The reception of the Bible comprises every single act or word of interpretation of that book (or books) over the course of three millennia. It includes everything from Jesus reading Isaiah, or Augustine reading Romans, to a Sunday School nativity play, or the appearance of '2COR4:16' as a stock number on military gun scopes. No one and nothing is excluded. Reception *history,* however, is a different matter. That is usually—although not always—a scholarly enterprise, consisting of selecting and collating shards of that infinite wealth of reception in accordance with the particular interests of the historian concerned, and giving them a narrative frame.[3]

What I find helpful about Roberts's words is the identification of the reception history task as the selecting and collating of particular examples of reception that can be shown to cohere in some way. Reception history is a meaning-making exercise, a way of storying the impact of biblical texts. Implicit in such storying is the analysis of the effects, which John Lyons indicates in his succinct definition, "Reception history aims to understand the interaction between a text, a context and an audience's response."[4]

---

2. Seow, *Job 1–21,* 110.
3. Roberts, "Introduction," 1 (emphasis original).
4. Lyons, "Hope," 213.

Roberts's definition above notes that reception is a very broad category, but his examples are largely written texts. One of the values of reception history is that it explores other forms of communication, such as music, drama, and art, that interpret biblical texts. Reception history is revealing the great breadth of the influence of the biblical text.

There are already a growing number of examples of the production of reception histories. Along with *The Oxford Handbook of the Reception of the Bible*, about half of de Gruyter's thirty-volume *The Encyclopedia of the Bible and Its Reception* has been published.[5] Commentary series such as the Blackwell Bible Commentary series and the IVP's *Ancient Christian Commentary on Scripture* have multiple published volumes. In addition, the theory and practice of reception history is being discussed and demonstrated in various journals and volumes such as the LOHBOTS *Scriptural Traces* series.[6]

Reception history has its roots in the work of Hans-Georg Gadamer, a German philosopher whose book *Truth and Method* (*Wahrheit und Methode*), first published in 1960, has been a significant influence on the theory of interpretation.[7] In *Truth and Method*, Gadamer pointed out that objective interpretation, as claimed by the science and literary theory of the time, was impossible. He argued that every person comes to a text with a mind shaped by his or her historical context. Gadamer said that a key factor in our interpretation of texts is our own awareness of our prejudgments or prejudices. That is, that the more we understand ourselves as interpreters, the more clearly we understand our differences from the historical text, the better chance we have of understanding the otherness of the text. The result is that the interpreter is able to see the text more closely to its own historical horizon and not according to the interpreter's own conditioned presuppositions. He argued that the interpretation of texts, including ancient texts like the Bible, involves the bringing together of two horizons, that of the reader and that of the text.

Gadamer did not propose a method of interpretation; rather, he claimed to be describing "the conditions in which understanding takes place."[8] He was interested in explaining the philosophical and theoretical aspects of what happens to an interpreter when that person seeks to make meaning of a text rather than in the mechanics. While Gadamer was not interested in method, his insights have influenced several hermeneutical

---

5. Klauck et al., *Encyclopedia*.

6. Examples of journals include *Journal of the Bible and Its Reception*, *Biblical Reception*, and the online journal *Relegere*.

7. Gadamer, *Truth and Method*.

8. Gadamer, *Truth and Method*, 295.

methods. One of those is reader-response theory, which focuses on the reader as meaning maker. Another approach that has grown out of Gadamer's ideas is reception history—how the text has been understood and the impact of that understanding.

Reception History Versus Historical Criticism

All new interpretive methods face challenges, and reception history is no exception. Over the past decades, various aspects of the approach have been critiqued and debated. One issue is whether it coheres as a hermeneutical method. Reception history is more a loosely linked set of methods than a cohesive method. Susan Gillingham, following the lead of Christopher Rowland, argues that the discipline is still in its infancy and that new hermeneutical models take time to develop.[9] She wrote that in 2015 and references Rowland's comment from 2004. While there are some benchmark works emerging, the field is too diverse to have any coherence beyond being a historical enterprise focused on reception. Although Gillingham speaks of reception history using a range of methods, she writes as if she expects an overarching hermeneutical model to arise in time. Given the great breadth of the potential receptions open to examination and the diversity of the biblical material, it is unlikely one model will be found to work. Note, for example, Chris Rowland's comments that the *Blackwell Bible Commentary* series did not start with a particular hermeneutical theory in mind and that experience had made clear that "one model will not suit every book."[10] Apart from the methodological issues, there is probably also a worldview one here. Modernists will look for the coherence of an overarching model, but postmodern scholars are unlikely to put so much store in essentialist models as the measure of a discipline or its value.

Gillingham notes that biblical studies as a discipline has undergone considerable change over her career, and even defining what the discipline is or what it does is difficult now.[11] When this factor is added to the current pressure on many university departments as humanities disciplines shrink, it is not surprising that methods that further diversify the field and appear to dilute its uniqueness cause disquiet in the academy. Yet the greater tension is probably more internal than external. One might say that pressure along the fault lines of biblical studies as a discipline have been building for several decades, and reception history has added yet more pressure to a growing

---

9. Gillingham, "Biblical Studies on Holiday?" 23.
10. Rowlands, "A Pragmatic Approach," 1–2.
11. Gillingham, "Biblical Studies on Holiday?," 18.

strain. Whether the result is a lengthy set of tremors and with an occasional larger jolt or a seismic shift of major proportions is yet to be revealed. Nevertheless, the assumed foundations of the discipline, the nature of the Bible as literature, and the goals of studying it are shifting.

These stress points seem to be underlying issues in some of the debate that goes on between the established king, historical criticism, and new pretender, reception history. An example of what I mean can be seen in a debate that is known in some circles as "Hurtadogate."[12] It started with comments by prominent NT scholar Larry Hurtado, who identified in his blog what he saw as essential skills for a New Testament PhD in the UK.[13] It amounted to the basic historical-critical skills, with relevant languages (Greek, Hebrew, German, and French) and ability to engage with text criticism. While Hurtado granted that approaches like reception history were valid endeavors, he indicated that they are supplementary to the foundational skills. Others, for a variety of reasons, saw his prescription as delimiting NT studies too narrowly.[14] Part of the response had to do with the current state of biblical studies as a discipline within the shrinking humanities curriculum in many universities. Yet another, as Hurtado noted, had more to do with worldview.[15] It is about with what biblical scholars think they are about and can achieve, which is clearly changing with postmodern influence.

Historical-critical scholarship begins by trying to obtain the most accurate text, that which most closely approaches what the author originally wrote. It then seeks to identify the various historical layers, categorizes the style and context of the text, and examines how it is shaped. This is supported and supplemented with philology, archaeology, history, and interpretive tradition. The goal is to understand *the* message of *the* text as accurately as possible. However, two key questions call this goal into question and thus the priority of the historical-critical method as the foundation upon which biblical interpretation is built. Those questions are: Is there *an original text*? And, is there *a meaning*? Reception history is reinforcing the answer "no" to both those questions, so widening the cracks in the foundations of the historical-critical method.

---

12. Morgan, "Visitors, Gatekeepers and Receptionists," 69.

13. Hurtado, "Tools of the Trade."

14. For example, see Crossley, "An Immodest Proposal"; Sandford, "Past and Future."

15. Hurtado, "On Diversity." See n. 21.

Where Is the Original Text?

One part of the response to the question about whether there is an original text or not intersects with the debate about where one starts the reception history task. Traditionalists argue that historical criticism is the foundation on which new methods should build.[16] Thus reception history, like all new interpretive methods starts after historical criticism has finished. Yet, it is obvious that the historical-critical method is itself is a form of reception and is as equally open to analysis as any other aspect of reception. The attempt to identify the most original text to interpret results in a scholarly creation, that is, a text that is a modern scholarly reception of the manuscripts that our critical texts are drawn from. Brennan Breed sums up the situation well with his description of the standard Hebrew OT:

> The *Biblica hebraica stuttgartensia*, the most commonly used critical edition of the Hebrew Bible, is a modern scholarly edition of a medieval manuscript with late antique vowels, written in an anachronistic script and surrounded by diachronous layers of paratextual symbols.[17]

He goes on to argue that the hermeneutical formulation of studying what is behind the text, in the text, and in front of the text, breaks down when the "in the text" element is drawn from a text, which is itself a complex mixture of things behind and in front of the text. Whether it is *BHS* or the Greek UBS/Nestle-Aland NT, the original text we draw on is a reception built on layers of reception.[18]

This line of thought needs to be taken a stage further. The Western church and scholarship has made the Masoretic Text its foundation for the

---

16. Hurtado appears to assume this, writing, "I think it is an asset to be able to read the Greek New Testament and draw upon scholarly investigation of its texts in tracing their subsequent reception history" ("On Diversity," 362). On the other hand, he earlier comments positively on Lyons's proposal to consider historical criticism a part of reception history ("Hope"). Some reception critics have also worked on this basis. John Sawyer comments that "the reception history of the Bible, is based on the premise that how people have interpreted, and been influenced by, a sacred text like the Bible is often as interesting and historically important as what it originally meant," in his series editor's preface in each of the *Blackwell Bible Commentary* series. However, in his own commentary in the series on Isaiah, he does not restrict himself to reception after the text reached an "original" state, but includes reception within Isaiah itself. See for example, Sawyer, *Isaiah*, 41–42.

17. Breed, *Nomadic Text*, 6.

18. While there are differences between the eclectic nature of the critical Greek NT and the reliance of *BHS* on the Leningrad codex, the key point that both represent receptions of the original language texts remains.

Old Testament, yet the Orthodox church has persisted with the Greek Septuagint used by the early church. That means that some books, such as Daniel and Jeremiah, differ quite significantly between branches of the church. So the form of the text that is used by Western scholars is a reception, as is the context in which the original language version is presented. The plurality of texts is not limited to Western scholarship, because the "received" nature of the biblical text is not something that begins with modern critical scholarship. Since the Dead Sea Scrolls gave us a Hebrew version of Jeremiah that is the equivalent of the Septuagint text of Jeremiah, it has been apparent that the shorter LXX form is not a result of translational editing. Rather, it is clear that some biblical books existed and were used in more than one form in overlapping time periods. The text of these books existed in different forms because they were still developing. Another example is that earlier Septuagint versions of 1 and 2 Samuel indicate that its *Vorlage* lacked some material that is now part of the Masoretic Text. Our current MT is an expansion, which leads James Harding to the following observation:

> . . . the layers of tradition history within 1 and 2 Samuel suggest that the process of telling and retelling the story of David and Jonathan, ... is already present *within the biblical text itself*. Indeed, it might be fairer to say that the very idea of a "biblical text itself" reflects an arbitrary and particular, though historically explicable attachment to one particular moment in the evolution of the story of David and Jonathan. This has further implications for reception history, because it suggests that reception history does not begin when there is a fixed text, but is already in process. In other words, the fixing of the text itself is a particular moment within its own history of reception.[19]

What is true for 1 and 2 Samuel and for Jeremiah is also apparent in other Old Testament books. These observations have forced text critics to abandon old ideas of recreating original autographs and to find other ways of defining what they are doing. In most cases, that seems to be to recreate an early version of the MT that the scholar understands to be authoritative in some form.[20] While I have focused on the Old Testament a similar set of issues also pertain to the New Testament. For example, Gospel studies is now so much more aware of the development trajectory that gives rise to four different versions of the same traditions. What we have in our Bibles are (re)created versions of texts taken at various stages in their development.

---

19. Harding, *Love of David*, 136 (emphasis original).
20. See for example, Tov, *Textual Criticism*, 161–69.

There are two conclusions worth noting here. First, as Harding notes, relegating reception history to the study of a finalized text is arbitrary when "[t]ext and reception are inseparable."[21] As Breed notes "the phrase 'the original text' actually means 'the text I have chosen to study for various contingent reasons.'"[22] John Lyons's argument that historical-critical methodologies need to relabel with the terminology of reception history is audacious, but it rests on a valid premise.[23] When it comes to the foundations of the biblical text, it is reception history all the way down.[24] This is not a statement in support of some kind of hegemony of reception history over historical-critical hermeneutics. It is simply an admission of the nature of the text. Secondly, given the fluidity of the text, the endeavor of producing the most accurate original text is relativized. What we are left with is developing traditions which means drawing a boundary line as to when those texts became "the original" is a matter of reception. These are not particularly new issues; they have been simmering for some decades, but reception history is highlighting them. Ironically, it is frequently the findings from historical criticism that reception history is using as the means to prize open the cracks in historical criticism's founding assumptions.

There have been attempts to create some debate around these issues, but they are not common conversations.[25] Most scholars are teachers, so continuing to push these issues to the background is not going to help our students or the discipline. For one, our students are increasingly postmodern in their presuppositions, so they don't see the problems those of us with modernist assumptions do. Secondly, they will increasingly encounter scholarly work that assumes a more fluid text and need to have some ideas about how to negotiate their reading. As someone who teaches hermeneutics, I find myself reflecting on the shape of my teaching program.

Finding Meaning

The related question to that about the text is the question about meaning. Reception history changes the dynamic in the interpretive process. The historical-critical method largely separated interpretation from the traditions of the past. It aimed to jump over all previous interpretation and go back to

21. Harding, "Reception History," 38.
22. Breed, *Nomadic Text*, 13.
23. Lyons, "Hope," 210.
24. Brennan Breed, "What Can a Text Do?" 97.
25. Lyons, "Hope," is aimed at provoking debate, which he argues needs to happen. He was prompted by the lack of response to Aichele et al., "Elephant in the Room."

the text in its ancient context. What did the original author mean, or what did the text mean to its earliest readers? There were always exceptions but if previous interpretations were noted it was usually to support the modern interpreter's understanding. Further, the focus is on one meaning. If options present themselves, scholars grapple with those options in order to choose the best alternative.[26] While multivalence may be recognized, it is usually accommodated into the wider themes of the text.

The focus of reception history is not one meaning but the many receptions. As Breed states, it is about tracing the "history of a text's unfolding capacities."[27] It confronts us with the history of interpretation in all its variety, but particularly as it is presented in the tradition of the church and synagogue. That which historical criticism jumped over, reception history requires us to reconsider. One of the key things it highlights is Gadamer's argument that all interpretation is bound to the interpreter's context. Whether a scholar is aiming to get as close to the meaning of the original context or not, every interpretation is influenced by the interpreter's own context. What we might want to pass judgment on as "misinterpretations" can become explicable in context.

Reception history opens us up to the richness of the text and its capacity to speak to myriad contexts. In a brief study of Daniel 7, Breed first notes how the vision of the four beast/kingdoms is itself a "redeployment of earlier symbolic patterns."[28] He then notes that even when interpreters are agreed on the identification of the kingdoms, the implications of that identification vary.[29] There is a long history of interpreting the fourth kingdom as Rome. Both Jews and Christians experienced Rome as the oppressor and saw the link to the fourth beast. For communities after the demise of the Roman Empire, from medieval Jews to twentieth-century Korean Christians, the fourth beast has symbolized their oppressors. Yet the same text has also been seen as a justification for the fifth kingdom. Read in conjunction with the emphasis on converting the monarch in Daniel 1–6, the fifth kingdom has been understood as a transformation of the fourth, rather than its destruction. Constantine's recognition of Christianity set in motion a wave of interpretations which saw the Roman Empire, or its putative successors, as

---

26. Tov, *Textual Criticism*, 164, notes that the inability to decide between variant readings does not mean one is not original; an evaluation must be made. The problem is the evaluation is made in terms of the critic's conception of the nature and context of the original, which is rarely acknowledged.

27. Breed, *Nomadic Text*, 142.

28. Breed, "What Can a Text Do?," 106.

29. Breed, "What Can a Text Do?," 106–09.

a transformed fourth kingdom. Agreed identification of the fourth beast is understood in opposite ways according to context.

This reinforces the idea that texts do not have one meaning, historically context has heavily influenced how the text is understood. Even if we aim for some original meaning, the context of the later interpreter in dialectic with the meaning observed in the text produces meaning that is shaped to the interpreter's context. This is evident in the way that Daniel 7 is appropriated by 4 Ezra, Revelation, and subsequent Jewish and Christian tradition. This is not an argument against attempting to understand the text as clearly as we can in the best context we can set it in but a reminder that all interpretations are contextual and contingent. Reception history presents us with other interpretations of a text, which are valuable and which relativize our claims about the meaning of the text.

Reception history demonstrates that a text in different contexts is interpreted differently. This again is nothing new, neither is it something that the historical-critical method ensures against. As with the discussion of the nature of the text above, historical criticism provides tools that reception history is using to challenge the base assumption of one meaning to a text.

In another study, Breed again provides a helpful example. He discusses Job 19:25–27, a passage notable for its various interpretative options.[30] At the base level it is very difficult to set the book of Job in a historical context. It might, in its present form, reflect either an exilic or Hellenistic context. It seems to be based in a folktale and likely developed over time. If anything, Job is multi-contextual rather than the product of one context. Breed sets his interpretive approach within a Persian-era Israelite context. The chapter 19 speech by Job in response to accusations by Bildad is also difficult to set in a literary context. It can be read in the context of the second cycle of speeches and with some intertexts as drawing on the trope of death, like a number of laments. In the last verses of the speech, Job presents himself as wrongly in Sheol with a potential way out. In this case, Job and his friends are debating who enters Sheol and why. Yet the text could also be read, in keeping with other texts in Job, in a forensic way, as Job's legal defense. In this case, Job imagines a court scene. In 19:24, Job writes his legal testimony before declaring his kinsman-redeemer will rise up to vindicate him in 19:25. These interpretive options are the result of historical-critical analysis of the passage.

Whereas historical criticism chooses an option, reception history lets alternative readings stand side by side. It is open to the semantic potentialities of the text. What is biblical scholarship about and what should we be

---

30. Breed, *Nomadic Text*, 143–48.

teaching and modeling to students? Do we say the text only has one meaning, in a similar way to Jülicher's insistence that parables only had one primary point of comparison, or do we say the text is contingent and capable of being multi-vocal?

Conclusion

Two underpinning assumptions of the historical-critical method, that of an original text and that of an original meaning in the text, have been background questions in biblical studies for several decades. Reception history adds weight to those questions by repeatedly highlighting the fluidity of the biblical text and the contingent nature of all interpretations. What is more, reception history is actively appropriating historical criticism to present its case. Biblical studies as a discipline cannot continue to overlook the widening cracks in the foundations of the historical-critical method. The answer is not a rejection of either method, nor the drawing of artificial borders between them, nor the hegemony of one over the other, but the acknowledgement that they are complementary and that reception history offers a means to deal with the fault lines in the foundations of historical criticism.

As someone who was educated in a modernist setting and who has looked to the historical-critical method to make sense of the biblical text, the trends in biblical studies can cause me some disquiet. Yet the evidence from reception history is compelling, not least because it draws so strongly on existing historical criticism and reinforces problems already acknowledged by that method. The world of biblical studies is changing, the strains in the fault lines have been growing for some time, and the discipline as a whole needs to acknowledge that more fully. The received nature of the text we study needs to be acknowledged, and choices justified, rather than making vague claims about originality. Issues of meaning need to be more widely acknowledged as contextual and the possibilities that individual texts may speak more than one message in any context more readily accepted. The discipline needs the clarity, and future scholars in the discipline need to start out with a better understanding of the nature of the biblical text and its interpretation.

Bibliography

Aichele, G., et al. "An Elephant in the Room: Historical-Critical and Postmodern Interpretations of the Bible." *JBL* 128 (2009) 383–404.

Breed, Brennan W. *Nomadic Text: A Theory of Reception History*. Bloomington: Indiana University Press, 2014.

———. "What Can a Text Do? Reception History as an Ethology of the Biblical Text." In *Reception History and Biblical Studies*, edited by Emma England and William John Lyons, 95–109. London: Bloomsbury, 2015.

Crossley, James G. "An Immodest Proposal for Biblical Studies." *Relegere* 2/1 (2012) 153–77.

Gadamer, Hans-Georg. *Truth and Method*. 2nd rev ed. Translated by J. Weinsheimer and D.G. Marshall. London: Continuum., 2004. German original *Wahrheit und Methode*. Tübingen: Mohr, 1960.

Gillingham, Susan. "Biblical Studies on Holiday? A Personal View of Reception History." In *Reception History and Biblical Studies*, edited by Emma England and William John Lyons, 17–30. London: Bloomsbury, 2015.

Harding, James E. *The Love of David and Jonathan*. Sheffield: Equinox, 2013.

———. "What is Reception History and What Happens to You if You Do It?" In *Reception History and Biblical Studies*, edited by Emma England and William John Lyons, 31–44. London: Bloomsbury, 2015.

Hurtado, Larry. "On Diversity, Competence and Coherence in New Testament Studies: A Modest Response to James Crossley's 'Immodest Proposal.'" *Relegere* 2/2 (2012) 253–64.

———. "Tools of the Trade." Accessed September 13, 2018. https://larryhurtado.wordpress.com/2011/09/04/tools-of-the-trade/

Klauck, Hans-Josef et.al. *The Encyclopedia of the Bible and Its Reception*. Berlin: De Gruyter, 2009–2018.

Lyons, William John. "Hope for a Troubled Discipline? Contributions to New Testament Studies from Reception History." *JSNT* 33/2 (2010) 207–20.

Moffat, Donald P. "Reception History: Signalling Changes in Biblical Studies." In *Essays in Recognition of the Retirement of Rev. Dr. Timothy Meadowcroft*, edited by Csilla Saysell and John de Jong, 42–50. *Pacific Journal of Baptist Research* 13/2 (2018).

Morgan, Jonathan. "Visitors, Gatekeepers and Receptionists: Reflections on the Shape of Biblical Studies and the role of Reception History." In *Reception History and Biblical Studies*, edited by Emma England and William John Lyons, 61–76. London: Bloomsbury, 2015.

Roberts, Jonathan. "Introduction." In *The Oxford Handbook of the Reception of the Bible*, edited by Michael Lieb et al., 1–8. Oxford: Oxford University Press, 2011.

Rowlands, Chris. "A Pragmatic Approach to Wirkungsgeschichte: Reflections on the Blackwell Bible Commentary Series and on the Writing of its Commentary on the Apocalypse." Accessed September 12, 2018. http://bbibcomm.info/?page_id=183

Sandford, Michael. "On the Past and Future of New Testament Studies: A Response to Larry Hurtado." *Relegere* 4/2 (2014) 229–40.

Sawyer, John. *Isaiah*. Hoboken: John Wiley & Sons, 2018.

Seow, Choon-Leong. *Job 1–21*. Grand Rapids: Eerdmans, 2013.

Tov, Emanuel. *Textual Criticism of the Hebrew Bible*. 3rd. ed. Minneapolis: Fortress, 2012.

19

Is There a Fish in this Cognitive Environment?

Relevance Theory, Interpretive Communities, and the Bible

STEPHEN PATTEMORE

TIM MEADOWCROFT AND I have several things in common. We both grew up in families involved in mission. And, during the 1970s, we were both influenced by our involvement in the Tertiary Students Christian Fellowship, which brought us together from time to time. Subsequent contact was infrequent until, in the mid-1990s, I ended up at the Bible College of New Zealand doing postgraduate biblical studies, where I found in Tim an able teacher and thesis supervisor. I benefited enormously from the relationship and thank Tim for his patient, humble, and incisive mentoring. I learned never to neglect the minutiae of spelling and grammar, never to ignore a pressing question, and to openly ask obvious questions even at the risk of appearing ignorant. It was in a class he taught on "Old Testament Narrative Theology" that I began to read widely (Ricoeur, Kristeva, and Derrida), beyond the bounds of my evangelical upbringing, and to grapple with what postmodern and deconstructive insights meant for our interpretation of the Bible. Tim gave me space and encouragement to investigate Relevance Theory, then (and perhaps still) a relatively unknown linguistic lens on textual meaning. It is with pleasure then, that I dedicate this essay on the topic to Tim in recognition of his academic collegiality and personal friendship.

Introduction

Stanley Fish's series of lectures entitled "Is there a text in this class?" have gained iconic status, due to Fish's lively wit and clarity of presentation and to the significance of his topic.[1] The lectures are in part a response to criticism of the apparent destabilization of the meaning of texts in the critical methodology of Fish, Derrida, and Bloom, who were accused of holding the self-contradictory position of wishing to apply their own interpretive strategy to other people's texts but insisting on normal logical interpretation of their own. To privilege the reader, their critics argued, leads to radical pessimism about the possibility of understanding human communication, and they defended a single, determinate, author-defined meaning. Fish's response is nuanced and operates on a number of levels, moving from direct spoken communication to the interpretation of communally owned texts. His position is well summed up by his statement that "understanding is always possible, but not from the outside."[2] This implies, first, that context is determinative for communication. Even face-to-face communication is ambiguous, and understanding is dependent on speaker and hearer participating in a common context of ideas that allow the text of the communication to find its interpretation. Secondly, a written text in particular has multiple meanings, dependent on the conventions and interests of the communities that interact with it. The range of possible meanings is limited—neither uniquely defined in advance, nor infinitely variable, but multivalent and dependent on the authority of the interpretive communities who address it, with their varying conventions and expectations.

Clearly such considerations of the interpretation of human communication are central to the task of biblical scholars as well as literary critics. How are we to understand these texts, which we hold to be of primary importance, when they were written for someone else in a totally different place and time and culture? Are we entitled to read straight off the page of the text, or do we need to stand in the shoes of the original hearers? Do these scriptural texts have one perspicuous meaning for all time and culture? Or does who you are and where you read from influence what it is you (validly) read? And how do biblical scholars relate their understanding to the wider Christian community?

1. Fish, *Is There a Text*.
2. Fish, *Is There a Text*, 303.

Linguistic pragmatics focuses on the way language is actually used in particular contexts.[3] One comprehensive pragmatic framework, with potential to assist both literary critics and biblical scholars, is Sperber and Wilson's Relevance Theory (RT).[4] Human communication, argue Sperber and Wilson, is geared towards efficiency, or the optimization of relevance. When the conditions of ostensive communication (that is, self-conscious, deliberate communication) are met, the receiver interprets the communication in the way that yields good results for an acceptable amount of processing effort. Central to the way in which this optimally relevant interpretation is reached is the idea of context as a negotiable, cognitive construct. In this essay, I attempt to bring RT alongside Fish's arguments to discover both convergences and divergences and to suggest the applicability of these ideas to the interpretation of biblical texts.[5]

Fish's argument is structured around several anecdotes, real and imagined. Two of the real anecdotes will be the focus of my interest. The first, which gave the title to the series of lectures, is a face-to-face verbal encounter between a professor and a student. The second lecture is titled "How to recognize a poem when you see one." Here we move from verbal to written communication and the issue of the interpretation of written texts. Using RT to examine what took place in each of these incidents, we will ask whether Fish has adequately explained the facts in his proposal that meaning is not inherent in the text but is brought to it by the interpretive community. We will show that RT supports the strategic importance of context for interpretation and the inherent asymmetry of any communicative act. But it does on the other hand provide a theoretical basis for the possibility of accessing the author's intended meaning within the context in which he or she communicated, and thus for according this meaning some priority over meanings brought to the text by other interpretive communities.

Relevance Theory

Defenders of a "single determinate authorial meaning" usually assume some variety of a code or conduit model of communication in which, by a process

---

3. Levinson, *Pragmatics*, 1–35.

4. Sperber and Wilson, *Relevance*. For a recent textbook see Clark, *Relevance Theory*. The breadth of application of RT can be seen at https://personal.ua.es/francisco.yus/rt.html

5. For more details see Pattemore, *People of God*. On the interaction of RT and literary theory see MacKenzie, *Paradigms of Reading*.

of coding and decoding, the recipient can reproduce the original thought.[6] This model is unable to explain the importance of inference, whereby what is communicated is something other than what is encoded in the message.

RT recognizes that coding take place, but holds that it is subordinated to a process of implication and inference:

> [T]he linguistic meaning of an uttered sentence falls short of encoding what the speaker means: it merely helps the audience infer what she means. The output of decoding is correctly treated by the audience as a piece of evidence about the communicator's intentions.[7]

> RT builds on the seminal work of H. P. Grice, which describes how communication creates the conditions for its own success.[8] "Grice put forward an idea of fundamental importance: that the very act of communicating creates expectations which it then exploits..."[9]

Successful communication depends on shared information, and RT calls this the *mutual cognitive environment*: a shared set of assumptions that communication participants are *capable* of making.[10] This cannot guarantee that communicator and audience *will make* a symmetrical choice of context and code to use in a communication situation. But Sperber and Wilson agree with literary critics that this asymmetry is inherent in communication.[11] Communication is, then, the attempt to change the cognitive environment of another person and to enlarge the scope of what is mutually manifest to both communicator and audience. No audience can explore and classify all possible contextual implications of an utterance.[12] RT explains the selecting and limiting process by means of "the presumption of optimal relevance":

a. The ostensive stimulus is relevant enough for it to be worth the addressee's effort to process it.

---

6. Since Shannon and Weaver, *Mathematical Theory*, especially 5, 95–113.
7. Sperber and Wilson, *Relevance*, 27.
8. Grice, "Logic and Conversation."
9. Sperber and Wilson, *Relevance*, 37.
10. Sperber and Wilson, *Relevance*, 39–42.
11. Sperber and Wilson, *Relevance*, 43.
12. A contextual implication is a conclusion derived from a combination of existing assumptions and new information. It is formed by the interpretation of new propositions within a particular context. See Sperber and Wilson, *Relevance*, 107–8.

b. The ostensive stimulus is the most relevant one compatible with the communicator's abilities and preferences.[13]

Recipients assume the *relevance* of a communication and bring to the text the most accessible elements of the mutual cognitive environment, choosing the meaning that produces adequate contextual effects for acceptable processing effort. The communicator, knowing this, produces the stimulus that will lead the receptor to the intended meaning.

Implicatures are assumptions that can only be derived by processing a text in a particular context. Sperber and Wilson assert that there is no sharp division between strong implicatures that are clearly intended by the speaker and weak ones for which the hearer "takes the entire responsibility."

> Clearly the weaker the implicatures the less confidence the hearer can have that the particular premises or conclusions he supplies will reflect the speaker's thoughts and this is where the indeterminacy lies. . . . The aim of communication in general is to increase the mutuality of cognitive environments rather than guarantee an impossible duplication of thoughts.[14]

This sliding scale of implicatures with corresponding movement of responsibility from speaker to hearer is precisely illustrated by the spectrum of hermeneutic strategies we are considering. Determinists accept the explicatures and perhaps strong implicatures. Fish and his colleagues focus on the responsibility of the hearer (or reader). But in RT, it is only in the limiting cases that the hearer assumes full responsibility. Weak implicatures are used by the communicator to achieve, among other things, a wide range of poetic effects.[15]

"Is There a Text in this Class?" —Reconstructing the Context

As a first step towards a relevance-theoretic understanding of the communication between professor and student in Fish's first anecdote, let us

---

13. Sperber and Wilson, *Relevance*, 270. Compare the original statement in Sperber and Wilson, *Relevance*, 158, in which the second clause stated, "The ostensive stimulus is the most relevant one the communicator could have used to communicate." The modified statement allows that the actual relevance may not be the absolute maximum but may be influenced by the speaker's aims, priorities, and abilities.

14. Sperber and Wilson, *Relevance*, 199-200.

15. Sperber and Wilson, *Relevance*, 222. See Wilson and Sperber, "Verbal Irony," and the symposium on irony in Carston and Uchida, *Relevance Theory*, 239-95.

attempt a dramatic reconstruction of the encounter.[16] What Fish describes as having taken place is something like this:

Setting: First day of semester at Johns Hopkins University. Teacher, T, is approached by student, S, who has previously taken a course with Fish.

1. S: Is there a text in this class?
2. T: Yes; it's the Norton Anthology of Literature.
3. S: No, no. I mean, in this class do we believe in poems and things, or is it just us?
4. T: (*thinks*) Ah, there's one of Fish's victims!
5. T: (*aloud*) Yes, there *is* a text in this class; what's more, it has meanings; and I am going to tell you what they are.

The teacher assumes the student's first question to be optimally relevant. It requires both decoding and inferential processing, mutually interactive processes which involve:

1. Disambiguation of

    Noun phrases: "a text" (a specific book, a book specified by syllabus, or an abstract concept?)

    "this class" (a room, a group of students, or an institutional structure for learning?)

    Verb phrase: "Is there" ("Does there exist?" Or "Is there specified?" Or "Do you believe in?")

    Preposition: "in" (located in, or among, or for the purpose of)

2. Reference assignment of the deictic demonstrative phrase "this class."

Teacher and student share a set of ideas, which each can call to mind and knows the other can call to mind, including concepts such as the nature of the academic institution, the enrolment of the student in the course of study, the relationship of student to teacher, and the expectations for clarifications on the first day of class. It is relatively easy to see that within this context, the interpretation of the first question that returns the best cognitive effects for the least processing effort is, "Is there a set textbook specified to be read by those participating in this course of study?"[17] The teacher's

---

16. See Fish, *Is There a Text*, 305, 313, 371.

17. Although the use of "in" rather than "for" is a little unusual and might be a trigger to suggest either that the student is less than precise in her grammar or that she intends something other than the most readily reached meaning.

response (line 2) shows that this is precisely how he understood it. It would have been possible for the teacher to recall that Stanley Fish taught courses at the same institution that had to do with the nature of texts, and that the question might be informed by this, but that would represent an excess of processing effort that appears unjustified. So far, RT agrees with Fish's analysis, and indeed provides a theoretical basis for his intuitive deductions. There is neither a single determinative meaning for the question, nor an infinite range of meanings, but a limited number, although RT would offer more than the two "literal" meanings Fish suggests.[18] The "institutional nesting" which Fish proposes is precisely due to the fact that the context of general academic requirements for courses is more easily accessible and more relevant than the context of Fish's literary-critical views.

But with the student's response (line 3), Fish's analysis starts to deconstruct. Fish argues that it is impossible to assign an absolute priority to either of the two meanings he considers for the first question, irrespective of context.[19] But he goes on to suggest that the meaning construed by the teacher is "more normal" than the alternative and more likely to be understood by "a random population." This assertion is only valid if we are concerned with an abstract, context-free decoding of a set of words. The utterance in question occurred in a particular space-time location, and in this specific context, it is possible to say that the meaning inferred by the teacher was the most *relevant* meaning to the teacher. But it was not the student's intended meaning. Her response begins, "No, no. I mean . . . " and clearly she is not saying "Bad luck, you picked the wrong one of two equally possible meanings" (as in a guessing game), but "You have misunderstood me." In RT terms, there has been a failure of relevance, and the student goes on to attempt a correction. This correction, and its sequels later in the exchange, are historical space-time consequences. The speaker's intention was in fact determinative for meaning in this context, and the teacher's deduction, though easily explicable, was simply wrong.

The student rephrases her question (line 3) in a sentence whose meaning is again not transparent, and which would be almost unintelligible to someone outside the specific context of literary-critical ideas. But she does disambiguate certain elements of her original statement. Thus "do we believe?" selects for "is there?" the meaning of literary-critical beliefs, while "poems and things" selects for "text" the abstract meaning.[20] This prompts the teacher to enlarge his cognitive environment to include not

---

18. See Fish, *Is There a Text*, 306–8.
19. Fish, *Is There a Text*, 308.
20. Contra Fish, *Is There a Text*, 311–12.

simply generalized academic course conditions but the specific concerns of contemporary literary-critical debate. However, his reported thoughts (line 4) reflect not a generalized inference about the academic context of the question, but a specific inference about the influence of Stanley Fish (rather than, say, Derrida or de Man). This is no doubt due to the readily available fact that Fish occupies a room "three doors down" and therefore has most likely been a prior influence on the student's understanding.[21] There *is* a Fish in this cognitive environment! The most relevant interpretation of line 3 is thus not simply "Do you believe in hermeneutic indeterminacy?" but "Do you agree with, and expect us to work with, the literary theory of Stanley Fish?" This more specific interpretation requires a little extra processing effort, but immediately returns a surplus of cognitive effects, arising from the history of his interaction with Fish and with students of Fish. The tone of both the thought and the audible statement of the teacher suggest a history of lively debate or disagreement. The teacher does not simply answer the question but implicitly draws swords with Fish.

Once again, Fish has himself traced this process in a way that, in its general outline, receives support from RT. His explanation of the process is less convincing, however. He rejects any idea of according precedence in interpretation to either the construal of sense or the identification of context.[22] RT agrees with him in de-privileging sense construal, but suggests that *optimal relevance* is assumed for the utterance and a context sought that gives the best cognitive effects (construal of sense) for the least processing effort. Thus, context does have a precedence over interpretation.

Fish concludes his chapter with a summary statement, which forms a useful backdrop against which to summarize the subtle relationship of RT to his theory:

> We see then that (1) communication does occur, despite the absence of an independent and context-free system of meanings, that (2) those who participate in this communication do so confidently rather than provisionally (they are not relativists), and that (3) while their confidence has its source in a set of beliefs, those beliefs are not individual-specific or idiosyncratic but communal and conventional (they are not solipsists).[23]

There is little here with which RT does not agree. The first point underlines the reality of context-based ostensive communication, the second expresses the principle of relevance, while the third describes the nature

21. See Fish, *Is There a Text*, 312.
22. Fish, *Is There a Text*, 313.
23. Fish, *Is There a Text*, 321.

of the mutual cognitive environment. RT agrees with Fish that there is no single determinative meaning to an utterance, and that meaning is not therefore unconstrained, but rather limited to alternatives provided by shared assumptions. But this does not imply that there is no privileged interpretation, corresponding to a privileged set of conventions and assumptions. Indeed, RT suggests that there is such a privileged interpretation, which is the one optimally relevant in the original communication situation. This is the one that leaves traces of its history.[24] Indeed, the way in which history constrains interpretation is evident in some of Fish's later illustrations. A non-ironic interpretation of Jane Austen's attitude to Mr. Collins could only be postulated on the basis of a hypothetical discovery of actual correspondence.[25] RT, like Speech Act Theory, sees communication as linguistic action, with the consequences and responsibilities (for both author and audience) inherent in actions.

That it is possible to *misunderstand* what a biblical author says is evidence that meaning is constrained. Certainly, such misunderstanding took place from the beginning and when authors had a chance, they attempted to correct this, much like the student in Fish's story (e.g., 1 Cor 5:9–10). If our question is "What was Paul saying to the Corinthians?" there remains (as always) a degree of uncertainty, but within constraints. If our question is "What did fifth-century Christians understand by it—and why?" then another set of criteria apply. And even more pertinently, if we ask, "What should it mean to us today?" then the contemporary context of the interpreting community will be equally relevant. RT provides a rationale both for the study of the original "meaning-in-context" and for an understanding of the history of interpretation.

How to Recognize a Poem—The Assumption of Ostensive Communication

With Fish's second historical anecdote, in which a class of students produces literary interpretations of a list of authors' names, we move from immediate face-to-face communication towards the interpretation of written texts. Sperber and Wilson developed RT largely with reference to short utterances of spoken language, in face-to-face contexts, and their spontaneous interpretation. But they already anticipated the change in scale, medium, and communication situation involved in considering written texts and found no difficulty with it: "We assume . . . that the lengthy and

---

24. Ricoeur's idea is discussed in Vanhoozer, *Biblical Narrative*, 100-3.
25. Fish, *Is There a Text*, 345-47.

highly self-conscious processes of textual interpretation that religious or literary scholars engage in are governed just as much by the principle of relevance as is spontaneous utterance comprehension."[26] The applicability of the principles of relevance to literary texts has been defended and applied by many in the decades since.[27]

Returning to our anecdote, Stanley Fish recounts how he ended one class on literary criticism with an assignment on the board, consisting of a list of authors' names arranged vertically. When the next class arrived to study seventeenth-century religious poetry, Fish had drawn a box around the list and given it a page number. He then told the second class that this was a religious poem and asked them to interpret it—which they did with amazing ingenuity. Fish's contention is that what began life as a rather prosaic list of authors becomes a poem in his students' act of so reading it. It is not that there are inherent properties in it that make it a poem or an assignment, or simply a list, but rather that the conventions of the interpretive community invest the text with predetermined properties. It is the community that makes the poem (or the assignment). But this is to ignore one very important feature of the incident. Before the students begin their work of interpreting the text of some supposedly unknown author there has been an overt act of ostensive communication: "Fish: This is a poem of the kind you have been studying. Interpret it."[28]

The students did not begin with the discovery of a text (like an archaeologist discovering an inscription); they began with an assertion by Fish which identified the text as a religious poem and thus activated a cognitive environment, which for them contained a large number of interpretive tools and resources, including the encyclopedic information from Fish's earlier lectures. Furthermore, Fish explicitly invited or instructed them to interpret it. Their ingenious interpretations were thus not primarily acts of discovery or of imposition but firstly acts of faith (in Fish) and secondly acts of obedience (to Fish and his previously taught methodology). Once again, there is a Fish in the cognitive environment, muddying the waters.

From an RT perspective, the students start with Fish's statement and instruction. Because he clearly had a communicative intent, they assume

---

26. Sperber and Wilson, *Relevance*, 75. (Also at 61).

27. See Gibbs, *Intentions*; Pilkington, *Poetic Effects*. I discussed this in some detail in Pattemore, *People of God*, 22–31. For more recent work see https://personal.ua.es/francisco.yus/rt.html#Lit

28. See Fish, *Is There a Text*, 323. I realize that I am in danger of short-selling Fish. His discussion of this incident is extensive and nuanced and repays careful reading. But the fact that he anticipated some objections similar to mine does not lessen their validity.

him to be communicating relevantly and, especially in this case where professorial authority is prominent, relevance entails truth.[29] The most relevant interpretation of his statement is thus that "seventeenth century religious poem" is an accurate characterization of the text on the blackboard. The students' interpretation was, "Here is what we think Fish would agree is the meaning of a text that Fish has told us is a religious poem." It was not their interpretation but his declaration that made it a poem. Once again, Fish has ignored the author—in this case, himself. He is in fact the author of both the assignment and the poem.

What does this amusing incident have to say about literary (and biblical) interpretation? Certainly, norms constrain interpretation. Whether the list was an assignment or a poem depended entirely on the ostensive communication from the author. Once the two audiences received the text in either way, their interpretation was constrained by the numerous conventions of academia. Some of these were taught by Fish, but others (e.g., how to handle a bibliography) came from the wider community of interpretation. The very conditions of ostensive communication constrain the interpretation. It is not hard to see the application to biblical studies. The first communities received texts from their authors, ostensively marked to be interpreted and understood in particular ways—a gospel or a letter—which themselves depended on broader social conventions. When later communities read them, their (spontaneous) interpretation is inevitably dependent on what they understand a *euanggelion* or an *apokalypsis* to be, constrained by their own (possibly different) norms. Even the very idea that a writing is inspired or authoritative (however you define that) is something received along with the text from the community. To read a text within a canon of which a community of faith has long said "this is the word of God" is to work with a *different* set of constraints than the first readers, but not an *unrelated* one. Let me elaborate a little.

Relevance Theory, Literary Texts, and the Absence of the Author

The anecdote of the poem is, of course, only half-way towards the context of normal literary interpretation, and of biblical interpretation, due to the author's physical and intellectual presence. The requirement under RT to treat texts as examples of ostensive communication in a mutual cognitive environment is sometimes seen to conflict with the dominant paradigm of contemporary literary criticism, namely that the author's context and

29. Relevance is here seen to encompass Grice's maxim of quality.

intentions are inaccessible and unnecessary to interpretation. Ricoeur's "threefold semantic autonomy" of the text suggests that a text is cut off from its author's intentions and from its original context and is no longer able to refer ostensively.[30] Fowler, however, points out the significance of RT's inferential understanding of communication for the problem of interpreting texts whose author is absent:

> True, old assumptions may be forgotten or unobvious. But while domains of assumption have changed in numerous ways, they have not changed beyond recognition. It is not in principle a hopeless task to learn enough to make sound inferences from the assumptions formerly taken to be optimally relevant.[31]

Two further points in favor of RT must be made, both of which are particularly pertinent to biblical interpretation.

First, RT does treat a text as a record of a genuine communication event. And in this regard, Gibbs has pointed out that the attribution of intentions is a normal part of the human understanding process: "We ordinarily attribute intentions to other people and animals in a wide variety of everyday interactions."[32] He goes on to argue that the same applies to the interpretation of texts, as well as utterances or even artworks.[33] There is no reason why the author's intentions should be either totally unrecoverable or irrelevant. This is encouraging for confessing communities reading biblical text. But the next point brings a note of caution.

Secondly, we should note that RT does not guarantee the recovery of the author's intended meaning. The one assumption that must be correctly conveyed for communication to take place is the communicative intention, which establishes the conditions for ostensive communication. Thereafter the form of the communication (e.g., the text itself) suggests a double responsibility for meaning. Thus, on the one hand, the communicator must "make correct assumptions about the codes and contextual information that the audience will have accessible and be likely to use in the comprehension process."[34] But on the other hand, "Fulfilment of the communicator's informative intentions is in the hands of the audience and this is itself mutually manifest."[35]

30. Ricoeur, *Interpretation Theory*, 30; Ricoeur, *Hermeneutics*, 145. See also Vanhoozer, *Biblical Narrative*, 109, note 7.

31. Fowler, "A New Theory," 17.

32. Gibbs, *Intentions*, 5.

33. Gibbs, *Intentions*, 15. See also his extensive treatment of literary interpretation, 234–72.

34. Sperber and Wilson, *Relevance*, 43.

35. Sperber and Wilson, *Relevance*, 60.

Central to both directions of interest is the mutual cognitive environment of communicator and audience. Thus, the original audience of a biblical text is entitled to use the text within the mutual cognitive environment to determine the author's informative intentions. But when later audiences use their own cognitive environments, unconnected to the author, there is no guarantee that they will recover the author's intended meaning.

The original readers or hearers of a biblical text would clearly have shared a large number of cognitive contexts with the author, including the life situations of the audience and author—some, though not all, aspects of these will be mutually manifest—and an array of other texts (oral and written) to which the author can assume the audience has access. Relevance is most certainly an operating principle in the author's construction of the text and in the audience's interpretation of it. Paul's letters, with their close dependence on a mutually manifest set of contextual assumptions, would be an example of this.

By virtue of committing a text to writing an author implicitly offers it to a wider and less clearly defined audience, or indeed to "anyone who finds it relevant." And indeed, some biblical texts, such as Gospels or general epistles, appear to begin at this level. But there may still be a considerable degree of shared cognitive environment. It begins with the text itself, but this context can be widened (contra Ricoeur). The author would assume the wider audience shares assumptions derived from membership in particular linguistic, cultural, or faith communities, within which other texts, ideas, traditions, and practices may well be assumed. Ostensive reference within such contexts is possible. The more removed the audience, the smaller is the extent of the mutual cognitive environment. This will not diminish the importance of the search for relevance in the audience's interpretation of the text, but it will mean a progressive loss in confidence that the derived meaning in any way represents the author's intentions.[36] Naïve interpretations of the Bible say more about the readers' cognitive environment than about the meaning of the text. But so do "interested" interpretations.

Scholars of biblical texts are more self-conscious in their search for meaning but are nonetheless guided both directly and indirectly by relevance.[37] Indirectly, the principle of relevance reaffirms the fundamental

---

36. The *limiting* case (rather than the normal) is when the audience's interests dominate, subvert, or eliminate the author's. This is similar to the "socio-pragmatic hermeneutics" extensively critiqued by Thiselton. See, e.g., Thiselton, *New Horizons*, 393–405, 545–50.

37. This is true even though the author can have had no intention to communicate to later scholars, nor to subject her communication to their scrutiny. Caird, *New Testament Theology*, 2, comments of the biblical authors: "They never dreamt that what they

importance of historical-critical research in order to discover the nature of the mutual cognitive environments within which the communication and its interpretations (both initial and subsequent) took place. Directly, relevance influences the work of scholars and critics even if they are unaware of it, because their conclusions will be those that, in their opinion, best explain the data available, i.e., are optimally relevant to them within the norms of their guild. But even more directly, to "use Relevance Theory" in the interpretation of texts is to bring this feature into conscious focus. It involves examining how the text might have achieved optimal relevance, interacting with the reader's cognitive environment(s) to produce good cognitive effects. It will involve careful analysis of the output of historical-critical research to determine which cognitive environments may have been more accessible than others, yielding good cognitive effects without gratuitous processing effort. Thus, by investigating the "readers' meaning," and with the assumption that the author is aiming for optimal relevance in his intended meaning, the scholar is provided with the best possible clues to the author's informative intentions.

Conclusions

Relevance theory has an interesting dialectic relationship with the critical theory of Stanley Fish. On the one hand, it undergirds some of his arguments with a plausible cognitive explanation, especially with respect to the importance of context for meaning and interpretation. But on the other hand, it calls into question his unwillingness to give priority to the author's meaning, or the meaning optimally relevant in the original context. RT provides a principled way of understanding the process of interpretation and the fact that it is context- and convention-dependent. But being a pragmatic theory, it also locates the text within a communication event that assumes an author and hence an "author-ity" about the meaning of the text. This is not to say that misunderstanding does not take place, whether in face-to-face or absent situations. Nor does it mean that the audience (or the reader) will necessarily arrive at the author's intended meaning. It is always possible that there will be a failure to obtain optimal relevance. And it is always possible for the reader's context to lead them to a different meaning. But in pragmatic theory a speaker "uses" an utterance to perform a "speech act," which, like

---

wrote would, centuries later, be subjected to the microscopic scrutiny of modern biblical scholarship, providing in every unusual phrase and every unexpressed assumption matter for a doctoral dissertation."

non-verbal acts, entails responsibilities and consequences.[38] There is nothing in texts that prevents this also being the case. The author may be removed, but it is nevertheless a "text act" and, as in all acts, brings with it responsibilities and consequences. The very anecdote Fish uses as his starting point contains an author and should lead him to assign a role and responsibility to the author of written texts as well as to their readers.

Whether in the study of literature in general, or the study of biblical texts, RT provides a *via media* between the determinists and the relativists. By accounting for the pragmatics of real communication, it successfully explains the power of interpretive communities while acknowledging the historical and hermeneutic priority of the original communication act. With respect to texts as old as the Bible, RT acknowledges—indeed, quantifies—the difficulty involved in a modern audience arriving at the author's intended meaning, and yet it does not write off this search as either impossible or unimportant. It takes seriously and accounts for the history of interpretation, and both explains and undergirds the interpretive strategies of contemporary communities who read the text within their own environment.

Bibliography

Caird, G. B. *New Testament Theology*. Oxford: Clarendon, 1994.
Carston, Robyn, and Seiji Uchida, eds. *Relevance Theory: Applications and Implications*. PBNS, 37. Amsterdam: John Benjamins, 1998.
Clark, Billy. *Relevance Theory*. Cambridge: Cambridge University Press, 2013.
Fish, Stanley. *Is There a Text in this Class?* Cambridge, MA: Harvard University Press, 1980.
Fowler, Alastair. "A New Theory of Communication." *London Review of Books* 11 (1989) 16-17.
Gibbs, Raymond W. *Intentions in the Experience of Meaning*. Cambridge: Cambridge University Press, 1999.
Levinson, Stephen C. *Pragmatics*. Cambridge: Cambridge University Press, 1983.
MacKenzie, Ian. *Paradigms of Reading: Relevance Theory and Deconstruction*. Basingstoke: Palgrave Macmillan, 2002.
Pattemore, Stephen. *The People of God in the Apocalypse*. Cambridge: Cambridge University Press, 2004.
Pilkington, Adrian. *Poetic Effects: A Relevance Theory Perspective*. Amsterdam: John Benjamins, 2000.
Ricoeur, Paul. *Hermeneutics and the Human Sciences*. Cambridge: Cambridge University Press, 1981.

---

38. This implication of Speech Act Theory, namely that a text, as a speech act, implies someone (an author) who is responsible for it, and similarly imposes responsibilities on its readers, is developed with respect to biblical texts by Wolterstorff, *Divine Discourse*.

———. *Interpretation Theory: Discourse and the Surplus of Meaning.* Fort Worth: Texas Christian University Press, 1976.

Shannon, C. E., and W. Weaver. *The Mathematical Theory of Communication.* Urbana: University of Illinois Press, 1949.

Grice, Herbert Paul. "Logic and Conversation." In *Studies in the Ways of Words.* Cambridge, MA: Harvard University Press, 1989.

Sperber, Dan, and Deidre Wilson. "On Verbal Irony." *Lingua* 87 (1992) 53-76.

———. *Relevance: Communication and Cognition.* Oxford: Blackwell, 1st ed. 1986; 2nd ed. 1995.

Thiselton, Anthony. *New Horizons in Hermeneutics. The Theory and Practice of Transforming Biblical Reading.* Grand Rapids: Zondervan, 1992.

Vanhoozer, Kevin. *Biblical Narrative in the Philosophy of Paul Ricoeur.* Cambridge: Cambridge University Press, 1990.

Wolterstorff, Nicholas. *Divine Discourse.* Cambridge: Cambridge University Press, 1995.

20

Linguistics and Hermeneutics

Stanley E. Porter

BEFORE I TURN TO the content of this essay, I wish first to congratulate my colleague Timothy Meadowcroft, the worthy recipient of this celebratory volume. Whether appropriately titled in German as a *Festschrift* or not, such a volume is designed genuinely to recognize and commend its recipient as one honored and feted by colleagues. Tim is certainly held in such regard by his friends and colleagues, and I know that those at Laidlaw College in Auckland, both students and academic staff, who have relied upon him over the years, will now miss him in his retirement. I here merely wish to add my congratulations to him and offer high hopes that these retirement years will be the productive ones that he has envisioned and anticipated.

When I had an invitation to lecture in New Zealand a few years ago, I enjoyed the opportunity to engage in discussion with a number of students and academic colleagues over a range of topics related to the field of hermeneutics in its various forms and expressions. This discussion came out of my own comments and approach to linguistics within the hermeneutical enterprise and especially as it relates to our common task as biblical interpreters. In honor of Tim, I thought that I would explore in this essay the relations among some of these notions in more detail, not because I believe that I have any great insights to offer but because I believe that the relationship of linguistics and hermeneutics, especially in relation to biblical interpretation, is one that merits clearer discernment than it has often garnered. In fact, the relationship—perhaps more of a distinction than a relationship—is one that usefully helps to understand some of the important interpretive issues that we as biblical scholars face.

Definitions of Hermeneutics

Before we are able to understand the relationship of linguistics to hermeneutics, we must first understand what we mean by hermeneutics, and this is where the problems begin. The definitions have varied considerably over the years, with sometimes narrow and sometimes very broad definitions obtaining. Richard Palmer in his (at one time) groundbreaking introduction to hermeneutics offers what he characterizes as "six modern definitions of hermeneutics."[1] I realize that he published these definitions in 1969, but so far as I can determine from more recent work, especially in New Testament studies, these definitions are still relevant and sufficient for my exposition of the issues. These six definitions provide a suitable platform for identifying various works of biblical hermeneutics and interpretation that follow these models, as a prelude to discussion of linguistics in relationship to hermeneutics.

The first definition is of hermeneutics as the "theory of biblical exegesis."[2] This conception predated invention of the word "hermeneutics" that was later formulated to describe "the rules for proper exegesis of Scripture."[3] Palmer traces such biblical exegesis from the Old Testament itself to the New and through the early church and the Reformers up to the time of the Enlightenment. In this sense, biblical exegesis or interpretation is as old as the Bible itself. This use of the term is precritical and concerned with determining "rules, methods, or theory" as distinct from doing exegesis (often focused in recent forms on trinitarianism as a basis),[4] although the definition of the term is sometimes also broadened to include nonbiblical

---

1. Palmer, *Hermeneutics*, 33–45, with this quotation the title of the chapter. Palmer's was one of the earliest introductions to hermeneutics that includes all six of his definitions within its scope of discussion (p. 66). Another such introduction is Schmidt, *Hermeneutics*, who in many ways mirrors Palmer's discussion.

2. Palmer, *Hermeneutics*, 34–38. Palmer traces the origins of the word hermeneutics to J. C. Dannhauer, *Hermeneutica sacra sive methodus exponendarum sacrarum literarum* (1654) and then, with increasing frequency of the word, to the nineteenth century.

3. Palmer, *Hermeneutics*, 34.

4. For this reason, I exclude the multitudinous volumes on New Testament exegesis, as they are for the most part and almost invariably rule-oriented treatments of how to do exegesis and often appear to be unaware of wider hermeneutical issues.

literature.⁵ Some volumes on biblical hermeneutics or interpretation still reflect this perspective, such as those by Milton Terry, Louis Berkhof, William Larkin, Gerhard Maier, Robert Thomas, Manfred Oeming, and probably Jens Zimmermann and Craig Bartholomew.⁶

The second definition is of hermeneutics as "philological methodology."⁷ This definition of hermeneutics emerged out of the Enlightenment and the development of historical criticism, as found in such authors as Johann August Ernest (1707-1781) and Johann Salomo Semler (1725-1791).⁸ This is called the philological method, because it parallels the first two major periods in modern language study, the rationalist and the comparative-historical, *before* the emergence of so-called modern linguistics, and it coincides with the emergence of historical-critical method seen in terms of applying general rules of philology and ascertaining determinate meanings. A recent figure closely associated with this view is the literary critic E. D. Hirsch.⁹ Many, if not most, recent volumes specifically on biblical hermeneutics or interpretation reflect this perspective, such as Berkeley Mickelsen, Bernard Ramm, Henry Virkler, Clayton Croy, Andreas Köstenberger and Richard Patterson, Craig Keener, and William Klein, Craig Blomberg, and Robert Hubbard.¹⁰

The third definition is of hermeneutics as "the science of linguistic understanding."¹¹ Palmer attributes this view to Friedrich Schleiermacher (1768-1834), who departed from the rule-based philological method and

---

5. Palmer, *Hermeneutics*, 34. See also a more recent book, such as Bacon, *Art of Interpretation*.

6. Terry, *Biblical Hermeneutics*; Berkhof, *Biblical Interpretation*; Larkin, *Biblical Hermeneutics*; Maier, *Biblical Hermeneutics*; Thomas, *Evangelical Hermeneutics*; Oeming, *Contemporary Biblical Hermeneutics*; Zimmermann, *Recovering Theological Hermeneutics*; and Bartholomew, *Biblical Hermeneutics* (the last two as surrogates for the entire Theological Interpretation of Scripture movement, the last by means of a revived form of *lectio divina*). Works that emphasize the historical progression of interpretation include Blackman, *Biblical Interpretation*; Grant with Tracy, *Interpretation of the Bible*; Neill and Wright, *New Testament 1861-1986*; Bray, *Biblical Interpretation*; Jasper, *Hermeneutics*; and Reventlow, *Biblical Interpretation*.

7. Palmer, *Hermeneutics*, 38-40.

8. Baird, *New Testament Research*, 1: 108-14, 117-27.

9. See Schmidt, *Hermeneutics*, 133 and 134-42, although he identifies this position with Schleiermacher, and he may well be correct, although Palmer sees it differently (see below).

10. Mickelsen, *Interpreting the Bible*; Ramm, *Protestant Biblical Interpretation*; Virkler and Ayayao, *Hermeneutics*; Croy, *Prima Scriptura*; Köstenberger and Patterson, *Biblical Interpretation*; Keener, *Spirit Hermeneutics*; and Klein et al., *Biblical Interpretation*. See also Corley et al., eds., *Biblical Hermeneutics*.

11. Palmer, *Hermeneutics*, 40.

introduced the notion of general hermeneutics as the science of describing the conditions for understanding. This is in some ways a problematic definition by Palmer, as the notion of linguistics held by Schleiermacher is significantly different from that of Ferdinand de Saussure and modern linguistics. By calling this view "linguistic," Palmer does not seem to mean the major tenets of Saussure's thought but instead indicates that Schleiermacher was concerned not just with language and its rules but with reconstructing the psychology of the author and hence with the author's thoughts expressed in the author's style. This shifted the interpretive emphasis from language to the human subject and its inward psychology and thought.[12] Even though Schleiermacher formulates what might be called a romantic hermeneutic, with emphasis upon the self, the subject, and experience, he sees language as fundamental to this psychological exploration, a factor not always appreciated in Schleiermacher's thought and apparently what is meant by "linguistic" in this definition, and as close as we are going to get to what is called modern linguistics. This approach would find recent representation in advocates of ordinary language philosophy and the Speech Act Theory of J. L. Austin and John Searle. If we adopt this expansive view of language and linguistics as related to Schleiermacher and those who have followed his path through modern linguistics (if such a path can indeed be found), we see that this approach to hermeneutics is found in a few biblical hermeneutical and interpretive works. These include the diverse theories of Severino Croatto, some of the work of Anthony Thiselton, Kevin Vanhoozer, Luis Alonso Schökel, Grant Osborne to a degree, Richard Briggs, David Holgate and Rachel Starr at least in part, and perhaps clearest of all, Petr Pokorny.[13]

The fourth definition is of hermeneutics "as the methodological foundation for the *Geisteswissenschaften*," or human sciences.[14] According to this definition, Wilhelm Dilthey sought to ground the human sciences in a method that was different from that of the natural sciences. He believed that they warranted a different hermeneutic based upon their historical, contextual, and personal dimensions. Few works of biblical hermeneutics or interpretation of which I am aware adopts this definition,

---

12. Palmer, *Hermeneutics*, 84–97.

13. Croatto, *Biblical Hermeneutics*; Thiselton, *New Horizons*, esp. 272–312; Vanhoozer, *Is There a Meaning*; Schökel with Bravo, *Manual of Hermeneutics*; Osborne, *Hermeneutical Spiral*; Briggs, *Words in Action*; Holgate and Starr, *Biblical Hermeneutics*; Petr Pokorny, *Hermeneutics*. See also Green, *Hearing the New Testament*, in particular the chapter by Max Turner on modern linguistics (189–217); and Black and Dockery, *Interpreting the New Testament*, esp. the chapters by Black on Greek grammar (230–52) and George Guthrie on discourse analysis (253–71).

14. Palmer, *Hermeneutics*, 41.

even if some of them might recognize a difference between the natural and human sciences, apart from that of Edgar McKnight, although there may be some that I have missed.[15]

The fifth definition is of hermeneutics as "the phenomenology of *Dasein* and of existential understanding."[16] This is the definition attributed to Martin Heidegger's interpretation and application of phenomenology, concerned with being in the world (*Dasein*). This position was later expanded by Hans-Georg Gadamer, who also came to recognize the importance of language as the means by which one confronts reality. Gadamer's perspective has come to be identified with what is called philosophical hermeneutics, and it has spawned a number of developments that continue to push the notion of hermeneutics forward even as far as poststructuralism and its related thought. This approach to hermeneutics, although widely accepted in the field of hermeneutics, is taken by relatively few in the field of biblical studies, but includes Thiselton, Stanley Porter and Jason Robinson, and Bradley McLean.[17]

The sixth definition is of hermeneutics as "a system of interpretation" that recovers meaning.[18] This view is represented by Paul Ricoeur, who argues in some ways for a return to the rule-driven exegesis of a previous era. However, rather than hermeneutics being confined to matters of language, other means are available for uncovering the deeper meanings of any complex symbol system, such as psychoanalysis. Hermeneutics focuses upon the symbolic meanings of texts to reveal their deeper meanings. Two hermeneutical approaches to these symbol systems may either sympathetically "demythologize" them, to use the language of Rudolf Bultmann, or seek to destroy them, as in the work of Marx, Nietzsche, and Freud. Those who sympathetically engage the text have the possibility of hermeneutically encountering the language, symbols, and myths that lie behind it. This approach to biblical interpretation and hermeneutics is taken by relatively few in the field of biblical studies, but includes the early work of Vanhoozer and the later work of Thiselton.[19]

These six definitions—if they are an accurate account of the six major current definitions of hermeneutics—provide a conspectus upon the various and broad definitions of hermeneutics, the distribution of a number of

---

15. McKnight, *Meaning in Texts*.

16. Palmer, *Hermeneutics*, 41.

17. Thiselton, *Two Horizons*; Thiselton, *New Horizons*; Thiselton, *Hermeneutics*; Porter and Robinson, *Hermeneutics*; and McLean, *Biblical Interpretation*.

18. Palmer, *Hermeneutics*, 43 and 43–45.

19. Vanhoozer, *Biblical Narrative*; Thiselton, *New Horizons*; Thiselton, *Hermeneutics*.

biblical interpreters according to this scheme, and a suitable point of departure for discussion of the relationship of linguistics to hermeneutics.

Linguistics and the Six Definitions of Hermeneutics

There are a number of different ways in which these six definitions may be examined in relationship to linguistics. Before doing that, however, I must clarify what I mean by linguistics. By linguistics, I am referring to what is often described as modern linguistics, the movement that fundamentally changed conceptions of language, beginning most especially in the early twentieth century with the work of Ferdinand de Saussure and then the Geneva School of Linguistics, the Prague Linguistics Circle, and the descriptive studies of Native American languages in North America. Most histories of linguistics point to at least Saussure, and often other influences such as mentioned here, as signaling the beginning of modern linguistics. Modern linguistics has continued to develop in a variety of ways since this early work, especially in the form referred to as structuralism. Structuralism had a widespread impact upon many intellectual disciplines, including not only linguistics but also other social sciences such as anthropology, the humanities in literary studies, and even the so-called hard sciences such as mathematics. Linguistic structuralism came to dominate the academic study of language, including both Europe and North America, until the field today is highly diverse, with a variety of competing models and theories.

There are a variety of ways that modern linguistics can be divided up, including seeing the division between syntactocentric and communication and cognition models, between formal, cognitive, and functional models, and between those focused upon language being in context, text, heads, or groups.[20] Most of these models would agree upon a number of factors that distinguish modern linguistics from the two major previous periods of language study. These would be synchrony over diachrony, language as system, the arbitrary nature of the sign, the distinction between *langue* and *parole* (with debate over which is to be emphasized), language as difference, the distinction between syntagmatic and paradigmatic relations, and language as a social entity (again, debated). The two earlier periods of importance were the rationalistic period of the Enlightenment to the eighteenth/nineteenth century, which was dominated by rationalism and empiricism, and the comparative-historical period of the nineteenth

---

20. These are three different ways of differentiating these schools of thought. See Van Valin and Lapolla, *Syntax*, 8–15; Banks, *Functional Grammar*, 1; Bateman, "Systemic Functional Linguistics," esp. 12.

century, which was dominated by historical, comparative, and source questions. This brief conspectus of linguistics sets the stage for an analysis of the varied definitions of hermeneutics.

The first observation to make is that, in light of these definitions, it is not surprising that there is such variety in books that use the terms "hermeneutics" and "biblical interpretation," as both are terms closely attached to the six definitions. The first three definitions are focused around language, and the second three on hermeneutics per se, even if language plays a role. Thus, half of the definitions of hermeneutics revolve around definitions of language, while half of them orient themselves to philosophical questions. The titles of the books written in these models reflect the diversity of orientations. Some books on hermeneutics focus upon matters of language, while others emphasize interpretation. They are simply reflections of different models of hermeneutics broadly defined. Hence, we can find books that reflect several varieties of hermeneutics, which is not surprising given that the topic is hermeneutics.[21]

Many of the most recent works on hermeneutics in biblical studies focus upon the work of Gadamer and Ricoeur, often without making the kind of differentiation made by Palmer or later by Schmidt. Thus, Thiselton's *New Horizons* devotes major sections to both Gadamer, whom he treated at length in *The Two Horizons*, and to Ricoeur, and the two of them recur in his introductory *Hermeneutics*. The two of them are also featured in Porter and Robinson's survey of hermeneutics, and in McLean's work as well. Matters of language have been important in the stream of thought from Heidegger to Gadamer to more recent developments. However, one probably cannot say that such thought accurately reflects modern linguistics, but more repeats theories regarding language and reality from the nineteenth century or uses linguistic notions to formulate philosophical statements. In 1920–21, Heidegger published an essay, "Introduction to the Phenomenology of Religion," in which he exegetes Paul in phenomenological terms.[22] In the course of doing so, Heidegger makes a distinction between two Greek words for time found in Paul, χρόνος and καιρός. Heidegger characterizes *chronotic* time as "historical time" and *kairotic* time as "a unified flow of life that opens up to future possibilities," in which there is a sense of the "present moment."[23] Those familiar with the discussion will note that similar

---

21. A good example is Porter and Stovell, *Biblical Hermeneutics*. This volume includes views that could be located in Palmer's first, second, and fifth categories.

22. Described in McLean, *Biblical Interpretation*, 130–32, as found in Heidegger, *Gesamtausgabe* 60, part 2. See also Fuller, "Philosophical Hermeneutics and Biblical Interpretation," esp. 186.

23. The language is from McLean, *Biblical Interpretation*, 130.

kinds of distinctions regarding words for time were a part of the Biblical Theology movement, especially the work of Oscar Cullmann, and soundly and decisively criticized, especially by James Barr, for their lack of support within the language and their violating sound principles of general linguistics.[24] Heidegger, however, goes even further than the biblical theologians, transforming the words for time into philosophical concepts that orient one to the world. In other essays, Heidegger makes clear that he believes that language mediates experience, and that the experiences we have are conveyed by language (to the point of making translatability impossible, something most modern linguists would not endorse) as language governs how we think—a form of linguistic relativity.[25]

Gadamer to a large extent follows Heidegger in his view of language, to the point where he says that language mediates reality in a subjective way.[26] Gadamer's major chapter on language in his *Truth and Method* speaks of it as a "horizon of a hermeneutic ontology," and includes a section on "language as experience of the world."[27] Gadamer, as Thiselton notes, reflects Wilhelm von Humboldt's views, developed further in the Sapir-Whorf hypothesis (though not mentioned by Gadamer), on linguistic relativism and determinism, in which languages differ and are reflective of the users' perspectives on the world. Jens Zimmermann characterizes Gadamer's view of language as somewhere between the Saussurean notion of it being an arbitrary system of signs to being a representative of reality (the earlier referential theory). Zimmermann goes on to note that Gadamer in his views of language draws analogies with trinitarian theology in which language becomes revelatory.[28] Language is thus epistemologically and even ontologically central to Gadamer's thought in a way that apparently moves far beyond what is found in modern linguistics. Bradley McLean refers to what he calls the "linguistic turn" as the transition from the precritical to the postcritical period in hermeneutics. He traces in particular the importance of the Sapir-Whorf hypothesis, found in various earlier forms in both Heidegger and Gadamer. This leads him to

---

24. James Barr, *Semantics of Biblical Language*.

25. See, for example, Martin Heidegger, *On the Way to Language*, 58–59, 112; Heidegger, *Poetry, Language, Thought*, esp. 189–210, esp. 189–90.

26. Thiselton, *New Horizons*, 323, citing Gadamer, *Truth and Method*, 411: "Whoever has language 'has' the world," but (this is Thiselton's interpretation of Gadamer) "language mediates this world intersubjectively rather than objectively." (Thiselton cites the above as from Gadamer's *Philosophical Hermeneutics*, but this reference is clearly incorrect).

27. Gadamer, *Truth and Method*, 397–447, esp. 397–414.

28. Zimmermann, *Recovering Theological Hermeneutics*, 170, citing Gadamer, *Truth and Method*.

identify the taxonomic power of language, that is, the power of language to divide up its world according to its own categories. For McLean, the linguistic turn involves recognition that in its taxonomic properties and symbolic systems language "shapes what we take to be reality."[29] The instability of the sign, and self-referentiality of every sign system, has been recognized by later thinkers. However, such poststructuralist thinkers as Jacques Derrida, Michel Foucault, and Roland Barthes, along with others, have also been severely criticized for many of the limitations of their modern linguistic knowledge, in particular what Thomas Pavel calls their "anti-referential and binary theses."[30] Thus, despite the use of language to make claims about language, this stream of hermeneutical thought cannot be characterized as robustly or modernly linguistic, despite their claims and intentions towards language and even, in some places, literary study.

Ricoeur is also well aware of developments regarding language, especially as the results of structuralism, and shares the belief with Heidegger and Gadamer that language mediates reality. Ricoeur's work is diverse and complex, so it is difficult to summarize his position on such an important topic as language. Nevertheless, there seems to be a common thread that runs through a number of his writings. In his early work, Ricoeur introduces the notion of semantics into his hermeneutical thought by means of the symbol, so that he endorses two levels of meaning.[31] The secondary and figurative meaning is accessed through the primary and literal level. However, Ricoeur is opposed to some of the fundamental tenets of structuralism, especially the structuralism of Saussure and some of the more rigorous linguists such as Louis Hjelmslev and his glossematics, and he takes a more functional approach. As a result, Ricoeur disputes the role of language as an object of scientific investigation, he gives priority to language as change (*parole*) over language as system (*langue*), and he questions the self-defining sign system of language and its autonomous self-referential nature—all clearly opposing the modern linguistic agenda. Ricoeur pursued many of these ideas later, among other volumes, in his volume on *Interpretation Theory: Discourse and the Surplus of Meaning*.[32] Ricoeur states that the problem of language stems from a distinction between language as code (system or structure) and language as it is used or functions. Ricoeur emphasizes language as discourse, which he equates with *parole*, over *langue*. *Parole* is heterogeneous, while *langue* is homogeneous. The sentence takes on significance within Ricoeur's

---

29. McLean, *Biblical Interpretation*, 169.
30. Pavel, *Feud of Language*, 104. His views are also held by Lord, *Words*.
31. Ricoeur, *Conflict of Interpretations*, 3–24.
32. Ricoeur, *Interpretation Theory*.

thought and is linked to propositions (having predicate structure). Ricoeur ends up rejecting Roman Jakobson's model of language and prefers instead the Speech Act Theory of Austin and Searle. For Ricoeur, authorial meaning is a property of the text, not of authors, hence Ricoeur takes a realist view of meaning in which language has an inherent referent and reflects reality. The symbolic and metaphorical extensions of meaning of a text are limited by probabilities. Even though Ricoeur acknowledges the role of language, he is much less sanguine about the role of linguistics, even if it is a more Saussurean structuralism.[33]

With Palmer's three more temporally recent hermeneutical definitions, numbers four to six, taking positions that do not provide a clear role for linguistics, we turn to the other three definitions. We can see from the six definitions above that three of the six definitions of hermeneutics are explicitly related to language, the first to the precritical period before the advent of post-Enlightenment studies of language and the second to the post-Enlightenment period of the rationalistic and comparative-historical study. The first and second of these definitions can hardly be called modern linguistic (at least as that term is usually understood) but would be associated with what is often referred to as traditional grammar. Traditional grammar is frequently linked with traditional exegesis and even with the early stages of language study up through both the rationalist and comparative historical periods. The linguist David Crystal has defined the major characteristics of traditional grammar, in a section in which he distinguishes linguistics from that which it is not. The things that it does not include are the tendency to equate linguistics with philology or the study of the history and development of language especially as seen in the classical languages, the all too ready attempt to equate linguistics with the ability to learn and to teach other languages, some confusion over whether a linguist is also a literary critic, and especially its distinctions from traditional grammar. Traditional grammar tends not to differentiate between spoken and written language, restricts its analysis to selected forms of the language (often formal in nature), provides a distorted view of the probabilities of language phenomena in light of its skewed sampling, utilizes the insights and even categories from other languages including Latin, and makes inappropriate value judgments regarding language such as its complexity, value, sophistication, or beauty.[34] The first and second definitions of hermeneutics clearly fit within the

---

33. Many of these characteristics are summarized in Porter and Robinson, *Hermeneutics*, 105–30.

34. Crystal, *What Is Linguistics?* 1–25.

parameters of traditional grammar, with their precritical and even rationalist and comparative historical approaches.

If we agree that the above description of the history of language study is reasonable—though admittedly very brief—then we have to acknowledge that only one of the six definitions of hermeneutics actually addresses the question of linguistics, and it does so in an admittedly unusual way by beginning with Schleiermacher and continuing through to Speech Act Theory. In other words, the strand that Palmer has identified follows the line of what one might call the author-oriented intentionalists. These intentionalists were given a foundation by Schleiermacher's location of meaning in the psychology of the author, and their lineage continued down through the ordinary language philosophers and then Speech Act Theory. There is no doubt that much modern linguistics would be equated with this strand of thought, especially if we expand the definition to include those linguistic theories that are equated with formalism and cognitive studies. To greatly simplify for the sake of the discussion, formalism, as found in the work of Noam Chomsky and his various and diverse followers, is a constituency-based phrase structure and transformational grammar that has expanded to include a variety of related grammatical models based upon constituency constructions. The cognitivists are concerned with the embodied mind. Palmer's definition, so far as it is representative of hermeneutics, neglects what might be called functional views of language, as mentioned by Ricoeur as his preference over structuralism. Functional grammars would include a variety of language models that emphasize the functions of language over its formal structures, as represented in such models as Systemic Functional Grammar, Tagmemics, Stratificational Grammar, and various forms of Functionalism (Continental, Northwestern, etc.). These functional approaches comprise major models within linguistics that do not seem to have a readily apparent home within the definitions of hermeneutics. In other words, as helpful as it is for one of the six definitions of hermeneutics to recognize a connection with developments in modern linguistics (definition five), the discussion is skewed by the framing of the definitions, and in fact is highly limited in its appreciation of the field of modern linguistics.

If my analysis above is correct, then it is no wonder that modern linguistics and hermeneutics have had much less significant critical interaction that two disciplines—no matter how abstractly construed they may be—focused upon texts might reasonably be expected to have. There is no doubt that hermeneutics recognizes the importance of language, to the point where three of the definitions recognize the history and role of language in the history of interpretation (definitions one to three), and to the point where even those definitions that do not align themselves with modern linguistics recognize the significance of language for hermeneutics to the point of seeing language as playing a significant role in mediating reality (definition six). However, there is little within these definitions to accommodate modern linguistics as usually defined.

Summative Observations Regarding Linguistics and Hermeneutics

In light of the previous discussion, one might legitimately ask regarding the relationship and hence future of linguistics and hermeneutics, or at least the future of linguistics and hermeneutics as disciplines that share legitimate interpretive concerns. Let me make three observations.

The first is that it appears that most theories of hermeneutics are not concerned with modern linguistics, or only concerned with modern linguistics as a small part of its overall perspective. In that regard, for hermeneutics, precritical and traditional language studies are at least as viable as modern linguistics. This is seen not only in the fact that several of the standard definitions of hermeneutics are based upon traditional conceptions of language but in the fact that the three definitions of hermeneutics most closely attuned to philosophical hermeneutics are only tangentially and peripherally engaged with modern linguistics. The major stream from Heidegger to Gadamer to the poststructuralists does not seem to have drawn seriously upon the modern linguistic tradition, but instead has, in its more recent forms, appropriated elements of the poststructural turn, arguably in ways that have not fully understood the linguistic issues involved. A similar comment might also be made regarding the tradition following in the line of Ricoeur.

The second observation is that—somewhat in defense of hermeneutics—much modern linguistics is not overtly and consciously concerned with hermeneutical matters. Hermeneuts may well wish to argue that if hermeneutics is concerned with theories of understanding and interpretation, then modern linguistics is, by default and definition, hermeneutical in nature. There is merit to this argument that should be taken seriously by those engaged in modern linguistic study. However, the number of modern linguists who overtly incorporate hermeneutics into their conceptual framework is very limited. If introductory linguistics books are any indication of how hermeneutics is treated within linguistics (and I realize that they may not be indicative, but I am not sure how else to test this hypothesis), then one would expect introductions to linguistics to attempt to situate their discipline within the wider history of interpretation and understanding. I surveyed twenty-five introductions to linguistics of various types that I happen to own, all published from 1970 (using Palmer as a point of reference, whose book was published in 1969) to the present (the latest was 2012), and not a single one included hermeneutics as an entry in its indexes (one volume did not have an index) and not a single one includes hermeneutics in a chapter title. Let me note that these volumes are full of discussion of such topics related to language (a major topic in hermeneutics) as meaning, semantics, pragmatics, culture, discourse, even structuralism, and the like—yet not a single one seems to have made a meaningful and explicit reference to hermeneutics. Thus, it is not just hermeneutics that does not appear to have a cognizance of its relationship to matters of linguistics, but linguistics itself seems to be oblivious to its hermeneutical relations.

The third and final observation is that the potential nexus of linguistics and hermeneutics is one waiting to be fully developed. There are many reasons, possibly even good ones, why the lines will not or cannot be drawn between the two fields concerned with interpretation, such as disciplinary isolation, academic specialization, the silo effect of contemporary academic institutions, and the like. However, both hermeneutics as a form of cultural philosophy and linguistics as dealing with forms of human communication are interdisciplinary in constitution, even if not always in execution and performance. The areas of overlap, especially around questions of the meanings and use of language, cannot be ignored, and merit much further exploration. It is difficult to speak for an entire discipline, especially one as diverse as linguistics, but linguistics tends to function with implicit intentionality, definitive meanings, and sometimes almost positivist knowledge of the structures of human communication. The discipline could benefit from realizing that assumptions about language, meaning, communication, function and the like also invoke larger questions of understanding. Hermeneutics tends to function with either entirely outmoded theories of language—as we have seen, hermeneutics accepts some theories of language more readily than others, especially, surprisingly, some that are clearly antithetical to more recent hermeneutical theories—or in ways that call into question some of the advances of modern linguistic theory, when various word fallacies or views of the relation of speaking and writing are simply asserted. There clearly is a lack of communication between the two that can and should be addressed.

Conclusion

The relationship of linguistics and hermeneutics represents relatively unexplored territory. They have many things in common, especially the concern for language and its functions, that demand further recognition of what each discipline could bring to bear on the other. I have not offered any clear guidelines on how this might be effected, but instead have been content simply to identify how both hermeneutics and linguistics have not yet apparently availed themselves of the potential resources that each could bring to the other. What might those next stages look like? I have no idea, but I think that neither linguistics nor hermeneutics will be able to do its work in the same way as before if each takes the other seriously and learns from what the other has already discovered about human language and communication.

Bibliography

Bacon, Wallace A. *The Art of Interpretation*. 2nd ed. New York: Holt, Rinehart, and Winston, 1972.
Baird, William. *History of New Testament Research*. 3 vols. Minneapolis: Fortress, 1992–2013.
Banks, David. *A Systemic Functional Grammar of English: A Simple Introduction*. London: Routledge, 2019.
Barr, James. *The Semantics of Biblical Language*. Oxford: Oxford University Press, 1961.
Bartholomew, Craig G. *Introducing Biblical Hermeneutics: A Comprehensive Framework for Hearing God in Scripture*. Grand Rapids: Baker, 2015.
Bateman, John A. "The Place of Systemic Functional Linguistics as a Linguistic Theory in the Twenty-First Century." In *The Routledge Handbook of Systemic Functional Linguistics*, edited by Tom Bartlett and Gerard O'Grady, 11–27. London: Routledge, 2017.
Berkhof, Louis. *Principles of Biblical Interpretation*. Grand Rapids: Eerdmans, 1950.
Black, David Alan, and David S. Dockery, eds. *Interpreting the New Testament: Essays on Methods and Issues*. Nashville: Broadman & Holman, 2001.
Blackman, E. C. *Biblical Interpretation*. Philadelphia: Westminster, 1957.
Bray, Gerald. *Biblical Interpretation: Past and Present*. Downers Grove, IL: InterVarsity, 1996.
Briggs, Richard S. *Words in Action: Speech Act Theory and Biblical Interpretation. Towards a Hermeneutic of Self-Involvement*. Edinburgh: T. & T. Clark, 2001
Corley, Bruce, et al., eds., *Biblical Hermeneutics: A Comprehensive Introduction to Interpreting Scripture*. 2nd ed. Nashville: Broadman & Holman, 2002.
Croatto, J. Severino. *Biblical Hermeneutics: Toward a Theory of Reading as the Production of Meaning*. Translated by Robert R. Barr. Maryknoll, NY: Orbis, 1987.
Croy, N. Clayton. *Prima Scriptura: An Introduction to New Testament Interpretation*. Grand Rapids: Baker, 2011.
Crystal, David. *What Is Linguistics?* 3rd ed. London: Edward Arnold, 1981.

Fuller, David J. "The Interface of Philosophical Hermeneutics and Biblical Interpretation: Towards a New Taxonomy." *MJTM* 19 (2017–2018) 178–98.
Gadamer, Hans Georg, *Truth and Method*. New York: Crossroad, 1975.
Grant, Robert, with David Tracy. *A Short History of the Interpretation of the Bible*. 2nd ed. London: SCM, 1984.
Green, Joel B. ed. *Hearing the New Testament: Strategies for Interpretation*. 2nd ed. Grand Rapids: Eerdmans, 2010.
Heidegger, Martin. *On the Way to Language*. Translated by Peter D. Hertz. New York: HarperOne, 1971.
———. *Poetry, Language, Thought*. Translated by Albert Hofstadter. New York: Harper & Row, 1971.
Holgate, David, and Rachel Starr. *Biblical Hermeneutics*. London: SCM, 2006.
Jasper, David. *A Short Introduction to Hermeneutics*. Louisville: WJK, 2004.
Keener, Craig S. *Spirit Hermeneutics: Reading Scripture in Light of Pentecost*. Grand Rapids: Eerdmans, 2016.
Klein, William W., et al. *Introduction to Biblical Interpretation*. 3rd ed. Grand Rapids: Zondervan, 2017 [1993, 2004].
Köstenberger, Andreas J., and Richard D. Patterson. *Invitation to Biblical Interpretation: Exploring the Hermeneutical Triad of History, Literature, and Theology*. Grand Rapids: Kregel, 2011.
Larkin, William J., Jr. *Culture and Biblical Hermeneutics: Interpreting and Applying the Authoritative Word in a Relativistic Age*. Grand Rapids: Baker, 1988.
Lord, Robert. *Words: A Hermeneutical Approach to the Study of Language*. Latham, MD: University Press of America, 1996.
Maier, Gerhard. *Biblical Hermeneutics*. Translated by Robert W. Yarbrough. Wheaton, IL: Crossway, 1994.
McKnight, Edgar V. *Meaning in Texts: The Historical Shaping of a Narrative Hermeneutics*. Philadelphia: Fortress, 1978.
McLean, Bradley H. *Biblical Interpretation and Philosophical Hermeneutics*. Cambridge: Cambridge University Press, 2012.
Mickelsen, A. Berkeley. *Interpreting the Bible*. Grand Rapids: Eerdmans, 1963.
Neill, Stephen, and Tom Wright. *The Interpretation of the New Testament 1861–1986*. New ed. Oxford: Oxford University Press, 1988.
Oeming, Manfred. *Contemporary Biblical Hermeneutics: An Introduction*. Translated by Joachim F. Vette. Aldershot: Ashgate, 2006.
Osborne, Grant R. *The Hermeneutical Spiral: A Comprehensive Introduction to Biblical Interpretation*. Rev. ed. Downers Grove, IL: InterVarsity, 2006.
Palmer, Richard E. *Hermeneutics*. NUSPEP. Evanston, IL: Northwestern University Press, 1969.
Pavel, Thomas. *The Feud of Language: A History of Structuralist Thought*. Translated by Linda Jordan and Thomas G. Pavel. Oxford: Blackwell, 1989.
Pokorny, Petr. *Hermeneutics as a Theory of Understanding*. Translated by Anna Bryson-Gustová. Grand Rapids: Eerdmans, 2011.
Porter, Stanley E., and Beth M. Stovell, eds. *Biblical Hermeneutics: Five Views*. Downers Grove, IL: InterVarsity, 2012.
Porter, Stanley E., and Jason C. Robinson, *Hermeneutics: An Introduction to Interpretive Theory*. Grand Rapids: Eerdmans, 2011.

Ramm, Bernard. *Protestant Biblical Interpretation: A Textbook of Hermeneutics.* Grand Rapids: Baker, 1970.
Reventlow, Henning Graf. *History of Biblical Interpretation.* 4 vols. Translated by Leo G. Perdue, 4 Atlanta: SBL, 2009–2010.
Ricoeur, Paul. *Interpretation Theory: Discourse and the Surplus of Meaning.* Fort Worth: Texas Christian University Press, 1976.
———. *The Conflict of Interpretations: Essays in Hermeneutics.* Edited by D. Ihde. Evanston, IL: Northwestern University Press, 1974.
Schmidt, Lawrence K. *Understanding Hermeneutics.* Stocksfield: Acumen, 2006.
Schökel, Luis Alonso, with José María Bravo. *A Manual of Hermeneutics.* Translated by Liliana M. Rosa, edited by Brook W. R. Pearson. Sheffield: Sheffield Academic, 1998.
Terry, Milton S. *Biblical Hermeneutics: A Treatise on the Interpretation of the Old and New Testaments.* Repr., Grand Rapids: Zondervan, n.d.
Thiselton, Anthony C. *Hermeneutics: An Introduction.* Grand Rapids: Eerdmans, 2009.
———. *New Horizons in Hermeneutics: The Theory and Practice of Transforming Biblical Reading.* Grand Rapids: Zondervan, 1992.
———. *The Two Horizons: New Testament Hermeneutics and Philosophical Description with Special Reference to Heidegger, Bultmann, Gadamer, and Wittgenstein.* Grand Rapids: Eerdmans, 1980.
Thomas, Robert L. *Evangelical Hermeneutics: The New Versus the Old.* Grand Rapids: Kregel, 2002.
Vanhoozer, Kevin J. *Biblical Narrative in the Philosophy of Paul Ricoeur: A Study in Hermeneutics and Theology.* Cambridge: Cambridge University Press, 1990.
———. *Is There a Meaning in This Text? The Bible, the Reader, and the Morality of Literary Knowledge.* Grand Rapids: Zondervan, 1998.
Van Valin, Robert D., Jr., and Randy J. Lapolla. *Syntax: Structure, Meaning and Function.* CTL. Cambridge: Cambridge University Press, 1997.
Virkler, Henry A., and Karelynne Gerber Ayayao. *Hermeneutics: Principles and Processes of Biblical Interpretation.* 2nd ed. Grand Rapids: Baker, 2007
Zimmermann, Jens. *Recovering Theological Hermeneutics: An Incarnational-Trinitarian Theory of Interpretation.* Grand Rapids: Baker, 2004.

21

A Mimetic Model of Hermeneutics

Martin Sutherland

CHRISTIANS WHO ENTER ACADEMIC life, particularly in the theological disciplines, are familiar with an "image problem," which too often surrounds their calling. It can manifest as a suspicion in congregational circles that our scholarly endeavors are inimical to sincere faith; that deep study is likely to eviscerate, rather than illuminate, Gospel commitment. It is possible that this is an especially acute problem in ex-colonial societies such as New Zealand, where a general anti-intellectualism has long been identified and lamented. However, the caricature of the scholar who has had his or her evangelical fire snuffed out under the weight of books is widespread and, sadly, relatively readily confirmed by individual anecdotes or high-profile cases.

That it doesn't have to be this way should go without saying. Stories of faithful scholars are legion in Christian history, but they somehow lack the impact of the counter-examples. Faithful discovery rarely carries the "bite" of apostacy—a tincture of scandal makes a better story. There is, moreover, a certain native satisfaction to be had in relegating the reputation of those who dwell in the gnostic-seeming realms of academe. Nevertheless, scholars remain who testify, through their very work, that faith can be built, mission can be enhanced, and the soul can be further entranced by the gospel, not in spite of scholarship, but by encountering the Spirit of God in it. The best of them work just as hard to bring the fruits of this discovery accessibly to the church as well as to their academic disciplines.

Tim Meadowcroft is one such: an exemplary Christian scholar. Tim has produced a list of publications to satisfy any panel. He has served his discipline well and never lost his thirst for knowledge and the joy of discovery. He has taught two generations, supervised their theses, and edited their writing. Throughout, he has retained the deep commitment of the scholar-priest, faithful to his parish and denomination, preaching, writing for non-technical outlets, engaging in (and being transformed by) mission settings.

Tim has never huddled in a narrow specialization. Indeed, he is notable for his thirst for interdisciplinary conversations. As friend and colleague over two decades, I have greatly benefited from this openness—always impressed with Tim's insight and determination to press into new ways of understanding. In Old Testament studies he has been master, and I the somewhat disappointing student, but in his interests in ecclesiology, history, hermeneutics, and systematic theology, we have enjoyed much fruitful engagement. The opportunity to continue this dialogue though the present volume is thus relished.

In 2006, Tim Meadowcroft published *Haggai* in the Sheffield Phoenix Press series, *Readings: A New Biblical Commentary*.[1] The biblical *Haggai* is a short book—one of the shortest, in fact, at just 38 verses. Tim's commentary is considerably longer—at nearly 250 pages. One can almost hear the naysayers muttering about over-analysis and wringing the life out of a living text, but that would be to totally miss the contribution of this fine volume. Especially impressive is the 40-page "Prolegomena: Reading Haggai as Scripture." The very title of this section signals the author's determination to model a faith-building scholarship of commentary. It is this extended statement of Tim's hermeneutical approach with which I intend to engage in this chapter.

After a brief exercise in claiming the significance of Haggai, the Prolegomena turns to the crucial task of explaining the "reading" approach which drives the series, and which characterizes the commentary itself. In doing so, Tim turns to the influential writings on hermeneutics of Friedrich Schleiermacher. In particular, he draws on Schleiermacher's "distinction between grammatical and psychological interpretation." The putative advantage of this distinction is that it identifies the mutually supporting roles of the technical discussion of a text (as found in modern commentaries and which will appear next, in the "Introduction" to Haggai) and the less quantifiable but no less real role of the reader.

> Psychological interpretation is the attempt to appreciate not so much how the text works as the effect on the text of the person

1. Meadowcroft, *Haggai*.

reading it and the experience and context that that reader brings with him or her to the reading of the text.[2]

In a creative use of Schleiermacher's notion of the "hermeneutical circle," the commentary does not abandon the role of the author or the text itself. The potential excesses of a reader-only focus are mitigated by constant reference to the context, grammar, even intent of the author/text. Nevertheless, the volume is "a 'readings' commentary, and so the opening contribution in the conversation with the text of Haggai is the reader and the questions the reader brings to the text. In that respect it is a 'reading' rather than an interpretation."[3]

Haggai of course, is Scripture, and Tim is a Christian scholar, so an unanchored "reading," even one qualified by the author's context, would be an inadequate hermeneutical approach. The commentary thus incorporates Speech Act Theory, valued because it "has made both intention and response, author and reader, indispensable to the understanding of the text."[4] This in turn is enhanced by Relevance Theory and its "emphasis on inference."

> I take inference to be the term that describes what happens when a hearer takes account of his or her own context, understands the speaker's context, assumes that the speaker is taking account of the hearer's context, and in light of all that is aware of what a speaker means by a particular statement.[5]

Crucially, Tim does not allow the task of interpretation to end with a merely intellectual grasp of meaning. "I suggest a further amendment to Relevance Theory, namely, that it need not be an exclusively cognitive function."[6] This opens the door to "connotative or affective functions." It is thus fitting that the Prolegomena concludes with the notion of "Interpretation as Performance," adopting Stephen Barton's call to "locate our work as exegetes in the wider context of divine and human action."[7]

The Prolegomena to *Haggai* is an unusually reflective and detailed discussion of the hermeneutical approach to be taken in a commentary. Rarely are these issues addressed at such depth in what remains a short commentary on an even shorter text. It is testimony to Tim Meadowcroft's scholarly

---

2. Meadowcroft, *Haggai*, 4.
3. Meadowcroft, *Haggai*, 6.
4. Meadowcroft, *Haggai*, 17.
5. Meadowcroft, *Haggai*, 21.
6. Meadowcroft, *Haggai*, 27
7. Meadowcroft, *Haggai*, 39.

commitment to conscious self-criticism and the philosophical underpinnings of his discipline. The success of the commentary proper, I leave to others more qualified than I am. I intend to take the opportunity presented by this *Festschrift* to engage with Tim's hermeneutical picture. My intent is not to reduce it, still less to refute it. Indeed, I find it a largely compelling and fruitful account of a Christian approach to holy Scripture. There is no need for me to repeat the insights Tim brings from speech Act and Relevance Theories. I happily accept them. I will, however adopt, a different starting point, as, for reasons I will explain, I consider Schleiermacher does not serve the case well. I hope what emerges is a new perspective on some of the issues, expanding some categories and suggesting a number of new aspects to the hermeneutical moment.

Given the clear importance of "the reader" to the commentary, the dependence on Schleiermacher is not as useful as it appears. To begin with, Schleiermacher's introduction of "psychological interpretation" is directed at the mind of the author, rather than the reader; to the utterance, rather than the encounter.

> As every utterance has a dual relationship, to the totality of language and to the whole thought of its originator, then all understanding also consists of the two moments, of understanding the utterance as derived from language [grammatical], and as a fact in the thinker [psychological].[8]

Secondly (and, ultimately, more importantly) Schleiermacher is at pains to *restrict* hermeneutics to a cognitive function. It is "only the art of understanding, not the presentation of understanding as such."[9] In the view of his first editor, in this Schleiermacher is carefully eschewing an alternative view that the act of interpretation rightly includes explication and application.[10] The conclusion of the Prolegomena, that scriptural interpretation, in particular, must reach beyond cognition to action, is of course built on theory provided elsewhere than by Schleiermacher. However, Schleiermacher's positive disavowal of this possibility further emphasizes his ambiguity as an ally.

In two other themes, Schleiermacher does point to important principles. He helpfully stresses the indivisibility of his hermeneutic schema. "Understanding is only a being-in-one-another of these two moments

---

8. Schleiermacher, *Hermeneutics and Criticism*, 8.
9. Schleiermacher, *Hermeneutics and Criticism*, 5.
10. Schleiermacher, *Hermeneutics and Criticism*, 5, n. 1.

(the grammatical and psychological)."[11] This is the hermeneutical circle and is a crucial concept. Indeed, though with a different framework, it is a principle I will heartily embrace and seek to develop. Schleiermacher also emphasizes the role of shared language. This coheres with elements of Relevance Theory and reminds us of the corporate nature of interpretation. Nevertheless, Schleiermacher remains, in my view, problematic in Tim's case. He provides no support to one key element Tim's approach (the role of the reader) and fundamentally denies the possibility of a second (performance). I therefore respectfully suggest that a more fruitful starting point than Schleiermacher is needed for building a hermeneutic for a "Readings" commentary such as *Haggai*. To this end, I will explore the religious epistemology of Blaise Pascal.

Pascal (1623–1662) was one of those creative geniuses that history (or providence) occasionally throws up. He contributed seminal ideas in philosophy, mathematics, physics, computing, game theory, and transportation. A convert to Jansenism, a radically Augustinian Catholicism, he also wrote some of history's most memorable religious thought—found in his *Provincial Letters* (1656–57—a polemic against the Jesuits) and unfinished notes for *A Defence of the Christian Religion*, gathered by his literary executors as *Pensées* (*Thoughts*).[12]

Pascal's world was the social and intellectual high culture of Western Europe. René Descartes (1596–1650) was a crucial figure, but more broadly this was the era of the first real flourishing of modern science, a development to which Pascal himself made important contributions. He was thus an individual who understood the implications of this "new philosophy" from its core. He rejected, for instance, all attempts to prove God from observation of design in nature—"nothing is more calculated to arouse [unbeliever's] contempt."[13] For Pascal, the discoveries of the new science exposed humans to an unprecedented sense of the universe—and themselves. Awed by the unfolding immensity of the world and the universe on the one hand, and discoveries of the microscopic world on the other, he was struck by the ambiguity of the human creature.

> For, in the end, what is man in nature? A nothing in comparison to the infinite, an everything compared to the nothing . . .

---

11. Schleiermacher, *Hermeneutics and Criticism*, 9.

12. There are numerous versions of *Pensées*. The quotations in this essay are taken from the Roger Ariew's translation—Pascal, *Pensées*. The individual fragments are variously arranged by editors. Two "standard" numbering systems are current. References here are to both Sellier's (S) and Lafuma's (L) editions.

13. *Pensées* S644/L781.

> What will he do then, but perceive [some] appearance from the middle of things, in an eternal despair at knowing neither their principle nor their end.[14]

Nonetheless, humans are different from the rest of creation. Impermanent, frail reeds to be sure, but "thinking reeds"—unique in the very capacity to realize both their greatness and their wretchedness.

> All our dignity consists, then, in thought. It is from there that we must raise ourselves, and not from space and duration, which we could not fill. Let us labor, then, to think well. This is the principle of morality.[15]

But what did it mean to "think well"? Pascal rejected the reliance on rationality that characterized Cartesian method. Indeed, he made a crucial division of thought processes, which has direct implications for the hermeneutical task. Pascal outlines his schema in one of the most important of the *Pensées*, entitled "Difference between the geometric and the intuitive mind."[16]

Addressing first the "geometric mind," Pascal suggests that in this way of thinking "principles are obvious, but removed from ordinary use, so that we find it difficult to turn our heads in that direction, for lack of habit."[17] By contrast,

> with the intuitive mind, principles are in common use and before everyone's eyes. You only have to look, and no effort is necessary; it is only a question of good sight. But it must be good, because the principles are so subtle and numerous that it is almost impossible but that some escape notice.[18]

Whilst geometric thinking is difficult, requiring training, it is precise. Broadly similar to Schleiermacher's grammatical approach, it will be to the fore, as Tim Meadowcroft notes, in a commentary's Introduction. But whereas, as argued, Schleiermacher's "psychological" category provides only tangential support for a Readings approach, Pascal's "intuitive mind" potentially informs all the categories of Tim's account. In contrast to the geometric, with intuitive processes "the principles are scarcely seen; they are

---

14. *Pensées* S230/L199.
15. *Pensées*, S232/L200.
16. *Pensées*, S670/L512.
17. *Pensées*, S670/L512.
18. *Pensées*, S670/L512.

felt rather than seen; there is endless difficulty in making them felt by those who do not themselves apprehend them."[19]

Pascal laments the tendency for one or other of these "minds" to dominate, though for different reasons. Geometric thinking is a skill, requiring training. Some who are naturally intuitive simply cannot "bend their thinking to the principles of geometry to which they are unaccustomed."[20] Such people,

> being thus accustomed to judge at a single glance, when presented with propositions of which they understand nothing and the paths to which consist of such sterile definitions and principles, which they are not accustomed to see in such detail, are so surprised that they are repelled and disheartened.[21]

Here is a picture of the suspicion that scholars sometimes encounter. Sometimes, Pascal would say, they must share the blame, as

> ["Geometers"] want to treat matters of intuition geometrically and make themselves ridiculous, wanting to begin by definitions and then by principles, which is not the way to proceed in this kind of reasoning. Not that the [intuitive] mind does not do this, but it does so tacitly, naturally, and without art, for its expression surpasses all men, and only a few can apprehend it.[22]

This was no mere theoretical exercise for Pascal. It was the structure of knowledge, in particular knowledge of God. Part of his objection to so-called "proofs" of God was that they drew only on geometric thinking. This achieves little, providing only the "God of the Philosophers," not the real God at all.

In the hermeneutical task both ways of knowing are essential. Pascal anticipates Schleiermacher's dictum, that "understanding is only a being-in-one-another of these two moments."[23] Importantly, in this integration, we encounter a direct link to "interpretation as performance." Indeed, in Pascal, the integration is complete. The hermeneutical circle moves in both directions.

In another of his *Pensées*, Pascal stresses the power of custom. Here he describes humans as "automata," a term deeply dislocating for

---

19. *Pensées*, S670/L512.
20. *Pensées*, S670/L512.
21. *Pensées*, S670/L512.
22. *Pensées*, S670/L512.
23. Schleiermacher, *Hermeneutics and Criticism*, 9.

twenty-first-century readers. For Pascal, caught in the mechanistic view of nature of the day, it had to do with instinct—that which springs from our animal nature.

> For we must not misunderstand ourselves: we are as much automata as minds. And thus the instrument by which we are persuaded is not solely demonstration. How few things are demonstrated! Proofs only convince the mind; custom provides our strongest and most firmly believed proofs . . . Finally we must have recourse to it once the mind has seen where the truth lies, in order to quench our thirst and to steep ourselves in this belief, which constantly escapes us. For always to have proofs before us is too much trouble . . . Both parts of us must be made to believe; the mind by reasons that need only to be seen once in a lifetime, and the automaton by custom, and by not allowing it any inclination to the contrary.[24]

Pascal's "custom" is the habits of life, which are both engendered by, and in turn embed, belief. Here are contained rituals of faith, but also ethics and morality—what Gisela Labouvie-Vief's would describe as "organismic forms of cognition."[25] A principal advantage of the geometric mind is that it produces observable ways of transmitting or communicating belief that the intuitive mind lacks. But this is not to suggest that custom lacks the power to promote belief. Indeed, the opposite is true. "Custom is our nature" and immensely powerful.[26]

In his most famous fragment, the "Discourse on the Machine," Pascal introduces the intriguing "wager" as a defense of the rationality of belief. However, he makes no claim that the wager argument itself creates belief. Something different, more intuitive, more active, is required. Something beyond mere cognition.

> You would like to be cured of unbelief and ask for the remedies? Learn from those who were bound like you, and who now wager all they have. These are people who know the way you wish to follow, and who are cured of the illness of which you wish to be cured. Follow the way by which they began: they acted as if they

---

24. Pascal, *Pensées*, S661/L821. The *Pensées* are notes, and as such display at times an unsurprising imprecision of terms. Here Pascal uses "mind" in an unqualified way. In terms of his discussion of the two types of mind, he clearly means the geometric mind in this context.

25. Labouvie-Vief, "Wisdom," 52–53. Pascal's proposals cohere quite closely with those of such as psychologist Labouvie-Vief, who, building on Piaget's theory of development, suggests a change is under way in perceptions of how wisdom was attained.

26. *Pensées*, S680/L419.

believed, took holy water, had masses said etc. This will make you believe naturally and mechanically [instinctively].[27]

In Pascal's account of religious epistemology, we find a far richer, more suggestive ground for understanding the reader's experience than in Schleiermacher. The interaction of the geometric and intuitive minds is suggestive of means to make sense of perlocutionary effect. The two-way link to communal custom coheres with Relevance Theory, shared language, and performance. It is far from a comprehensive hermeneutical theory, but it does offer vectors of thought, touching matters on which Schleiermacher is silent.

Of course, the warning inherent in Pascal's schema is that a "comprehensive hermeneutical theory" is ultimately unattainable. That would be to imagine the geometric can supplant the intuitive. As Pascal (later to be echoed by Wittgenstein) declares, "reason's last step is the recognition that there are an infinite number of things which are beyond it."[28] Conversely the geometric impulse is not to be abandoned. We can understand better, and Pascal at least provides resources for the task.

Can we do better? If, as I suggest, Pascal provides a more fertile base for a hermeneutics of reading than Schleiermacher's relatively barren ground, then perhaps a thin layer of coral can be added to Tim Meadowcroft's already impressive structure.[29]

Fittingly, we may begin as Tim leaves off, with "Divine Discourse" and "Interpretation as Performance." These two, I will suggest, lead us to the same point.

At stake in Tim's account, and in this essay, is the interpretation of holy Scripture. In its discussion of divine discourse, the Prolegomena contends that we do not need to resort to a naïve anthropomorphic caricature of inspiration to make the legitimate claim that God is author of Scripture. This is a belief statement, but not invalid for that. In Nicholas Wolterstorff's argument, such knowledge claims are legitimate if subject to the testing of "doxastic practice."[30] As Tim puts it,

> It is in the entitlement of the human authors to convey a narrative in which God is [a] character, and in a similar entitlement

---

27. *Pensées*, S680/L418.

28. *Pensées*, S188/L267. See the concluding sections of Wittgenstein, *Tractatus*, esp. 6.54.

29. See Tim's evocative picture of the progress of scholarship (after Michael King) in the Preface to *Haggai*, ix.

30. Meadowcroft, *Haggai*, 34–35. See Wolterstorff, *Divine Discourse*, especially 261–80.

of readers to see in the discourse so created a divine discourse, that the claim that God speaks is realized.[31]

As will be seen, I will argue that Wolterstorff's framework is too narrowly cognitive. For now, the assertion of the legitimacy of a belief in divine utterance is key.

This element of divine discourse joins Stephen Barton's already discussed location of interpretation in "a wider context of divine and human action."[32] Here we are fortunate to have a magisterial, but strangely underrecognized, exploration of that nexus by one of the most significant contributors to hermeneutical debate, Anthony Thiselton.

In his 2007 work, *The Hermeneutics of Doctrine*, Thiselton sets out to break down the theoretical and practical distinctions between hermeneutics and systematic theology.[33] Three elements are key to making this possible. First, the recognition, in terms similar to those of Wolterstorff, that theology and the doctrines that emanate from it are reflections on divine discourse, on revelation. But revelation is not propositions; rather, it is an encounter with the living God. Crucially, the Judaeo-Christian witness is that God is God of history. Citing Brevard Childs, Thiselton endorses the view that "the God of Israel makes known his being in specific historical moments, and confirms in his works his ultimate being by redeeming a covenant people."[34]

This leads to the second element in Thiselton's account. Revelation is story, a narrative, and as such temporally defined. So, in turn, is doctrine. "If doctrine reflects the nature of God and derives ultimately from God, *doctrine will be no less 'living' and related to temporality than God*, who acts in human history."[35] This lends a natural structure to the theological/doctrinal/hermeneutical task. Here, Thiselton picks up Ricoeur's work on narrative.

> The coherence and continuity of narrative depends in part on the mind's performing "three functions: those of expectation . . . attention . . . and memory"; these together make possible interactively the temporal hope of emplotment. Christian doctrine relates closely to memory of God's saving acts in history; attention to God's present action in continuity with those saving acts; and trustful expectation of an eschatological fulfillment of divine promise.[36]

31. Meadowcroft, *Haggai*, 35.
32. Cited in Meadowcroft, *Haggai*, 39.
33. Thiselton, *Hermeneutics*.
34. Childs, *Exodus*, 76, cited in Thiselton, *Hermeneutics*, 63.
35. Thiselton, *Hermeneutics*, 63 (emphasis original).
36. Thiselton, *Hermeneutics*, 65, quoting Ricoeur, *Time and Narrative*, 1:20.

If temporal, in this sense, doctrine is also "communal." It is not a matter of individual mental assents, but rather doctrine should be seen "in terms of living out the 'narrative of God'" and, moreover, asking "what kind of community the church must be to rightly tell the stories of God."[37]

A third and crucial element in Thiselton's account is a move away from belief defined in propositional terms to belief understood in *dispositional* terms. Belief is acknowledged, not in an individual's opinions, but in their ways of life—more particularly, their communal ways of life. In Speech Act terms, the perlocutionary effect is not merely to convince, but to transform. In Pascal's terms, true belief is when understanding ceases to mere merely geometric and becomes intuitive. As Thiselton summarizes, belief reflects a narrative structure, a communal setting and consists of dispositions, rather than propositions. As such belief "is *action oriented, situation related*, and embedded in the *particularities and contingencies* of everyday living . . . *Action, contingency, particularity* and the *public world of embodied life*, constitute part of what it is to *believe*."[38]

Such an account of belief should come as no surprise in a religious tradition that includes in its Scriptures such passages as Isa 1:10–17; John 14:15; 2 Tim 3:5; 1 John 2:3–6 and, of course, Jas 2:14–26.

All of this requires a reset of our approach to scriptural hermeneutics. It can no longer be described in terms of process but, rather, as event. Process relates to the geometric, event to the intuitive. The event sits in a wider communal narrative, which itself is a response to the divine narrative created by the God of history. Most importantly, the outcome for the reader(s), the perlocutionary effect, the very nature of the event, is action.

In what remains of this essay, I will sketch a possible response to these issues. Specifically, I propose the elements of a "mimetic" model of hermeneutics.

"Mimesis" or "imitation" provides a useful model of a Christian hermeneutic that issues in action. The action generated is not merely any activity, but action which reflects the character of God, which is itself revealed in narrative. Christ reveals the Father because he is like the Father; indeed, representing the Father is core to his ministry (John 5:31–47; 14:7–14). The believer is called to imitate Christ (1 John 1:6) or even another of his followers (1 Cor 14:6; 2 Thess 3:9; Heb 6:12).

The virtue or otherwise of mimesis, or imitation, has been debated since the ancient world. With roots in drama and other arts, mimesis is

---

37. Thiselton, *Hermeneutics*, xix, citing Stanley Hauerwas, *A Community of Character*, 1.

38. Thiselton, *Hermeneutics*, 21 (emphasis original).

essentially the representation of something else. Ancient debate was mostly about its limitations. The artist represents a scene, but the painting is not the landscape. The actor represents a historical figure, but the character is not the person. A play may represent an event, but it is not real life. Put simply, the copy always diminishes the original. So, Plato: "imitation is far removed from truth, for it touches only a small part of each thing and a part that is itself only an image."[39] This Platonic concern, of course, springs from the doctrine of Forms, which means that any observable object, such as a table or a bed, is already at one remove from the original; any further copy can only be a further distortion.

The Christian can acknowledge this, even celebrate it. Our representation of God succeeds only by virtue of the Spirit's presence with us. Moreover, we can distinguish mimesis from mere replication. Samuel Taylor Coleridge insisted that imitation is not copying, in that "it of necessity implies and demands difference."[40] The imitation is not and should not be the original. It will be no less faithful to the original, but it will not be a reproduction. Simple replication would not recognize context or narrative. Indeed, it would be a reversion to a Platonic idealism. As Thiselton puts it, "'Plots,' or 'emplotment,' allow for reversals, conflicts, surprises, complexities, hopes, frustrations, and fulfillment. They are the very stuff of human life (not theoretical thought), with which Christian doctrine interacts."[41]

The proposed Mimesis Model requires further teasing, as the outcome of the hermeneutical event (belief as action or disposition) does not of itself explain its inner dynamics. For this we this look beyond the disposition, to the narrative structure, specifically to Ricoeur's proposal that it requires of the mind "three functions: those of expectation . . . attention . . . and memory."

I elect to change Ricoeur's order, proposing the following understanding of the hermeneutical event, namely, that the event contains within it three inter-laced "moments," inalienable from each other. My mimetic model posits three such moments:

1. Remembering
2. Anticipating
3. Presenting

---

39. Plato, *Complete Works: The Republic,* Book X, 1202.
40. Coleridge *Collected Letters,* III:501.
41. Thiselton, *Hermeneutics,* 66.

I will outline the posited function of each. The third—"presenting"—is perhaps intuitively out of place, but it will be dealt with last, with greater attention, as it is the moment most open to a new approach.

Remembering

Christianity is a historic faith—indeed, with a heritage that takes it back into prehistory. It has always been recognized that a recalling of the acts of God in the past is natural to our existence. Our rituals and forms, and of course Scripture itself, find their place in Christian experience for this very reason. The Christ event has an especial paradigmatic role in our action/belief. The function of the canon is in part to ensure that authentic remembering continues. But this is not merely for antiquarian benefit. The remembering function is transformative when it provides comfort and assurance but also in that calls us to imitation (mimesis). In this it is a *mnemonic* moment. Mnemonics are aids that enhance our ability to retrieve memories that don't necessarily come naturally to us. Mnemonics are devised to facilitate the appropriation of memory for application in the present. They are, moreover, an intriguing example of the importance of *difference* in mimesis. Mnemonics work by adding an element (a place, anagram, face, or number sequence) which is additional or foreign to the thing being remembered. It is the association that enables the remembering. Christians are called to shape their ways of life, not in slavish repetition of the past, but in continuity with it, living out the same calling to follow Christ, but in a way authentic to the specifics of their context.

Anticipating

It is hardly news that Christianity, as well as being historical, is an eschatological faith. Thiselton summarizes this function as "trustful expectation of an eschatological fulfillment of divine promise."[42] This is too soft. In the same way as the remembering moment in a mimetic model is more than just a source of comfort, the anticipating moment involves more than just psychological hope, based on the promises of God. This is a *proleptic* function and therefore, in that sense, also mimetic. A primary call of the church is to model the world to come. If Christ is first fruits of the eschatological plan of God, so the church carries on that role. Importantly—we must conclude, inherently—the picture afforded us of the world to come is unspecific, defined by

---

42. Thiselton, *Hermeneutics*, 65.

generalities rather than details. Christ himself is an example of mimesis at work in this respect. Yes, first fruits, but not a ministry of apocalyptic fire. Instead it is specific and contextual: relationships with real people are built and sustained, discrete disorders are healed, local authority structures are challenged. The very opaqueness of the eschatological vision requires the church, likewise, to employ its communal imagination. The result will not be an imitation that replicates what is to come, but the church's proleptic anticipating will nonetheless point authentically to the promises of God.

Presenting

Thiselton, following Ricoeur, cites "attention to God's present action" as the immediate narrative imperative of Christian doctrine. This, too, I am proposing to be too soft a description of this function. "Presenting" is offered for a number of its connotations. First, (coincidentally, but somewhat usefully) it enables a direct counter to Schleiermacher's reduction of hermeneutics to "only the art of understanding, not the presentation of understanding as such." The effect of Schleiermacher's exclusion was to locate hermeneutics as a purely cognitive technique. Perhaps the strongest thesis of this essay is that this limitation is not only mistaken but misshapes the discipline. Pascal suggests to us that cognitive functions are an inadequate vehicle for response to divine discourse. Thiselton's account argues convincingly that "belief" cannot be distinguished from "disposition." The ideal response to the gospel is not mere understanding but "faith which shows itself in action" (1 Thess 1:3 NEB).

Secondly, and simply, "presenting" reminds us of the temporal and spatial imperatives. It insists on live action, in the present. It is not open to Christians merely to live in the past or withdraw into eschatological dreams. Each generation is called to its own. This "making present" of God requires continuities but demands contemporary forms and contextual relevance. It also means embodiment. The power of the NT image of the church as the body of Christ includes this: that flesh and blood stand before the powers of this age to declare the counsel of God.

Thirdly, and most profoundly perhaps, "presenting" carries the sense of "performance" sought in the final section of the Prologue to Tim Meadowcroft's *Haggai*. The church is to present God's narrative and character to the world. This is properly understood as a "doxastic" moment in the hermeneutical event.

"Doxastic" in this sense requires some explication. Doxastic logic is an established form of logic that addresses beliefs. It draws on the ancient

Greek meaning of δόξα as "belief" or "opinion." It is in this conventional sense that Wolterstorff insists on "doxastic practice" as a safeguard for human discourse about God. Human entitlement to such discourse is in part guaranteed by believers' willingness to critically examine their beliefs in the light of experience. This of course is sound and wise as far as it goes. However, it fails to embrace the profound redefinition of δόξα brought about first in the LXX and the Hellenistic Apocrypha, where it becomes the favored word to replace כבוד or "honor," especially in relation to God. By the time it reaches the NT, δόξα is invested with a sense of "the divine mode of being." Δόξα as "belief" or "opinion" is entirely absent. Δόξα has instead become a shorthand for the nature and character of God. Moreover, the term is applied directly to Christ, in terms which parallel its application to God. Believers too can participate in δόξα and, crucially the church participates in the of God (Eph 3:21).

Doxastic, in the sense employed here, thus means presenting the glory of God as a principal function of the church. It is, like other functions, inherently mimetic in nature. How else is the church to glorify God but to present in its communal ways of life the gospel and the divine character that lies revealed within it? Moreover, although like any mimetic function it is expected to be anchored in its time and place, this most aspirational of imitation moments is called upon to undergo the self-critical exercise intended in Wolterstorff's "doxastic practice." Only in this, the principal examination will not be the logic or coherence of belief, but the faithfulness of the picture of God presented in this time and this place. As such, it will be informed by the acts of Remembering and Anticipating, together with which Presenting constitutes a mimetic hermeneutical event.

A mimetic model of hermeneutics draws together in one event the functions of Remembering, Anticipating, and Presenting. It is a hermeneutic of embodiment and action, calling us away from cognitively defined models to one that in its very exercise acknowledges and lives out the character of God.

The church has institutionalized something of this dynamic in its regular celebration of the eucharist. The event of course has the elements of remembering, presenting, and anticipating at its core. It is mimetic of both past event (last supper) and future (wedding feast of the lamb) but it does not purport to be a copy of either. It is not (or should not be) merely a Passover gathering, nor does it claim to be the moment in time of eschatological triumph. We have, moreover, properly reduced it in most traditions to a stylized form. Our wafers or small cups are no meal but serve a mnemonic function of evoking the feast, even when they are clearly not one. More deeply, bread and wine remind us of body and blood. The eucharist is, further, a clear presenting of the story and the inherent declaration of the sacrificial love of God. Finally, it also serves as a moment of doxastic practice, properly understood in the Christian fashion outlined above, as all participants and the community together are called to examine their practice and ways of life. Do they align with the event? Do they glorify God?

This Mimetic Model is respectfully offered in conversation with Tim Meadowcroft's account of the hermeneutical challenge, as outlined in the Prolegomena to his fine commentary on Haggai. It is fitting, therefore, to conclude with a reflection on a portion of the biblical text itself: Haggai 1:15b—2:9.

Haggai's fourth oracle is redolent with the themes discussed above. The reader immediately notices the pattern of memory, attention, and expectation as the leaders and the people through the prophet are called to recall the former splendor of the temple, take courage in the present and look forward to even greater splendor to come. The implication of the remembering is that the hearers are to look for the return of this "glory" (כבוד), motivating their efforts in restoration. If splendor was due to beauty and fine furnishings, then it is no wonder that in its early state of rebuild it is, in their sight, "as nothing" (2:3c). But, of course, the splendor is not the result of human effort; it is doxastic; the glory is all God's and derives from his presence. God was present in former days and is present now.

> Yet now take courage
>
> ... for I am with you.
>
> ... my spirit abides among you; do not fear" (2:4–5).

Present action reflects the memory, but the mimetic call is to "be that now," only in a different way. In former days, the presence/glory of God was signified by the temple. Now there is no physical temple, but the presence is as real—the Spirit abides among them. As Tim Meadowcroft notes,

> What is unique here is the verb 'md, translated by NRSV as "abides." As a result, this is a stronger statement than that found anywhere else in the Old Testament of a permanent present of the spirit of Yahweh among the people.[43]

Because the splendor is God's it has in fact never faded. As people of that God they are to act in that light. The anticipation in vv. 6–9 has similar import. World-shaking things will happen, the treasures of the nations will come to Jerusalem, but it will be God who "will fill this house with splendor" (again, כבוד). In keeping with the mimetic theme, and reinforcing

---

43. Meadowcroft, *Haggai*, 161.

the message of the remembering and the presenting, this reference to the future is proleptic. The splendor is because of God, not of the building. When the temple was at its finest in the past, the splendor was due to God. When, in the future, it is restored, the splendor will be due to God, not the building. So, in the present, "all you people of the land" (2:4) identify splendor with God's presence. Don't be discouraged by a broken building; celebrate the ongoing presence of God.

The mimetic model proposed in this essay emphasizes the call to *live* as people of divine discourse. As the call is to our entire beings, it cannot be broken down to a process. It is an event. The elements in it that I have described—remembering, presenting, anticipating—are not like movements in a symphony, able to be played and enjoyed in isolation. Rather they are like the partials in a harmonic series. The music is in the combination. Isolated, they decline to mere noise.

Tim Meadowcroft hears the music. As he draws his commentary to a close, he put it this way:

> As we engage in this exercise, we step into a delicate dance with time. While a theology of restoration lives constantly with a sense of the realized future in the face of exile, the fuel for this hope is a remembered past. Just as Haggai constantly draws the remembered story of Yahweh and Yahweh's people into the present, so we are called to do the same.[44]

This commitment to hold such elements as one whole is the mark of the Christian scholar.

Worth imitating.

Bibliography

Childs Brevard. *Exodus: A Commentary*. London: SCM, 1974.
Coleridge, Samuel Taylor. *Collected Letters of Samuel Taylor Coleridge*. Edited by E. L. Griggs. 6 vols. London and New York: Oxford University Press, 1956–71.
Labouvie-Vief, Gisela. "Wisdom as Integrated Thought: Historical and Developmental Perspectives." In *Wisdom: Its Nature, Origins and Development*, edited by Robert J. Sternberg, 52–83. Cambridge: Cambridge University Press, 1990.
Meadowcroft, Tim. *Haggai*. Sheffield: Sheffield Phoenix, 2006.
Pascal, Blaise. *Pensées*. Translated by Roger Ariew. Indianapolis: Hackett, 2005.
Plato, *Complete Works*. Edited by John M. Cooper. Indianapolis/Cambridge: Hackett, 1997.
Ricoeur, Paul. *Time and Narrative*. Translated by K. McLaughlin and D. Peliauer. 3 vols. Chicago and London: University of Chicago Press, 1984–88.

44. Meadowcroft, *Haggai*, 232.

Schleiermacher, Friedrich. *Hermeneutics and Criticism and Other Writings*. Cambridge: Cambridge University Press, 1998.
Thiselton, Anthony C. *The Hermeneutics of Doctrine*. Grand Rapids: Eerdmans, 2007.
Wittgenstein, L. *Tractatus Logico-Philosophicus*. ET London: Kegan Paul, 1922.
Wolterstorff, Nicholas. *Divine Discourse: Philosophical Reflections on the Claim that God Speaks*. Cambridge: Cambridge University Press, 1995.

22

The Bible as Sacred Re-Membering

Yael Klangwisan and Lisa Spriggens

And what shall I more say? for the time would fail me to tell of Gideon, and of Barak, and of Samson, and of Jephthae; of David also, and Samuel, and of the prophets: Who through faith subdued kingdoms, wrought righteousness, obtained promises, stopped the mouths of lions, Quenched the violence of fire, escaped the edge of the sword, out of weakness were made strong, waxed valiant in fight, turned to flight the armies of the aliens . . . Wherefore seeing we also are compassed about with so great a cloud of witnesses, let us lay aside every weight, and the sin which doth so easily beset us, and let us run with patience the race that is set before us, Looking unto Jesus the author and finisher of our faith; who for the joy that was set before him endured the cross, despising the shame, and is set down at the right hand of the throne of God. (Hebrews 11:32—12:1 KJV).

What the Bible does for us is to make us live all along the generation ladder. With the Bible, we climb up and down through generations.[1]

---

1. Cixous, *Three Steps*, 67.

According to the psychotherapeutic theory developed by Michael White, the work of being human is the work of identity formation.[2] Through White's narrative lens on psychological wellbeing, this project of identity formation or identity reformation may be entered into from a multitude of positions, through all the experiences and events that bring people into relationship, including experiences of faith and religious practice. Regardless of what a person seeks or brings into any relationship, the ultimate consequence of human interaction inevitably becomes one of identity. In this frame, relationship becomes the primary storying of a person in the world. Thus, White's narrative lens is particularly focused on practices in which stories support preferred identities. Narrative acts to uncover how people navigate their discursive contexts and how they are positioned within discourse, and this includes textual worlds like the Bible. Emerging from social constructionist thought, narrative therapists are particularly interested in language and how this is used to shape and understand the world within which people function.

Given the constitutive nature of language, story then becomes the metaphor through which identity and relationship is constructed. In this way people shape and are shaped by language. The stories that we and others tell about us become critical to how we experience ourselves in all contexts of life. An important component of the story is the audience. A story can evolve and change through the rich engagement of the audience. There is potential for new understandings of a story to emerge when it is heard and responded to by an audience. Thus, sacred texts play a role in the identity development of their readers. The telling of stories, sacred stories, on behalf of shaping preferred identities, is a critical component of human development. We all share moments or events in life that reflect what is important to us—the hopes, values, dreams we may hold, which reflect who we understand ourselves to be, where we have come from, and where we are going. This reflects an underlying premise that a person, and their identity, is not static but is able to shift and change in response to context and relationship.

Religion, among other human cultural phenomena, consists of developed practices that invite the observant into the storying of one's life. In these practices or rituals, audiences are chosen as those who would thicken and support preferred stories. Definitional ceremonies, outsider witness practices and re-membering are all therapeutic practices arising as social/communal phenomena and are utilized in therapy to actively invite an audience into the therapeutic conversation. In therapy these are intentional, explicit practices, conducted with clients through group process, or via reflection on

2. White, *Re-Authoring Lives*.

documentation and letters, or through evoking the client's memory and experience of a relationship. The Bible plays an important role here in Judaism and Christianity, where its narrative annals of a people, the sacred poetry, law, prophecy, and letters to the faithful, can be seen as belonging to the reader's thought world or journeying with the reader through life in a number of different ways. The overall intent of these storying practices is to give the client an experience of their story being witnessed and responded to in a way that makes explicit the meaning it holds for the audience.

One such religious observance with particular relevance to Jewish readers is the Passover celebration *chag hammatzot*, which consists of a week-long commemoration of an ancient and pivotal experience of liberation from slavery. The observance commencing annually at sunset marking the end of the 14th day of Nissan and the beginning of the 15th (Lev 23:5–8). The first evening of this memorial is replete with ritual, including ritual cleansing, prayers, washings, lighting, ritual meal, ritualized foods and drink, and other ritual acts all centered on the remembering of the exodus and the associated commandments of observance in the books of the Torah. The observance includes a reading of the biblical texts, specifically Exodus and Deuteronomy.

> [Ritual] dwells in an invisible reality and gives this reality a vocabulary, props, costume, gesture, scenery. Ritual makes things separate, sets them apart from ordinary affairs and thoughts. Rituals need not be solemn, but they are formalized, stylized, extraordinary, and artificial. In the name of ritual, we can do anything. We can do astonishing acts. In the end, ritual gives us assurance about the unification of things.[3]

The term "definitional ceremony" was first used by Barbara Myerhoff in her work in elderly Jewish communities.[4] The definitional ceremony is a structured process through which stories are told, witnessed by an audience who then respond to the story by reflecting back to the teller the knowledge, skills, values, and hopes that they have heard present in the story. Within narrative therapy, definitional ceremonies are understood as practices that use community (both past and present) as a source of acknowledgment and authentication of a persons' experience and knowledge.[5] For the Passover, there is most often a naturally occurring audience for this ritual observance—the family—while in Narrative Therapy settings the therapeutic practice of

---

3. Barbara Myerhoff, cited by Broner, *Bringing Home the Light*, 37.
4. Myerhoff, "Life History."
5. White, *Re-Authoring Lives*.

bringing together an "artificial" audience developed.[6] The audience is known as an outsider-witness group, and their response follows a particular structure, which maintains the focus on the story being told and keeps the conversation away from advice-giving, analysis, or judgment of what has been shared. These tellings and re-tellings bring forward preferred ways of being known and invite the teller to experience their story differently.

In the Passover Seder, these tellings and re-tellings (readings and re-readings) are thousands of years old and serve to reconnect the community and the individual observer to the formative event of the exodus. These tellings and re-tellings are generational. The extended family and guests gather, and the primordial story is read and told again with the next generation. In the eating of the ritual meal after sunset that marks the beginning of the 15th of Nissan, each year, a time when the moon is full and round, the story of liberation from Egypt is vicariously relived by those at the table. As Myerhoff asserts, housed in this ritual is the belief that "the Torah has no beginning and no end."[7] It cycles through our generations, shaping and forming the individual and the community, shaping our futurity through an ancient memory of the past.

Narrative Therapy's "outsider witness" practices evolved from Myerhoff's studies on "definitional ceremonies" and were further developed by Michael White.[8] These conversations are intended to provide a space where the telling and retelling of "story" can be noticed and acknowledged. Rather than the story being told in a therapy context where the story, and consequently the individual, can be subject to assessment or interpretation, the outsider witness process structures the conversation around noticing and acknowledging the expressions of telling: the images that came to mind when hearing these expressions; how these connect to the personal experiences of the audience; and about how the audience's lives might have been altered, touched, or moved by the hearing of this expression.[9] This kind of therapeutic conversation provides an opportunity for bringing forward the voices of clients in ways that center the knowledge they hold about their lives and also creates a generative space for new knowledge to emerge.

When the reader engages the text as cultural and sacred "outsider" witness, each reading becomes a journey through that witness, and this changes the reader's experience of themselves in response. This in turn has real-world effect, changing the reader in lesser, greater, or ongoing ways,

---

6. Myerhoff, "Life History"; White, *Narratives of Therapists*.
7. Myerhoff and Kaminsky, *Remembered Lives*, 134.
8. White, *Narrative Practice*.
9. White, *Maps of Narrative Practice*.

impacting how others might see us, how we experience ourselves and our interactions with others, subtly changing the ways in which we participate in our communities or circles. Entering into the text as a community of witness influences who the reader becomes as a person and as a contemporary community, underlining the profound effect of the meanings we make of life. The effect on personal identity and group identity is pervasive. This is a narrative view of life that sees our identities as being shaped by "many voices." Along with the maternal call of the spirit of God, the Bible is another of the myriad voices calling us in and reflecting our world back to us. We can think of the Bible as offering a revelation on the road of life. This was the experience of the two that walked with the stranger to Emmaus in the gospel of Luke. That stranger was Christ and he invited the two into a kind of textual witnessing through the stories of the Bible. As they walked and talked of the sacred text, from Moses all the way through to the Prophets, they responded, "Didn't our hearts burn within us?" as a description of an inner awakening to new possible ways of being and ways of seeing themselves (Luke 24:32).

Psalm 105:8 makes the extraordinary statement that God remembers, *zakhor*, his covenant for a thousand generations: זכר לעולם בריתו דבר צוה לאלף דור.[10] "Remembering" within Narrative Therapy is a critical concept related to identity development. Re-membering is the intentional practice of bringing back in to consciousness significant figures in the life of an individual. In doing so there is an opportunity to weave these figures in to the past, present and future, in an on-going participation in relationship.[11] Re-membering conversations intentionally invite in the voices, stories, and memories of others and resist the individualist notion of self that dominate Western psychology. Re-membering becomes more than a tool of cognition but a practice that can be intentionally engaged in ways that promote identity restoration and development. Re-membering can be a proactive strategy that supports the grieving process, to be able to hold loss (both personal and cultural). Rather than "moving on" and "disconnection" as paradigms for managing loss, re-membering practices work to provide a space for a re-vision of the relationships considered important in a person's life. They stem from a social constructionist position that holds that identity is constructed in relationship rather than inherently based on a core self.[12]

10. "He is ever mindful of His covenant,/ the promise He gave for a thousand generations." All Scripture translations are from *Tanakh*.

11. Myerhoff, "Life History," 111. Myerhoff introduced the term re-membering in her work with elderly members of a Jewish senior citizens community centre in the United States of America.

12. White, *Maps of Narrative Practice*.

From this position, a person is able to have some choice about how another person or a relationship informs their own sense of identity. While often used when talking about personal loss (death of a loved one), re-membering conversations are not limited to this context. Bringing forward the value of past relationships and recognizing their contribution to the shaping of identity can bring an experience of connectedness and support for a person. Yerushalmi writes of biblical literature in this regard—in light of fresh tragedy for a people, the biblical text provides a certain solace: ". . . while the horror remained vivid it was no longer absurd, and grief, though profound, could be at least partly assuaged."[13]

Drawing on both White and Myerhoff in terms of personal/communal identity reformation, the book of Deuteronomy's emphasis on memory and the exodus holds remarkable resonance. As in the everlasting and perpetual divine remembrance of Psalm 105, the biblical text of Deuteronomy in particular invites the reader to practice remembering particularly around the pivotal events of the exodus commemorated in the Passover Seder. This biblical text invites the reader to remember repeatedly. For example, Deuteronomy asks us to take to memory the time when we were once an embattled minority in Egypt, וזכרת כי-עבד (5:15),[14] what he did to Pharaoh, זכר תזכר את אשר-עשר יהוה אלהיך לפרעה (7:18),[15] and how God brought us out, led us through the desert, וזכרת את-כל-הדרך (8.2),[16] the promises he made to our Fathers, וזכרת את-יהוה אלהיך . . . למען הקים את-בריתו אשר-נשבע לאבתיך (8:18),[17] the failings and rebellions, זכר אל-תשכח את אשר-הקצפת את-יהוה אלהיך במדבר (9:7).[18] Moses, given voice in Deuteronomy, invites God to call to mind certain ancestors, זכר לעבדיך לאברהם ליצחק וליעקב (9:27),[19] then the reader, to set aside an appointed time to reflect on our redemption וזכרת כי עבד היית . . . ויפדך יהוה אלהיך (15:15, 24:18),[20] the day of our liberation:

13. Yerushalmi, *Zakhor*, 39.

14. "Remember that you were a slave in the land of Egypt and the Lord your God freed you from there with a mighty hand and an outstretched arm . . ."

15. "You have but to bear in mind what the Lord your God did to Pharaoh and all the Egyptians . . ."

16. "Remember the long way that the Lord your God has made you travel in the wilderness these past forty years . . ."

17. "Remember that it is the Lord your God who gives you the power to get wealth, in fulfillment of the covenant that He made on oath with your fathers . . ."

18. "Remember, never forget, how you provoked the Lord your God to anger in the wilderness . . ."

19. "Give thought to Your servants, Abraham, Isaac, and Jacob, and pay no heed to the stubbornness of this people, its wickedness, and its sinfulness."

20. "Remember that you were a slave in Egypt and that the Lord your God redeemed you from there . . ."; "Bear in mind that you were slaves in the land of Egypt

תזכר את־יום צאתך (16:3),[21] and the disturbing witness of Miriam and Amalek (24:9, 25:17)[22] as a cautionary tag. Deuteronomy's final chapter closes with the instruction to the reader, the inheritor of the text, to remember, but not only to remember but to reflect and critique within the family and among kin, to ask and to retell, זכר ימות עולם בינו שנות דור־ודור שאל אביך ויגדך זקניך ויאמרו לך (32:7).[23]

How is this kind of remembering different to the day to day tasks of memory? Why the special emphasis on the ever more distant past if every person is responsible for their own actions in the present, especially given we are living in a contemporary world so grounded in the now? The biblical text seems to invite a special type of recollection or "re-membering" by which we might touch with fingertips our people and our histories through text replete with all those implicit or explicit successes and failures, and sometimes devastating witness.

Yerushalmi writes that "... [o]ur texts are paradigmatic... because the issues they raise transcend their Jewish contexts, because the phenomenology of collective memory and forgetting is essentially the same for all social groups, though the details may vary widely."[24] Deuteronomy is an extraordinary text, that represents the blood and breath of sacred memory that casts itself back into the past and forwards into the future from its own time of codification. This textual memory of a community of faith in Deuteronomy (and the Bible writ large) function like sacred genealogies—not in terms of an aggrandizing of antecedents but as the community or family into which the reader is invited. This is a particularly Jewish perception of the tree of life. In this tree of life, as the textual tree that holds this community, its leaves are its vignettes, songs and poems, branches its seferim, megillot and ketuvim, and the whole, into which we are welcomed as a family that reconstitutes itself through the witness of the text, and that continues to offer us an embrace that stirs reflection regarding our own identity. "The vision of the moment signifies the power of memory over time, loss and death."[25]

---

and the Lord your God redeemed you..."

21. "You shall not eat anything leavened with it; for seven days thereafter you shall eat unleavened bread, bread of distress—for you departed from the land of Egypt hurriedly—so that you may remember the day of your departure from the land of Egypt as long as you live."

22. "Remember what the LORD your God did to Miriam on the journey after you left Egypt"; 'Remember what Amalek did to you on your journey, after you left Egypt."

23. "Remember the days of old,/ Consider the years of ages past;/ Ask your father, he will inform you,/ Your elders, they will tell you."

24. Yerushalmi, *Zakhor*, 113.

25. Ginsberg and Ron, *Shattered Vessels*, 133.

If we were to pursue the text developmentally as reader, it then becomes a kind of inheritance. The kind of encountering of the sacred text would not be one of prescription, but as the narrative reader encounters these genealogies—stories of the generations—we experience a thickening of our relation to a certain heritage or inheritance, a natural relation or an adoption, brought into a community who chose God, or whom God chose, as the implied reader of Deuteronomy. We see this in some of the characters themselves who were brought in and became kin: Ruth the Moabitess who became a mother and Boaz a father in the line of David in Ruth 4; Rahab in Josh 6:25. This kind of belonging is deeply formative, as said of Rahab—ותשב בקרב ישראל עד היום הזה—she dwells in Israel to this day.[26] Or, as in other biblical stories, characters who belong to the people ethnically but who have experienced radical marginalization from the same community. In Cixous's account of her own readerly encounter of the story of Moses, a young Hebrew living in a foreign palace, and then as a refugee in Midian, she describes ways in which this touched her own childhood in a Jewish family in Algeria:

> There is no one more ordinary than Moses; he is a man who experiences all manner of unexpected passions himself... The Bible's Moses cuts himself while shaving. He is afraid... He does many a thing under the table before being Up There with the other Tables... We are those who later on transform, displace, and canonize the Bible, paint and sculpt it another way.[27]

This kind of quickening that the reader experiences in reading is that deep sense of belonging to which the reader is heir. The biblical narrative contributes to a sense of community, the kind outlined by Paul in Hebrews 11 where he speaks of a great cloud of witnesses spanning from the text's past to the present. The reader develops a deep connection with that past and is shaped by the future towards which the text casts itself. The reader literally becomes the people of the book whether by blood, by humanity, or by faith, as the Bible's myriad stories intersect with the reader's thought-life or lived-life in myriad ways. The text for the reader can be a forest of green and verdant leaf, or a forest of bare limbed trees, or even a desert. As in Narrative Therapy, the intentionality of the reader to develop a preferred identity and take responsibility for this is key; the narrative reader may choose to embrace that stream in the text where the leaves are most green and verdant for them. Thus, the reader might encounter the text as an orchard of pomegranates (Song 4:13), a garden full of comfort (Isa 51:3),

26. Josh 6:25 "... and she dwelt among the Israelites—as is still the case..."
27. Cixous, *Three Steps*, 67.

and hanging gardens where the trees have leaves that heal (Rev 22:2). And equally, the reader may need to make certain choices, choosing at times to forget, as Luria suggests:

> [W]e must know the right time to forget as well as the right time to remember, and instinctively see when it is necessary to feel historically and when unhistorically. This is the point that the reader is asked to consider: that the unhistorical and the historical are equally necessary to the health of an individual, a community, and a system of culture.[28]

Meadowcroft wrestles with this kind of readerly responsibility in his chapter on "The Covenant Remembered" in *The Message of the Word of God*. Meadowcroft enters the politically complex territory of the relation of the biblical text and biblical memory to contemporary territorial concerns in Israel today and ways in which these concerns become part of an identity of the people it impacts.[29] He assures the reader that the words of Deuteronomy, the re-membered Book of the Law found in the temple, are the inheritance spoken of and the call to the land must not arise within our communities dressed in violence, a closed vocabulary of possession and dispossession, and that the words of the Prophets arising from the same era in which Deuteronomy was written, add to the paradigmatic mythos of the promised land, the messianic call to peace: "Ultimately the book of Deuteronomy is part of a story that belongs to all those families," he writes, " . . . so it is part of a story that is bigger than possession of one particular parcel of land . . . "[30] Furthermore, in Deut 4:20 the reader discovers the people of the inheritance are vastly more than the sum total of what they have, but inheritors in who they become.

Regarding the meanings that we make of the text and those pressing existential questions: We find ourselves in a certain place and time. A certain century. At a certain locus in the world history. How did we arrive here, and where are we going? We find in the biblical story that we are not alone. We touch fingertips with many patriarchs and matriarchs, who become ours—Abraham, Isaac, and Jacob; Sarah, Rebecca, and Rachel—through the texts that become windows into their lives, ladders into heavens upon which the angels ascend and descend. A narrative reading is a spiritual and cultural encounter; how blessed is the reader to have the cultural memories of the garden, the rainbow, the exodus, Sinai, the promised land, and of the incarnation, the Passover, and Yom Kippur, heralding the promise of the

---

28. Isaac Luria, *The Mind of a Mneumonist*, cited in Yerushalmi, *Zakhor*, 107.
29. Meadowcroft, *The Message*, 113.
30. Meadowcroft, *The Message*, 125.

Messianic age. We remember the legacy of these sacred histories through memory, each an apple tree. We must continue to ask anew what these stories mean for us now. The highs and lows, ebbs and flows, tragedies and griefs are all there in the pages. There is a rich land of text that marks our sacred heritage, shadow and also light in its pages—all the vulnerability of the human condition. It speaks to that of which we are a part; a continuation of this green forest of the sacred text marks us irrevocably.

Where do we go from here in terms of this yearning? Our journeys into the text as cultural and sacred memory must never end. This renegotiation of identity that occurs when confronted by the text will continue through life, if we let it, as we participate in the biblical imagination, and its dream of a Messianic future to come. This possibility of *tikkun olam*, the restorative choices, values, meanings that make us who we are and who we will be, are then the promise of a color and hue of the leaves of our part of the tree of life. And, if the narrative reader embraces it, also the memory or torah that we will become as part of this very special tree of life. Our torah is then a leaf or a stem on the tree that we leave in trust for the next generation.

> ... because we know since the Bible that in due time the walls yield. The dream is to be there, at the first hour, to be able to respond, to be witness to one's own birth, to arrive where Esther was, Esther my mother, Wo Esther war soll ich gehen—my mother the proof, my mother who circulates in me, my mother who is in me as I was in her, what a strange bond, strange and red, contained, and which does not collect itself, does not stop, which goes by, escapes, follows its course across generations, carrying our colors well beyond ourselves. Here, in the invisible inside, I no longer know if I am the subject of verbs in the past, in the present, or if already today is the day before yesterday while days of old are part of the future.[31]

Bibliography

Broner, E. M. *Bringing Home the Light*. N.p.: Council Oak, 1999.
Cixous, Hélène. *Rootprints: Memory and Life Writing*. New York: Routledge, 1997.
———. *Three Steps on the Ladder of Writing*. New York: Columbia University Press, 2003.
Ginsberg, Michal, and Moshe Ron. *Shattered Vessels: Memory, Identity, and Creation in the Work of David Shahar*. Albany: SUNY, 2004.
Meadowcroft, Tim. *The Message of the Word of God*. Nottingham: Inter-Varsity, 2011.

---

31. Cixous, *Rootprints*, 129.

Myerhoff, Barbara. "Life History Among the Elderly: Performance, Visibility and Re-Membering." In *A Crack in the Mirror. Reflective Perspectives in Anthropology*, edited by J. Ruby, 99–117. Philadelphia: University of Pennsylvania Press, 1982.

———. "Life History as Integration." *The Gerontologist*. 15/6 (1975) 541–43.

Myerhoff, Barbara, and Marc Kaminsky. *Remembered Lives: The Work of Ritual, Storytelling, and Growing Older*. Ann Arbor: University of Michigan Press, 1992.

White, Michael. *Maps of Narrative Practice*. New York: W. W. Norton & Company, 2007.

———. *Narratives of Therapists' Lives*. Adelaide: Dulwich Centre, 1997.

———. *Narrative Practice: Continuing the Conversations*. New York: W. W. Norton & Company, 2011.

———. *Re-Authoring Lives: Interviews and Essays*. Adelaide: Dulwich Centre, 1998.

Yerushalmi, Yosef. *Zakhor: Jewish History and Jewish Memory*. Seattle: University of Washington Press, 1996.

Subject Index

Abraham, 41, 71, 80, 127, 131, 154–57, 165, 179, 220–21, 224, 246, 323, 326
adultery, 54, 153, 175, 186–87, 192, 195
allusion, 25–26, 28, 33, 58, 106, 122, 124, 126, 131, 144–45, 220
Amos, 139–41, 150, 217, 226
ancestor, 7, 33, 35–36, 41–42, 152, 155, 165–66, 203, 218, 220–21, 225, 323
angels, 111, 128–30, 133, 250, 253, 326
anthropology, 45, 166, 208, 211–13, 241, 289, 328
apocalypse, 69, 83, 267, 282
apocalyptic, 128, 313
Apocrypha, 153, 155, 166, 314
apostle, 86–87, 89–90, 94–95, 97, 107–8, 110, 112–13, 115, 197, 251
Aramaic, 22, 30, 229–30, 232, 234–41
Aristotle, 104–5, 189
atonement, 44, 46–49, 51–52, 56, 71, 104
Augustine, 13, 189, 257

Babylon, 4, 6, 8–9, 125
Bethlehem, 33–37, 40–41, 118, 159–60
Bethlehemite, 34, 39
Bethsaida, 234–35
Boaz, 33–41, 160–61, 165, 325

colonialism, 6, 169, 172, 175–76, 178, 215–17, 221, 225, 300
commandments, 70–76, 78, 80, 164, 185, 187–91, 196–97, 320
covenant, 12, 34–35, 76, 81, 124–25, 127–32, 155–56, 158, 163–65, 191, 195, 217, 219–21, 224, 226, 309, 322–23, 326
creation, 19, 58–67, 71, 100–102, 147, 191, 195, 201, 215–22, 261, 305, 327
creature, 24, 59–61, 71, 217–19, 221–22, 224–25, 304
crucified, 17, 71, 87, 92, 97, 109, 113, 115, 209–210, 251

Daniel, 3–16, 106, 262, 264–65
David, 33, 35–36, 39, 50, 138, 154n15, 155, 165, 177, 179, 262, 267, 318, 325
defiled, 4, 44–45, 47–51, 53–55, 57, 207
Deuteronomy, 61, 141, 145, 186, 188–90, 197–98, 219–20, 320, 323–26
disciples, 9, 17, 68, 85, 114, 116, 204, 208–9, 212, 234–36, 239–40, 250–51
discourse, 143, 169–70, 182, 196, 205, 209, 211, 239, 282–83, 287, 292, 296, 299, 307–9, 313–14, 316–17, 319

doctrine, 29, 71, 215, 221, 226, 255, 309–311, 313, 317

education, 9, 139, 150, 170–73, 176, 178, 182, 189, 199, 241
Egypt, 10–11, 66, 144, 157, 223, 232, 321, 323–24
Elohim, 218, 220, 223–25
empire, 4, 6, 8–9, 11–13, 108, 215, 225, 230, 239, 264
Ephesians, Ephesus, 13, 92–93, 99, 107, 224, 253
Ephraim, 35, 139–42, 144–49
epistemology, 182, 291, 304, 308
Erasmus, Desiderius, 198, 245–46, 253
eschatology, 119, 121–22, 124, 126–27, 129–32, 309, 312–14
Esther, 31, 37, 42, 153, 156, 161–66, 327
ethics, 18, 40, 78, 80, 108–9, 113, 150, 219, 225, 307
ethnicity, 38, 77, 119, 127, 169, 178, 237, 325
evangelical, 9–10, 181, 268, 300
evangelism, 98–99, 102, 106, 108–9, 111, 113–17, 253, 255
evangelists, 107, 234, 236, 240
exile, 7, 37, 119, 121–25, 130–31, 265, 316
Exodus, exodus 46, 50–51, 56, 201, 226, 309, 316, 320–21, 323, 326
expiation, 44–46, 48–49, 51–53, 56
Ezekiel, 41, 154–55, 174–75, 218, 226
Ezra, 23, 35, 39, 65, 131, 265

families, 32, 34, 40, 139, 157, 182, 194–96, 205, 268, 326
foreigner, 6, 36, 38, 79–80, 83, 160

Galatians, Galatia, 87, 93, 109–110, 252
Galilee, 105, 232–34, 239, 242
Genesis, 33, 35–36, 41, 58–67, 101, 157, 167, 174–75, 180–81, 184, 191, 195, 218, 220, 225
genre, 27, 33, 42, 153–54, 238
gentile, 87, 90, 94, 107, 119, 129, 131, 220–21, 251, 253

glory, 55, 101, 107–9, 124, 153, 199–201, 204, 207–9, 211–13, 248, 250, 253, 314–15
Griesbach, Johann, 244–45, 247–48, 250, 252–55

Haggai, 301–2, 304, 308–9, 313, 315–16
Hannah, 156, 163–65
Hebrews, 118–22, 124, 126–34, 250, 318, 325
Heidegger, Martin, 288, 290–92, 295, 298–99
Hellenistic, 232, 234–35, 241, 265
holiness, 50, 72, 85, 89–91, 95–97, 104, 108, 113, 126, 185, 187
Homer, 104–5, 110, 112
homosexuality, 28, 168–69, 171, 173, 177, 182, 193–95
honor, 33–34, 155, 200, 209–212
Hosea, 137, 139–41, 144–51, 174–75
humanity, 11, 53–55, 81, 111, 139, 170, 189, 195, 210, 218, 224, 304–6, 325
human rights, 169–70, 181–82

ideologies, 18, 134, 171, 173–74, 178–79, 217, 238
idols, 148–49, 187
impure, 45–48, 51, 53–57
incarnation, 68, 71, 299, 326
injustice, 25, 82, 180, 190
integrity, 23, 25, 27, 29, 99, 176, 178
intercultural, 218, 220–21
intertextual, 3, 106, 117, 141, 265
Isaac, 9, 41, 62, 122–24, 130–34, 148, 154, 257, 261, 267, 323, 326

Jacob, 41, 56, 63, 119, 123, 141, 154, 198, 323, 326
James, 17, 30, 97, 117, 133, 167, 241, 244, 255, 267, 297
Jeremiah, 3–16, 19, 62, 103, 121–22, 124–25, 132–34, 154, 262
Jericho, 77, 158–59, 165
Jerusalem, 3, 5–6, 11, 50, 66, 77, 90, 119–25, 127–28, 130–34, 232, 315

SUBJECT INDEX 331

Jesus, 76, 78, 80, 84–86, 89–90, 92–95, 129, 209–210, 232, 235, 237–38, 241–42, 249, 251, 255
Jonah, 141, 150
Jonathan, 56, 133, 179, 229, 234, 242, 262, 267
Joseph, 97, 114, 154, 199, 207, 210, 247
Josephine, 212
Josephus, 65, 105, 112–13
Joshua, 24, 154–55, 158–59, 166
Josiah, 9, 124, 154–55
Judah, 4, 9, 11, 13, 35–36, 38, 122–23, 155, 159, 241, 309
Judaism, 56, 70, 116–17, 127, 131–32, 174, 185, 192, 320
Judaizers, 106, 108–9
Judas, 179, 209
Judean, 36, 79
judgment, 7, 50, 79, 103, 121–22, 124, 129, 131, 142, 146–47, 225, 246, 264, 293, 321
justice, 5, 10–12, 22, 25, 29, 51, 69, 72–74, 78, 80–81, 83, 132, 138, 170–71, 182, 185, 188–93, 195–98
justification, 264

Kingitanga, 216

Laidlaw College, 68, 84, 98, 114, 116, 214, 268, 284
law, 76, 169, 174, 179, 181–82, 186, 188, 195, 219, 299
Lazarus, 208
Leviticus, 4, 46–49, 51–54, 56–57, 61, 76, 185, 196, 198
liberation, 181–82, 320–21, 323
logic, 44–45, 47, 49, 51, 53, 55, 57, 81, 126, 185, 271, 283, 313–14, 317
love, 77, 139, 151, 164, 184, 194, 267
Luke, 17, 36, 72, 74–75, 78–79, 83, 97, 100, 103, 110, 114, 192, 225, 235, 249, 251, 322

mana, 199–209, 211–12
Māori, 170, 178, 199, 201–7, 210, 211–13, 215–16, 225–26

marriage, 34, 36, 38–39, 41, 54, 139, 146, 149–51, 161, 169–70, 174, 177, 181, 184–88, 190–96
Matthew, 12, 36, 38, 75, 191–93, 197–98, 223–24, 241–42, 248–51
mercy, 12, 49, 53, 55–56, 83, 147, 152, 189, 193
messiah, 35–36, 326–27
metaphor, 8, 14, 24–26, 28, 53, 90, 109–110, 117, 127, 139–42, 146, 148–50, 174–75, 179, 187, 200, 293, 319
mimesis, 301, 303, 305, 307, 309–317
mission, 9–10, 68, 99, 102–110, 113–17, 193, 215, 217, 243, 255, 268, 300–301
Moab, 33, 36–37, 39, 42, 159–60, 325
model, 45, 212, 300, 311
Molech, 47, 54, 196
monotheism, 63, 65–66, 72, 218
morality, 48, 56, 79, 299, 305, 307
Moses, 17, 41, 47, 51, 55, 105, 126–27, 134, 154, 185–87, 195, 208, 219–21, 322–23, 325
mother, 137, 143–44, 146–48
multilingual, 231, 233–34
multivalence, 264, 269

Naomi, 34, 37–41, 156, 159–61, 164–66
nations, 7–8, 114, 119, 121–25, 131, 185–87, 218, 220, 222, 225, 315
Nebuchadnezzar, 4, 6, 11–12, 14–15, 121
Nehemiah, 124, 152, 154

obedience, 15, 73–76, 94, 113, 145–46, 188, 191, 277
offering, 44–46, 48–49, 52, 56–57, 145
Orthodox, 70, 262

Pākehā, 178, 202, 212, 215–16, 226
Palestine, 79, 118, 229–32, 234, 236–37, 240–42
parable, 72, 77–83, 223–24, 239, 266
paradigm, 71, 73, 169, 223, 270, 278, 282, 289, 312, 322, 324, 326
Pascal, Blaise, 304–8, 310, 313, 316
Pasifika, 170, 178

Passover/Seder, 314, 320, 321, 323, 326
patriarchal, 127, 160, 170, 174, 177–78, 181, 326
patronage, 199, 212, 215
Paul, 9, 13, 65–67, 85–101, 103, 106–117, 121, 132, 185, 191–95, 197, 201, 212, 220–21, 223, 276, 280, 290, 325
peace, 68–70, 72, 77, 82
Pentateuch, 46, 56, 220, 225
Pentecost, 235, 298
performance, 73, 296, 302, 304, 306, 308, 313, 328
Persia, 7–8, 163, 165, 265
Peter, 97, 103, 117, 132–34, 197, 211–12, 234, 298
Philemon, 93, 253
Philippians, Philippi, 89, 92–93, 98–113, 116–17
Plato, 104–5, 111, 193, 311, 316
pollute, 5, 47–48, 53–54, 56, 203
postcolonial, 3, 6, 115
postexilic, 50, 119, 131
postmodern, 3, 115, 256, 259–60, 263, 268
poststructural, 288, 292, 295
poverty, 169, 190, 233
prayer, 12–13, 15, 40, 62, 106, 114, 163, 248, 320
priest, 9, 28, 46–47, 50–52, 57, 78, 129–30, 133, 152, 219–21, 223–24, 301
prophecy, 8, 13, 16, 155, 320
prophets, 7, 9, 13, 15, 17, 62, 103, 120–21, 134, 141, 145, 148, 150–52, 154, 165, 174, 179, 187, 251, 315, 318, 322, 326
Proverbs, 42, 156, 164–66, 187, 219
Psalms, 17, 19, 21, 62, 69, 71, 120–21, 126, 133–34, 153, 163, 217–19, 226, 322–23
purification, 46–48, 51, 54–56, 251
purity, 35, 54–56, 97

Qumran, 128, 133

rangatira, rangatiratanga 203–4, 206, 215–16, 226

rationalism, 198, 286, 289, 293–94, 305, 307
reception, 3, 257–67, 272
reconcile, 68–69, 82, 132, 221, 226
redeem, 39–41, 62, 95, 124–25, 265, 309, 323–24
redemption, 68, 71, 95, 179, 250, 323
Reformation, 246, 285, 319, 323
relativism, 79, 263, 265, 275, 282, 291
remarriage, 191–92, 195, 197–98
repentance, 12, 114, 125–26, 145, 192
resurrection, 11, 17–19, 28, 68, 71, 101, 208, 210
Revelation, 7, 121, 265, 309
revelation, 12–13, 39, 209, 291, 309, 322
rhetoric, 25, 99, 107, 116, 133, 146, 150, 153, 174, 205, 209, 212
Ricoeur, Paul, 268, 276n24, 279–80, 282–83, 288, 290, 292–95, 299, 309, 311, 313, 316
righteous, 36, 95, 106, 115, 129, 223–24, 318
ritual, 44–49, 51, 53–56, 307, 312, 319–21, 328
Romans, 84–87, 89–91, 93–97, 109, 114, 121, 185, 193, 234, 252, 257
Rome, 8, 30, 67, 84–85, 87, 89, 94, 99, 107, 112, 119, 128, 131–32, 264
Ruth, 31–43, 153, 156, 159–61, 163–67, 179, 325

Sabbath, 4–5, 129
sacred, 5, 38, 46–47, 50, 88, 174, 177, 179–80, 203–4, 215, 224, 246, 261, 319–25, 327
sacrificial, 45–46, 71, 81, 110, 315
salvation, 72–73, 88, 90, 92–94, 96, 100–101, 106, 108–9, 113–14, 120, 142
Samson, 179, 318
Samuel, 137–38, 145, 149, 154–55, 163, 166, 174–75, 179–80, 215–16, 262, 318
sanctification, 5, 19, 84, 90–92, 94–96, 129, 170
sanctuary, 47–48, 50–51, 54–56
Sarah, 156–57, 164–65, 326
Saussure, Ferdinand, 231, 241, 287, 289, 291–93

SUBJECT INDEX   333

Schleiermacher, Friedrich, 286–87, 294, 301–6, 308, 313, 317
semantics, 211, 265, 291–92, 296–97
Septuagint/LXX, 64 86, 97, 102–3, 105–6, 122–25, 130, 167, 200–201, 262 314
Simeon, 152, 155
Sinai, 25, 54, 126–27, 130, 326
Sirach, 103, 152–55, 164–67
slavery, 11, 174–75, 320
sociolinguistics, 229–33, 236–37, 239, 242
Solomon, 50, 154–55, 255
speech, 24, 27, 29, 35, 40, 102, 130, 164, 168, 206, 216, 224, 241, 265, 281–82, 303, 310
speech act, 276, 282, 287, 293–94, 297, 302
spiritual, 5, 13, 54, 70, 98, 110, 125, 173, 195, 202–4, 217, 220, 223, 225–26, 326
structuralism, 289, 292–94, 296
symbol, 4–5, 8, 35, 45, 54, 56, 126–28, 130, 133, 212, 261, 264, 288, 292
synagogue, 18, 118–19, 121, 131, 264

Tanakh, 59–60, 322
tapu, 201–4, 206, 212
Targum, 21, 121
Temple, 47–48, 50, 54, 56, 65, 77, 91, 119–21, 126, 128–33, 187, 210, 217–18, 315–16, 326
testimony, 177, 241, 244, 265, 300, 302
textual criticism, 21, 23, 30, 243, 255, 262, 264, 267
theodicy, 19–20, 30, 56
therapy, 319–22, 325, 328
Thessalonians, 93, 108, 110–11, 117, 251
Timothy, 68, 89, 99, 103, 108–9, 251, 253
Torah, 4, 70, 73, 77, 80–81, 119, 123, 134, 164, 219–20, 230, 320–21, 327
tradition, 8, 21, 23, 28–30, 36, 63, 71–72, 75, 83, 99, 116, 128, 133–34, 167, 171, 212, 218–
translator, 21, 85, 95, 200, 212, 236
transmission, 27, 232, 234, 236–37, 255

Treaty of Waitangi, Te Tiriti o Waitangi, 202, 211–12, 215–16, 217, 224, 226
Trinity, 71, 221, 253, 255, 285, 291
truth, 7–8, 29, 68, 72, 83, 101, 127, 251, 258, 267, 278, 291, 298, 307, 311

unbelief, 83, 108, 113, 192, 304, 307
unclean, 48, 54, 57, 61, 203
unity, 69–72, 99, 108–9, 115, 191, 197
utterance, 22, 271, 274–77, 279, 281, 303, 309

victim, 18, 24, 51, 77–80, 82, 170, 173, 176–77, 180, 273
violence, 6, 10, 69, 82, 137, 139, 149, 151, 168–83, 210–11, 222, 318, 326
virtue, 6, 34, 41, 157–58, 164, 280, 310–11
vision, 7–8, 11, 119, 123, 134, 216–17, 219–21, 223, 264, 313, 322, 324
vocation, 9–10, 92, 96, 115, 214–15, 217, 219, 221–25

Waikato, 216, 226
wealth, 33, 103, 201, 205, 257, 323
Wiremu Tāmihana, 215–16, 219, 221, 224, 226
wisdom, 64, 87, 95, 103, 114, 137, 141, 153–55, 164, 166–67, 187, 200, 213, 219–21, 226, 307, 316
wives, 32, 41, 138, 153, 160, 164–65, 190
womb, 62, 137, 139–41, 143–49, 151, 157, 219, 221
workers, 107–8, 114–15
worldview, 13, 153, 174, 178, 189, 259–60
worship, 10, 14–15, 18, 24, 45, 47, 49, 54, 62, 69, 71, 79, 81, 120–21, 125, 127–30, 172
Yahweh/YHWH, 9–15, 24, 26, 34–35, 40, 48, 54, 62–63, 65, 119–21, 123–25, 130, 141–43, 148, 149, 155–56, 158–61, 163–65, 185, 218–21, 224–25 315–16
Yahwistic, 218–19

Zion, 118–34, 156

Author Index

Abegg, Martin G., 152n3, 155n16, 166
Alter, Robert, 18n2, 23, 29, 41

Barr, James, 230, 232, 241, 291, 297
Bartholomew, Craig, 66, 286, 297
Barton, Stephen C., 89n22, 96-97, 302, 309
Bauckham, Richard, 63, 65-66, 235n22, 240n33, 241
Breed, Brennan, 261, 263-64, 265, 267
Bretherton, Luke, 221-23, 225
Bruce, F.F., 102n18, 116, 126n49, 128n59, 132

Cixous, Hélène, 318, 325, 327
Croy, Clayton N., 235n22, n24, 241, 286, 297

Derrida, Jacques, 268-69, 275, 292
DeSilva, David A., 127n55, 132, 153n8, 155n21, 166
Dickson, John P., 102n17, 103, 105-6, 116
Dunn, James D.G., 89n22, 90n30, 97, 167

Eidevall, Göran, 141-43, 149
Ellingworth, Paul, 124n30, 126-29, 132

Feder, Yitzhaq, 45n3, 48-49, 51-53, 56

Fee, Gordon D., 87n13, 89, 91, 95, 97, 99n3, 100n12, 102n18, 106, 107n47, 116
Fiddes, Paul S., 219n17, 224n26, 226
Fitzmyer, J.A., 30, 89n23, n25, 94, 97, 231n5, n8, 232, 235n25, 238, 241

Gadamer, Hans-Georg, 258-59, 264, 267, 288, 290-92, 295, 298-99
Glueck, Nelson, 157n28, 158n33, 166
Greenstein, Edward L., 22-23, 25, 30

Havea, Jione, 221, 226
Holladay, William L., 121n16, 124-25, 133
Houts, Margo G., 139n10, 145n40, 147, 148n57, 150
Hurtado, Larry 260, 261n16, 267

Johnson, Luke Timothy, 126n48, 127n51, n53, 133

Kawharu, I. H., 203, 212
Keefe, Alice, 139n14, 145n39, 146n45, 150

Landy, Francis, 140n16, 141, 145n41, n43, 146n44, 150
Levin, Saul, 21n10, 23n14, 28n25, 30

Lightfoot, Joseph Barber, 103n24, 104n28, 110, 117
Lyons, William John, 257, 261n16, 263, 267

Malina, Bruce J., 205n36, 207n51, n52, 208n57, 212
Malina, Bruce J., and Richard Rohrbaugh, 205n39, 206, 207n51, n54, 208, 209n59, 210n61, 212
McKenzie, John L., 141, 142n26, 148, 150
McLean, Bradley H., 288, 290n22, n23, 291, 292, 298
Mead, Hirini Moko, 202n21, 203n26, 207n52, 212
Metge, Joan, 201, 202, 204, 206, 212
Metzger, Bruce M., 110n61, 117, 245n8, 255
Metzger, Bruce M., and Bart D. Ehrman, 245-47, 253n27, 255
Milgrom, Jacob, 46-51, 53-54, 56, 196, 198

Oakes, Peter, 85n1, 90-91, 97, 102n16, 103, 117

Palmer, Richard E., 285-88, 290n21, 293-94, 296, 298
Pere, Rangimarie Rose, 201-3, 207n52, 212

Roberts, Jonathan, 257-58, 267

Seow, Choon-Leow, 24-28, 30, 257, 267
Shirres, Michael P., 202, 203n27, 204n34, 212
Sperber, Dan, and Deidre Wilson, 270-72, 276-77, 279, 283

Thiselton, Anthony, 90-91, 95, 97, 192-93, 198, 280, 283, 287-88, 290-91, 299, 309-313, 317
Tuhiwai Smith, Linda, 169n7, 182

Vanhoozer, Kevin J., 276n24, 279n30, 283, 287-88, 299

Wallace, Daniel B., 64, 67, 101, 117, Waltke, Bruce, 62, 67, 164, 167
Ware, James, 99n3, 102-6, 108, 117
Weinfeld, Moshe, 123-24, 134, 201n15, 213
Wenham, Gordon, 46n9, 57, 62n7, 67, 157n26, 167
Williams, H.W., 203n24, n25, n30, 213
Williamson, H.G.M., 122n23, n24, n25, 123, 134
Wolterstorff, Nicholas, 282n38, 283, 308-9, 314, 317
Wright, David P., 49n20, 54n34, 55, 57

Yee, Gale A., 139n13, 141n19, 144n37, 145n38, 151
Yerushalmi, Yosef, 323-24, 326, 328

Zimmermann, Jens, 286, 291, 299

www.ingramcontent.com/pod-product-compliance
Lightning Source LLC
Chambersburg PA
CBHW061423300426
44114CB00014B/1513